The cookbook for people who want wholesome, nutritious food, from the Kitchens of Keepers at Home Readers

ISBN 10-digit: 1-933753-12-9
ISBN 13-digit: 978-1-933753-12-6

Text Design: Amy Diane Wengerd
Design: Brenda Troyer
Cover Photograph: Jason Weaver

First Printing December 2009   10M
Second Printing May 2010   10M

Carlisle Press
WALNUT CREEK

2673 Township Road 421
Sugarcreek, OH 44681
800.852.4482

Dedication

To all mothers who make the sometimes difficult food choices and lifestyle sacrifices for the sake of their own or another's health.

III

IV

Acknowledgments

Thank you to all *Keepers at Home* mothers who spent hours in their kitchens perfecting these recipes. You belong to a dedicated group of mothers determined to provide your families with the best. You prove yourself willing to do without the short-term pleasure of compliments that often come with food that, while it pleases our taste buds, ruins our health. You are willing to sacrifice that short-term pleasure of compliments for the long-term benefit of feeding your family food that sustains life. You're willing, even if the boys cautiously take only a small helping the first time around and your husband asks what you used to make it or suggests that you work on it a little before serving it to company. Thank you for serving a dinner that our taste buds and conscience both enjoy.

"The heart of her husband doth safely trust in her, so that he shall have no need of spoil. She will do him good and not evil all the days of her life." Proverbs 31:11 & 12

Marvin & Miriam Wengerd
Keepers at Home

V

Introduction

My interest in healthy eating began when I met Marvin. At the time, he had arthritis, which was triggered off by a knee injury that occurred when he was seventeen years old. For ten years, daily, debilitating pain was his close companion. During this time we got married and our two oldest children were born. I tried to make healthy foods and learn all I could about what causes sickness and what I could do to help Marvin get better. When I began baking 100% whole wheat bread, I didn't know of a single other person who had any interest in it. I used a recipe out of a cookbook given to me by Eloise Wright, a friend whom I had done housecleaning for. She was a wonderful cook, originating from Louisiana. I still remember sitting in her large old-fashioned farmhouse kitchen, feasting on a delicious chicken and rice dish she made. She gave me the *Ten Talents* cookbook when I was still single. I put this information in the back burner of my mind and after we married began using it. My No-Crumble Whole Wheat Bread recipe is on page 56. I made this bread by hand for eight years, then Marvin bought me a Bosch mixer. Now I use a recipe that came along with the mixer, making a few changes to suit my personal tastes better. This recipe is on page 57, called Perfect Whole Wheat Bread.

In 1991 I started reading about fasting for your health. I became convinced that Marvin needs to go on an extended fast and tried to persuade him to do so. He agreed it was a good idea, but it looked like a mountain to him as it necessitated going away from the family for a few weeks. So he was reluctant to commit himself to doing it. I kept trying to persuade him until one day God spoke to my heart and said, "It is not your business to make Marvin go on a fast, you are not his conscience. Stop nagging him!" So I went to Marvin and told him what God said to me. I told him I won't bring up fasting again, but will only talk about it if he initiates the discussion. Not long after this, possibly two weeks later, he informed me that he has made up his mind to go!

An amazing chain of events then took place. A very unique job opportunity came his way, so he quit his job and planned to go to Dr. Scott's Natural Health Institute in Strongsville, Ohio, to do an extended fast, knowing that upon his return his new job would be waiting. It turned out that my parents left on a trip to Europe during the time he was at the clinic. They asked me to stay at their place, caring for my youngest sister while they were gone. The timing of the whole deal came off perfectly! Marvin and I traveled to Strongsville on September 3, 1991, and he stayed, then I came home and went overnight to my parents, who left the next day. It was a blessing for me to be there because it kept me busy and sidetracked from my loneliness. He was gone nearly two weeks and came home the day before my parents arrived. Talk about God's timing! This fasting experience was life changing. Marvin hasn't known a day of arthritis pain since then. To God be the glory, great things He hath done!

VII

After Marvin was healed we became very zealous to maintain this precious gift of health which God so graciously granted us. We hope those of you who have never suffered daily pain are not critical of our zeal to maintain our family's health. We are very grateful to have learned what a great difference healthy food choices can make, and it is our desire to pass on the things God has taught us so others too may partake of the benefits.

Miriam Wengerd
June 24, 2009

Table of Contents

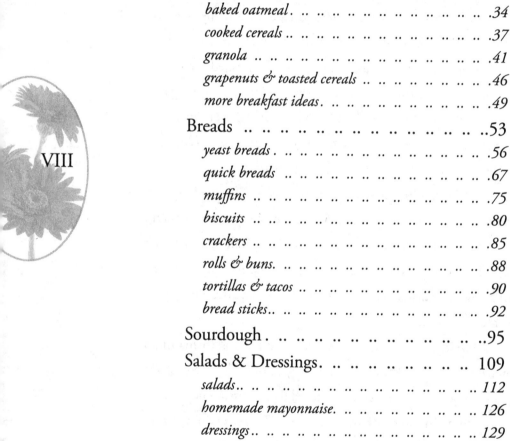

About Keepers at Home Magazine

Started in 1993, *Keepers at Home* had a mission to encourage mothers in their God-given calling of being mothers and homemakers. Our banner verses were and still are Titus 2:4-5. Speaking to women, Paul encourages, "That they may teach the young women to be sober, to love their husbands, to love their children, to be discreet, chaste, **keepers at home**, good, obedient to their own husbands, that the Word of God be not blasphemed. Four times a year we seek to bless and encourage close to 16,000 readers across the world with homemaking articles, recipes, gardening topics, homemade creations and spiritual nourishment, all written by our readers and editors.

We live "down the hill" from Walnut Creek, Ohio, a little town famous for its Amish Kitchen Cooking and other tourist amenities. We invite you to stop at our house if your travels bring you by!

Marvin & Miriam Wengerd family
Amy (Josh), Leah, Rosetta, Emily, David, Lisa, Heidi, Carrie & Jonathan

Ben Jr. & Mary K. Troyer family
Jolene (Conrad), Jessica (Charles), Bethany (Daniel), Vonda, Ben Lindan, Justin & Josiah (in heaven)

X

Beverages

WHO DOESN'T ENJOY COOLING OFF WITH A TALL GLASS of iced garden tea on a sticky July day? We all enjoy something good to drink.

Unfortunately there are not many healthy options in grocery stores. All those many different kinds of pop would be better off down your drain rather than down your throat!

So what can we moms do to make sure we have satisfying thirst-quenchers on hand that everyone will enjoy?

Our family cans around 100 quarts grape juice concentrate each year. This lasts until about the beginning of summer. We have friends who have an orchard, so each fall we enjoy drinking fresh apple cider from them. Last year we often drank five gallons a week, totaling at least fifty gallons.

In the summertime I make lots of iced mint tea. Then we often make smoothies too. These we enjoy with sandwiches for summer suppers.

Stock your freezer with strawberries, blueberries, black raspberries, peaches and frozen bananas, have maple syrup or agave nectar on hand for a sweetener, add a liquid such as rice milk or raw milk, and you have a winner for an energizing cooler that can even replace ice cream (another sugar-laden "avoidee") in summer. So, moms, don't reach for the pop cans, reach for healthy drink choices instead!

Healthy

Grape Juice Concentrate

MRS. MIRIAM WENGERD, SUGARCREEK, OH

You will need a steamer juicer for this recipe:

Wash grapes and pick off stems. Fill water reservoir. Fill steel basket inset with grapes. Turn on high and let boil for 45 minutes. Meanwhile prepare cans and lids. After 45 minutes drain juice into jars with attached hose. Put on lid and screw on band tightly. Set on towel on countertop they will seal as they cool. Continue cooking and draining off juice until grapes look rather colorless. Dump into steel strainer and set into large bowl, letting it drain overnight. Next morning there'll be some nice juice in the bottom yet. Use right away or set in jar in fridge to use later.

To use, open jar, empty into pitcher, refill jar with water and dump into pitcher. Add ice cubes. Add sweetener if you wish. I use a lot of 2 quart jars when canning this grape juice. It is the best grape juice I've ever tasted! We get our grapes by the box from a local farm market.

Strawberry Daiquiri

MARY BETH HEISEY, PUEBLO WEST, CO

3 cups frozen strawberries
2 cups apple juice
1 Tbsp. lemon (or lime) juice

1 tsp. vanilla
honey or stevia to taste

Combine in blender. Blend until smooth. Serve immediately. We enjoy this especially during the summer.

Banana Smoothie

ELIZABETH STALTER, MILLERSBURG, OH

2 cups milk
2 bananas, peeled
(opt.)
2 Tbsp. honey or fructose

¼ tsp. vanilla
other ingredients for extra nutrients,

Blend in blender. Keep in freezer until ready to serve. Serves 2.

Strawberry Milk Shake

ELIZABETH STALTER, MILLERSBURG, OH

1½ bananas
12 frozen milk cubes
¼ cup cream, optional

¼ cup fructose, (opt.)
1 quart fresh or frozen strawberries

Blend in blender until smooth. Add milk until you have a consistency you like, at least 1-2 cups. Variation: Replace strawberries with 1-3 tablespoons chocolate powder.

Fruity Breakfast Juice

MRS. RHODA MILLER, SUGARCREEK, OH

2 cups orange juice
1 frozen banana

½ cup frozen strawberries
1 tsp. honey

Combine all ingredients in a blender until smooth. Pour into glasses.

Slushy Fruit Juice

MRS. RHODA MILLER, SUGARCREEK, OH

2 cups cranberry juice
1 cup pineapple juice

½ cup orange juice

Mix the three juices, then put in blender with ice cubes.

Barley Water

VICKY SCHILLING, SCOTLAND, UK

2 pints boiling water
4 Tbsp. honey
4 sliced lemon rinds

juice of 5 lemons
1 Tbsp. pearl barley

Scald the barley; drain off water. Put barley, lemon rinds, and honey in a pan with two pints boiling water; simmer for five minutes. Press through strainer and add the fresh lemon juice.

Healthy

Lemon Water

VICKY SCHILLING, SCOTLAND, UK

2 pints boiling water
3 lemons, rinds and juice

2 Tbsp. honey

Put lemon rinds, juice and honey in a bowl; pour on boiling water; leave to sit 10 minutes. Serve hot or cold.

Pear Sunshine Nog

MRS. CLARA YODER, MILLERSBURG, OH

1 large fresh pear
4 eggs
2 Tbsp. + 1 tsp. honey

1 cup cold orange juice
2 cups milk
nutmeg

Pare and core pear. Cut up and put in blender or salsa maker. Separate one egg, reserve white. Add yolks along with remaining whole eggs to pear; also add 2 Tbsp. honey, juice and milk. Blend until smooth. Pour into four beverage glasses. Beat egg white stiff and add 1 tsp. honey. Top nog with egg white meringue and dust with nutmeg.

Alice's Fruit Soup

ELIZABETH STALTER, MILLERSBURG, OH

Place in large bowl:

12 oz. frozen raspberries
16 oz. frozen strawberries

12 oz. frozen blueberries or blackberries

Add and stir to combine:

20 oz. pineapple chunks,
    unsweetened, undrained
16 oz. peach slices, unsweetened, undrained

16 oz. pear halves, unsweetened, undrained

Let stand about two hours or overnight in refrigerator for frozen fruit to thaw, and juices to mingle. Variation: Vary any fruit except raspberry, but substitute frozen for frozen, and canned for canned.

beverages

5

Fruit Smoothie

ELIZABETH STALTER, MILLERSBURG, OH

Place all in blender and blend until smooth:

1 cup Alice's Fruit Soup
(preceding recipe)

3 ice cubes

Fill to the ½ cup mark with water. Variations: In place of Alice's Fruit Soup, add 2 bananas, broken in chunks (may be frozen if desired), 2 oranges, peeled, cut in chunks (or 4 tangerines), 1 apple, cut in chunks, ¼ cup frozen juice concentrate, optional, and 6 dates, chopped, optional. Add water to the 1 cup mark. 1½ cups fresh pineapple, peeled and chopped, can be substituted for oranges and apple. Use up to ⅓ cup frozen juice concentrate, and combine two different kinds if desired.

Strawberry Milk Shake

MRS. MIRIAM WENGERD, SUGARCREEK, OH

2 cups milk
25 whole, large frozen strawberries

⅓ cup maple syrup
3 Tbsp. fresh lemon juice (opt.)

Pour milk in blender. Put in strawberries, maple syrup and lemon juice. Blend on high until smooth. Serve in glass tumblers with straws—yummy! Can be used to make popsicles. Makes a good summer supper served with popcorn and banana bread or served with egg sandwiches. Can use 1 teaspoon lemon flavoring instead of lemon juice. Serves two.

Carob Banana Smoothie

JULIA ENGLE, OKLAHOMA CITY, OK

1-12 oz. pkg. MORI NU tofu (soft)
2 bananas
1 Tbsp. carob powder

1 cup milk
3 cups ice

Place all ingredients in blender and blend on high until smooth.

Hot Cocoa Drink

SUSAN STALTER, MILLERSBURG, OH

1½ rounded cups fructose
¾ rounded cup cocoa
1½ cups warm water

1 gallon milk
½ tsp. vanilla, (opt.)

Combine fructose and cocoa. Mix well. Add water and boil for one minute, stirring constantly. Add milk and heat, stirring occasionally. Add vanilla and serve. Reheats well, but boils over very easily. Serves 16.

Healthy

Hot Cranberry Cider

MARY BETH HEISEY, PUEBLO WEST, CO

3 quarts apple juice or cider

1 quart cranberry juice

2-3 whole cloves

1 cinnamon stick

Simmer together for ½ hour. Remove spices and serve hot.

Hot Cider

MRS. RHODA MILLER, SUGARCREEK, OH

2 quarts cider

¾ tsp. cloves

¾ tsp. cinnamon

¾ tsp. allspice

dash of nutmeg

In saucepan combine spices and cider. Mix well. Bring mixture to boil over medium heat. Cook for 3 minutes and serve.

Peppermint New Year's Eve Tea

MARY BETH HEISEY, PUEBLO WEST, CO

1 quart boiling water

6 Tbsp. peppermint tea (or 6 tea bags)

½ tsp. saffron

2 cinnamon sticks

Add tea, saffron and cinnamon to boiling water. Cool and strain. Refrigerate. To make tea, use 1 cup concentrate to 6 cups boiling water. Sweeten with honey, if desired.

Homemade Eggnog

MARY BETH HEISEY, PUEBLO WEST, CO

6 eggs

⅓ cup honey

¼ tsp. salt

2 quarts milk

1 Tbsp. vanilla

½ tsp. nutmeg

1 cup cream or milk

Blend everything together except the vanilla and nutmeg. Heat in saucepan to 160-170°. Add vanilla and nutmeg. Cool. Refrigerate and enjoy!

Choices

Eggnog

LEAH GARBER, TUOLUMNE, CA

2 egg yolks
¼ tsp. salt

4 cups milk

Beat and cook together, just to boiling.

2 egg whites
1 tsp. vanilla

½ tsp. liquid stevia, scant
nutmeg

Beat egg whites until almost stiff. Add vanilla and stevia. Stir into hot mixture. Sprinkle with nutmeg. Chill, then serve. This is my mother's recipe, which I changed from white sugar to stevia. If you don't like the foam, you can omit the egg whites; just add vanilla and stevia to hot mixture.

Honey Lemonade

MRS. MIRIAM WENGERD, SUGARCREEK, OH

15 cups water
¾ cup honey

3 med. lemons, thinly sliced
2⅓ cups lemon juice

Heat 3 cups water and honey in a pan over medium heat until honey dissolves. Set aside to cool. Mix together in bowl 12 cups water, lemon juice, and honey-water mixture. Add thinly sliced lemons. Refrigerate for 4-5 hours; serve over ice cubes. Very refreshing! Makes 1¼ gallon.

Minty Cooler

MRS. MIRIAM WENGERD, SUGARCREEK, OH

15 cups water
¾ cup maple syrup

9 cups mint leaves

Put 5 cups cold water in blender. Add 3 cups mint leaves. Blend on high until leaves are all chopped up. Pour through strainer into pitcher. Repeat twice. Stir in maple syrup. Chill thoroughly. Serve over ice. Optional: Substitute 2 cups orange mint tea and 1 cup lemon balm leaves for 3 cups mint tea leaves. Cooling and refreshing!

Iced Tea Concentrate

Mrs. Rhoda Miller, Sugarcreek, OH

4 cups water
¾ cup honey

1½ quart tea leaves

Boil water and add tea leaves, tightly packed. Turn off heat and let steep 15 minutes, then strain. Add honey, stirring until dissolved. Put in freezer boxes. Mix one part concentrate to three parts water.

Hot Dandy (coffee substitute)

Ida Edwards, Linden, TN

4 med. dandelion roots

milk

Wash dandelion roots, then roast until dry. Once dry, grind them. Take 1 tsp. of ground root to 1 cup hot milk; let steep with saucer on top for 6 minutes, then strain. Sweeten to taste.

Spicy Milk Drink

Mrs. Joe Garber, Prattsburgh, NY

1 quart milk
½ cup sucanat
pinch of salt

1 tsp. vanilla
1 tsp. cinnamon
⅓ tsp. nutmeg

Beat well. Serve chilled.

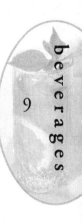

Strawberry Rice Milk Shake

Mrs. Miriam Wengerd, Sugarcreek, OH

2 cups rice milk
1 cup water
⅓ cup maple syrup

1 large frozen banana
1-2 tsp. lemon flavoring
25-30 frozen whole strawberries

Put rice milk and water in blender. Add 25 frozen strawberries and maple syrup. Blend on high speed. Add chunks of banana and 1 tsp. lemon flavoring. Blend on high until smooth. Add strawberries according to taste and thickness, and more lemon flavoring if desired. Can be used to make popsicles. Serves two.

Rice Milk

MRS. SAMUEL BRUBAKER, DUNDEE, NY

¼ cup brown rice flour
3 cups water
¼ tsp. salt

1 Tbsp. oil
4 Tbsp. brown rice syrup (opt.)

Cook water and rice flour. Cool. Blend, then add salt and syrup. With blender on high slowly add oil.

Almond Milk

MRS. RHODA MILLER, SUGARCREEK, OH

3 cups cold water

½ cup raw almonds

Blend together for several minutes. Strain. Delicious with cereal. Will stay fresh in refrigerator for three days.

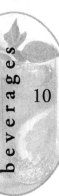

Breakfast

Healthy

MOST SATURDAYS WE ONLY HAVE TWO MEALS TO SAVE US

time. For many years we've made pancakes and eggs, sometimes waffles and on special occasions omelets for Saturday morning brunch. For a long time we used the Whole Grain Pancake Mix on page 22. Very handy to have on hand. Lately we've been using the Whole Wheat Pancakes recipe on page 22. My sister-in-law Marianna made these when we visited them in Tennessee. I never forgot those perfect pancakes! They're soft and fluffy—a winner!

For years I struggled to find a granola recipe I really liked, that didn't feel so heavy in my stomach. One day a thought came into my mind, "Why not use a crumb recipe that was intended as a pie topper and just make a healthy version of it?" So I tried it. The result is on page 41.

Serving eggs rounds out your meal of pancakes or waffles. Want an easy way to make enough for a large family? Try Simply Eggs on page 18. Fuss free!

Breakfast foods can make a fast meal for supper as well. During summer you can serve fresh fruit with yogurt and granola for a light supper. It might not be enough for a farmer, but it works for our family!

Last time when we had Sunday evening supper and hymn singing, we served a breakfast meal. You can make the Overnight Breakfast Casserole (page 16) the day before. In order to prevent your eggs from turning green, scramble them, heating just until done. Then immediately spread out on cookie sheets to cool off quickly before layering in casserole.

So really, "breakfast" foods can be used at other times too, not just mornings. Try them for special events or anytime.

When your family is happily munching away on your homemade granola you can have the quiet satisfaction of knowing they are beginning their day with a healthy choice.

Choices

Breakfast Main Dishes & Casseroles

Breakfast Haystacks

CHRISTY NOLT, DODGE CENTER, MN

grated potatoes, fried
ground sausage, browned
diced green peppers
diced hard boiled eggs

diced onions
diced tomatoes
cheese sauce
salsa

Place each ingredient in separate serving bowls. Make "haystacks" by layering ingredients in order given.

Hidden Eggs for Breakfast

ELIZABETH STALTER, MILLERSBURG, OH

4 Tbsp. butter
bread
6 or 7 eggs

salt and pepper
shredded cheese

Melt butter in a Pyrex pie pan. Save half of melted butter for top. Break up bread to cover bottom of pan. Drop eggs on bread. Sprinkle with salt and pepper. Break up one or two more slices of bread on top of eggs. Drizzle with butter and dot with shredded cheese. Bake 15-20 minutes or until eggs are done, at 375° or higher.

Soft Grits Casserole

KAYLENE HARTZLER, TENNILLE, GA

1 lb. sausage, fried	1 tsp. salt
½ lb. bacon, fried and crumbled	1 cup yellow grits, cooked
10 eggs, beaten	2 cups cheddar cheese
2½ cups milk	½ tsp. pepper
2 tsp. dry mustard	½ cup chopped onions

Mix together. Bake at 350° for 60 minutes or until brown on top and set. Makes one 9 x 13" pan.

Breakfast Stack

MRS. RHODA MILLER

toasted wheat bread cubes	peppers
scrambled eggs	mushrooms
gravy	onions
fried potatoes	cheese sauce

Prepare each ingredient. Sauté peppers, onions, and mushrooms together. Serve in order given.

Broccoli Cheese Soufflé

MRS. MIRIAM WENGERD, SUGARCREEK, OH

1½ lb. broccoli (5½ cups)	½ cup butter
1 cup onions	½ cup + 1 Tbsp. barley or wheat flour
2 cups shredded cheddar	2 tsp. salt
6 eggs, separated	½ tsp. garlic salt
2 cups milk	½ tsp. dry mustard
½ tsp. cream of tartar	¼ tsp. pepper
1 lb. bacon, fried and crumbled (optional)	

Wash broccoli. Cut in chunks, place in a little water in kettle. Chop onions and pour over broccoli. Cover and cook over low heat, just until bright green. Meanwhile, melt butter, stir in flour and heat until bubbly. Pour in milk. Add salt, garlic salt, pepper and dry mustard. Stir in egg yolks and shredded cheese. Remove from heat. Beat egg whites with cream of tartar until stiff. Fold into first mixture gently. Now stir in broccoli and onions (drained). Pour into ungreased 3 quart casserole. Set on cookie sheet with 1" water in cookie sheet. Bake at 350° for 50-60 minutes or until golden brown. Serves 12. Variations: This is good with spicy vegetable yogurt cheese instead of cheddar. You can also substitute chicken, cauliflower or cheese for the broccoli. This recipe x 2 fits nicely into a Lifetime-sized roaster and feeds 24. It is a delicious breakfast!

Simply Eggs

Mrs. Marvin Wengerd, Sugarcreek, OH

Melt butter in large skillet. Add three tablespoons water. Crack the number of eggs you wish into skillet, sprinkle with seasonings, put lid on. Turn on very low heat. For a dozen eggs check after twenty minutes. The handy thing about this recipe is there is no need to flip the eggs! They are soft and tasty if made just until done. Overcooked eggs are rubbery. When eggs are done, pinch bread bag twisty between lid and pan to keep lid from sealing. These eggs are a lot like poached eggs, but you avoid the extra chore of washing all the little egg cups.

Scrambled Eggs

Mrs. Miriam Wengerd, Sugarcreek, OH

12 eggs	4 Tbsp. butter
1 cup cream	¼ cup onions, minced (opt.)
1½ tsp. salt	¼ cup green peppers, finely diced (opt.)
½ tsp. pepper	¼ cup fresh mushrooms (opt.)

Beat eggs thoroughly. Add cream, salt, and pepper. Stir well. Melt butter in skillet. Pour in eggs and cook on low constantly. Do not overcook. May sprinkle with cheese and let melt before serving. If using onions, peppers, and mushrooms, sauté and add after eggs are beaten and cream is stirred in.

Omelets

Mrs. Miriam Wengerd, Sugarcreek, OH

2 eggs, beaten	pepper
salt	cheese slices

For filling, your choice of:

onions	green peppers
sausage	mushrooms

Chop and sauté onions, peppers, sausage and mushrooms. Beat eggs. Pour in buttered omelet pan; sprinkle with salt and pepper. Cook over low heat until beginning to set. Lift edges with pancake flipper and let unset eggs run underneath. Cook a little longer, then flip and immediately lay cheese on top and spread filling on one half of omelet. Now fold other half on top of filled portion, and carefully slide out on warmed plate. When making omelets for a large family, use large platter and keep warm in 150° oven until ready to serve. Serve with toast and orange juice. A favorite at our house!

Healthy

Breakfast Sandwiches

Mrs. Miriam Wengerd, Sugarcreek, OH

buns/bread   12 eggs
cheese

Toast buns or bread on pan with butter. Beat eggs with 1 cup homemade cream cheese, 1 tsp. salt, and ½ tsp. pepper. Pour into buttered 12" skillet, put lid on. Cook over low-medium heat for 15-20 minutes or until set. No need to flip! If they are puffy when you remove the lid, let them set until they flatten. The cream cheese makes them soft and fluffy—perfect for sandwiches. Divide into ten pieces. If using bread, make open-face sandwiches with one slice of cheese on top. If using buns, place egg on toasted bun half, place cheese slice on top and finish with bun top. Something about the toasting makes these sandwiches special! This is the perfect amount with our family of mostly girls and little children, and thus smaller sandwiches, but it would take more with more adults and/or boys. Serves 10.

Breakfast Burritos

Mrs. Miriam Wengerd, Sugarcreek, OH

10-8" honey wheat tortillas   1 cup onions, chopped
2 lb. bulk sausage, fried   1 cup green peppers, chopped
7½ cups cooked, cooled & grated potatoes

Cheese Sauce:

4 Tbsp. butter   ¾ tsp. salt
4 Tbsp. barley flour   ¼ tsp. pepper
2 cups milk   2 cups cheddar cheese

Fry and chop sausage. When it's nearly done, add onions and green peppers. When done frying, drain in colander. Scrub potatoes, cut in half if large, steam until tender. Cool and shred. Make cheese sauce. Melt butter, whisk in flour, then milk, and cook while stirring until it thickens. Turn off heat. Add cheese, salt and pepper. Cover until cheese is melted, then stir until smooth. Stir in drained sausage liquid to thin a little, or use water. Lay 10 tortillas on flat surface. Spoon 2 heaping Tbsp. sausage mix down center of each. Spread ¾ cup potatoes on top. Roll up tortillas and place seam side down in two glass 9 x 13" pans—5 tortillas per pan. Pour cheese sauce over top of each filled pan, dividing evenly between the two. Sprinkle the rest of the sausage mixture over the top. Bake at 350° for 30-45 minutes or until hot. Serves 8-10 people.

French Toast & Waffles

French Toast

MRS. IVAN YODER, MILLERSBURG, OH

2 eggs
1 cup milk
1 Tbsp. honey

⅛ tsp. salt
4-6 slices bread

Beat eggs, milk, honey and salt. Heat lightly greased skillet. Dip bread in egg mixture and fry on both sides. Serve with maple syrup.

Delicious French Toast

MRS. LEONA MILLER, ODON, IN

3 eggs
½ cup milk
1 Tbsp. plain yogurt
1 Tbsp. honey

½ tsp. cinnamon
½ tsp. vanilla
dash of salt

Beat all ingredients together well. Dip slices of your favorite homemade bread into egg mixture and fry on hot griddle coated with natural canola oil. Spray until golden brown. Delicious served with maple syrup or may use topping of your choice.

Quick French Toast

MRS. RHODA MILLER, SUGARCREEK, OH

6 slices whole wheat bread
2 eggs

1 cup milk
½ cup whole wheat flour

Combine eggs, milk, and flour. Dip bread in egg mixture. Fry on lightly greased griddle. Serve with maple syrup, honey or fruit.

Healthy

World's Best Waffles

B. Garber, Fayetteville, PA

1 pkg. active dry yeast	1 tsp. vanilla extract
1 Tbsp. sweetener	2½ cups whole wheat pastry flour
2 cups warm milk	½ tsp. salt
4 eggs, separated	½ cup butter, melted

Dissolve yeast and sweetener in warm milk. Beat egg yolks lightly; add to yeast mixture with vanilla. Combine flour, salt, and nutmeg; stir into yeast mix, just until combined. Add butter; mix well. Beat egg whites until stiff peaks form; fold into batter. Cover and let rise until doubled, about 45-60 minutes. Bake in a preheated waffle iron until golden. Yield: 12-16 waffles.

Waffles

2 cups rye flour	1 Tbsp. baking powder
¾ tsp. salt	1 tsp. wheat gluten (opt.)

Mix all together. Then mix separately:

1 small egg	¼ cup olive oil
2 Tbsp. honey (mixed with 2 Tbsp. hot water)	2 Tbsp. egg replacer
	1¾ cup rice milk

Stir with dry ingredients briefly. Makes 10-12.

Waffles

Mrs. Miriam Wengerd, Sugarcreek, OH

2 cups wheat flour	2 tsp. cinnamon
2 cups barley flour	6 eggs, separated
4 tsp. baking powder	3 cups milk
1 tsp. salt	½ cup butter, melted

Measure flour, baking powder, salt and cinnamon into large bowl. Separate eggs; beat egg whites and set aside. Beat yolks, milk, and melted butter together. Add to flour mixture, beating until thoroughly mixed. Fold in egg whites. Preheat waffle iron, grease lightly. Pour in ¾ cup batter, bake 5-7 minutes. Makes 20-5" waffles. Keep warm on platter in oven turned to 150°. Serve with frozen blueberries, hot maple syrup, and Peanut Butter Topper. (Peanut Butter Topper: 1 cup fresh ground peanut butter and ½ cup maple syrup mixed together in food processor until creamy.) After years of struggling to make good whole grain waffles, I came up with this recipe that works. Light, yet full of flavor.

Pancakes

Whole Grain Pancake Mix

Mrs. Miriam Wengerd, Sugarcreek, OH

3 cups wheat flour
2½ cups buckwheat
½ cup oatmeal
1 cup wheat germ

1 cup cornmeal
5 Tbsp. baking powder
1 Tbsp. salt
2 Tbsp. lecithin granules

Mix and store in cool place. To make panckes:

2 cups milk
2 eggs
2 cups mix

½ cup oil
2 tsp. cinnamon

Combine milk, eggs, oil and cinnamon, Add to mix and stir well. Fry on buttered griddle.

This is the pancake recipe we used for many years. Very handy to have on hand! A good quickie for supper too. Serve with fresh ground peanut butter and maple syrup and/or frozen blueberries. Yummy and satisfying! Tip: Grind 2 cups wheat berries to make 3 c. flour, 2 c. buckwheat to make 2½ c. flour.

Whole Wheat Pancakes

Mrs. Miriam Wengerd, Sugarcreek, OH

2 eggs
2 cups buttermilk
4 Tbsp. oil
1½ cup wheat flour

1 tsp. salt
2 Tbsp. sweetener
2 tsp. baking powder
1 tsp. baking soda

Mix all ingredients and fry on buttered skillet.

When we visited Marvin's brother Dean in Tennessee, his wife Marianna served these pancakes. They are perfectly delicious! Sour milk can be used instead of buttermilk.

Pumpkin Pancakes

MRS. RAEDELLA WENGER, CHAMBERSBURG, PA

3 eggs
1 cup pumpkin
½ cup milk

2 tsp. baking powder
1 tsp. salt
1 cup wheat flour

Beat eggs. Add cooked pumpkin and milk. Stir in dry ingredients. Fry in electric skillet. Makes 7 pancakes.

Whole Wheat Pancakes

JULIA ENGLE, OKLAHOMA CITY, OK

3 eggs
3 cups milk
¼ cup canola oil

3 cups whole wheat flour
2 Tbsp. baking powder
1 tsp. salt

Beat eggs lightly, then add milk and canola oil. Stir in dry ingredients and mix until smooth. Cook pancakes in a non-stick skillet over medium heat. Serves 7.

Cornmeal Pancakes

MRS. SUSAN RABER, BRINKHAVEN, OH

1⅓ cup wheat flour
⅓ cup cornmeal
2 Tbsp. sweetener of your choice
4 tsp. baking powder

1 tsp. salt
2 eggs
¼ cup oil
1⅓ cup milk

Combine flour, cornmeal, sweetener, baking powder and salt. In another bowl whisk eggs, milk and oil. Stir into dry ingredients just until moistened. Pour batter by ¼ cupfuls onto lightly greased hot pan. Turn when bubbles form on top. Cook until second side is golden. Good!

Pumpkin Spice Pancakes

MARY BETH HEISEY, PUEBLO WEST, CO

2¼ cups whole wheat flour
1½ tsp. baking powder
1 tsp. baking soda
½ tsp. salt
½ tsp. cinnamon
¼ tsp. nutmeg

¼ tsp. cloves
½ cup oil
3 eggs, beaten
¼ cup honey
1 cup pumpkin
1 cup milk or water

Mix together and drop by ¼ cupfuls onto preheated griddle. Serve with applesauce and maple syrup.

Oatmeal Pancakes

MONICA BAZEN, GRAND RAPIDS, MI

Soak five minutes:

2 cups milk	2 cups quick oats

Add:

2 eggs, beaten	¼ cup oil

In separate bowl, mix:

½ cup flour	1 tsp. baking powder
½ tsp. salt	½ tsp. cinnamon
1 tsp. baking soda	1 peeled and chopped apple

Gently mix the dry and wet ingredients until just moistened. Fry by ¼ cupfuls on a hot pancake griddle.

Pancakes

DEB FUNK, DALLAS CENTER, IA

1 egg, beaten	1 tsp. baking powder
1 cup whole wheat flour	¼ cup vegetable oil
¾ tsp. salt	1 cup sour milk or buttermilk
½ tsp. baking soda	

Mix all ingredients. Add additional milk if necessary. Note: If you don't have sour milk, add 1 tsp. vinegar. I just use plain milk sometimes.

Corn Cakes

1 cup white cornmeal	1 Tbsp. egg replacer*
1 tsp. baking powder	

Can be stored in refrigerator for months.

Cakes:

1 cup mix	Braggs
½ cup water	

Heat frying pan. Add a dab of butter. Divide batter into fourths and spoon onto pan. Brown and flip. *Egg replacer: Mix 1 cup potato starch, 1 cup tapioca flour and 2 tsp. baking powder together well.

Everyday Pancakes

MRS. LEONA MILLER, ODON, IN

1 cup whole wheat pastry flour
2 Tbsp. canola oil
2 Tbsp. raw honey
1 egg

½ tsp. salt
1 tsp. vanilla
¾-1½ cup milk
2 Tbsp. aluminum-free baking powder

Mix all ingredients together well, adding baking powder last. Fry on hot griddle, greased with natural canola oil spray, until golden. Serve with maple syrup or topping of your choice.

Syrupy Pancake Bake

MRS. REBECCA ZOOK, MYERSTOWN, PA

1 egg
1 cup buttermilk, scant
½ tsp. salt

2 Tbsp. melted butter or oil
1 cup whole wheat flour
1 Tbsp. baking powder

Mix and cover. Let stand overnight. Grease 13 x 9" pan. Pour maple syrup in to slightly cover bottom. Pour mixture on top. Bake at 350° for 20 minutes or until pancake is done.

Whole Grain Pancakes

DARLA REENA STOLL, ODON, IN

1 cup wheat pastry flour
¾ to 1 cup rolled oats
1¾ to 2 cups buttermilk
¼ cup oil

¾ cup brown rice flour
1 tsp. baking soda
2 eggs

Mix all dry ingredients together. Beat eggs well, then add eggs and remaining ingredients to dry mixture, mixing only until blended. Add quarter-size drop of oil to pan. Fry until brown on both sides. My husband likes these, and he usually doesn't like whole grain foods too well.

Favorite Pancakes

SUSIE NISLEY, DANVILLE, OH

2 eggs
2 cups buttermilk
1 tsp. soda
2¼ cups spelt flour

2 tsp. baking powder
1 tsp. salt
3 Tbsp. coconut oil

Beat eggs until light. Add buttermilk and soda. Add flour, salt and oil, then last add baking powder. Stir until smooth; fry on hot griddle.

Choices

Graham Breakfast Cakes

MRS. REBECCA ZOOK, MYERSTOWN, PA

2 cups whole wheat flour
1 cup oatmeal
½ cup honey
¼ cup unsulfured baking molasses
1 cup buttermilk

⅓ cup oil
1 tsp. soda
½ tsp. salt
½ tsp. cinnamon
1 tsp. vanilla

Mix together, cover and let set overnight. Bake at 375° for 15-20 minutes or until done.

Prairie Gold Pancakes

ROSEMARY SHOWALTER, DAYTON, VA

2 eggs
2½ cups milk
½ cup oil
¼ cup honey

3 cups Prairie Gold wheat flour
1 tsp. salt
4 tsp. baking powder

Beat together eggs, milk, oil and honey in bowl. Mix flour, salt and baking powder. Pour together, mix well. Fry on hot griddle. This is the best pancake recipe that we've tried!

Whole Wheat Oatmeal Pancakes

MRS. JEREMY (ROSE) MILLER, ST. IGNATIUS, MT

2 eggs
1½ cup milk
4 Tbsp. olive oil
2 Tbsp. honey

1 cup oatmeal
1 cup whole wheat flour
1½ Tbsp. baking powder
½ tsp. salt

Beat eggs until fluffy; add milk, oil, and honey. Stir in dry ingredients. Let set a few minutes before frying. If mixture thickens too much, add a little more milk. Delicious!

Sourdough Pancakes or Waffles

Mix together:

½ cup starter	1½ cup fresh ground flour
½ cup oat flour	1½ cup water or buttermilk

Let soak overnight in a covered bowl. Next morning, stir in:

1 egg	½ tsp. sea salt
2 Tbsp. olive oil	1 tsp. baking soda
2 Tbsp. raw honey	

Let set 30 minutes then fry on hot griddle. You can use coconut oil for frying.

Waffles & Pancakes

KATHY SCHWEIHOFER, CHINA, MI

2¼ cups flour	½ tsp. salt
4 tsp. baking powder	

Add dry ingredients to liquid items:

3 eggs	2 Tbsp. oil
2 cups milk	

Fry in greased skillet, or pour ¾ cup in waffle iron. Top with butter, maple syrup, honey, or homemade preserves.

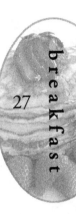

Whole Wheat Pancakes

MRS. KATHRYN HERSHBERGER, CLARE, MI

2 cups whole wheat flour	2 eggs, beaten
1 tsp. soda	1¾ cup milk
2 tsp. baking powder	¼ cup melted butter or olive oil
½ tsp. salt	2 Tbsp. vinegar
3 Tbsp. maple syrup	

Add ingredients in order given. Don't beat too much. For fluffier pancakes, beat egg whites separately and fold in last. I like to drizzle fresh or frozen blueberries over them while frying.

Pancake Cake

ELIZABETH STALTER, MILLERSBURG, OH

3¾ cups flour

1 Tbsp. sweetener

1 cup melted butter

2¼ tsp. salt

3¾ cups milk

6 eggs

3 Tbsp. baking powder

Beat eggs slightly. Add butter and milk. Add dry ingredients. Beat only until flour is mixed. Batter should be lumpy; do not overmix. Bake in greased 9 x 13" pan at 375° for one hour, or until center is done.

Variation: Use your favorite pancake/waffle recipe and experiment to find the baking time and temperature.

Sour Cream Pancakes

LUCIA LAPP, BENTON, IL

4 eggs

1 cup flour

½ tsp. stevia powder

½ tsp. vanilla

¼ tsp. salt

⅔ cup sour cream or plain yogurt

6 Tbsp. milk

Mix dry ingredients together. Beat egg whites until stiff. Stir sour cream, yolks, and milk into dry ingredients. Fold in egg whites. Fry pancakes about 3-4 minutes per side.

Cornmeal Pancakes

LUCIA LAPP, BENTON, IL

1⅓ cup whole grain flour

⅔ cup cornmeal

1 Tbsp. fructose

4 tsp. baking powder

1 tsp. salt

2 eggs

1⅓ cup milk

¼ cup oil

Mix just until moistened. Fry on hot griddle.

Sourdough Pancakes

Lucia Lapp, Benton, IL

1 cup sourdough
1 cup flour
¾ tsp. salt
¾ tsp. soda
2 Tbsp. sucanat

1 tsp. baking powder
⅓ cup oil
2 eggs
½ cup milk

Mix well and fry. Makes approximately 15 pancakes.

Egg Pancakes

Marie Bear, Patriot, OH

12 eggs
3 cups milk

2 cups quick oats
¼ cup oil

Beat eggs well and add rest of ingredients. Melt a little butter in frying pan. Pour enough batter into pan (on medium heat) to cover the bottom. Cut into fourths or sections small enough to flip. Serve like regular pancakes.

Corn Mush Pancakes

Mrs. Urie Miller, Middlebury, IN

1½ cup precooked cornmeal mush
¾ cup whole grain flour
3 eggs

½ tsp. salt
2 tsp. baking powder
½-¾ cup milk

Put all ingredients into bowl and beat up with a potato masher. Add milk as needed to make a batter of the right consistency. Bake on moderately hot griddle, using butter as needed. These pancakes are very tender and delicious, served with syrup or honey, applesauce or sausage gravy.

Oatmeal-Buttermilk Pancakes

Cynthia Korver, New Oxford, PA

Mix:

½ cup milk	1 Tbsp. honey

Add:

2 cups buttermilk	1½ cups oatmeal

Beat in:

1 cup whole wheat flour	½ tsp. salt
1 tsp. baking soda	2 eggs

More milk may need to be added. May be made right away or put into the refrigerator from 1-24 hours. Drop by ¼ cup onto hot skillet and fry. Note: This was my mother-in-law's recipe. She is no longer living so it's special.

Pancakes

Mrs. Linda Troyer, Guthrie, KY

4½ cups whole wheat flour	4½ cups milk
9 tsp. baking powder	5 eggs, separated
1⅛ tsp. salt	

Stir together dry ingredients and separate eggs. Beat egg yolks with one cup milk and add all the milk and yolks to dry ingredients. Beat egg whites until stiff and fold in last.

Pancakes

Walter Sauder, Latham, MO

1 cup buckwheat flour	1 egg
1 cup buttermilk	1 tsp. soda
pinch of salt	

Soak flour in buttermilk for seven hours, or overnight. Stir in salt, egg, and soda. Fry in a hot pan.

Healthy

Pancakes

MRS. REBECCA SCHLABACH, BURTON, OH

2 cups spelt (or whole wheat) flour
2 cups yogurt
2 eggs
½ tsp. sea salt
1 tsp. baking soda
2 Tbsp. melted butter

Soak flour in yogurt (those with milk allergies may use 2 cups water with 2 tablespoons whey or lemon juice) in a warm place (70-80 degrees) for 12-24 hours. Stir in remaining ingredients and thin to desired consistency with milk and water. Cook on a hot, oiled griddle or cast-iron skillet. These pancakes cook more slowly. Delicious! Variation: Drop a few blueberries on each pan of batter for blueberry pancakes.

Buckwheat Buttermilk Pancakes

INA SCHROCK, GAP MILLS, WV

1 cup buttermilk
4 eggs, beaten
½ cup fruit juice

Combine in a large bowl. Then add:

¾ cup buckwheat flour
2¼ cups whole grain flour
2 tsp. salt
2 tsp. soda
½ tsp. baking powder

Mix well with a spoon but do not beat! If batter is thick, add yogurt or milk until batter easily runs off spoon. Fry in hot skillet. Makes 16-4" cakes.

Dry Pancake Mix

INA SCHROCK, GAP MILLS, WV

3¾ cups buckwheat flour
11¼ cups whole grain flour
    (oat, rice or barley)
10 tsp. salt
10 tsp. soda
2½ tsp. baking powder

Combine and store in airtight container in freezer. To use: 3⅔ cups pancake mix. Wet ingredients same as original recipe (preceding recipe). Performs well over a campfire!

Diligent Student Pancakes

CINDY TURNER, BRADFORD, OH

1½ cup whole wheat flour
¼ cup wheat germ
3 tsp. baking powder
2 Tbsp. oil
1 egg

½ tsp. salt
1 tsp. molasses
1¼ cup milk
2 Tbsp. honey

Mix and fry as you would your favorite pancakes.

Blender Waffles or Pancakes

MARLENE ZIMMERMAN, ORCHARD, IA

1½ cup buttermilk
1 egg
1 tsp. vanilla
½ cup raw brown rice

½ cup rolled oats
2 Tbsp. olive oil
2 Tbsp. honey
½ cup wheat flour

The secret to light and tender waffles is the thinness of the batter. This is very important. The batter should always swirl about a vortex in the blender. If not, add a little liquid until the hole reappears. Blend above ingredients for 3-5 minutes or until smooth. Blend in briefly just before baking:

½ tsp. soda
2 tsp. baking powder

1 tsp. salt

Pour thin batter onto a hot waffle iron or pancake griddle sprayed with olive oil. Makes 4-5 servings or 4 large Belgian waffles.

Honey Wheat Cakes

CINDY TURNER, BRADFORD, OH

1 cup wheat bran (or oat bran, all bran)
¼ cup wheat germ
½ tsp. soda
½ cup hot water
¼ cup honey

¼ cup oil
1 cup whole wheat flour
1½ tsp. baking powder
½ tsp. salt
1 cup buttermilk
1 egg

Preheat oven to 425°. Beat all ingredients until smooth. Pour into a greased 15 x 10" jelly roll pan. Bake 8-10 minutes. Cut into squares and serve with maple syrup. (These will be thin like pancakes.) Variations: Sprinkle ⅔ cup browned sausage and blueberries over batter, then bake. Or sprinkle chopped bacon pieces (3 slices) and chopped apple (¾ of an apple) over batter, then bake.

Healthy

Whole Wheat Pancakes

MRS. RHODA MILLER, SUGARCREEK, OH

3 eggs
3 cups milk
¼ cup vegetable oil
3 cups whole wheat flour

2 Tbsp. baking powder
1 tsp. salt
2 Tbsp. honey
cinnamon (opt.)

Beat eggs; add milk and oil. Stir in dry ingredients. Makes many pancakes!

Oatmeal Pancakes

MRS. URIE MILLER, MIDDLEBURY, IN

2 cups cornmeal
2 cups whole wheat flour
2 cups quick oats
1 Tbsp. baking powder
1 Tbsp. soda

1 Tbsp. salt
3 eggs, separated
½ cup melted butter or coconut oil
1¼-1½ qt. sweet milk

Mix dry ingredients thoroughly. Add egg yolks, butter or oil, and milk that is warmed to lukewarm and mix. Fold in beaten egg whites. Bake on greased griddle, turning once.

Yorkshire Pudding

MABEL ZIMMERMAN

1 cup flour
1 cup milk

3 large eggs
½ tsp. salt

Put 2 Tbsp. butter and 2 Tbsp. coconut oil in a 9 x 13" baking dish. Put in oven at 375° to melt. Meanwhile stir together other ingredients, then pour into butter and oil. Bake 25 minutes or until edges brown.

Choices

Baked Oatmeal

Baked Oatmeal

SUSAN STALTER, MILLERSBURG, OH

½ cup butter, melted
¼-½ cup fructose

2 eggs

Beat together. Then add:

3 cups oats (rolled or quick)
2 tsp. baking powder

1 tsp. real salt
1 cup milk

Bake in an 8 x 8" pan at 350° for 30 minutes.

Baked Oatmeal

JODY NOLT, MYERSTOWN, PA

½ cup butter
1 cup maple syrup
2 eggs, beaten
3 cups oats

2 tsp. baking powder
1 tsp. salt
1 cup raw milk

Cream together first three ingredients. Add rest to creamed mixture. Bake in 10 x 10" pan at 350° for 20-30 minutes.

Whole Wheat Ocean Cake

LINDSAY ZEHR, HALSEY, OR

⅓ cup butter
5 eggs
1 cup whole milk

¾ cup whole wheat flour
⅓ cup whole rolled oats

Heat oven to 425°. Melt butter, and pour into 7 x 11" pan. Beat eggs until thick, add flour, milk and oats. Stir and pour over butter in pan. Bake 20-25 minutes, until crusty and medium brown. It will puff and look like ocean waves. Serve warm with real maple syrup.

Healthy

Baked Oatmeal

BETH WEAVER, NARVON, PA

½ cup milk
½ cup olive oil
3 cups oatmeal
1 tsp. salt
1 Tbsp. cinnamon

2 eggs
½ cup sucanat or honey
2 tsp. baking powder
1 Tbsp. vanilla

If using honey, decrease milk to ¼ cup. Put in 8 x 8" pan or pie dish. Bake at 350° until nice and brown, about 30 minutes.

Delicious Baked Oatmeal

MRS. LEONA MILLER, ODON, IN

2 cups organic quick oats
½ tsp. real salt
1 tsp. (heaping) aluminum-free
   baking powder
⅓ cup butter (melted)

⅓ cup raw honey
1 tsp. vanilla extract
1 egg
¾ cup milk

In a small saucepan, melt the butter, remove from heat, and add the honey and vanilla. Stir well. Combine rest of ingredients in a mixing bowl and add the butter mixture. Mix well. Pour into a greased 9 x 13" baking pan. Bake at 350° for 25-30 minutes or until edges are golden brown. Immediately spoon into serving bowls and sprinkle with sucanat or honey and serve with warm milk and fresh fruit if desired. Our favorite is blueberries. We also like to sprinkle with sliced almonds or any chopped nuts of your choice.

Baked Oatmeal Breakfast

MRS. NANCY PEIGHT, McVEYTOWN, PA

2 eggs
½ cup sucanat
½ cup oil
2½ cups oatmeal
½ cup fine coconut
2 Tbsp. ground flax seeds

2 tsp. baking powder
1 tsp. salt
½ tsp. cinnamon (opt.)
½ cup raisins, chopped apples
   or frozen blueberries

Mix eggs, oil, and sucanat together. Add remaining ingredients and stir until well mixed. Pour into a greased 9 x 13" pan. Bake at 350° for 30 minutes. Serve with milk or your choice of canned or frozen fruit.

Baked Oatmeal

MRS. RHODA MILLER, SUGARCREEK, OH

3 cups oatmeal
½ cup honey
2 eggs, beaten
½ cup oil or melted butter

1 cup rice milk or water
2 tsp. baking powder
1 tsp. cinnamon

Mix all ingredients together. Spoon into greased 9" baking dish. Bake at 350° for 30-45 minutes. Serve warm with fruit and/or milk. Variation: Use ½ cup applesauce to replace the ½ cup oil.

Baked Oatmeal

MRS. MIRIAM WENGERD, SUGARCREEK, OH

4½ cups oatmeal
3 tsp. baking powder
2¼ tsp. cinnamon
¾ cup melted butter

¾ cup sorghum molasses
1½ cup milk
3 eggs, beaten
1½ tsp. salt

Mix dry ingredients. Add all wet ingredients at once and beat thoroughly. Pour into greased 9 x 13" glass pan. Bake at 350° 30-40 minutes. Serve with maple syrup, plain yogurt, and frozen blueberries for a delicious, quick breakfast! Or serve with Peach Cream as a topping. Serves 10. Peach Cream: 1 qt. peaches, drained, 1½ cup plain yogurt, sucanat to taste, optional. Pour into blender and blend until smooth. A yummy way to use up peaches that are old or discolored.

Healthy

Cooked Cereals

Overnight Baked Porridge

B. Garber, Fayetteville, PA

4½ cups water
3 cups quick oats
2 eggs, lightly beaten
2 apples, peeled and chopped (1 cup)
½ cup sucanat
½ cup milk
½ cup vegetable oil
½ cup raisins (opt.)
2 tsp. baking powder
1 tsp. salt
½ tsp. cinnamon

Boil water and add oats. Return to a boil and cook for 1 minute. Remove from heat, cover and let stand for 5 minutes. Combine remaining ingredients. Stir in oatmeal. Spoon into a greased 9" square pan. Cover and refrigerate overnight. Remove from refrigerator 30 minutes before baking. Bake, uncovered, at 350° for 60-65 minutes or until a knife inserted comes out clean. Cut into squares. Pour milk over each serving if desired. Yields: 9 servings

Fried Corn Mush

Ida Edwards, Linden, TN

2 cups cornmeal
1 cup flour
2¼ cups cold water
9 cups boiling water
6 tsp. salt

Mix cornmeal, flour and cold water. Boil 9 cups water in a large cast-iron Dutch oven, add salt. Once you're sure it's boiling, stir in the cornmeal mixture. Cook, stirring constantly, until mixture thickens and comes to a boil. Reduce heat, cover and let simmer 10 minutes, stirring occasionally; remove from heat and stir until smooth. Pour into a greased 9 x 13" cake pan and chill overnight. In the morning, slice the firm mush, and fry lightly floured slices in butter until crispy on both sides. Serve with butter and maple syrup.

Cornmeal Mush

Christy Nolt, Dodge Center, MN

1 cup cornmeal	1 cup cold water or milk
1 tsp. salt	3 cups boiling water

Mix cornmeal, salt, and cold water or milk. Add to boiling water. Cook until thick, then simmer 10 minutes, covered. Serve warm with a little milk and butter or maple syrup. Or pour mush into a greased loaf pan and refrigerate overnight. Invert loaf, slice into ¼" slices, and fry in butter until lightly browned.

Creamy Corn Cereal

Mrs. Vernon Schrock, Lewistown, IL

2 quarts whole milk	1 tsp. salt
1½ cups cornmeal	

Heat 5 cups of the milk to boiling. In a bowl, mix cornmeal and salt with remaining milk. Add to boiling milk and stir until mixture boils. Serve with sweetener and milk. This is enough for our family of ten. It is a favorite hot cereal.

Country Breakfast Cereal

Ina Schrock, Gap Mills, WV

1 cup brown rice, uncooked	2¼ cups water
¼ tsp. salt	milk or cream
1 Tbsp. butter	honey
½ cup raisins	fresh fruit
1 tsp. cinnamon	

Combine rice, salt, butter, raisins, cinnamon, and water in a 2-3 qt. casserole dish. Bake at 350° for 1 hour. Fluff with fork. Serve with milk or cream, honey, and fresh fruit, if desired. Serves 6.

Cornmeal Mush

MARTHA STOLTZFUS, BLAIN, PA

2 cups + 5 cups water
2 cups cornmeal

1 Tbsp. salt

Using a 3 quart pot, mix together 2 cups water with cornmeal and salt, stirring until all is dissolved. Add 5 cups water and cook on medium heat until starting to thicken. Reduce heat to low and continue to simmer for 20-30 minutes or until consistency of thick applesauce. Pour into two small ungreased bread pans. Store in refrigerator after cooling. At breakfast time, slice in ¾" thick slices and fry in a skillet with butter until browned on both sides. Serve with maple syrup if desired. Can also be eaten warm as a pudding with breakfast.

Breakfast Whole-Grain Cereal

MRS. MIRIAM NOLT, PINE GROVE, PA

½ cup wheat berries
¼ cup cracked wheat
½ cup rolled oats

½ tsp. sea salt
¼ tsp. cardamom (opt.)
4 cups water

In a 4 quart crockpot, combine all ingredients. Cover and cook on low for 6-8 hours or overnight. Stir in ½ cup raisins or dried cranberries just before serving, if desired. Serve with maple syrup and milk.

Cooked Corn Mush

MRS. ALLEN R. BYLER, SMICKSBURG, PA

3 cups water
1 cup cornmeal
¾ cup milk

1 tsp. salt
¼ cup whole wheat flour

Bring 3 cups water to a boil in a 3 quart saucepan. Mix cornmeal and flour together, add milk and salt. When water starts to boil, slowly pour cornmeal mixture into kettle of boiling water, stirring constantly. Reduce heat and boil slowly for ten minutes. Pour into two bread pans and let set overnight until cold. Then slice and fry in hot olive oil. I sprinkle my pans of olive oil with flour before adding mush. Makes a hearty breakfast!

Maple Oatmeal

MRS. MIRIAM WENGERD, SUGARCREEK, OH

4 cups cold water
2 cups oatmeal

1 cup maple syrup

Put everything in kettle, stirring well. Bring to boil over high heat, stirring occasionally. Now turn on low and simmer about ten minutes. Turn off heat. Let set until ready to serve. Serve with Crunchy Topper and cream. (Crunchy Topper: ¼ cup butter, 1 cup ground pecans, 1 cup coconut, ¼ cup sucanat. Melt butter in saucepan. Stir in pecans and coconut. Next stir in sucanat. Heat on low for 10-15 minutes, stirring occasionally, until toasted. Serve warm on top of bowl of oatmeal.)

Multi-Grain Breakfast Porridge

MRS. LEONA MILLER, ODON, IN

¼ cup organic rolled oats
½ tsp. real salt

¼ cup water
1 heaping tsp. plain yogurt

Mix all ingredients in a small bowl and let soak for 8 hours or overnight. Next morning in a small saucepan, bring one cup of water to a boil. Add ½ tsp. salt, ¼ tsp. cinnamon, and soaked oat mixture. Boil gently for about one minute. Remove from heat and add 6 tsp. of any combination of oat bran, ground flax seed, raw wheat germ, or any other grain of your choice. I also add ¼ tsp. vanilla or maple flavoring. Mix well. Sprinkle with stevia, sucanat, or sweetener of your choice. May also add fruit and milk if desired. May also add raisins or chopped nuts. Makes one serving.

Apple-Banana Oatmeal

MRS. LEONA MILLER, ODON, IN

1 cup water
1 Tbsp. orange juice concentrate
½ cup chopped, unpeeled, apple
¼ cup sliced, firm banana
¼ cup raisins

¼ tsp. salt
⅛ tsp. cinnamon
⅔ cup organic quick oats
¼-⅓ cup oat bran

In a saucepan, combine water, orange juice concentrate, apple, banana, raisins, salt, and cinnamon; bring to a boil. Stir in oats and oat bran. Cook for 1-2 minutes, stirring occasionally. Sprinkle with sweetener of your choice and milk if desired. Yield: 2 servings.

Granola

Peanut Butter Granola

B. Garber, Fayetteville, PA

10 cups oatmeal
2 cups raw sunflower seeds
½ cup ground flax seed
1 cup honey

1 tsp. salt (opt.)
2 cups peanut butter
¾ cup oil
1 cup warm water

Mix dry ingredients. Mix remaining ingredients in a pan and heat and stir occasionally until mixed. Pour into dry ingredients and mix well. It will be slightly chunky. Spread on two baking sheets with sides and bake at 325° for 1-1½ hours, stirring every 15 minutes. Many things can be substituted to make up the 12½ cups dry matter in this recipe. I have used coconut, oat bran, and wheat germ.

Golden Crispies Cereal

Martha Wise, Seneca Falls, NY

8 cups rolled oats
4 cups wheat germ
4 cups oat or wheat bran
¾ cup oil

¾ cup water
4 Tbsp. vanilla
⅔ cup honey

Mix all together. Bake at 350° for 40-45 minutes, stirring every fifteen minutes. When cool, add 1 cup raisins.

Granola

Mrs. Miriam Wengerd, Sugarcreek, OH

4 cups wheat flour
6 cups rolled oats
3 cups flake coconut (unsweetened)
3 cups pecans (ground)

3 cups sucanat
3 tsp. cinnamon
3 cups butter (melted)

Mix the first six ingredients in a bowl. Melt butter, pour over dry mixture and mix until crumbly. Put on cookie sheets with sides. Bake at 300° until golden brown, stirring every 20 minutes. Takes about one hour. I tried to make granola for a long time, but never found one I like as well as this. It's crunchy and delicious. Divide between three 11 x 17" cookie sheets when toasting. Makes one gallon.

Cinnamon Nut Granola

SUSAN STALTER, MILLERSBURG, OH

12 cups rolled oats
1½ cups coconut
3 cups nuts (walnuts/pecans)
1¾ tsp. salt
1 Tbsp. cinnamon
1¼ cups bran

½ cup fructose
1½ cups honey
1 cup butter
¾ cup oil (olive or canola)
1½ tsp. vanilla

In a large bowl, combine dry ingredients. Melt liquid ingredients together over medium heat. Add to dry ingredients and mix well. Bake in two 9 x 13" pans, uncovered, at 275°, stirring every 20-30 minutes. Bake until golden.

Granola

MIRIAM STOLTZFOOS, GARNETT, KS

breakfast

42

Stir and heat together the following:

1 cup maple syrup
1½ cup butter
1 Tbsp. cinnamon

1 cup honey
1 Tbsp. maple flavoring
1 tsp. salt

In a large bowl mix the following:

12 cups rolled oats
3 cups unsweetened coconut

1 cup sesame seeds
3 cups nuts

Pour the wet ingredients over the dry ingredients and mix well. Bake on cookie sheets at 350° for 20-30 minutes, stirring every 10 minutes. Can add raisins or other dried fruit before storing. Makes about 24 cups.

Granola Cereal

CHRISTY NOLT, DODGE CENTER, MN

4 cups old-fashioned oats
1 cup coconut
½ cup sunflower or sesame seeds
1 cup wheat germ, bran, or other
   whole grain
1 tsp. cinnamon

½ cup honey
½ cup oil
½ cup water
1 Tbsp. vanilla
1 cup nuts (opt.)
½ cup raisins (opt.)

Mix dry ingredients. Blend liquid ingredients and stir into dry ingredients. Mix well. Spread thinly on cookie sheets and toast at 350° until slightly brown; stirring every five minutes.

Granola Cereal

MRS. REBECCA ZOOK, MYERSTOWN, PA

1 cup honey
¾ cup maple syrup

12 Tbsp. butter
4 Tbsp. peanut butter

Melt honey, maple syrup, butter, and peanut butter in saucepan. In a big bowl, mix:

1 cup unsweetened coconut
2 tsp. real salt

2 heaping quarts oatmeal
4 quarts spelt flakes, crushed

Pour syrup over cereal. Mix together well. Bake at 225°, stirring occasionally, for one hour. Dried fruit, raisins, etc. can be added after baking.

Crunchy Granola Cereal

KIM BROWN, GOODRICH, MI

4 cups rolled oats
1 cup chopped almonds
½ cup honey
2 Tbsp. maple syrup

⅓ cup canola oil
2 Tbsp. water
1-1½ cup mixed dried
 cherries and raisins

Preheat oven to 325°. In a large bowl, mix oats, almonds, honey, maple syrup, oil and water. Mix well and spread on a baking sheet (with sides) that has been covered with parchment paper to prevent sticking. Bake until golden brown (30-35 minutes), stirring every 5-10 minutes. Let cereal cool on pan, then stir in fruit and store in an airtight container. It will keep for almost a month, but it doesn't last that long at our house. You can also substitute whatever nuts or seeds or fruits your family likes. Changing them also adds variation to the cereal.

Granola Cereal

RACHEL YODER, MILLERSBURG, OH

13 cups regular oats
1 cup wheat germ
2 cups oat bran
½ cup flaxseed meal

1½ cup melted butter
1 cup honey
1 tsp. cinnamon
pinch of salt

Mix the first four ingredients, then heat remaining ingredients and pour to first mixture. Stir well. Spread on three cake pans and toast for one hour at 300°. Stir every 15 minutes until golden. Cool. Put in airtight container. Can also be frozen. Delicious!

Granola

DOREEN OTTO, GRAYSON, KY

4 cups quick oats	½ cup melted butter or oil
4 cups rolled oats	¼ cup olive oil
¼ cup flax seed	⅔ cup honey
¼ cup sesame seeds	⅓ cup apple concentrate
2 cups oat bran	2 tsp. vanilla or maple flavoring

Bake at 212° until done (or 170° all night). When cooled, add:

⅔ cup sunflower seeds (opt.)

Store in an airtight container.

My Own Peanut Butter Granola

MARY BETH HEISEY, PUEBLO WEST, CO

breakfast

44

20 cups rolled oats	¼ cup ground flax seed
2 cups flaked coconut	2 cups chopped nuts
2 tsp. salt	

Stir together in a large roaster.

1½ cups oil	1½ cup peanut butter
1½ cups water	1 cup maple syrup
½ cup butter	1 cup honey

Melt in large saucepan. Add 1½ tsp. vanilla. Pour over dry oat mixture and stir until well coated. Dry in slow oven until slightly brown and still a little chewy. Note: You can mix it up and let it set on the counter overnight, then toast the next morning.

Granola

BETTY LONON, MARION, NC

5 cups rolled oats	2 tsp. vanilla
⅔ cup ground flax seed	⅓ cup oil
1 cup unsweetened coconut	¾ cup maple syrup
1 Tbsp. ground cinnamon	⅔ cup chopped nuts

Mix all ingredients together and bake in an ungreased 9 x 12" baking pan at 250° for about an hour, stirring once during baking. Remove from oven, add any dried fruit you like (such as raisins, dates, chopped apricots). Cool and store.

Healthy

Granola Cereal

Sharon Hochstedler, Kokomo, IN

4 cups rolled oats
1 cup slivered almonds
1 cup sunflower seeds, ground fine
1 cup pumpkin seeds, ground fine
1 tsp. cinnamon

¼ cup unsweetened coconut
½ cup wheat germ
1 tsp. vanilla extract
1 cup sweetener (raw unfiltered honey or
    pure maple syrup)

Place all dry ingredients in a large bowl and mix well. In a separate bowl combine the wet ingredients and mix well. Pour over dry ingredients and mix well to coat all nuts and seeds. To bake: Spread mixture on a non-stick cookie sheet. Bake 20 minutes in preheated oven set at the lowest temperature. Stir mixture and continue to bake another 20 minutes. Stir mixture periodically to prevent burning.

Granola

Mrs. Rhoda Miller, Sugarcreek, OH

1 cup honey
2 cups melted butter
8 cups oatmeal
4 cups whole wheat flour

½ tsp. salt
1 tsp. soda
4 cups coconut
2 pkgs. graham crackers, crushed

Mix all together. Bake at 250° until browned, stirring often. Chocolate chips may be added while still warm.

Low-Fat Granola

6 cups fine oatmeal
3 cups unsweetened coconut
2 cups bran
3 cups wheat germ

½ tsp. salt
1 cup nuts or seeds
⅓ cup olive oil

Mix ingredients together. Add a small amount of molasses or honey if desired. Place in shallow pans and toast in a slow oven until golden brown and dry. Will be crispy, do *not* over brown. Cool and store in an airtight container. Variations: ½ tsp. cinnamon, powdered milk or flour, ½ cup dates after baking, or use butter instead of oil.

Grapenuts & Toasted Cereals

Grapenuts

IDA EDWARDS, LINDEN, TN

7 cups whole wheat flour
1 cup maple syrup
1 cup sorghum molasses
2¼ cups buttermilk

½ cup butter
1 Tbsp. salt
2 Tbsp. soda

Mix flour and salt, then add maple syrup, molasses, butter, salt and the soda dissolved in ¼ cup buttermilk. Pour two cups of buttermilk over all and stir well. If you need to add more buttermilk to make it smoother, that's fine, but a thick dough is expected. Pour into two greased 9 x 13" pans and bake 1½ hours at 450°. Let cool then crumble and toast on cookie sheets. Store in tight containers, keeps for months.

Grapenuts

SUSIE ANN STOLTZFOOS, BIRD-IN-HAND, PA

7 cups whole wheat flour
3 cups sweetener (honey or
   maple syrup)
2¼ tsp. baking soda
1 tsp. salt

2½ cups buttermilk
6 Tbsp. melted butter
2 tsp. vanilla
½ tsp. maple flavoring

Combine dry ingredients, add sweetener, milk, butter, and flavorings. Stir until well mixed. Spread into two jelly roll pans. Bake at 350° for 35 minutes. Cool; grate. Return to pans and bake at 250° for one hour, stirring every 15 minutes. I divide them into 3 pans after they are grated. These keep a long time if dried well. You can also freeze them.

Grapenuts

BARBARA SUE TROYER, EVART, MI

7¾ lb. whole wheat flour
1½ Tbsp. salt
2 cups honey
2 cups maple syrup
3 Tbsp. soda
3 quarts buttermilk
¾ lb. butter, melted

Stir soda into buttermilk, then mix all ingredients except butter. Add that last. Pour into 4 greased 9 x 13" pans. Bake at 350° for one hour or until well done. The grapenuts can be pushed through a sieve to grate them, then dry in a 250° oven. Or they can be cut into strips, dried, then ground.

Grapenuts

CHRISTINE SLABAUGH, FARMINGTON, NM

1 quart buttermilk
1 Tbsp. soda
2 cups sorghum molasses
½ cup oil
1 tsp. maple flavoring
2 tsp. vanilla
1½ tsp. salt
8 cups whole wheat flour
2 cups raw wheat germ

In a large bowl, combine soda with buttermilk, then add molasses and oil. Add flavorings, salt, and six cups of the flour. Beat until well blended. Add wheat germ and remaining flour. Spread on two well-greased cookie sheets. Bake at 350° for 35 minutes. Grind when cool. Spread grapenuts on shallow pans and toast in slow oven until crisp. Stir every 15-20 minutes during toasting process.

Grapenuts Cereal

MRS. URIE MILLER, MIDDLEBURY, IN

1 quart cream
1 quart buttermilk or sour milk
4 cups sorghum
2 Tbsp. baking soda
1 Tbsp. salt
2 Tbsp. vanilla
8 cups oatmeal
16-17 cups whole wheat flour

Mix first six ingredients. Add oatmeal, then flour. Put into 3 greased 9 x 13" pans. Bake at 350° for about 1 hour or until done. When cool, crumble through a ¼" mesh screen or by some other means of your choice. Put on pans and dry and toast in a 150-250° oven. Stir occasionally. When dry, store in airtight containers.

Choices

Wheat Germ Crunchies Cereal

MRS. LORENE MAST, DALTON WI

2 cups whole wheat flour
1 cup wheat bran
1 cup oat bran
1½ cup butter, melted
1½ cup fructose (sugar substitute)
3 eggs, beaten

3 tsp. baking powder
2 cups coconut
3 cups oatmeal
1 tsp. salt
1½ tsp. vanilla and maple flavoring
2 tsp. cinnamon

Melt butter and add eggs and flavorings and add to dry ingredients. Bake on cookie sheet for 20 to 30 minutes in 350° oven, then crumble and toast until dry. I have used maple syrup for sweetening and then used only 1 cup butter.

Wheat Germ Crunchies

MRS. VERNON SCHROCK, LEWISTOWN, IL

3 cups rolled oats
2 cups whole wheat flour
½ cup honey
2 cups coconut
1 cup wheat germ
1 cup wheat bran
1 cup oat bran

3 tsp. baking powder
1 tsp. cinnamon
1 tsp. salt
½ cup melted butter or oil
2 eggs, beaten
1 tsp. maple flavoring

In large bowl, mix dry ingredients. Mix together honey, butter, eggs and maple flavoring and add to the rest. Toast in 250° oven on cookie sheets.

Grapenuts

MRS. RHODA MILLER, SUGARCREEK, OH

8 cups whole wheat flour
2 cups honey
1 tsp. salt
3⅓ cups sour milk

½ cup butter, melted
½ tsp. maple flavoring
1 Tbsp. vanilla
1 Tbsp. soda

Mix soda in milk. Mix all ingredients together. Spread in two greased 9 x 13" pans. Bake at 350° until well done. Cool, cut in strips and grate into fine crumbs. Toast at 300° in shallow layers until golden brown, stirring often.

More Breakfast Ideas

Peanut Butter Syrup

MATILDA BEAR, PATRIOT, OH

½ cup butter
½ cup honey
½ cup peanut butter
¼ cup carob powder

Combine in a saucepan and cook until boiling. Good on pancakes, pudding and ice cream. For fudge: Boil a few minutes until thick. Pour into a buttered pie pan and refrigerate.

Cranberry Sauce

LISA REYNOSO, WESLACO, TX

1 bag of cranberries, fresh or frozen
1 cup water
¾ cup honey, or to taste

Combine and bring to a boil. Turn down heat and simmer about 10 minutes, stirring occasionally as needed. If you wish, you can use 1 tsp. of stevia, a naturally sweet herb, to sweeten instead of honey. My mother is diabetic, and we made it that way for her, and it tasted delicious and not one bit sour, without any sugar. The sauce is great on waffles or pancakes, and I also like to use it to flavor yogurt. I start it before I start my waffles and it will be cool (if I put it in the freezer) by the time I have enough to serve breakfast.

Maple Fruit Dip

MARY BETH HEISEY, PUEBLO WEST, CO

1-8 oz. pkg. cream cheese
1-8 oz. plain yogurt
⅓ cup maple syrup
½ tsp. vanilla

Mix well and chill. Serve with fruit tray.

Yogurt Breakfast

MRS. MIRIAM WENGERD, SUGARCREEK, OH

plain yogurt, unsweetened
your favorite granola
frozen blueberries
maple syrup

Serve yogurt in bowls and pass toppers. Scrumptious and satisfying! One of my favorites.

Breakfast Yogurt

Darla Reena Stoll, Odon, IN

1 cup plain yogurt
3 dates, sliced
½ small banana, sliced
honey, maple syrup, or sucanat to taste

1 Tbsp. chopped nuts
¼ red apple, diced
¼ cup granola cereal

Spoon yogurt into breakfast bowl and top with remaining ingredients. Reserve sweetener to pour on top.

Pancake & Bisquick Mix

Barbara Sue Troyer, Evart, MI

8 cups wheat flour
⅓ cup baking powder

2 tsp. salt
2 tsp. cream of tartar

Mix together and store in airtight container. For pancakes and Bisquick, add one egg to ¾ cup mix, ½ Tbsp. oil, and enough milk to make it the right consistency.

Sausage Gravy

Raedella Wenger, Chambersburg, PA

½ lb. ground sausage
¼ cup flour

¼ cup butter
2½ cups milk

Fry sausage in 2 quart kettle. When browned, add butter. Stir together and add flour. Stir well and add milk. Stir until it is thick and bubbly. Serve over pancakes or potatoes.

Hamburger Scramble

Mrs. Cindy Wilkinson, Dixon, FL

¼ lb. lean ground beef
2 Tbsp. finely chopped onion
2 Tbsp. olive oil

1 tsp. salt
4 eggs
¼ cup milk

Brown ground beef and onion lightly in hot oil in skillet. Beat salt, eggs, and milk until well-blended. Pour egg mixture over meat mixture. Cook slowly, stirring gently to keep mixture in large, soft lumps. Do not brown. Serve hot on, or with toast.

Healthy

Cheese Sauce

Mrs. Miriam Wengerd, Sugarcreek, OH

4 Tbsp. butter
4 Tbsp. barley flour
2 cups milk or water
½ tsp. salt
⅛ tsp. pepper
2 cups shredded cheddar

Melt butter in saucepan; add flour, stirring with whisk until smooth. Add liquid, stirring continually until boiling. Turn off heat; add salt, pepper, and cheese. Cover until cheese melts. Stir in with whisk.

Muesli

Mrs. Miriam Wengerd, Sugarcreek, OH

1 cup wheat germ
1 cup oatmeal
1 cup pecans, ground
1 cup coconut, unsweetened
2 apples, peeled and sliced
2 bananas, sliced
2 quarts peaches, undrained
32 oz. plain yogurt
maple syrup or sucanat

Put dry ingredients in bowl. Add fruit and yogurt and sweetener and stir together gently until evenly moist. Serve with sucanat sprinkled on top or drizzle with maple syrup. This recipe was given to us by a visitor from Germany. We like it for breakfast. Can be made the evening before and chilled. Can also be served as a summer supper when it's too warm to cook.

Breads

TWENTY-TWO YEARS AGO, WHEN I BEGAN TO BAKE OUR OWN bread, I didn't know anyone who baked 100% whole wheat bread. My first attempts were not so great, but gradually I got the hang of it. When Marvin bought me a Bosch mixer it became so easy I could do it with a child on one hip! The right tools can make such a difference.

Good, fresh ingredients will make your finished product taste better. We use Lira extra virgin olive oil in our bread which we buy in one gallon metal containers. This is the best olive oil I've found. It has a mild flavor. Others I've tried have not had such a light, fresh taste.

I use Prairie Gold and Bronze Chief wheat berries which I grind fresh just before baking. When I make bread for others, I often just use Prairie Gold because it makes a lighter bread, but for us I like to use some red wheat too because it adds more flavor.

Healthy

Hints for successful bread making:

• I prefer using wheat gluten rather than dough enhancer because dough enhancer contains whey and the bread smells old sooner.

• Using lecithin will improve the keeping quality of your bread.

• After bread is mixed let set in mixer five minutes before putting in pans. This makes a spongy, light bread.

• Don't use too much oil on the counter when rolling out dough - it causes your loaves to have holes in the middle. A pool of oil the size of a quarter is enough.

• Use stainless steel bread pans. They are more expensive but they will never rust! Aluminum pans have a peculiar smell and aren't healthy even though they bake nicely.

• I don't grease the bread tops after baking; it just makes your bags sticky. Your crust will soften if your bread is put in plastic bags and closed with twisties.

• Someone gave us a Cutco bread knife. It makes perfect slices of bread! Make sure you have a good sharp bread knife that doesn't "saw" your bread flat.

• If you are discouraged about your previous attempts at baking whole grain bread, take fresh courage, it is possible! It takes practice. Ask God to help you learn how to make good bread that your family enjoys. Then when your family gets hungry between meals, experience the satisfaction of watching them reach for a homemade slice of bread! Because you made a healthy choice, they can too.

Yeast Breads

No Crumble Whole Wheat Bread

Mrs. Miriam Wengerd, Sugarcreek, OH

Put:

⅓ cup sorghum	1 Tbsp. lecithin
1 Tbsp. oil	1 Tbsp. dry active yeast

Into:

2 cups lukewarm water

Stir until dissolved. Add slowly, mixing in well:

6 cups whole wheat flour

Add last:

2 tsp. salt

Knead on lightly floured surface until smooth and elastic. Let rise until double in bulk in a warm place. Punch down and let rise again. Shape into loaves. Let rise until almost double. Bake in 350° oven for 50 minutes.

I would add salt with first step. I would bake at 300° for 30 minutes, then check for doneness.

This is the first 100% wheat bread recipe I used.

TIP

Flax seed Substitution—Ground flax seed is easily added to quick breads, cakes, and cookies in place of nuts. ⅓ cup ground flax instead of ½ cup nuts. Can also be added along with nuts, ¼ cup of each. Add ¼ cup ground flax to bread recipes that make 2 loaves. Put 1-2 spoonfuls ground flax on salads, sprinkle on casseroles right before serving. Store ground flax in freezer or refrigerator. Whole flax can be stored in a cool place and ground as needed.

—Kari Wendt, Lake Ariel, PA

Healthy

Perfect Whole Wheat Bread

Mrs. Miriam Wengerd, Sugarcreek, OH

4½ cups lukewarm water
¾ cup olive oil
½ cup honey
3 Tbsp. instant yeast

2 Tbsp. lecithin granules
2 heaping Tbsp. wheat gluten
1 Tbsp. sea salt
12-14 cups wheat flour*

Put water, oil, and honey in Bosch mixer. Mix briefly. Now add next four ingredients. Mix briefly. Next add 6 cups flour. Mix well. Add 5 more cups flour and mix well again. Continue adding flour ½ cup at a time (while mixer is on speed 1) until dough starts cleaning side of bowl. Mix for 10 minutes on speed 1. Let set 5 minutes. Divide dough into five 1 lb. 6 oz. loaves. I always use a rolling pin and roll out my dough (about ¾ inch thick) into a rectangular shape. Then roll up and tuck in sides and place in pan. Prick tops with fork to remove air bubbles. Place in greased loaf pans and set in oven on pilot to rise for 30 minutes. Turn oven to 300° and bake for 30-35 minutes or until golden brown. Remove from pans and let set on cooling racks for 20 minutes before putting into bread bags.

*Use fresh-ground flour for best results. Can grind a mixture of 6 cups Prairie Gold wheat and 3 cups Bronze Chief wheat, or for a really light bread, use all Prairie Gold wheat.

This bread recipe passes the wrap-around-a-hot-dog test! The girls and I have baked thousands of these loaves; it is our most used bread recipe. This bread recipe can also be used to make hamburger buns. Roll out about ½-¾" thick and cut with wide-mouth screw-on ring. Let rise for 30 minutes and bake 15-20 minutes at 300°. Sesame seeds can be rolled in with rolling pin before cutting. After cooling, split in half and use as sandwich buns. Soft and yummy! We also use ¾ lb. of this dough to make a thin, round pizza crust. Let rise 30 minutes, bake 12 minutes at 300°, and put on your family's favorite toppings and bake until ready.

#1 Whole Wheat Bread

2½ cups very warm water
⅓ cup olive oil
1 tsp. honey
1/16 tsp. white stevia powder
¼ cup mashed potatoes
2 tsp. salt

½ of one egg, beaten
¼ cup ground flax seed
2 cups whole wheat flour
⅛ cup instant yeast
4-4½ cups whole wheat flour

Combine water, oil, honey, stevia, potatoes, salt, and egg, mix well with wire whisk. Add flax and 2 cups whole wheat flour. Mix well and bring to gluten stage. Mix instant yeast with remaining flour. Add to mixture gradually and knead until it isn't sticky, yet not too dry, having somewhat of a moist texture. Pour olive oil (1-2 Tbsp.) in bottom of big stainless steel bowl. Put dough in and flip around to top, having dough all covered with a touch of oil. Cover with tea towel and let rise in a warm place for one hour, then shape loaves. This makes 3-4 loaves. Put in greased pans and stab with a fork to bottom of pan to remove air bubbles. Let rise 45 minutes-1 hour, until bread is nicely rounded above pan. Do not let over rise. Bake at 350° for 25 minutes or until done. Brush with olive oil and cool. It has a nutty taste. I always double this recipe; it makes 7 loaves. A doubled recipe also fits into a Kitchen Aid mixer.

58

breads

Whole Wheat Bread

Mrs. Jeremy (Rose) Miller, St. Ignatius, MT

4¾ cups warm water
1¼ cup olive oil
1 cup honey
3 eggs, optional

1 Tbsp. salt
⅓ cup instant yeast
13-14 cups whole wheat flour*

Mix first 5 ingredients. Add some flour and the yeast, then add the rest of the flour, a little at a time, mixing well after each addition. Dough should be sticky. Put bowl in warm place and let rise 20 minutes. Punch down; let rise another 10 minutes. Makes 6 loaves. Let rise ½ hour then put in 350° oven. Bake 15-30 minutes (until loaves have started to brown), then turn oven to 250°. I usually bake it for a total of one hour.

*I use Bronze Chief.

TIP

Instead of using only one kind of whole grain flour, try using a blend. For example, we use oat, rice, and barley flour for pancakes, shortcake, cobblers, biscuits, etc.

—Ina Schrock, Gap Mills, WV

Healthy

Honey Whole Wheat Bread

MARLENE ZIMMERMAN, ORCHARD, IA

3½ cups hot water
½ cup honey
¹/₆ cup gluten
1½ Tbsp. yeast

½ cup oil
1 Tbsp. lecithin
1 Tbsp. salt
10 cups whole wheat flour

Mix ingredients together. Let rise, punch dough down and shape into 3 big or 4 small loaves. Let rise again and bake at 300° for 25-30 minutes.

Whole Wheat Bread

MRS. VERNON SCHROCK, LEWISTOWN, IL

6 cups warm water
⅔ cup olive oil
2 Tbsp. salt
⅓ cup sugar, honey or molasses

2 Tbsp. liquid lecithin
2 Tbsp. instant yeast
16-18 cups whole wheat flour
  (fresh ground)

Mix first 5 ingredients, then add 6-8 cups of flour, and mix hard with wire whip for 3 minutes. Add 2 more cups of flour with yeast, and mix. Keep adding flour and mixing until dough is slightly firm but still soft. Let rise ½ hour, punch down, let rise until double, then shape into 6 loaves. Let rise 45-60 minutes, then bake for 25-30 minutes in 325° oven.

Whole Wheat Bread

JOYCE STRITE, COCHISE, AZ

1 cup warm water
2 Tbsp. yeast
2 cups milk
1½ Tbsp. salt

½ cup olive oil
½ cup honey
1 egg
8 cups whole wheat flour

Dissolve yeast in warm water. Scald milk and add olive oil and honey. Beat egg and add enough water to make 1½ cups. Cool milk mixture to warm and then pour it over 4 cups flour and salt. Add egg and yeast mixture. Mix and add flour to right consistency. Grease 4 loaf pans. Bake at 350° for 40-45 minutes.

Quick & Easy Whole Wheat Bread

ELIZABETH STALTER, MILLERSBURG, OH
SUSAN STALTER, MILLERSBURG, OH

10½ cups Golden 86 wheat berries
6½ cups hot water
3 rounded Tbsp. wheat gluten
3 slightly rounded Tbsp. dough enhancer
½ cup olive oil
½ cup honey
2 Tbsp. liquid lecithin
3 rounded Tbsp. instant yeast
1 rounded Tbsp. real salt

Grind 2½ cups wheat berries. Put that flour in Bosch mixing bowl, turn to speed 1 and add rest of ingredients except salt. Grind 8 more cups wheat berries. Add 7 cups flour, then add salt.* Add approximately 6 more cups flour, until dough starts pulling away from sides. Knead with lid on for 8 minutes. Working with greased hands, divide into 6 smooth balls and let set for 5 minutes. (Meanwhile, wash up Bosch and get bread pans out and spray grease. Using spray will keep the oil suspended and help not to get too much on, so the loaves will pop out.) Gently make up loaves and put in greased pans and let rise 25 minutes on warm with oven door open one notch. (Or 150-170° with door closed for 10-15 minutes.) Bake at 325° for 25-30 minutes. Brush tops with butter, milk or water. Makes 6 loaves. Prep time: 45 minutes. This recipe is so quick and easy that we can turn around and make a second batch immediately (timing is right) and make 12 loaves, including slicing, ready for the freezer.

*Note: This step is tricky until you get the hang of it. Dough should be very soft and almost sticky (not hard or stiff, that means you put in too much flour). With patience, getting this step right results in soft, beautiful bread.

Whole Wheat Bread

SUSIE ANN STOLTZFOOS, BIRD-IN-HAND, PA

4 cups lukewarm water
2 Tbsp. yeast
½ cup oil or butter
½ cup honey or maple syrup
2 eggs
2 tsp. salt
10 cups whole wheat flour

Beat well, adding flour one cup at a time until not too sticky. Let rise one hour. Punch down every 15 minutes. Divide into 6 loaf pans, let rise about 30 minutes. Bake at 350° for 30-35 minutes.

TIP

Spelt is a low-carbohydrate, low-gluten grain. I buy it in bulk and grind my own flour. It is an excellent substitute for white and wheat flour in cream sauces, gravies, breads, and cookies. We like the flavor of it better than whole wheat. Bread will be a little more crumbly, but cookies, muffins, and cakes are more tender with all or part spelt.

—B. Garber, Fayetteville, PA

Healthy

100% Whole Wheat Bread

MRS. KATHRYN HERSHBERGER, CLARE, MI

3 eggs
5½ cups water
¾ cup olive oil
¾ cup honey
3 Tbsp. salt

3 heaping Tbsp. wheat gluten
2 heaping Tbsp. lecithin
3 heaping Tbsp. yeast
12 cups whole wheat organic flour

Beat together eggs, honey, oil, salt, and water with rotary beater. Beat well, then add 2 cups flour, yeast, gluten, and lecithin. Beat on high for 5 minutes. Using a wire whisk, add 2 more cups flour, stirring well after each addition until dough is too stiff to use whisk. Mix rest of flour with hands and knead well. Dough should be quite sticky. Use olive oil to knead it. Punch down at 15 minute intervals, 3 times. Cover and let rise about one hour. After dough is in pans, let rise until just a little higher than pans (about one inch). Put in oven and bake at 350° for 30 minutes. Yield: 5 loaves. Freeze while slightly warm if you wish.

Light Whole Wheat Bread

KAYLENE HARTZLER, TENNILLE, GA

¾ cup oil
¾ cup honey
5 tsp. salt
2 Tbsp. lecithin
2 Tbsp. dough enhancer

2 Tbsp. wheat gluten
6 cups warm water
4½ Tbsp. yeast
½ cup potato flakes (optional)
13-14 cups whole wheat flour

Mix together first six ingredients. Then mix and add water, yeast, potato flakes (can also use additional ½ cup flour instead of flakes), and flour. Knead 10 minutes with Bosch mixer. Let rise 15 minutes then punch down. Let rise another 15 minutes then punch down and shape into 6 or 7 loaves (I use glass bread pans—4½" x 8½"). Let rise 30-45 minutes. Bake at 325° for 30 minutes. I use this recipe for everything—rolls, hamburger buns, pizza crust, sticky buns, cinnamon rolls, bread sticks, any recipe calling for frozen dough. This will freeze well unbaked if you get it in the freezer *right away* before the yeast starts working.

Shenk's Whole Wheat Bread

Cynthia Korver, New Oxford, PA

5 cups warm milk (or buttermilk)   ¾ cup honey
⅔ cup oil

Combine ingredients. In mixer bowl run mixer on low. Mix well, then add about 5 cups fresh-ground whole wheat flour. Then add:

⅓ cup gluten   1 Tbsp. salt
2 Tbsp. lecithin granules   ¼ cup yeast

Mix well. Then add more whole wheat flour, one cup at a time, letting mixer mix flour in until it's all mixed in before adding next cupful. Make it take about 10 minutes to mix in flour until your machine can't handle it anymore (3-5 cups, depending on machine). In large bowl, put one cup whole wheat flour. Scrape out bread dough from mixer bowl into large bowl. With hands, work dough, kneading in the flour. Add flour sparingly, until dough is just not sticky. Dough should be soft, smooth, and elastic, not dry. Shape into ball. Leave in bowl. Grease top of dough; let rise 15 minutes. Punch down. Let rise 15 minutes again. Shape into 4 loaves. Put in greased pans, turning once to grease tops. Let rise to tops of pans. Bake at 350° for 30-35 minutes. Bread will sound hollow when tapped. Note: I use a Kitchen Aid mixer. This recipe was made for a Bosch mixer. I've redone it for other mixers. It works best if you have fresh ground wheat. Wheat that has been ground and stored in freezer or elsewhere results in a heavy loaf.

Whole Wheat Bread

Mrs. Rhoda Miller, Sugarcreek, OH

5 cups warm water   ¼ cup yeast
⅔ cup vegetable oil   1 Tbsp. salt
¾ cup honey   1 egg
¼ cup wheat gluten   11-14 cups wheat flour
2 Tbsp. lecithin

Mix thoroughly. If using a mixer, mix for 10 minutes. Put in pans, let rise in oven 30-45 minutes. Bake at 325° for 20-25 minutes. Yield: 6 large loaves. Also good for pizza crusts.

Turtle Bread

MRS. VERNON SCHROCK, LEWISTOWN, IL

3-3½ cups fresh-ground whole wheat flour ⅓ cup milk
1 Tbsp. instant yeast
1 Tbsp. honey
1 tsp. salt
½ cup warm water

1 Tbsp. melted butter
1 egg
2 raisins

Heat water, milk, and butter until warm. Add honey, salt, and egg and beat with wire whisk. Then add 2 cups flour and yeast, beating until elastic. Add remaining flour or enough to make dough easy to handle. Knead well. Let rise for 10 minutes. Shape a 2" piece of dough into a ball for turtle's head. Shape 5 walnut-sized pieces into balls for feet and tail. Shape remaining dough into a ball for body; place on greased cookie sheet and flatten slightly. Attach head, feet and tail by placing one end of each under edge of body. Press raisins into the head for eyes. Make crisscross cuts in body ⅛" deep, to look like a turtle's shell. Let rise 20 minutes. Bake at 325-350° for 20-25 minutes. This is a fun bread to make and the children enjoy watching and helping, then eating the turtle!

Spelt Bread

MRS. ALLEN R. BYLER, SMICKSBURG, PA

4½ cups warm water
4 Tbsp. molasses
3 Tbsp. yeast
½ cup olive oil

1 Tbsp. salt
2 beaten eggs
10 cups spelt flour

Dissolve 1 Tbsp. molasses in water. Sprinkle yeast over it and let stand until bubbly. Beat in 4 cups spelt flour. Beat 5 minutes with egg beater. Let set until it rises to double. Add eggs, salt, and 3 Tbsp. molasses, then 6 more cups spelt flour. Stir well, then add oil. Stir for 10 minutes. Let rise to double, divide into 3 bread pans. Let rise a little, then place in 350° oven, bake for 25-30 minutes. Cool, slice and enjoy.

Spelt Bread

3 Tbsp. honey
3 Tbsp. oil
1 tsp. salt
1 Tbsp. yeast

1 small egg
1 cup warm water
3 cups spelt or rye flour

Punch down 3 times every ½ hour. Add a little extra flour. Makes one loaf. Bake at 350° for 25-30 minutes.

Whole Spelt Bread

WALTER SAUDER, LATHAM, MO

6 cups warm water
2 Tbsp. salt
⅔ cup olive oil

⅔ cup honey
3 Tbsp. instant yeast
12-15 cups spelt flour

Mix the dry ingredients first, including yeast, using only 4 cups spelt flour. Add the wet ingredients and mix thoroughly. Gradually add more flour until proper thickness is reached but dough is still a little sticky. Knead 5-10 minutes. Cover and let rise until double. Punch down and bake at 350° for 30 minutes. Note: One portion can also make 5 dozen hamburger buns. Let dough rise like usual and then form into balls. With the palm of your hand punch ball down into a circle on a pan. Let rise until nice size and bake at 350° for 15 minutes.

Caraway Rye Bread

MRS. MIRIAM WENGERD, SUGARCREEK, OH

3¾ Tbsp. instant SAF yeast
4 cups warm milk
½ cup sucanat
2 Tbsp. caraway seed, ground

2 Tbsp. olive oil
4 tsp. salt
5 cups rye flour
6 cups wheat flour

Grind 3¼ cups rye berries to make 5 cups flour. Warm milk, put in Bosch mixer. Add yeast, mix to dissolve. Add sucanat, caraway seed, oil, and salt. Mix again. Add rye flour, mix until smooth. Add wheat flour until dough cleans bowl sides. Mix on speed 1 for 10 minutes. Let dough rise 5 minutes. Divide into 4 equal portions (1 lb. 6 oz. each). If you want round loaves, shape into balls and place in greased 8" round pan and pat into 6" round. If you want regular loaves roll out into rectangular shape, then roll up and place in greased bread pans and prick with fork. Let rise until double, approx. 40 minutes. Bake at 300° for ½ hour. Let set 5 minutes, remove from pans. Serve with Creamy Spread. (8 oz. cream cheese, softened, 2 tsp. water, 2-3 tsp. lemon juice, 1 tsp. garlic powder, 1 tsp. basil, dried, ¼ cup Parmesan. Put all into food processor and blend until creamy.)

Honey Oatmeal Bread

LISA WEAVER

4 Tbsp. yeast	⅔ cup butter
1½ cup warm water	4 eggs
½ cup honey	1½ cup water
2 cups oatmeal	9-10 cups flour
1 tsp. salt	

Mix warm water and yeast and let set for about 5 minutes. Then add rest of ingredients and mix and knead real well. Allow to rise, then shape into loaves and place dough in greased pans. Let rise in pans. Bake at 350° for 30 minutes. Makes 4 or 5 loaves. Delicious!

Yeasted Sprout Bread

MRS. BRAD GRANT

3 cups hard wheat berries
1 heaping tsp. active dry yeast
2 Tbsp. warm water

3 Tbsp. honey, scant
2 tsp. salt

To sprout the wheat:

Place the wheat berries into a large jar and fill the jar with lukewarm water. (I usually make enough for two loaves at once and put 6 cups wheat berries in a gallon jar.) Let sit at room temperature overnight, or for most of the day. Drain off the water and rinse with fresh water. An easy way to do this is to cover the jar with a piece of cheesecloth stretched over the top and secured with a rubber band. Leave the jar tipped so the water can drain off. Rinse a couple times a day until the wheat berries sprout. It's very important that the grain is sprouted just until the tiny sprout is barely beginning to show and the grain itself is tender. It rarely takes more than 48 hours. Drain the sprouts well and cool them on the refrigerator for several hours.

To make bread using a food processor:

Note: The food processor both grinds the sprouts and kneads the dough in just a few minutes. However, most food processors can only handle about a third of a loaf at once.

Dissolve the yeast in the warm water. Put the regular double stainless steel blade in the food processor and add ⅓ of all the ingredients: just over 2 cups of the sprouted wheat, about 2 tsp. of the yeast water, a scant Tbsp. of honey, and about ⅔ tsp. salt. Process until a ball is formed, about a minute. Scrape the sides of the bowl, and process a couple more minutes. It should be thoroughly kneaded, but stop processing before the ball completely falls apart. If it does, check the time and stop a little sooner for the next two batches. Place the small ball of dough in a bowl. Repeat the grinding/kneading two more times using the remaining ingredients. Knead the dough balls together with your hands. Form into a ball and place it in a bowl. Cover and let it rise. After about an hour and a half, gently poke the center of the dough about ½" deep with a wet finger. If the hole doesn't fill in at all, or if the dough sighs, it is ready for the next step. Using water on your hands to prevent sticking, divide in half and gently knead into rounds. Let them rest for a few minutes to regain suppleness. Form into loaves and place into greased loaf pans. Let rise in a warm, draft-free place until the dough slowly returns a gently made fingerprint. Bake about 40-60 minutes at 350°.

To make bread without a food processor:

Grind the wheat sprouts using something that is capable of handling moist substances like a powerful blender or a meat grinder. A regular grain mill will not work. After the sprouts are ground, mix the remaining ingredients in and knead. It is possible to knead by hand, but it takes much time and effort to fully develop the gluten. Knead until dough is really elastic, considerably longer than the usual amount of time. Proceed with the rising and baking instructions above.

After reading about the health benefits of sourdough, sprouted, and soaked breads, I made several attempts at sourdough, but couldn't seem to make anything my family enjoyed. I was thrilled when I came across a recipe for sprout bread in a library book. It's not a light and fluffy loaf, but we like its flavor and dense, chewy texture. It took some effort to get used to a totally different way of making bread, and like all bread making, there is an art to it. It takes some planning ahead, but really doesn't take too much more time than a standard yeast bread recipe.

Quick Breads

Cornbread

MRS. MIRIAM WENGERD, SUGARCREEK, OH

2¼ cups cornmeal
¾ cup barley flour
6 Tbsp. butter, melted
3 tsp. baking powder
1½ tsp. salt

¾ tsp. baking soda
3 eggs
¼ cup sucanat
2¼ cups milk

Put all dry ingredients in a mixing bowl and stir with whisk. Add all wet ingredients at once, beating well with whisk until well blended. Pour in greased 9 x 13" pan and bake at 400° for 25 minutes or until center springs back. Serve in squares. Split square and spread with soft butter. Drizzle with honey. Yummy! Delicious eaten with Sorghum Baked Beans. These two make a simple supper.

Cornbread

MRS. MIRIAM WENGERD, SUGARCREEK, OH

1½ cups cornmeal
½ cup wheat flour
¼ cup olive oil
2 tsp. baking powder

1 tsp. salt
½ tsp. baking soda
2 eggs
1½ cups water

Mix dry ingredients in bowl. Add wet ingredients and stir until well mixed. Pour in greased 8 x 8" pan. Bake at 400° for 20 minutes or until center springs back. I like to use a glass pan. Serve warm, cut in squares. Split and top with softened butter and honey.

Cornbread

MRS. JOHN (EVA MAY) YODER, CLARE, MI

1 cup cornmeal
1 cup flour

4 tsp. baking powder
½ tsp. salt

Mix together, then add:

¼ cup lard or soft butter
1 egg

¼ cup maple syrup
1 cup milk

Stir until just mixed. Immediately put into a greased 8 x 8" pan and bake in 425° oven for 20-25 minutes.

Choices

Sour Cream Cornbread

MRS. URIE MILLER, MIDDLEBURY, IN

¾ cup cornmeal
1 cup whole grain flour
1 tsp. soda
1 tsp. cream of tartar
1 tsp. salt

2 Tbsp. sweetener
1 egg
2 Tbsp. melted butter
1 cup thick sour cream
4-6 Tbsp. milk

Sift flour and cornmeal; measure and add soda, cream of tartar, and salt. Sift into bowl. Add remaining ingredients, using milk as needed to make a batter of the right consistency. (You may omit the butter and milk and use only cream if desired.) Stir only enough to blend well. Pour into greased 9" square pan. Bake at 425° for 20-25 minutes or until tests done.

Cornbread

SUSAN STALTER, MILLERSBURG, OH

1½ cups cornmeal
½ cup whole wheat flour
3 eggs
⅓ cup honey

1 Tbsp. baking powder
¼ tsp. salt
1 cup milk
½ cup soft butter (optional)

Mix all ingredients together. Put in greased 9 x 13" pan. Bake at 350° for 20 minutes or until set. Serve warm.

Honey Cornbread

LUCIA LAPP, BENTON, IL

1 cup whole wheat flour
1 cup yellow cornmeal
1 Tbsp. baking powder
½ tsp. salt

2 eggs
1 cup cream or milk
¼ cup oil
¼ cup honey

Mix dry ingredients. Beat eggs, add milk, oil and honey. Combine and stir just until moistened. Pour into a 12" greased muffin pan. Bake at 400° for 20 minutes or until done.

TIP

I like to substitude plain yogurt in cornbread for the buttermilk. It makes it so much softer and moister. You have to bake it at 400° for 30-45 minutes.

—Kaylene Hartzler, Tennille, GA

Healthy

Dutch Apple Bread

Mrs. Leona Miller, Odon, IN

½ cup butter
1 cup raw honey

2 eggs
1 tsp. vanilla

Cream together well.

2 cups whole wheat pastry flour
1 tsp. baking soda

½ tsp. salt

Stir together and add in alternately with:

½ cup buttermilk

Fold in:

1 cup chopped, peeled apples

¼ cup chopped nuts

Spread into a greased bread pan. Topping:

½ cup whole wheat pastry flour
2 Tbsp. honey
2 Tbsp. sucanat

½ tsp. cinnamon
2½ Tbsp. butter

Crumble together. Sprinkle on top of loaf and bake at 350° until browned and springy and toothpick tests done.

Dutch Rye Bread

Monica Bazen, Grand Rapids, MI

3 cups cracked rye (fresh)
1 cup whole wheat flour (fresh)
1 tsp. salt

½ cup molasses
2½ cups hot water

Stir together ingredients. Pour into bread pans (I use two small bread pans), cover with foil. Bake at 325° for 40 minutes to 1 hour (depending on pan size). Remove foil. Cool 30 minutes before removing from pan. Great with a slice of cheddar. This is a very dense bread.

Baked Pumpkin Bread

Sharri Noblett, Port Arthur, TX

1 lb. can of pumpkin
½ tsp. ginger
½ cup molasses
butter

1 tsp. cinnamon
¼ tsp. allspice
1 cup milk
2 eggs

Beat eggs with fork until light and fluffy. Add pumpkin. Mix well. Add spices, molasses, and milk. Mix well. Grease loaf pan or casserole dish with butter. Pour mixture into pan or dish and bake 1 hour at 350°.

Banana Nut Bread

5 overripe bananas	⅓ cup butter
1 egg	1 cup pure maple syrup

Mash bananas and set aside. In separate bowl, cream together butter, egg, and maple syrup. Then add:

2 cups whole wheat flour	½ tsp. baking soda
3 tsp. baking powder	½ tsp. sea salt

Slowly mix together ingredients trying to avoid any lumps, and add mashed bananas. To this mixture add ½ cup walnuts or pecans. Pour batter into well-greased 7 x 11" loaf pan. (Use cooking spray for easy coating. Make sure your cooking spray is pure vegetable oil and propellant—nothing else.) Use a knife to mound the batter slightly around the edges to make a nice even top. Bake at 350° for 25 minutes and then at 300° for another 30 minutes. Test for doneness with a toothpick. Spread walnut or pecan butter on top of loaf for a delicious, natural icing. If serving warm from the oven, the nut butter will melt slightly, making this delicious bread even more moist.

Banana Bread

KARI WENDT, LAKE ARIEL, PA

2 cups whole wheat flour	1 cup mashed bananas
1½ tsp. baking powder	½ cup oil
½ tsp. baking soda	2 Tbsp. yogurt or buttermilk
½ tsp. salt	⅓ cup maple syrup
½ cup nuts (or sunflower seeds)	2 eggs

Preheat oven to 350°. Mix wet and dry ingredients separately, then mix together. Pour into greased 8 x 4" loaf pan. Bake for 45-55 minutes or until toothpick inserted into the center comes out clean. Variation: ⅔ cup sucanat instead of syrup, ½ cup brown rice flour instead of ½ cup of the wheat flour.

Healthy

Whole Wheat Banana Nut Bread

CHRISTY NOLT, DODGE CENTER, MN

⅓ cup oil
½ cup honey
1 tsp. vanilla
2 eggs
1 cup mashed bananas

1¾ cups whole wheat flour
½ tsp. salt
1 tsp. baking soda
¼ cup hot water
½ cup chopped walnuts

Preheat oven to 325°. Beat oil and honey together. Add eggs and mix well. Stir in bananas and vanilla. Stir in flour and salt. Add baking soda to hot water, stir to mix then add to batter. Blend in chopped nuts. Spread in a greased 9 x 5" loaf pan. Bake for 55-60 minutes. Cool on wire rack for ½ hour before slicing.

Moist Banana Bread

MRS. KATHRYN HERSHBERGER, CLARE, MI

2½ cups whole wheat flour
2¼ tsp. baking powder
¾ tsp. salt
¾ tsp. baking soda
½ tsp. nutmeg
3 eggs
¾ cup nuts

¾ cup butter
3 Tbsp. milk
1 tsp. lemon juice
¼ cup honey
¾ cup maple syrup
4 medium bananas

Beat butter, honey, and maple syrup together. Add lemon juice, milk, and eggs, mix well. Add bananas and mix again, add nuts and other ingredients. Don't overmix. Bake at 350° for 40-45 minutes in two loaf pans or one 9 x 13" pan for 50 minutes.

73
breads

Blueberry Applesauce Bread

KARI WENDT, LAKE ARIEL, PA

⅔ cup sucanat or ⅓ cup maple syrup
1 cup applesauce
½ cup oil
2 eggs
2 Tbsp. yogurt or buttermilk
1½ cup blueberries

2 cups whole wheat flour
1½ tsp. baking powder
½ tsp. baking soda
½ tsp. salt
½ cup nuts

Preheat oven to 350°. Mix wet and dry ingredients separately, then mix together. Pour into a greased 8 x 4" loaf pan. Bake for 45-55 minutes or until toothpick inserted into center comes out clean.

Choices

Rice Bread

INA SCHROCK, GAP MILLS, WV

1½ cups brown rice flour
½ cup oat flour
¼ tsp. salt

Mix well. Then add:

2 Tbsp. honey
2 eggs, beaten
½ cup yogurt

1 tsp. baking powder
½ tsp. soda

⅓ cup water
¼ cup melted butter

Combine only until moistened. Pour into greased 9 x 13" pan. Bake at 350° for 30-35 minutes.

Zucchini Bread

MRS. JEREMY (ROSE) MILLER, ST. IGNATIUS, MT

breads

74

2 eggs
¾ cup honey
½ cup olive oil
½ tsp. salt
½ tsp. baking soda
½ tsp. baking powder

¼ tsp. ground ginger
¼ tsp. cinnamon
⅓ tsp. vanilla
1 med. zucchini squash, grated
1½ cup whole wheat flour

Beat eggs, honey, and oil together. Mix in rest of ingredients, adding flour last. The zucchini should be about 1½ cups, loosely packed. Can also add nuts if you wish. Bake in greased loaf pan for 1 hour at 350°.

Spoon Bread

MARY BETH HEISEY, PUEBLO WEST, CO

1 pint milk
6 Tbsp. butter
1 cup cornmeal

1 tsp. salt
3 eggs, separated

In a saucepan, heat milk, do *not* boil. Stir in butter, cornmeal, and salt. Cook, stirring occasionally, until thickened. Cool to lukewarm. Beat egg yolks and add to cornmeal mixture. Mix thoroughly. Beat egg whites until stiff. Fold into cornmeal and mix gently but thoroughly. Pour into 2 quart baking dish. Bake at 375° for 1 hour or until top is golden brown. Serve immediately. Serves 6.

Corn Pone

Mrs. Ruth Wanner, Conneautville, PA

1 cup whole wheat flour
1 cup cornmeal
½ cup honey
⅛ cup sorghum (optional)
½ cup oatmeal
⅓ cup butter (softened)

2½ Tbsp. coconut oil or 2½ Tbsp. butter
2 tsp. baking powder
1 tsp. soda
1 cup buttermilk
1 egg

Mix well. Bake in greased 9 x 13" cake pan at 350° until nicely browned. Serve warm with milk and fruit. A simple summer meal—delicious!

Muffins

Breakfast Muffins

Yvonne Sommers, Oswego, KS

3 cups whole wheat flour
2 cups oat bran
2 tsp. soda
½ tsp. salt
2 tsp. cinnamon
1 cup honey
1 cup skim milk

3 cups finely shredded carrots
2 large apples, shredded
½ cup raisins
½ cup chopped pecans
½ cup olive oil
4 eggs
½ tsp. vanilla

Mix together and bake in muffin tins. Bake at 350° for 25-30 minutes. Delicious!

Banana Nut Muffins

Mrs. Rhoda Miller, Sugarcreek, OH

2 eggs
⅓ cup butter, melted
2 ripe bananas, mashed
¼ cup honey
¼ cup apple juice concentrate

2 cups whole wheat flour
1 Tbsp. baking powder
1 tsp. cinnamon
½ cup chopped nuts

Beat eggs, butter, bananas, honey, and juice. Add dry ingredients and mix lightly. Fill muffin tins ¾ full. Bake 20-25 minutes at 350°.

Choices

Banana Muffins

MRS. JOHN SZKLARZ. DEVINE. TX

4½ cups whole wheat flour
1½ cup evaporated cane juice sugar
  (organic)
2½ tsp. baking soda
1 tsp. salt
1 cup soft butter (mixed with ½ cup
  olive oil)

6 eggs
3 cups bananas
½ cup raisins
2½ tsp. vanilla
½ cup unsweetened coconut chip flakes
1 cup chopped nuts

Combine flour, sugar, soda, and salt, then cut in butter and oil in a big bowl. Mix bananas, vanilla, and eggs together and add to dry ingredients. Stir in coconut, nuts, and raisins. Bake at 325° for 20 minutes. Makes about 4½ dozen muffins.

Pumpkin Muffins

MRS. MIRIAM WENGERD, SUGARCREEK, OH

2½ cups wheat flour
1 tsp. cinnamon
2½ tsp. baking powder
1 tsp. salt

1 tsp. nutmeg
1 cup oatmeal
2 cups sucanat

Mix together. In a separate bowl, mix the following:

1 cup honey
4 eggs
1½ cups milk

1 cup pumpkin
½ cup olive oil
1 tsp. vanilla

Add to first mixture. Stir until well mixed. Pour batter into pitcher then fill muffin pans ⅔-¾ full. I use cupcake liners. These are very moist and delicious! If you want to frost them take cream cheese (softened) and whip honey and cinnamon in until it is spreadable and has the right taste.

Healthy

Pumpkin Bran Muffins

JUANITA WEAVER, JOHNSONVILLE, IL

2 eggs
½ cup honey
¾ cup oil
1 cup soft wheat flour
2 cups oat or wheat bran
2 tsp. soda

2 tsp. baking powder
1 tsp. salt
1 Tbsp. cinnamon
2 cups pumpkin
2 cups milk or water
1 cup raisins

Boil raisins with 2 Tbsp. water for 1 minute. Add all ingredients together in mixing bowl and beat on high 2-3 minutes. Fill muffin cups or cupcake papers ⅔ full. Bake at 350° for 20 minutes. Makes around 24. Variation: 2 cups flour, 1 cup bran.

Maple Bran Muffins

FRIEDA YODER, MILLERSBURG, OH

¾ cup wheat bran
½ cup milk
½ cup maple syrup
1½ tsp. maple flavoring
1 egg, slightly beaten

¼ cup oil
1¼ cup whole wheat flour
3 tsp. baking powder
½ tsp. salt
⅓ cup chopped nuts

Combine first four ingredients. Add egg and oil. Combine remaining ingredients in separate bowl. Add bran mixture and stir just until moistened. Divide batter into twelve greased muffin tins and bake at 400° for 18-20 minutes. Heat a small amount of maple syrup to 230° to drizzle over top of muffins. Serve warm. Enjoy!

77

breads

Whole Wheat Apple Muffins

MONICA BAZEN, GRAND RAPIDS, MI

2 cups (freshly ground) whole wheat flour
2 Tbsp. sweetener (opt.)
3 tsp. baking powder
¼ tsp. salt

1 tsp. cinnamon
1¼ cup apple cider or juice
½ cup applesauce
1½ cup chopped apples

Combine dry ingredients in large mixing bowl. Combine juice and applesauce in another bowl. Add apples to dry ingredients and mix to coat apples. Add juice mixture to dry ingredients. Mixture will be somewhat thick. Spoon into muffin pan lined with muffin papers. Bake at 425° for about 20 minutes or until lightly browned.

Apple Muffins

Mrs. Rhoda Miller, Sugarcreek, OH

2 eggs
½ cup applesauce
½ cup apple juice
¼ cup honey
¼ cup oil
1¾ cup whole wheat flour

¼ cup bran
2 tsp. soda
1 tsp. cream of tartar
1 tsp. cinnamon
¼ tsp. nutmeg
1 cup chopped apples

Beat liquid ingredients together. Add dry ingredients. Mix lightly just until moistened. Fold in apples. Fill greased muffin tins ¾ full. Bake 20 minutes at 400°.

Rhubarb Muffins

Mrs. Rhoda Miller, Sugarcreek, OH

2 eggs
¼ cup oil
1½ cup apple juice or milk
3 cups whole wheat flour

2 Tbsp. baking powder
½ cup honey
½ tsp. salt
1½ cup fresh chopped rhubarb

Beat eggs, oil, juice, and honey. Add flour, baking powder, salt, and rhubarb. Mix very lightly. Bake 20-25 minutes at 375° in greased muffin tins.

Blueberry Muffins

Mrs. Uriah (Rebecca) Schlabach, Burton, OH

3 cups spelt (or whole wheat) flour
2 cups yogurt
2 eggs
1 tsp. sea salt
¼ cup maple syrup

2 tsp. baking soda
1 tsp. vanilla
3 Tbsp. melted butter
1 cup blueberries

Soak flour in yogurt for 12-24 hours. Muffins will rise better if soaked for 24 hours. Blend in remaining ingredients, except blueberries. Pour into well-buttered muffin tins, filling about ¾ full. Place 5-7 blueberries on top of each muffin tin. Bake at 350° for about 1 hour or until a toothpick inserted comes out clean. Variation: For fruit spice muffins, add 1 cup fresh or canned fruit of choice, ½ tsp. cinnamon, ⅛ tsp. cloves, and ⅛ tsp. nutmeg.

Molasses Rye Muffins

MRS. ABBY ABBOTT RIDER, DELPHI, IN

1½ cups rye flour
½ tsp. baking powder
¼ cup oil
¼ cup molasses

1 egg
6 Tbsp. orange juice
¼ cup raisins

Preheat oven to 375°. Prepare 10 muffin cups, greased or lined. Add liquids to dry ingredients until just moistened. Bake for 20 minutes. These are good combined with homemade strawberry jam, apple butter, or honey orange butter. (Honey Orange Butter: ½ cup butter, ⅓ cup extra virgin olive oil, ¼ cup raw honey, 2 tsp. orange juice, grated rind of one orange. Beat together until fluffy.)

Boiled Raisin Muffins

MRS. JOHN (NORLEEN) HOOVER, OWEN, WI

1½ cups raisins
1½ cups water

½ cup honey
½ cup butter

Bring the above ingredients to a boil; simmer for 2 minutes and leave for an hour or so. Then add:

1 egg
1½ cups wheat or whole grain flour
1 tsp. baking powder

1 tsp. baking soda
1 tsp. vanilla

Mix all together and place in muffin tins and bake at 400° for 15 minutes or until done.

79

breads

Cappuccino Muffins

MRS. CONRAD (MARTHA) KUEPFER, PLEASANTVILLE, OH

2 cups whole wheat flour
¾ cup honey
2½ tsp. baking powder
1 tsp. cinnamon
¾ cup milk

2 Tbsp. instant coffee granules
½ cup melted butter
1 egg, beaten
1 tsp. vanilla
¼-⅓ cup carob powder

Combine milk and coffee granules and stir until coffee is dissolved. Add butter, egg, and vanilla. Stir in dry ingredients just until moistened. Fill muffin cups ⅔ full. Bake at 375° for 17-20 minutes or until muffins test done. Spread for muffins:

4 oz. cream cheese, cubed
1 Tbsp. honey
½ tsp. instant coffee granules

½ tsp. vanilla
¼ cup chocolate chips
    or 1 Tbsp. carob powder

In a food processor or blender, combine spread ingredients. Blend until smooth. Serve with muffins. Yield: one cup.

Biscuits

Sweet Potato Biscuits

MRS. MIRIAM WENGERD, SUGARCREEK, OH

2 cups sifted whole wheat flour
4 tsp. baking powder
pinch of salt
⅓ cup butter

⅓ cup oil
1 rounded cup mashed sweet potatoes
2 Tbsp. rice milk

Preheat oven to 400°. Sift dry ingredients, cut in butter and oil. Blend in potatoes. Add milk to make a moist dough. Drop by ¼ cup measures on a dry cookie sheet. You can also use a large cookie scoop instead of a measuring cup. Bake for 15-20 minutes. Note: Unbaked biscuits can be frozen on cookie sheet for several hours, then stored in airtight container until needed. Bake frozen for 20-25 minutes at 400°. These are moist and delicious served with butter and honey!

Fluffy Biscuits

MRS. MIRIAM WENGERD, SUGARCREEK, OH

2 cups sifted wheat flour
4 tsp. baking powder
½ tsp. salt
½ tsp. cream of tartar

½ cup butter
¾ cup milk
3 Tbsp. sucanat (opt.)

Sift dry ingredients into a bowl. Cut in butter; mix until crumbly. Mix in milk. Form a ball with dough. Place on floured surface and roll to ¾" thickness. Cut with biscuit cutter and place on cookie sheets. Bake 10-12 minutes at 350° or until golden brown. Makes 12-14 biscuits. We double this recipe for our family of 10. These are delicious split and spread with butter and honey, or can be served with chicken gravy.

Whole Wheat Biscuits

SUSAN STALTER, MILLERSBURG, OH

2 cups whole wheat flour
4 tsp. baking powder
½ tsp. cream of tartar (opt.)
½ tsp. salt
½ Tbsp. dough enhancer

1 Tbsp. sweetener
½ cup butter
1 egg, unbeaten
½ cup milk

Combine dry ingredients. Add shortening and blend until it has a cornmeal-like consistency. Add milk and egg. If necessary, add more flour until dough reaches rollable consistency. Roll to ½" thick. Cut out biscuits with floured rim of glass. Bake 10-15 minutes at 450°. Serve warm.

Whole Wheat Biscuits

MRS. KATHRYN HERSHBERGER, CLARE, MI

2 cups whole wheat flour
1 Tbsp. baking powder
½ tsp. salt

⅓ cup butter or lard
½ cup sour milk
2 Tbsp. maple syrup

Mix flour, baking powder, and salt. Cut in butter or lard. Add milk and maple syrup (which has been mixed together). Mix thoroughly but do not overmix. Drop on cookie sheet and bake at 425° for 10-15 minutes.

Whole Wheat Buttermilk Biscuits

BARBARA SUE TROYER, EVART, MI

2 cups whole wheat flour
1 tsp. soda
½ tsp. salt

⅓ cup butter
1 cup buttermilk

Use finely ground flour and sift it well to lighten it. Mix flour, soda, and salt. Cut in butter. Add buttermilk. Mix thoroughly, but do not overmix. Pat into ¾" thickness on floured board or cookie sheet. Cut biscuits, and if desired, dip into melted butter. Bake at 425° for 15-20 minutes. To save time, biscuits may be dropped.

Whole Wheat Popovers

ELIZABETH STALTER, MILLERSBURG, OH

3 large eggs
1½ cups whole wheat flour

¾ tsp. salt

Preheat oven to 450°. Grease or spray muffin pan. Place above ingedients in blender and blend on high for 30 seconds. Fill muffin cups about ¾ full, stirring batter a couple of times, as flour has a tendency to quickly settle. Bake at 450° for 15 minutes, then turn oven down to 350° and continue to bake for 20 minutes longer, or until golden brown. Cool 5 minutes in pan before removing, then serve immediately. It is normal for the tops to sink after removing from oven, and for the insides to be hollow. Delicious served with jam or butter.

Scones (Biscuits)

ELIZABETH STALTER, MILLERSURG, OH

2 cups whole wheat pastry flour
1 Tbsp. fructose
1 tsp. cream of tartar

¾ tsp. salt
½ tsp. baking soda

Mix. Work in 2 Tbsp. butter to make a crumbly mixture. Stir in ½ cup milk. Roll out in a circle, ¾" thick. Cut into 6 triangle-shaped scones. For regular round biscuits, cut out with 2" cookie cutter. Do not re-roll scraps. (This toughens the gluten, making it heavier and less tender.) Bake at 400° for 12-15 minutes or until nicely browned.

Biscuits

BETTY LONON, MARION, NC

2 cups whole wheat pastry flour	1 tsp. honey
1 Tbsp. baking powder	1 cup yogurt
¼ tsp. baking soda	¼ cup oil
¼ tsp. salt	

Mix dry ingredients together in bowl. Mix in oil with pastry blender until mixture resembles coarse crumbs. Add honey and yogurt, stirring with fork. Knead lightly on floured surface. Roll out to ⅜" thickness and cut. Place on ungreased cookie sheet, sides touching. Bake at 425° for 13-15 minutes, until golden.

Biscuits Supreme

LEAH NISLEY, DANVILLE, OH

2 cups flour (spelt or wheat)	4 tsp. baking powder
½ tsp. salt	½ tsp. cream of tartar
½ cup shortening	

Sift dry ingredients together. Cut in shortening until mixture resembles coarse crumbs. Add to milk all at once; stir until just mixed. Let stand a little. Roll out; cut with biscuit cutter. Place on cookie sheet. Bake at 450° for 10-12 minutes or until brown.

83

breads

Bisquick Mix

MRS. REBECCA ZOOK, MYERSTOWN, PA

8 cups flour	2 tsp. salt
½ cup baking powder	1¾ cup lard
2 tsp. cream of tartar	

Mix together until crumbly and store in tight container in refrigerator. To make biscuits:

2¼ cups Bisquick mix	⅔ cup buttermilk

Mix together. It will be sticky. Drop by tablespoons on greased cookie sheet. Bake at 450° for 8-10 minutes.

Choices

Melt in Your Mouth Biscuits

MARTHA WIDEMAN, LISTOWEL, ON

2 cups sifted whole wheat pastry flour
2 tsp. baking powder
½ tsp. cream of tartar
½ tsp. salt
2-3 tsp. dried parsley

½ cup shortening
1 egg, unbeaten
⅔ cup milk
onion or garlic salt (optional)

Sift dry ingredients together and cut in shortening until mixture resembles coarse meal. Pour milk in slowly. Add egg and stir well. Knead on lightly floured surface. Roll out and use biscuit cutters for different shapes. Bake 10-15 minutes at 450°.

Baking Powder Biscuits

MARTHA WIDEMAN, LISTOWEL, ON

2 cups whole wheat pastry flour
3 tsp. baking powder
½ tsp. salt
2 tsp. chicken soup base

1 tsp. sage
1 tsp. curry
¼ cup shortening
¾ cup milk

Sift dry ingredients together. Cut in shortening. Add milk and knead. Roll out dough. Use cookie cutters to cut dough to make various shapes. Bake at 450° for 12-15 minutes.

Biscuits Supreme

MRS. JOHN (EVA MAY) YODER, CLARE, MI

2 cups flour
½ tsp. salt
2 tsp. maple syrup
½ cup lard or soft butter

4 tsp. baking powder
½ tsp. cream of tartar
1 cup milk

Mix dry ingredients; add lard until crumbly. Add liquid all at once; stir until just mixed. Depending on the flour, you may need to use more or less milk. Roll into balls and press flat on cookie sheet. Bake at 450° for 10-12 minutes.

Buttermilk Biscuits

Susan Doty, Lobelville, TN

3½ cups spelt or whole wheat flour
1 cup soured buttermilk
¼ cup butter or lard

1½ tsp. salt
2 tsp. soda

Mix flour and buttermilk to thick dough. Cover in warm place 12-24 hours. Knead in remaining ingredients. Roll to ¾" thickness. Bake at 350° for 40 minutes.

Crackers

Graham Crackers

2 cups spelt flour (or wheat)
2 tsp. baking powder
1 tsp. salt

⅔ cup water
¼ cup oil

Shape into round balls and press flat on greased cookie sheet. Bake at 350° until desired crispness (20-30 minutes).

Graham Crackers

Martha Wise, Seneca Falls, NY

½ cup oil
2 tsp. vanilla
1 tsp. baking soda
½ cup honey
½ tsp. salt

1½ tsp. cinnamon
⅓ cup milk
1 Tbsp. molasses
1½ tsp. baking powder
3½ cups oat flour

Mix liquids first, except milk, then add dry ingredients alternately with milk. If sticky, add more flour. Roll out to completely cover a 10 x 15" jelly roll pan. Cut into squares and prick with fork. Bake at 300° for 18-20 minutes, until edges are brown. Break squares apart and return to oven. Turn oven off and allow them to toast 2-3 hours. These can be frozen.

Homemade Graham Crackers

MARTHA BEILER, QUARRYVILLE, PA

1 cup oil
1 cup honey
2 Tbsp. molasses
4 tsp. vanilla
1 tsp. salt
7 cups whole wheat flour

3 tsp. baking powder
2 tsp. baking soda
4 tsp. cinnamon
⅔ cup milk
½ cup wheat germ

Mix liquids first, except milk, then add dry ingredients, alternating with milk. If dough is sticky, add more flour. Divide dough in quarters then roll to ¼" thickness with rolling pin. Use pizza cutter to cut into squares. Place on greased cookie sheets and prick with fork. Bake at 300°. Cool a little before removing.

Cheese Wheat Thins

MRS. ABBY ABBOTT RIDER, DELPHI, IN

2 cups whole wheat flour
¼ tsp. baking soda
1 Tbsp. sweetener of your choice
½ cup butter

⅓ cup milk
1 Tbsp. cider vinegar
½ cup grated cheese

Combine milk and vinegar and set aside. This makes a sour milk similar to buttermilk. Combine the rest of ingredients in a mixer and mix with wire whips until it resembles coarse meal. Add milk mixture until just combined. Turn out on oiled counter and knead into a ball. Roll thin on a baking sheet and cut into pieces. Prick with fork. Bake at 375° for 12-15 minutes.

Oatmeal Crackers

MRS. LAMAR (NANCY) ZIMMERMAN, STEVENS, PA

3 cups rolled oats
1 cup raw wheat germ
2 cups whole wheat flour
½ cup sesame seeds (opt.)

3 Tbsp. honey
¾ cup oil
1 cup water

Mix dry ingredients in a large bowl. Heat water, oil, and honey until warm. Pour over oat mixture. Mix well and roll out on a floured board until ⅛" thick. Cut in squares. Put on cookie sheet and salt lightly. Bake at 300° for 20-25 minutes, until crisp, but not too brown.

Wheatless Crackers

Mrs. Abby Abbott Rider, Delphi, IN

1 cup brown rice flour
1 cup oat flour
1 tsp. salt
2 tsp. baking powder

2 tsp. sweetener of your choice
½ cup butter
⅓ cup milk

Mix dry ingredients together and cut in the butter. Add the liquid. Dough will seem dry. Roll out on ungreased cookie sheet, cut and prick with a fork. Bake at 375° about 10-12 minutes or until lightly browned.

Vegetable Thins

Martha Wideman, Listowel, ON

2 cups whole wheat pastry flour
1 tsp. baking powder
¼ cup finely grated cheese
¼ cup finely grated carrots
2 tsp. dried parsley

1 tsp. seasoned salt
2 tsp. finely grated onion
6 Tbsp. butter
1¾ tsp. cheese powder
⅔ cup tomato juice

Mix everything together. Roll out on cookie sheets or use cutters to make cute shapes. Prick tops with a fork and bake for 10-15 minutes. Tips for crisp crackers: Crackers are *much* crisper again if put in a 200° oven for a few hours the next day.

Choices

Date Crackers

BETTY LONON, MARION, NC

2 cups whole wheat flour
2 cups rolled oats
1 tsp. salt
⅔ cup chopped nuts
⅓ cup shredded coconut

2 cups chopped dates
⅔ cup oil
⅔-1 cup water
¼ cup orange juice concentrate

Combine dry ingredients and dates. Add oil, water, and orange juice concentrate. Make pliable dough, and divide dough into two portions. Put dough on ungreased cookie sheets, place waxed paper on top of dough, roll out, and cut into squares. Bake at 350° for 15 minutes. Note: I place the dough on a long jelly roll pan and a round pizza pan. Both of these pans have an edge to them to contain the dough. You can use any size pans you have, just divide the dough between them so they are rolled out to similar thicknesses, about ⅛-¼". After making these a time or two, you will discover what thickness you like for the finished cracker. The purpose of the waxed paper is to keep the dough from sticking to the glass when rolling out. I use a drinking glass for a rolling pin so I can get the dough rolled into the corners, and the edges on the pans do not interfere with the rolling when using a glass. You can cut the dough into the size squares you want your crackers to be. Mine are usually about 2 x 2". I use a pizza cutter to make fast work of the cutting.

Rolls & Buns

Yorkshire Sticky Buns

MABEL ZIMMERMAN

Bake 2 pans of Yorkshire Pudding,* very lightly browned. Loosen pudding and dump out on cookie sheets while still quite warm. Spread generously with softened butter. Mix 2 tablespoons rappadura with 1 tsp. cinnamon, sprinkle onto butter. Roll up each pudding like jelly roll, wrap with parchment paper or plastic wrap, tightly, and put in refrigerator to chill. After rolls are chilled, heat in saucepan:

3 Tbsp. cream (or milk)
⅓ cup butter

⅓ cup rappadura
2 Tbsp. honey or maple syrup

Pour into 2 square pans or 1 larger and 1 smaller (it all depends on how thickly you slice the rolls). Lay the rolls into syrup, firmly against each other to keep from rolling open. Put into 350° oven and heat until very bubbly and lightly browning. Dump onto cookie sheets, letting syrup drip on top. Scrape syrup and spread onto rolls, wherever needed.

*For Yorkshire Pudding see page 33.

Healthy

Cinnamon Rolls

MRS. MIRIAM WENGERD, SUGARCREEK, OH

½ cup maple syrup
1 tsp. cinnamon
½ cup water

2 Tbsp. butter
1 cup chopped pecans
1½ lb. bread dough

In saucepan, melt butter, add maple syrup, water and cinnamon, stir with whisk. Pour into 9 x 13" pan. Sprinkle pecans over syrup. Roll out bread dough ½" thick in rectangular shape. Spread with 2 Tbsp. melted butter using pastry brush. Sprinkle sucanat evenly over this then sprinkle generously with cinnamon. Roll dough together the long way and divide evenly into 12 slices about 1¼" thick. Cut with bread knife and place on top of syrup and nuts, 3 in a row in 4 rows. Let rise until almost double. Bake at 350° for 25-30 minutes. Invert on a large platter while still warm.

Overnight Sticky Buns

JUANITA WEAVER, JOHNSONVILLE, IL

2 Tbsp. yeast
2 eggs
½ cup honey
¾ cup butter

2½ tsp. salt
2½ cups warm water
7-8 cups wheat flour

Stir wet ingredients, salt, and yeast in large bowl. Knead in flour to make a soft dough. Let rise at least 8 hours in fridge. Roll out as usual and let rise 1 hour. More flour can be added if needed. Bake at 325° for 15-20 minutes. You can double the honey and just spread dough with butter and sprinkle with cinnamon and roll, or drizzle sorghum over dough instead of brown sugar. Topping:

1 cup butter
⅔ cup sorghum

⅓ cup honey
¾ cup nuts

Boil syrup ingredients for 1½ minutes. Spread in bottom of two 9 x 13" pans. Lay cinnamon rolls on top. Time saver tip: Drop dough on topping in tablespoon size globs. Add 2 Tbsp. of cinnamon to syrup topping.

Three-Grain Pan Rolls

KENDRA ROKEY, SABETHA, KS

2 cups water
½ cup bulgur
1 Tbsp. active dry yeast
1 cup warm milk
½ cup quick cooking oats
⅓ cup honey
2 eggs
2 tsp. salt

¾ tsp. pepper
5-6 cups whole wheat flour
2 Tbsp. olive oil
2 tsp. celery seed
2 tsp. fennel seed
2 tsp. sesame seed
1 tsp. poppy seed

In a saucepan bring water to a boil. Stir in bulgur. Reduce heat; cover and simmer for 15 minutes. Drain. In large mixing bowl, dissolve yeast in warm milk. Add the oats, honey, eggs, salt, pepper, bulgur and ½ of the flour. Beat until smooth. Stir in rest of flour to form soft dough and knead until elastic, about 6-8 minutes (dough will be lumpy). Place in a greased bowl, turning once to coat top. Cover and let rise in a warm place until double, about 1¼ hours. Punch dough down. Turn onto a lightly floured surface, divide into 22 pieces. Roll into balls. Arrange 11 balls in one 9" round greased pan. Put the other 11 balls in another round pan. In a bowl, combine seeds. Brush roll tops with oil and sprinkle seeds over top. Cover and let rise in a warm place until double, about 40 minutes. Bake at 375° for 18-22 minutes or until golden brown. Remove from pans to wire racks to cool. Yield: 22 rolls.

breads

90

Tortillas & Tacos

Taco Shells

MRS. IVAN J. YODER, MILLERSBURG, OH

1½ cup cold water
1 cup white spelt flour (or wheat)
½ cup cornmeal

¼ tsp. salt
1 egg

Mix all together and beat well and fry like pancakes. Pour scant ¼ cup dough into greased hot skillet. Cool. Serve with sour cream, shredded lettuce, shredded cheese, salsa, tomatoes and hamburger seasoned with taco seasoning.

Chapatties (or Tortillas)

MRS. HARRY (CINDY) WILKINSON, DIXON, IL

1 cup whole wheat flour
1 cup corn flour
⅛ tsp. salt
1 cup cold water

Mix flours and salt together. Add water gradually, adding just enough to keep dough from sticking to hands (about one cup). Divide into 8 portions and roll out each portion with a rolling pin as thin as possible. Toast over medium heat in a dry cast-iron skillet for about 30 seconds on each side, or until lightly toasted and cooked through. Yield: 8 chapatties, about 5" in diameter.

Whole Wheat Tortillas

MARY BETH HEISEY, PUEBLO WEST, CO

3 cups whole wheat flour
1 tsp. salt
⅓ cup oil
1 cup warm water

Mix flour and salt in a bowl. Add oil and warm water all at one time. Stir with a fork. Work into a soft dough. Let rest for 30 minutes in covered bowl. Cut into 12 pieces. Roll out on slightly oiled counter. Cook on non-stick skillet on both sides. Put into plastic bag. You can refrigerate or freeze these. Then reheat on a non-stick skillet and place in kitchen towel to serve.

91

breads

Whole Wheat Flour Tortillas

MRS. RUBY SHETLER, HOMER, MI

5 cups whole wheat flour
2 tsp. salt
2 Tbsp. olive oil
½ tsp. baking powder
1⅔ cup warm water

Stir together dry ingredients, then add the oil and water. Mix well and knead lightly. Pinch off walnut-sized pieces of dough and roll out very, very thinly on a floured pastry cloth or on a floured board or counter. Aim for a round tortilla, but it really doesn't matter much if they are misshapen. Heat an ungreased griddle or frying pan to very hot, and cook on one side until bubbles form, then turn over and cook the other side until brown "freckles" appear. You can accentuate the bubbling and air pockets by pressing down with a dry cloth after it has been turned over. Store in plastic bag. Makes 20 or more.

Whole Wheat Tortillas

KAREN MILLER, PARTRIDGE, KS

2 cups whole wheat flour
½ tsp. salt

¼ cup canola oil
⅔ cup warm water

Rub flour, salt, and oil or shortening together with your fingers until completely incorporated and fine crumbs form. Pour water into dry ingredients and immediately work it in with a fork. Dough will be in large clumps. Sprinkle with flour and knead until smooth, about 2 minutes. Allow dough to sit, covered, for 20-30 minutes or more, and then divide into 6-8 equal pieces. Roll out thinly with a bit of flour. Bake each tortilla about 45-60 seconds on each side on hot griddle or skillet or tortilla maker. Makes 6-8 tortillas. Easily doubled or tripled. Note: May use pastry, hard red, 7-grain, or Kamut flour.

Bread Sticks

Italian Bread Sticks

ELIZABETH STALTER, MILLERSBURG, OH

⅔ cup warm water
1 Tbsp. active dry yeast

½ Tbsp. fructose

Blend all and let set for 5-10 minutes, until it begins to bubble up. Blend in:

1 tsp. salt
½ cup soft butter

1 cup whole wheat pastry flour

Stir in an additional cup of flour, kneading about 5 minutes. Cover in bowl and let double. Punch down and divide into 8 balls. Divide each ball into 6 pieces. Roll out like a pencil (6-10" long). Sprinkle with sesame seeds (optional). Place 1" apart on a greased cookie sheet; lightly brush tops with 1 beaten egg yolk. Bake at 400° for about 20 minutes or until lightly golden. Do not overbake.

Creamy Italian Breadsticks

MRS. MIRIAM WENGERD, SUGARCREEK, OH

1 Tbsp. instant yeast
1 cup warm water
1 tsp. sweetener of your choice
1 Tbsp. olive oil

1 tsp. salt
3 cups fresh-ground wheat flour
⅓ cup Italian dressing (see below)

Mix the first 3 ingredients and let stand for 5 minutes. Add next 3 ingredients. Knead until smooth. Roll out on greased 14" pizza pan. Spread with dressing. Mix the following and sprinkle on top:

¼ tsp. garlic powder
¼ tsp. oregano
¼ tsp. thyme

¼ tsp. chili powder
1 cup cheddar cheese, shredded
¼ cup Parmesan

Bake at 450° for 15 minutes. Cut into strips. Serve with pizza sauce as dip. Our family enjoys this as a simple winter supper. I double the recipe for our family of 10.

Breadstick Italian Salad Dressing

MRS. MIRIAM WENGERD, SUGARCREEK, OH

¼ cup lemon juice
¼ cup apple cider vinegar
½ tsp. garlic powder
½ tsp. onion powder
1 tsp. sea salt

½ tsp. green mustard
½ tsp. oregano
½ tsp. basil
¼ tsp. paprika

Whisk everything together well or shake in jar.

Corn Sticks

KAREN MILLER, PARTRIDGE, KS

⅓ cup butter, melted
2¼ cups whole wheat flour
5 tsp. baking powder
2 Tbsp. sweetener of your choice

1 tsp. salt
1 cup creamed corn
¼ cup milk or buttermilk

Pour melted butter into 10 x 15" jelly roll pan. Mix dry ingredients; stir in corn and milk. Mix, then turn out on a floured surface. Knead lightly; roll to ¼" thickness. Cut in strips (2 x 5" or to desired size.) Lay each strip in butter on pan, turning to coat both sides. Bake at 450° until golden brown. A wonderfully crunchy addition to chili soup!

Italian Bread Wedges

MARTHA WINGERT, CHAMBERSBURG, PA

3 tsp. yeast
1 cup warm water, divided
1 tsp. sweetener of your choice

2 Tbsp. canola oil
1 tsp. salt
2½-3 cups flour

Dissolve yeast in ¼ cup warm water. Add sweetener; let stand for 5 minutes. Add oil, salt, remaining water and 2 cups of flour; beat until smooth. Add enough of remaining flour to form a soft dough. Turn onto a floured surface, knead until smooth and elastic. Put in greased bowl; let rise until doubled. Punch dough flat onto a pizza stone or 12" pizza pan. Let rise for 5 minutes. Topping:

⅓ cup Italian dressing
¼ tsp. garlic powder
¼ tsp. oregano
¼ tsp. thyme

dash of pepper
1 cup shredded mozzarella
¼ cup grated Parmesan

Spread dough with Italian dressing. Combine the garlic powder, thyme, oregano, and pepper. Sprinkle over dough. Top with cheese. Bake at 450° for 15-20 minutes or until golden brown. Serve warm.

Sourdough

THERE SEEMS TO BE A GROWING INTEREST IN LEARNING to bake with sourdough. I've been bitten by the bug myself and am currently experimenting with using sourdough. By the amount of flops I've had, I can tell it will take some practice to get something our family enjoys! Lots of people have problems with eating too much processed yeast, thus their interest in sourdough. Strange as it may sound, sourdough catches wild yeast out of the air.

Sourdough is made by stirring flour and liquid together and letting it sour on your countertop, keeping it covered with a clean cotton cloth. Every day you add flour and water again. After seven days your starter should be bubbly. Put it in a glass bowl (no metal) and keep it covered with the cotton cloth. Always use a wooden spoon when stirring in your daily flour and water. If you use metal it will kill the yeast. Always leave at least one cup starter to grow within its glass bowl again.

Try something new today—give your family another healthy choice!

Old-Fashioned Sourdough Starter

Mrs. Anthony (Nora) Mast, Baltic, OH

1 cup warm water
1¼ cup bread flour
1 tsp. salt

1 tsp. sweetener of your choice
1 med. raw potato, grated

Mix together and put in a crock or wide-mouth jar. Cover with cheesecloth for 24 hours. Then cover with lid and let ferment for 2 weeks. Always store in a jar. Use 1 cup starter with any sourdough bread recipe. This recipe was used before any yeast was available.

Sourdough Starter

Mrs. Daniel (Verna) King, Pembroke, KY

Put 1 cup raw milk in a glass jar or crock (no metal) and let stand at room temperature for 24 hours. Stir in 1 cup flour. Fresh ground rye is about the best flour to use for sourdough starters. Spelt or whole wheat flour may be used to finish the bread. Cover with a cheesecloth and place in a warm place (80° is ideal) for 2-5 days, depending on how long it takes to bubble or sour. Through the summer you may set it outside to expose your starter to the wild yeasts, or spores, in the wind. This may speed fermentation. If it starts to dry out, stir in enough moderately warm water to bring it back to its original consistency. It should not have a crust on top; this will slow it down somewhat. Once it has a sour aroma and is full of bubbles it is ready to use. This starter is best if used once a week. If not used for several weeks, spoon out and discard about half and replenish with equal amounts of milk and flour. If you don't plan on using it for several weeks, freeze it. Freezing slows down action. Leave it at room temperature for 24 hours to thaw. Each time you use part of your starter, replenish it with equal amounts of milk and flour. Leave at room temperature for several hours until it becomes full of bubbles. Then cover and store in refrigerator.

Sourdough Starter

Mrs. Daniel (Verna) King, Pembroke, KY

Mix 1 cup flour with 1 cup lukewarm water in a scalded pot or jar. Cover with cheesecloth and let stand in a warm place to sour. This is the most primitive starter, and the results can be uncertain with regards to odor, texture, and flavor.

Sourdough Culture

Joanne Martin, Brooten, MN

1 cup milk

1 cup flour

Allow milk to stand in a warm place for 24 hours. Using a wooden spoon, stir in flour (never use metal utensils when mixing sourdough). Allow to stand in a warm place until it bubbles and becomes sour. When ready, place in a large, loosely covered container and refrigerate. Replace or feed every 4 days by adding 1 cup milk, 1 cup flour, and ¼ cup sweetener of your choice. Do not use for at least 24 hours after feeding. If it doesn't increase fast enough, divide into two bowls. When you use your culture, always allow 1½ cup to remain in the container. If you can't use your culture for a while, freeze it. Thaw for 24 hours or until bubbly again. The longer a culture is kept, the better it will get. If it's well cared for, it can be kept for years.

Sourdough Starter

Cynthia Korver, New Oxford, PA

1¼ cups unbleached flour
1 cup lukewarm water

1 glass quart jar

Mix flour and water in jar and let stand until the batter bubbles and rises. (May take anywhere from overnight to 1 week.) Tips: Place a rubber band on the jar at the level of liquid when you begin, so you know when it rises. Keep in a warm place. Cover jar with cheesecloth to keep out bugs and keep starter from drying out. Stir only if liquid rises to the top. The aroma should be pleasantly sour. If it gets a bad smell, throw it away, scald jar, and try again. To use, "double" it first by mixing up another flour and water batter (may use whole wheat) and stir in the live starter. Let set in warm place until it is bubbly. Return ½ to jar and use the other ½. Works wonderfully if kept unrefrigerated.

Sourdough Starter

The B Sisters, Oregon City, OR

1 Tbsp. dry yeast
2½ cups warm water

2 tsp. honey
2½ cups flour

Let ferment for 5 days, stirring daily. Sourdough contains microorganisms that grow in the dough, giving it its characteristic taste. It can be tricky to get your own starter going. It is best if you can get a couple cups of starter from a friend.

Sourdough Starter

To <u>reactivate</u> the starter from the powdered form:

In a glass or plastic bowl (*not* metal) dissolve the contents of the packet in ¾ cup warm (90°) water. Add ¾ cup unbleached flour and 1 tsp. sweetener of your choice. Place bowl in warm place (85°). Cover with damp towel for up to 48 hours. It will get bubbly from the fermentation. It's alive! Mix in ¾ cup water and 1 cup unbleached flour. Stir well and let the mixture sit another 2-4 hours. When mixture expands slightly and gets bubbly again it is ready to use. Now you can store it in the refrigerator until needed. It may develop a clear liquid on top. If so, simply stir it back in. This is alcohol. The starter will need feeding once every couple of weeks. To do this, either use a cup of it or discard a cup and replace with ¾ cup water plus 1 cup unbleached flour. Sometimes your starter might seem inactive, but by adding 1 Tbsp. of apple cider vinegar, you'll give it a good kick. Whenever you are ready to use your starter, take it out of the refrigerator and let it warm up to room temperature. Remove 1 cup and feed it. Let the starter recover before putting it back in the refrigerator. Be sure to share with friends.

Sourdough starter is available for $10 pp. Order from L. Kevin Johnson, 4402 Gilead Road, Clinton, LA 70722

Sourdough Pancakes or Waffles

½ cup storage culture	1½ cups fresh ground wheat flour
½ cup oat flour	1½ cups water or buttermilk

Let this soak overnight in a covered bowl in order to ferment. Next morning, stir in:

1 egg	½ tsp. Celtic sea salt
2 Tbsp. olive oil	1 tsp. baking soda
2 Tbsp. raw honey	

Let mixture sit for 30 minutes, then cook on hot griddle. You can use coconut oil for cooking. This is my favorite breakfast along with buckwheat lettuce, scrambled egg, cultured butter, homemade pancake syrup and fruit. Yum!

Sourdough Pancakes

LUCIA LAPP, BENTON, IL

1 cup sourdough	1 tsp. baking powder
1 cup flour	⅓ cup oil
¾ tsp. salt	2 eggs
¾ tsp. soda	½ cup milk
2 Tbsp. sucanat	

Mix well and fry. Makes approximately 15 pancakes.

Choices

Sourdough Pancakes

Mrs. Jason Byler, Lobelville, TN

2 cups flour
2 cups lukewarm water
½ cup starter
1½ Tbsp. honey
½ tsp. soda dissolved in 1 Tbsp. water

1 tsp. salt
½ tsp. baking powder
3 Tbsp. cooking oil
2 eggs, slightly beaten

Mix flour, water, and starter in a glass bowl. Cover with a towel and let stand in a warm place overnight. Next morning, add other ingredients and cook pancakes on a lightly greased griddle. This makes a thin type of pancake with a delicious pancake taste.

Sourdough Waffles

Kendra Rokey, Sabetha, KS

In the evening, combine:

½ cup sourdough starter
2 cups milk

2 cups whole wheat flour

In the morning, gently add:

2 eggs, beaten
1 Tbsp. honey
½ tsp. salt

1 tsp. soda
2 Tbsp. oil

Mix all well together and bake in waffle iron.

Sourdough Bread

Mrs. Anthony (Nora) Mast, Baltic, OH

1 cup warm water
1 cup starter
2 Tbsp. honey
5-5½ cups flour

½ tsp. soda
2 egg yolks
2 tsp. salt
¼ cup shortening or oil

Combine all ingredients, except only ½ cup flour. Mix well. Add flour to make a soft dough. Knead until smooth. Shape into 2 loaves in greased pans. Let rise until double. Bake at 350-400°, approximately 1 hour.

Sourdough Bread

MRS. DANIEL (VERNA) KING, PEMBROKE, KY

1 cup sourdough starter
2 cups warm water

2½ cups flour, sifted

Combine ingredients in a large glass bowl (about 2 quart size). It needs room to rise. Leave set for at least 14-36 hours. You won't need salt if the mixture is sour enough. It will be somewhat thick and lumpy, but will thin down during fermentation.

After fermentation and before you finish the bread, return 1 cup, or the amount you borrowed, to the pot again for future use in starting another starter. To finish your bread add enough flour so you can knead it. Sourdough bread will turn out best if you keep it on the soft side rather than stiff. Knead 10-15 minutes, then let rest 10 minutes. Form into loaves. Cover with a slightly damp towel. Let rise until doubled in size. Rising may take 3-6 hours. Bake for 20 minutes at 400°, or until it shrinks from sides of pan.

Sourdough Bread

JOANNA KLINE, CANASTOTA, NY

Mix 1 c. starter with 1 c. wheat flour and ¾ c. cold water (regular tap). Let stand at room temperature for 2-3 hours until bubbly. Add 2½ c. wheat flour and 1½ c. water, mix well and add 2 tsp. salt and an additional 3 c. wheat flour. Mix just until flour is moistened. Let set for 6-8 hours. (I let it rise overnight.) Knead in Bosch for 5 minutes. Let rest 10 minutes then repeat twice (adding flour as needed). Divide in three loaves and let set on countertop for 30 minutes. Shape in tight round loaves and place in bowls lined with cloth. Sprinkle cloth with flour or loaves will stick. Let rise until double (2-4 hours). Invert on baking stone or glass pie pan. Sprinkle with corn meal. With a sharp knife make two slashes through top of loaves. Bake in hot oven, 500°, for 10 minutes. Turn oven temperature back to 400° for rest of the time (about 12 minutes). For thin crust moisten heat with a pan of water on bottom of oven and squirt oven a few times with water while baking.

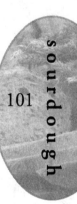

Choices

Sourdough Bread

sourdough starter (recipe on pages 97-99)	18 cups whole wheat flour
1 cup safflower oil	2½ Tbsp. salt
juice of 1 lemon	½ grated carrot (optional)
7½ cups water	¼-½ cup gluten flour

The night before, put water in a very large bowl or machine that can knead. (We use a Bosch Universal Mixer.) Slowly add 9 cups whole wheat flour, mixing well. Then mix in all sourdough starter. Discard any brown liquid that may have formed when starter was in fridge. Let sit on counter, covered, overnight.

The next day, stir dough well. (It is all starter now.) Take out approximately 2 cups dough and put in a glass jar in the fridge for next time. THIS IS AN IMPORTANT STEP! Add salt, oil, lemon juice, carrot, and gluten flour, mixing well after each addition. Add flour in medium amounts, kneading well (you will need to turn up the speed of your mixer at this point), until dough pulls away from sides of bowl and is no longer sticky. (Pinch the dough between your fingers and see how it feels. This takes experience. Too much flour makes dense bread and too little makes it hard to handle. Too little flour is better than too much, as you can always add flour when you are shaping the loaves. We add somewhere near 9 cups of flour.) After all flour is added, knead for five minutes. (Optional: At this point, dough can be left to rise for a few hours.) Turn out dough onto an oiled or floured surface and cut into four pieces with a large knife. Shape into loaves. We spread dough into a round rectangle, fold into thirds, and then roll up. Pinch all seams shut and place in bread pan. Repeat with all sections. Cover with a damp towel and let rise in a warm place for two hours. Heat oven to 350°. Brush top of loaves with beaten egg. Cut three slits crosswise along top of loaves. Baking times will vary on ovens and bread pans. We have heavy clay pans and bake for 1 hour at 350° and then turn off the oven and leave in oven for another 20 minutes.

Notes: Can be formed into rolls. We use starter once a week, but it probably could be used up to three times a week. If you do not use your starter for over two weeks, it tends to get too sour! You can solve this by pouring off brown liquid and then discarding ¼-⅓ cup of dough. Mix ⅓ cup water and ⅓ cup flour back in jar and return to fridge. We have made delicious variations by rolling up cinnamon, honey, nuts and raisins, etc. in the loaves. Another variation is to replace safflower oil with ½ cup melted butter and ½ cup olive oil. Mix chopped olives into the dough.

Hi-Fiber Sourdough Rice Bread

MABLE ZIMMERMAN, NEW ENTERPRISE, PA

3 cups brown rice flour   2½ cups kefir or yogurt*
1½ cups sweet rice flour

Mix the above ingredients 12-24 hours before baking. *If dairy-free, use 4 Tbsp. vinegar or lemon juice and add water to make 2½ cups. Soak in a glass bowl or other glass container in a warm place with a plate or plastic wrap on top. When ready to mix the bread, beat for 5-10 minutes:

8 large eggs

To the sourdough, mix the following in while it's warm:

3 Tbsp. coconut oil

Stir in the remaining ingredients:

½ cup flax seed, ground   ¼ cup frozen apple juice
½ cup coconut flour   concentrate
2 tsp. baking soda   ½ cup cooked pumpkin
2 tsp. salt   or applesauce

Fold sourdough mixture into beaten eggs just until thoroughly mixed. Pour into 2 small greased loaf pans. Bake at 350° for 45 minutes or longer. (Check with toothpick before removing from oven.) Let cool 15 minutes before removing from pans. Cool completely before slicing, then freeze what isn't used the same day, as it gets dry quickly. Notes: This is a heavy, moist bread. Experiment until it's like you want it. It could be improved by adding tapioca, potato, and/or cornstarch for part of flour, or the gums (guar or xanthan) but we choose to avoid these high-carbohydrate ingredients. The flax seed and coconut flour give this bread excellent fiber. Coconut flour is exceptionally high in fiber and can be purchased in some health food stores. Two known brands are Tropical Traditions and Bob's Red Mill. Apple juice improves the flavor and gives it some sweetness. Sweet rice is more glutenous than other rice, and gives more moisture, as also does the pumpkin, applesauce, etc.

Rice Flax Sourdough Bread

MABLE ZIMMERMAN, NEW ENTERPRISE, PA

Twelve to twenty-four hours before baking, stir together: 1½ cups brown rice flour and 1½ cups kefir or yogurt. (If dairy-free, use 3 Tbsp. vinegar or lemon juice in a measuring cup and add water to a total of 1½ cups.) Soak in a glass bowl or jar, covered, for 12-24 hours. Before baking, add 4 extra-large eggs or 5 smaller eggs, and 1 tsp. salt. Mix with a whisk. Put 1 Tbsp. butter and 1 Tbsp. coconut oil in each of two 9 x 13" pans and put in 375° oven until melted. Pour the batter, divided, into the two pans. Bake approximately 25 minutes until lightly browned. Cool slightly, then cut into 8 or 10 pieces. Delicious served warm, as jelly bread or sandwiches. The bread holds together well because of the top and bottom crust. Freeze what you don't plan to use in a day or two.

Sourdough Bread

Mrs. Jason Byler, Lobelville, TN

1 cup sourdough starter	1 Tbsp. salt
½ cup sorghum	1½ cups warm water
½ cup oil	6 cups flour

Mix first 5 ingredients and half of the flour. Beat vigorously for several minutes. Knead in the rest of the flour. Grease bowl and let rise until double. Punch down and shape into loaves. Let rise until almost double. Bake at 375° for 40-45 minutes. Grease tops with butter. Yield: 2-1½ lb. loaves. Note: I usually don't measure the starter, but dump in whatever I have extra. More sourdough only makes it better. To feed sourdough starter for bread: ½ cup starter, ½ cup flour, ⅜ cup sweetener, ½-¾ cup very warm water, 1½ Tbsp. instant potato flakes. Mix dry ingredients. Add water and stir well. Add sourdough; let set at room temperature for 12 hours. Reserve ½ cup for next baking; use the rest for bread. It's best to "feed" it no less than once a week to keep it active. Always keep starter refrigerated. Use only wooden, plastic, or glass bowls when feeding sourdough.

Sourdough Bread

Mrs. Mose A. Yoder, Fresno, OH

1 cup starter	1½ cups warm water
2 Tbsp. oil	1 tsp. salt
2 eggs	2 Tbsp. liquid lecithin (opt.)

Mix all ingredients with whole grain spelt flour or any other flour you wish. Make consistency of regular dough. Let rise in covered bowl for 4 or 5 hours. Work out in pans, and let rise another hour or until high enough to bake. Bake at 350° for 30 minutes or until done. Sourdough starter: 1 cup starter (we bought this at an organic health food store). Feed, then set in room temperature for 12 hours. Take out all but approximately 1 cup. Return to refrigerator on bottom shelf, so it's not at the coldest spot. Store in plastic or glass. Do not use metal spoon. Feed starter once a week, then take out a cup and put in fridge. When feeding, add: ¾ cup sweetener, 3 Tbsp. potato flakes, 1 cup hot water.

Sourdough Bread

MELISSA HORST, TUNAS, MO

The evening before, combine 3 cups whole wheat flour and 2¼ cups water; cover and refrigerate overnight. (When combining mixture, stir until all flour is moistened. May add a little more water if necessary.

In the morning, bring soaked flour to room temperature. (I often set it in warm water until it's warmer than room temperature but not hot.) Meanwhile, combine 1½ cups sourdough culture with 1 cup plus 2 Tbsp. warm water and 1½ cups whole wheat flour. Set it someplace warm, but not hot (as you would yeast dough), until there are small bubbles here and there, should be 2-4 hours or less. Combine soaked flour with the sourdough mixture, stir well, then add:

4½ cups whole wheat flour	3 tsp. salt
3-5 Tbsp. honey	½ cup water

Mix this stiff dough together until well moistened. More water may be added if it seems too dry. Cover with a damp cloth and set in warm spot (maybe 80°-100°) to ferment for 6-8 hours, or until expanded with small bubbles here and there.

Gently knead the dough on floured surface for about 5 minutes. (I just put a handful or two of whole wheat flour on my countertop, and another on top of the sticky dough, and knead until the flour is used up.) Repeat two more times (knead dough 5 minutes, let rest 10 minutes).

Cut the dough into 2 lumps. Shape into loaves just as you would yeast dough. Place in 2 greased 9 x 5" bread pans. I like to use a toothpick to poke holes down through the loaf, which helps release air bubbles. Let it rise in warm spot for 2-4 hours or until it's expanded and looks fat enough to bake. Allow extra time if necessary. (When ready, it looks almost ready to overflow the pans.) Bake at 350° for about 40-45 minutes. Crust should be medium brown and bread may pull slightly away from pan. Remove from pans to cool. Store in paper bag or loosely wrapped plastic bag; tends to get moldy if stored too tightly covered. May be frozen if it won't be used in 3 or 4 days. May use all white, all whole wheat, or a combination of flours, but the sourdough culture must always be fed with white flour, preferably unbleached. You may wish to set your glass quart jar of culture into a bowl or container of some sort, as sometimes the bubbling culture may overflow a little in fridge.

My first few attempts at sourdough bread were flops—I told husband Travis, if we want to brick the outside of our house, I can just keep baking this bread! It was HARD and sour. I kept feeding the culture every week or two and used it occasionally, and after 2-3 months suddenly it seemed I was turning out wonderful bread! So please don't despair if you have some flops—just persist—I'm glad I did! Lots of people have enjoyed ours and I like to give it away. I can feel good about giving our sons this for a snack or eating lots of bread myself now! I usually use regular brown flour or Prairie Gold. This bread is *really* easy and simple once you master it. Happy baking!

105

sourdough

Sourdough French Bread

Kendra Rokey, Sabetha, KS

1 Tbsp. yeast
¼ cup warm water
1 Tbsp. honey
2 tsp. salt
1 cup water

2 Tbsp. oil
½ cup sourdough starter
½ cup milk
5½ cups whole wheat flour

Dissolve yeast in water. Add honey, salt, water, oil, starter, and milk, and mix together. Add 2 cups flour; mix. Then add remaining flour and knead until smooth and elastic (5-8 minutes). Put in greased bowl, turning once. Let rise in warm place until double. Punch down and divide in half. You may now put in loaf pans for regular bread or roll into rectangle 8 x 12" and roll up starting on wide side. Seal edges. Let rise to double again. Before baking make diagonal slashes ¼" deep across top of loaf. Bake at 400° for 20 minutes.

Sourdough Chocolate Cake

Mrs. Jason Byler, Lobelville, TN

½ cup sourdough starter
1½ cups flour
1⅓ cup honey
¾ cup powdered cocoa
1 tsp. baking powder
2 tsp. soda

2 eggs
1 cup milk
½ cup vegetable oil
¾ cup cold coffee
1 tsp. vanilla

Let starter stand at room temperature until active, at least 1 hour, then add remaining ingredients, beating well after each addition (batter will be thin). Pour into two 9" round cake pans, and bake at 350° for 30 minutes. This cake has a fudge-like quality you can't get any way except with sourdough.

sourdough

106

Sourdough Cornbread

Mrs. Miriam Wengerd, Sugarcreek, OH

3 cups cornmeal	1 egg
1 cup barley flour	¼ cup butter, melted
2 cups boiling water	1 tsp. soda
1 cup warm milk (can use sour)	½ cup honey
1 tsp. salt	¼ cup sucanat

Put 1 cup cornmeal and 2 cups boiling water in bowl and stir thoroughly. Add milk, barley flour, 1 cup cornmeal, and salt. Mix well. Cover and let stand at room temperature for 24 hours. At baking time, add egg, butter, soda, honey, sucanat, and 1 c. cornmeal. Mix well. Pour into greased 9 x 13" pan and bake at 350° for ½ hour or until done. This cornbread is soft and moist! Delicious with butter and honey.

This is not true sourdough since it doesn't use starter. But it's very good. Soaking the cornmeal seems to make it moist instead of gritty.

Sourdough Biscuits

Mrs. Daniel (Verna) King, Pembroke, KY

1 cup sourdough starter	2½ cups flour, sifted
2 cups warm water	

Mix ingredients thoroughly. Cover and leave in a warm place for 12 hours. Reserve 1 cup for future starters before adding ingredients. Add:

1½ cup flour, sifted	1 tsp. baking powder
1 tsp. salt	

Mix together. Roll out dough to about 1" thick and cut with biscuit cutter, dip in warm melted butter and press biscuits against each other in a cake pan. Let rise 30 minutes, then bake at 375° for 30 minutes.

Choices

Sourdough English Muffins

KENDRA ROKEY, SABETHA, KS

2 cups whole wheat flour
2 cups milk
½ cup sourdough starter
1 Tbsp. honey
2 tsp. salt
1 tsp. baking soda

Beat all the above ingredients together until smooth. Cover loosely with waxed paper and let stand in a warm place for 18 hours. Add:

2 Tbsp. oil
1 Tbsp. active dry yeast
3-4 cups whole wheat flour

Add the oil and yeast and stir to blend. Add flour to make a moderately stiff dough. Sprinkle work surface with cornmeal and roll dough on cornmeal until it is ⅜" thick. Cut with biscuit cutter and let rise until double. Grease a griddle preheated to 275°. Bake muffins 10-15 minutes on each side. Split when cool.

Sourdough Yorkshire Pudding

MABLE ZIMMERMAN, NEW ENTERPRISE, PA

Twelve to twenty-four hours before baking, stir together 1 cup flour and 1 cup kefir or yogurt. (If dairy-free, use 2 Tbsp. vinegar or lemon juice in a cup and fill to 1 cup with water.) Soak in glass bowl or jar, covered, for 12 to 24 hours. Before baking, add 3 large eggs and ½ tsp. salt, and whisk together. Put 2 Tbsp. butter and 2 Tbsp. coconut oil in 9 x 13" pan and put in oven at 375° until melted. Pour batter onto melted butter and oil. Bake for 25 minutes or until lightly browned. Serve with blueberries and maple syrup if desired. Or add a cut-up apple or two, or blueberries or other fruit before baking.

Sourdough Rice Pie Crust

MABLE ZIMMERMAN, NEW ENTERPRISE, PA

Seven to twenty-four hours before baking pies, mix:

2½ cups brown rice flour
¾ cup water
¼ cup kefir or yogurt

Soak in a glass bowl or container in a warm place with a plate or plastic wrap over top. When ready to mix in the rest of ingredients, add:

¾ cup butter
¾ cup pecan or almond flour
¼ cup ground flax seeds
½ tsp. salt
1 large egg, beaten

Mix well. Chilling can help to make easier handling. Roll between waxed paper and fit into 3 medium pie plates. Bake at 350° for 8-10 minutes. If putting in a filling, either prebake or bake at 425° for 10 minutes, then at 350° for 10 more minutes or until done, on the lowest shelf of the oven.

sourdough

Salads & Dressings

WHAT IS BETTER THAN A CRISP HEAD OF GREEN GARDEN

lettuce? You simply can't beat the taste!

Our family enjoys Buttercrunch, Tom Thumb, Green Ice and Red Sails. In the spring we plant a wide row of lettuce seeds. As soon as they are big enough we transplant them. This year we transplanted 500 lettuce heads!

We eat lots of lettuce sandwiches, and of course we use it in salads too.

The secret to making good salads is fresh ingredients. Don't expect limp old vegetables to make a tasty salad.

Some kitchen gadgets I like to use are a salad spinner, V-slicer, Salsa Master and a handheld chopper that makes wavy patterns as it cuts.

Try serving your salads in new and different ways. One day shred your carrots, next day cut in matchsticks, next time slice in thin rounds. Use different ingredients and techniques to add variety and to spice up your salads.

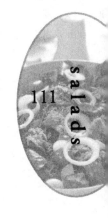

salads

For example pecans can be sautéd in a little butter, cooled and used as a salad topper. Make croutons from leftover bread and drizzle with butter and add herbs and seasonings and toast in oven. Cook eggs, slice and toss on salad. If you've never raised basil before, do it next year and add it to your salads. Our family really enjoys the sweet unique flavor it adds. Baby beet tops make a pretty addition to a salad because they are red-veined. Spinach is another easy to raise and simply delicious salad ingredient. There is no end to the possibilities!

A good dressing will add the crowning touch. Get used to making your own dressings. It is simply absurd how many unhealthy ingredients are in most dressings you buy. Anything from lots of sugar to food colorings, additives and preservatives. Experiment until you find a few that your family enjoys and make them often. Children seem to prefer familiar salad dressings.

It is a good idea to have a daily salad. It gets you in practice and provides your family with another healthy choice!

Salads

Taco Salad

Mrs. Miriam Wengerd, Sugarcreek, OH

2 heads lettuce
1-15.5 oz. can kidney beans (1½ cups)
4 cups Bulgur Burger (page 168)
1 cup sweet onions

2 cups chopped tomatoes
2 cups shredded cheddar
1 pkg. taco chips

Drain beans. Chop lettuce, onions, and tomatoes, and crush chips. If cooking beans yourself, soak the night before, next morning drain water, replace with fresh water, bring to boil and cook until tender (about 1 hour). Drain. Season with garlic salt and chili powder to taste. Put everything in a large bowl except chips and mix well. Just before serving, add chips and taco dressing and mix well.

Dressing for Taco Salad

Mrs. Miriam Wengerd, Sugarcreek, OH

1½ cup oil
½ cup tomato juice
½ cup vinegar
sweetener to taste
4 Tbsp. homemade mayonnaise (pages 126-127)

2 Tbsp. taco seasoning mix
4 tsp. mustard
1½ cup cooked kidney beans
    or 1-15.5 oz. can, drained

Put all ingredients in blender and blend on high speed until smooth. Taco Seasoning Mix: 1 Tbsp. chili powder, 1 tsp. garlic powder, 1 tsp. paprika, 1 tsp. oregano, ½ tsp. salt, 2 tsp. onion powder, 1 pinch stevia, optional. Mix all ingredients together. Can make large batches and keep on hand. 3 Tbsp.= 1¼ oz. pkg. store-bought.)

BLT Salad

Monica Bazen, Grand Rapids, MI

2 lbs. medium/thick bacon
¾ cup homemade Miracle Whip
　(pages 128-129)
½ cup Ranch dressing
¼ cup red onion, finely chopped
1 Tbsp. sweetener of your choice
4 cups cubed Roma tomatoes

12-15 cups torn romaine lettuce
2 cups cauliflower
¼ cup shredded cheddar
croutons (opt.)
broccoli (opt.)
hard-boiled eggs (opt.)

Cook bacon until crisp. Cool and crumble. Mix dressings, onion, and sweetener in small bowl. Refrigerate at least 1 hour. At serving time, toss vegetables and bacon in large bowl. Add cheese to dressing mixture. Carefully fold into vegetables, then put in serving bowl. Serve immediately.

Crunchy Floret Salad

R.M.Z., Thorp, WI

3 cups broccoli florets
1½ cup cauliflowerets
½ lb. sliced bacon, cooked and crumbled
1 cup homemade mayonnaise
　(pages 126-127)

2-3 Tbsp. sweetener of your choice
2 Tbsp. cider vinegar
¼ tsp. salt
6 oz. shredded cheddar

In a large bowl, combine the broccoli, cauliflower, and bacon. In a small bowl, whisk the mayonnaise, sweetener, vinegar, and salt. Pour over salad and mix well. Cover and refrigerate until serving. Stir in the cheese.

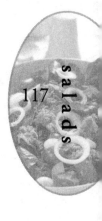

Summer Salad

MARK & BETH WEAVER, NEWAYGO, MI

1 large tomato	2 tsp. basil
1 sweet pepper	¼ tsp. garlic salt
1 small onion	¼ cup Italian dressing

Cut vegetables in coarse chunks. Mix all ingredients together. This is a delicious salad available even after the lettuce season is past. Serves 2.

Mediterranean Cafe Salad

MARY BETH HEISEY, PUEBLO WEST, CO

Vinaigrette:

¼ cup oil	½ tsp. salt
3 Tbsp. red wine vinegar	¼ tsp. parsley
1 garlic clove, minced	¼ tsp. onion powder
2 Tbsp. honey	½ tsp. prepared mustard

Blend together in a blender. Toss with salad. Salad:

1 cucumber, diced	2 cups chopped cooked chicken
1 cup sliced black olives	romaine lettuce
1 red pepper, chopped	1 can Great Northern beans, drained
1 red onion, chopped	½ cup crumbled feta cheese
1 carrot, grated	

salads

118

Romaine Lettuce Boats

MRS. ERVIN (ELIZABETH) BEACHY

small canoe-shaped lettuce leaves	nutritional yeast
raw lacto-fermented sauerkraut	coconut or olive oil

Spoon sauerkraut on leaves. Sprinkle with yeast, drizzle with oil. Variations: browned beef, cheese, bacon, grated eggs, grated carrots, cottage cheese, raw sour cream, raw cream cheese, chopped tomatoes. Use your imagination!

Garden Salad

EUNICE HALTEMAN, NEWVILLE, PA

1 tomato
2 cucumbers
½ onion
1 pepper

2 Tbsp. light olive oil
2 Tbsp. vinegar
salt to taste

Slice cucumbers and layer them on a plate. Top with sliced tomatoes next, onions and peppers. Sprinkle with oil and vinegar. Add salt to suit your taste. Another way would be to chop the veggies and put them in a bowl. Add dressing and toss. If the dressing isn't strong enough, just add a little more. My children love this dressing on cucumbers and peppers. This kind of dressing can be used with lettuce, radish, and cabbage salad too. If you slice your cabbage real thin, it adds crunch to your lettuce salad. They use this dressing for salads in Paraguay, South America.

Simple Cucumber Salad

LINDSAY ZEHR, HALSEY, OR

3-4 6" cucumbers
10-12 sweet cherry tomatoes
1 small sweet onion

1 Tbsp. black pepper
1 Tbsp. salt
2 tsp. dill weed

Peel and slice cucumbers. Cut tomatoes in half. Finely slice half of onion. Toss together with spices. Add more or less of all ingredients to size and taste. This salad is very simple and refreshing.

119

salads

Cucumber Salad

MRS. VERNON SCHROCK, LEWISTOWN, IL

Slice several cucumbers with Salad Master and add a few Tbsp. soy sauce, ½ tsp. garlic powder, and ⅛ tsp. black pepper. Mix and let set for a while before serving. We learned this while traveling, from our driver, and it's good. Try it for a different taste.

Wheat Berry Salad

KENDRA ROKEY, SABETHA, KS

2 cups whole wheat berries
1 pomegranate or ¾ cup raisins

honey to taste
cinnamon to taste

Soak the berries overnight in water. In the morning, bring to a boil and simmer, uncovered, until berries are tender—about 45 minutes to 1 hour. Drain. Add the pomegranate seeds or raisins, honey, and cinnamon. Stir to mix well.

Favorite Broccoli Salad

Mrs. Conrad (Martha) Kuepfer, Pleasantville, TN

2 bunches broccoli
8 strips bacon, fried and crumbled*
⅓ cup chopped onion

1 cup chopped, seeded tomatoes
½ cup shredded cheese
2 hard-boiled eggs, chopped

Dressing:

1 cup salad dressing
⅓ cup sweetener of your choice

2 Tbsp. vinegar

Separate broccoli into small bite-sized pieces. Add rest of ingredients. Mix dressing until smooth and pour over salad just before serving.

*You may also substitute chicken or other favorite meat.

Mandarin Salad

Mrs. Robin Chase

¼ cup sliced almonds
1 Tbsp. sweetener of your choice
¼ head lettuce
¼ bunch romaine lettuce

2 medium stalks celery
2 Tbsp. green onions, sliced
1-11 oz. can mandarin oranges

Cook almonds and sweetener over low heat, stirring constantly, until sweetener is melted and almonds are coated. Cool and break apart. Store at room temperature. Break lettuce into bite-sized pieces and place in plastic bag, add celery and onions. Pour sweet sour dressing (recipe follows) into bag, add oranges. Shake until well coated, add almonds and shake. Serves 4-6. Sweet Sour Dressing: ¼ cup vegetable oil, 2 Tbsp. sweetener, 2 Tbsp. vinegar, 1 Tbsp. snipped parsley, ½ tsp. salt, dash of pepper. Shake in tightly covered jar and store in refrigerator.

Raw Cranberry Salad

Ina Schrock, Gap Mills, WV

2 bags fresh cranberries, washed
1 cup raw pumpkin seeds
1 apple, chopped
1 cup raw pineapple tidbits
2 stalks celery, chopped

¾ cup yogurt, plain
½ cup maple syrup
¼ tsp. stevia
juice of 1 lemon

Chop cranberries in food processor. Grind pumpkin seeds fine. Put all chopped ingredients in a large bowl. In a smaller bowl combine dressing ingredients. Stir all together gently but thoroughly. Serves 10.

Healthy

Green Bean Gourmet Salad

Mrs. John (Norleen) Hoover, Owen, WI

1½ lbs. fresh whole green beans
⅓ lb. cheese
½ cup chopped ripe olives

½ cup thin sliced green peppers
½ cup thin sliced red peppers

Dressing:

½ cup fresh lemon juice
½ cup olive oil
2 large cloves freshly crushed garlic
1 Tbsp. apple cider vinegar
pinch of cayenne
½ tsp. dried tarragon

½ tsp. dried dill
½ tsp. salt
freshly ground black pepper
2 tsp. Dijon mustard
½ cup freshly chopped parsley

Wash and top and tail beans. Place in bowl and pour boiling water over the beans. Immediately drain and place in bowl of ice cold water. Drain. Add dressing and cheese. Toss well and marinate for 2-3 hours. Add olives and peppers and chill overnight or for a few hours.

Three Bean Salad

Mrs. Heidi Peyton, Westfield, IN

In a large bowl add 10 oz. of fresh or frozen green beans, 10 oz. of yellow wax beans and drain and rinse 1-15 oz. can of red kidney beans. Whisk together ¼ cup apple cider vinegar and ⅓ cup extra virgin olive oil; season with salt and ground pepper. Toss to combine and let marinate in the refrigerator for 30 minutes. This salad will serve 6 guests nicely, and can be ready in 40 minutes. I especially like to serve this in the summertime when I have access to fresh garden vegetables.

Fresh Corn Salad

Mrs. Heidi Peyton, Westfield, IN

6 ears of sweet corn
1 yellow pepper, chopped
1 red pepper, chopped
1 red onion, minced

½ cup chopped cilantro
¼ cup olive oil
¼ cup lime juice
salt and pepper to taste

Cut the fresh corn off the cob and steam for 3-5 minutes in ¼ cup water. Continue to cook until water evaporates. Combine corn and other ingredients in a large bowl and chill.

Fiesta Corn Salad

Mrs. Urie Miller, Middlebury, IN

2 cups whole kernel corn, drained
1 cup chopped fresh tomato
1 cup chopped cucumber

½ cup diced celery
½ cup diced sweet pepper
¼ cup diced onion

Dressing:

2 Tbsp. olive oil
¼ cup honey

3 Tbsp. vinegar
½-¾ tsp. salt

Mix dressing ingredients. Combine with vegetables. Chill several hours before serving. Yield: 4-6 servings.

Potato Salad

Dressing:

1 onion, sautéed
1½ Tbsp. flour
1 cup water
2 Tbsp. vinegar
1 Tbsp. butter

2 scoops stevia
1 Tbsp. Braggs
¼ tsp. dry mustard
½ tsp. lemon juice (opt.)
¼ tsp. paprika

Sauté onion, stir in flour. Add rest of ingredients and cook until thick. Cool. Add to:

2 lb. cooked, diced potatoes
2 eggs, chopped (opt.)
2 large celery ribs, chopped
2 tsp. onion salt

½ cup homemade mayonnaise (page 126)
½ Tbsp. mustard
1 scoop stevia
¼-½ cup potato juice

salads

124

Healthy

Dawn's Potato Salad

Mary Beth Heisey, Pueblo West, CO

4 cups red potatoes

Do not peel potatoes. Quarter and cook in salted water until tender, not mushy. Dressing:

⅓ cup homemade sour cream (page 265)
⅓ cup homemade mayonnaise (pages 126-127)
4 oz. cream cheese
½ tsp. dill weed

1 tsp. honey
1 Tbsp. mustard
½ tsp. garlic, minced
¼ tsp. salt
¼ tsp. pepper

Mix together and fold in cooled potatoes. Add topping just before serving if desired. Topping:

2 Tbsp. fresh chopped parsley
2 Tbsp. chopped green onion

6 slices bacon, fried and crumbled

Fresh Summer Salsa

Mrs. Ervin (Hannah) Hostetler, Pleasantville, TN

4 large, ripe tomatoes
1 small sweet onion
2 banana or ½ bell pepper
2 Tbsp. vinegar

1 tsp. sweetener
3 sprigs cilantro
1 clove fresh garlic
salt to taste

Put tomatoes, onion, garlic, and pepper in food chopper. Chop and add vinegar, salt, and sweetener. Last, cut up cilantro in it. Chill. Serves 8.

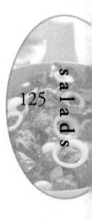

125

salads

Croutons

Mrs. Rhoda Miller, Sugarcreek, OH

Toast 8 cups of bread cubes in a roaster at 375° for 20 minutes. Sprinkle with seasonings of your choice (seasoning salt, garlic salt, VegeSal, celery salt, etc.). Drizzle with melted butter over all and toss well. Toast until golden brown. Great for salads and soups!

Salad Croutons

MRS. ERVIN (HANNAH) HOSTETLER, PLEASANTVILLE, TN

1 Tbsp. Italian seasoning
2 tsp. garlic salt
1 tsp. black pepper
2 Tbsp. parsley flakes

1 Tbsp. Parmesan cheese
butter or olive oil
1 loaf bread

Cut bread into cubes. Drizzle with melted butter or olive oil. Sprinkle on seasonings. Mix. Bake at 250° until crispy. (Toasted sesame or sunflower seeds are great on salads, also.)

Homemade Mayonnaise & Miracle Whip

Note: Throughout *Healthy Choices* whenever a recipe asks for homemade mayonnaise or Miracle Whip you may choose from the following eight recipes. Simply find the one your family likes best, then substitute it for the store-bought variety.

Homemade Mayonnaise

ANNA RUTH KING

4 eggs
1 tsp. honey
1 tsp. vinegar
½ tsp. salt

¼ tsp. pepper
2 cloves garlic
2 cups olive oil
1 tsp. dried herb mix (opt.)

Put first 6 ingredients in blender and blend until smooth. While continuing to blend, add oil slowly, until thick. We add a tsp. of a dried herb mix we made that has a strong basil flavor.

Homemade Mayonnaise

MRS. REBECCA ZOOK, MYERSTOWN, PA

1 cup oil

Make a paste of:

⅓ cup flour
⅓ cup xylitol
⅛ tsp. stevia
1 tsp. salt

2 egg yolks

1 tsp. dry mustard
2 Tbsp. vinegar
2 Tbsp. lemon juice

Add 1 cup hot water, cook and stir until clear and pour over egg mixture. Beat until stiff. This is also good to use as a salad dressing. I usually add some pickle juice to thin it a little and add some herbs and spices, etc.

Homemade Mayonnaise

SANDRA SMUCKER, JOHN DAY, OR

2 eggs
1-2 tsp. mustard
1-2 tsp. apple cider vinegar

1 tsp. garlic
2 tsp. lemon juice

Add any other seasonings you wish. If you want it extra tart, add the second teaspoon of the mustard and vinegar. Blend these ingredients in blender until frothy. Add approximately 2 cups oil while blender is still on, drizzling a pencil-thin line until it is too thick to take more. May need less than 2 cups. I have tried olive oil and the taste was too strong. Grapeseed oil may be used. Store in refrigerator.

Homemade Mayonnaise

WALTER SAUDER, LATHAM, MO

1 very fresh egg
½ tsp. salt
½ tsp. dry mustard
¼ tsp. paprika

1 Tbsp. vinegar
1 Tbsp. lemon juice
1 cup olive oil

In blender, blend all but oil. Slowly add oil while blending.

Cooked Mayonnaise

WALTER SAUDER, LATHAM, MO

1 Tbsp. honey (opt.)
2 eggs, beaten
¼ cup lemon juice (may use less)
2 Tbsp. oil (opt.)
½ tsp. salt

1 tsp. celery salt or seed
1-2 tsp. dry mustard
3-4 Tbsp. flour
1½ cup water or nut milk

Bring water to a boil. Combine the rest of ingredients and pour into boiling water. Cook until thick, stirring often. Cool.

Homemade Miracle Whip

MIRIAM YODER, LaGRANGE, IN

1¾ cup water
½ cup vinegar
⅔ cup flour
1 egg
¾ cup butter, softened

2 Tbsp. honey
2 Tbsp. maple syrup
2 tsp. salt
1 tsp. lemon juice
1 tsp. mustard

Cook water, vinegar, and flour until thick. Process the rest of ingredients in blender on high until creamy. Add cooked mixture and blend on high until creamy.

salads

128

Miracle Whip

SUSIE NISLEY, DANVILLE, OH

1 qt. water
¾ cup molasses or maple syrup

1 cup sifted spelt flour, slightly rounded
½ cup clear jel or cornstarch

Mix clear jel with 1 cup water. Add to first part and boil 3 minutes. Remove from heat. Meanwhile, melt 3 cups coconut oil. Put in bowl:

1 cup vinegar
4 egg yolks
1 tsp. paprika

1 tsp. mustard powder (opt.)
1 tsp. onion powder (opt.)
3 tsp. salt

Add oil and first part to last part. Beat all together; add 1 cup safflower oil. Put in blender until whipped and turns white. Put in jars warm, and put in cool place and it will seal. Makes approximately 3 quarts.

Miracle Whip

Mrs. Miriam Wengerd, Sugarcreek, OH

1¾ cup water
½ cup raw apple cider vinegar
⅔ cup wheat flour
1 egg
¾ cup butter, softened
2 Tbsp. honey

2 Tbsp. maple syrup
2 tsp. salt
1 tsp. lemon juice
1 tsp. mustard
1 tsp. paprika (opt.)
2 tsp. basil (opt.)

Cook water, vinegar and flour until thick, stirring constantly with whisk. Put other ingredients in blender and process until smooth. Add cooked mixture and blend until creamy. Pour in glass wide-mouth jar and store in fridge. Use instead of store-bought Miracle Whip. Very good recipe with a delightful flavor!

Salad Dressings

All-Purpose Dressing

Martha Wideman, Listowel, ON

⅓ cup oil
½ tsp. garlic powder
1 tsp. soya sauce (opt.)

½ tsp. lemon juice
½ tsp. salt
sprinkle of pepper

For dandelion salads, lettuce, etc.

Salad Dressing

Blend and cook until clear:

1½ cup cold water
½ cup vinegar

½ cup clear jel

Take a little at a time and mix with first part in blender:

1 egg (add water to make ¾ cup)
1 tsp. lemon juice
½ tsp. dry mustard
¾ cup oil

dash paprika
⅓ cup honey
2 tsp. salt

Blend well. Refrigerate.

Vinegar & Oil Salad Dressing

MRS. JR. KAUFFMAN, REDDING, IA

⅓ cup vinegar
1 tsp. salt
½ cup honey
1 tsp. dry mustard
dash of celery seed
¼ cup onion, chopped
1 cup oil

Put all ingredients in blender except oil. Add oil slowly while blending. Keep refrigerated.

Grandma's Salad Dressing

IDA EDWARDS, LINDEN, TN

8 cloves garlic
8 Tbsp. grated onions
8 tsp. salt
2¼ cups honey
4 cups olive oil
2 cups vinegar
2⅔ cups catsup
4 tsp. paprika
½ cup lemon juice

Put all ingredients into a half-gallon jar and shake well. Pour into serving or storing containers.

salads
130

Honey French Dressing

SUSIE NISLEY, DANVILLE, OH

1 cup oil
½ cup catsup
⅓ cup vinegar
⅓ cup honey
1 tsp. salt
1 tsp. paprika
1 tsp. grated onion
1 clove garlic, halved

Mix honey, vinegar and catsup, very slowly add oil and seasonings. Let stand 10 minutes, remove garlic. Keeps indefinitely.

Creamy French Dressing

MRS. JEREMY (ROSE) MILLER, ST. IGNATIUS, MT

1 cup ketchup
½ cup homemade mayonnaise
   (pages 126-127)
3 Tbsp. cider vinegar
3 Tbsp. honey
2 Tbsp. water
1 Tbsp. olive oil
1 tsp. lemon juice
½ tsp. ground mustard
¼ tsp. salt

Mix in blender. Yield: 1¾ cup.

Healthy

Maple Syrup Salad Dressing

VICKY SCHILLING, SCOTLAND, UK

1 tsp. mustard powder
½ tsp. dried basil
2 Tbsp. maple syrup
3 Tbsp. balsamic vinegar
1 Tbsp. lemon juice
1 minced garlic clove
1 cup virgin olive oil
1 tsp. salt
¼ tsp. pepper

Place all ingredients in jug and whisk well until mixed, pour into a bottle to store, and shake well before each use.

Mexican Salad Dressing

MRS. CRIST (SUSIE) NISLEY, DANVILLE, OH

¾ cup honey
⅓ cup vinegar
3 tsp. liquid mustard
1 tsp. salt
1 tsp. celery seed
¼ tsp. black pepper
1 cup oil
½ med. onion (opt.)

Mix everything except oil together gradually; add oil slowly while beating, so oil doesn't separate. Keeps well.

Mexican Salad Dressing

MRS. DENNIS (MIRIAM) NOLT, PINE GROVE, PA

1 medium onion
⅓ cup honey
1 tsp. sea salt
⅛-¼ tsp. black pepper
1 tsp. celery seed
2 tsp. prepared mustard
⅓ cup vinegar
1 cup olive oil

Put all ingredients in blender except olive oil. Blend slowly. Add olive oil while blender is running and then blend on full speed until smooth. Makes about 2½ cups.

Italian Dressing

1 cup oil
¼ cup lemon juice
¼ cup vinegar
1 tsp. salt
stevia
½ tsp. oregano

½ tsp. dry mustard
½ tsp. onion salt
½ tsp. paprika
⅛ tsp. thyme
2 cloves garlic (or powder)

Drain pinto beans. Add fresh cucumbers, tomato wedges, etc. Add dressing to taste. Chill.

Italian Dressing

IDA EDWARDS, LINDEN, TN

¾ cup olive oil
⅓ cup vinegar
2 Tbsp. finely chopped onion
1 tsp. honey
1 tsp. dry mustard
1 Tbsp. fresh basil (or 1 tsp. dry)

1½ tsp. salt
2 tsp. fresh oregano
   or ½ tsp. dry oregano
1 tsp. black pepper
2 cloves crushed garlic

Shake all ingredients in a tightly covered container. Shake well before using. Yield: 1½ cups.

Italian Dressing

MRS. JOHN (EMMA) MULLET, BURTON, OH

1 cup oil
⅓ cup vinegar
2 Tbsp. lemon juice
1 tsp. garlic salt
1 tsp. sweetener of your choice

½ tsp. dry mustard
½ tsp. oregano
¼ tsp. basil
¼ tsp. black pepper

Mix well and serve. We like this for marinating chicken and pork chops.

Simple Fruit Dressing

SUSIE NISLEY, DANVILLE, OH

½ cup homemade mayonnaise
  (pages 126-127)
1 Tbsp. honey

1 tsp. grated lemon peel
2 Tbsp. cream cheese
1 Tbsp. lemon juice

Chill mayonnaise. Combine honey, lemon juice, peel, and cheese. Mix with mayonnaise. Raw honey should be heated and cooled, as it has enzymes that tend to thin puddings. If used soon it is okay.

Spring Salad Dressing

MRS. AARON (CYNTHIA) WISE, WATERLOO, NY

¾ cup homemade mayonnaise
  (pages 126-127)
¼ cup vinegar
½ cup oil

⅓ cup honey
¼ cup ketchup
½ tsp. salt
1 tsp. mustard

Shake all together and pour over salad.

The Voeller Dressing

MIRIAM STOLTZFOOS, GARNETT, KS

1 cup olive oil
3 Tbsp. Dijon mustard
2 Tbsp. Braggs liquid aminos
2 Tbsp. honey

2 Tbsp. lemon juice
1 Tbsp. dried thyme
½ tsp. pepper

Whisk all ingredients together. Makes about 1½ cups. This dressing stores well in refrigerator. It's also good on baked potatoes.

Salad Dressing

LOVEDA BEAR, PATRIOT, OH

2 eggs
½ cup vinegar
½ cup honey
½ tsp. dry mustard

2 Tbsp. onion
1 tsp. salt
½ tsp. liquid smoke (opt.)
1½-2 cups oil

Mix everything in blender except oil. Add oil slowly, until mixture is thickened. Serve on tossed salad.

Choices

Just Perfect Salad Dressing

Joyce Strite, Cochise, AZ

⅛ cup honey
¼ tsp. salt
1½ Tbsp. vinegar

2 Tbsp. homemade mayonnaise
(pages 126-127)
⅓ cup milk

Mix together honey, salt, mayonnaise, and vinegar with a whisk. Stir in milk. Makes about 1-1½ cups.

French Dressing

Jessica Strite, Cochise, AZ

1 cup honey
1 Tbsp. minced onion
2 tsp. dry mustard
2 tsp. paprika

2 tsp. celery seed
2 tsp. salt
½ cup vinegar
2 cups oil

Put everything except the oil in blender. Mix. Pour in oil slowly. Beat for 10 minutes. Makes 3 cups.

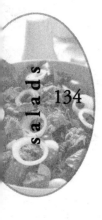

salads

134

Caesar Salad Dressing

Ina Schrock, Gap Mills, WV

2 garlic cloves, chopped
1 Tbsp. vinegar
1 Tbsp. lemon juice
6 Tbsp. olive oil

⅜ tsp. salt
½ tsp. black pepper
small pinch oregano (opt.)

Combine all ingredients in blender. Blend on medium speed until creamy. Pour over salad and toss gently before serving. Will nicely coat a bowl of salad for 7 people.

Cooking with Herbs

RIGHT NOW THE PATH IN OUR HERB GARDEN IS OVERRUN
with volunteer dill and tall red poppies. It looks a little wild, but I think
an herb garden should look a little more unstructured! Herbs are so
interesting with their many different flavors, textures and scents. I raise
some for use in the kitchen and some as medicinals.

We made a path up the middle of a small rectangular garden plot. On
the left I planted kitchen herbs, and on the right I planted medicinals.
Along the front I left room for flowers, and around the path on either
side is creeping thyme. At the end of the garden is a small flat area
with a red bench. Behind the bench are assorted teas in small patches.
For use in the kitchen I like chives, parsley, garlic, perennial onions,
oregano, sage and of course lots of basil! Basil is a family favorite so
we raise plenty. Last year I had tarragon which I used to make herbal
vinegar. You can do the same with basil; this makes a tasty addition to
marinades or salad dressings.

Oregano is a wonderful attraction to bees. They come-a-buzzing if you
let it flower. If you want to harvest it, don't wait until it flowers. Take
it off, wash it (or hose off the evening before harvesting) and lay it on
clean sheets in some suitable drying place. Ours dries beautifully in the
attic. When dry, strip off leaves into a bowl crushing gently to make
it fit into a glass jar with tight fitting lid. You can easily raise a year's
supply of oregano, parsley and basil without much effort. This became
more important to me after I learned that many kitchen herbs you buy
are treated with radiation to prolong their shelf life.

Don't worry if you don't know a lot about using herbs. Just designate
a small plot and start growing them. If you have them growing fresh
you're more apt to start using them and your children will grow up
familiar with them.

Healthy

Potato Appetizers

ANNA RUTH KING

potatoes   butter, melted
paprika (opt.)

Cut potatoes in wedges and dip into melted butter. Sprinkle with paprika. Bake in 375° oven for 30 minutes, turn over and bake for 25 minutes longer, or until crisp. Serve with dipping sauce. Dipping Sauces: plain yogurt, watercress, chickweed, or purslane, and green onions. Or use: cream, sour cream, chili powder, and greens. Mix sauce ingredients in blender until smooth.

Green Pesto

ANNA RUTH KING

4 oz. Parmesan cheese	¼ cup olive oil
6 sprigs parsley	½ tsp. dried basil
1 clove garlic, minced	or 1-2 stems fresh
2 cups lamb's-quarter or purslane	¼ tsp. salt

Put first four ingredients in blender and process 20 seconds. Add oil, basil, and salt and process until smooth. Serve over hot, cooked noodles or spaghetti. Variation: Use lemon balm instead of other greens, then serve with fish. Pesto freezes well.

137

herbs

Wilted Salad Greens

ANNA RUTH KING

6 slices bacon, cut up	1 tsp. salt
4 eggs	dash of pepper
¼ cup honey or maple syrup	1 quart dandelion, endive,
⅔ cup cream or milk	or early wild greens
¼ cup chopped onion	¼ cup vinegar

Fry bacon until crisp. Beat eggs and sweetener, add cream, blend well. Add to bacon and drippings. Cook slowly, stirring constantly, until thick. Combine greens, onion, salt, and pepper and pour dressing over all; add vinegar; blend well. Garnish with hard-boiled egg slices and croutons if desired.

TIP

Keep a small basket or container with garlic bulbs close to the stove, use some every day in meat dishes, soups, and casseroles. Use cilantro or turmeric in soups and casseroles.

—Mrs. Vernon Schrock, Lewistown, IL

Choices

Wild Strawberry Crepes

ANNA RUTH KING

Crepes:

2 cups flour	5 eggs
1 Tbsp. honey	1½ cups rich milk
pinch of salt	3-4 Tbsp. melted butter

Filling:

1 qt. wild strawberries, sweetened with honey	⅔ cup whipping cream
3 oz. cream cheese	⅛ tsp. almond extract

Mix flour and salt. Blend eggs and honey. Do not beat. Add to flour and stir until smooth. Gradually add milk and melted butter. Heat small skillet. Add ½ tsp. oil. When bubbly pour in small amount of batter. Tilt pan immediately so batter covers bottom. Brown lightly on both sides. Place between paper towels to keep warm. Mash cream cheese and almond extract. Add cream, beat until thick and creamy. Fold in strawberries. Place 3 Tbsp. on each crepe and roll. Top with sweetened whipped cream and a whole strawberry. These wild strawberries are tiny but nothing can beat their flavor.

Nettles and Eggs on Toast

ANNA RUTH KING

8 large egg yolks, beaten	pepper
6 Tbsp. melted butter	2 cups chopped nettles
2 cups milk	paprika
salt	

Sauté nettles in butter. In a double boiler, stir yolks, butter, and milk until thickened (use whisk). Add salt, pepper, and paprika to taste. Last, stir in nettles. Serve over toast.

Blender Chickweed Crepes

ANNA RUTH KING

1½ cups milk	2 Tbsp. butter, melted
3 eggs	2 cups chickweed
1¾ cups flour	

Put everything in blender and process until smooth. Pour 3 Tbsp. at a time on hot skillet. Tilt skillet so crepe is thinly distributed. Brown about ½ minute, then turn to brown other side. Stack with wax paper between every 4 crepes, cover with lid or towel to keep warm and moist. Spread with crepe sauce and fill with watercress and grated radishes.

Weed Chips

ANNA RUTH KING

5 oz. frozen lamb's-quarters
2 Tbsp. butter
½ cup onion, chopped
3 eggs
1 tsp. oil
1 tsp. warm water
2 cups wheat flour

1½-2 Tbsp. salt
3 Tbsp. grated cheese
1 Tbsp. garlic, minced
½ tsp. black pepper
1 Tbsp. fresh oregano
  or ½ tsp. dried

Sauté greens and onion in butter. Put in blender with eggs, oil, and water. Prepare seasonings in bowl, mix with flour. Make a well. Add green mixture. With fork, work flour from side of well into green mixture, then knead with your hand. Let rest 10 minutes, knead another 10 minutes. Let dough rest 30 minutes. Roll out on lightly floured surface $^{1}/_{16}$" thick. Sprinkle lightly with flour, let rest 15 minutes then cut into 1" x ¾" rectangles or triangles. Deep fry 3-5 seconds. Drain. Makes about 12 dozen.

Watercress & Parsley Soup

ANNA RUTH KING

2 Tbsp. butter
½ cup onion, chopped
¼ cup wheat flour
2¼ cups chicken broth
2 cups milk

2½ cups parsley
2 cups watercress
⅛ tsp. nutmeg
¼ tsp. salt
¼ tsp. pepper

Melt butter, add onions, sauté briefly. Add flour and cook 3 minutes. Gradually stir in the stock and milk and bring to a boil, whisking constantly. Lower heat, then add your parsley and watercress, nutmeg, salt, and pepper. Cover and cook for 5 minutes or less. (Greens should be chopped fine or processed with milk in blender before adding.) Variation: Replace parsley and watercress with 4 cups sorrel. Add garlic and rosemary instead of nutmeg. Add 1 bag peas and chopped chicken.

Crepe Sauce

ANNA RUTH KING

1 cup homemade mayonnaise
  (pages 126-127)
1 tsp. horseradish
1 tsp. dry mustard

1 tsp. curry powder
dash lemon juice
2 Tbsp. sour cream
yogurt or blended cottage cheese

Spread crepes with crepe sauce then put on two spoonfuls of nettle sloppy joe filling (recipe follows) on one side. Wrap up and enjoy!

Choices

Nettle Sloppy Joes

1 lb. ground deer meat
1 onion, chopped (opt.)
5 cups chopped nettles
1 cup oatmeal
1 cup pizza sauce or ketchup
1½ Tbsp. honey or maple syrup

1½ Tbsp. vinegar
1½ Tbsp. mustard
½ tsp. chili powder
1 tsp. salt
pepper to taste

Fry meat and onion together. Add nettles, simmer 10 minutes, then add oatmeal, pizza sauce, and rest of ingredients. Stir well. This can be used to fill crepes. Wrap up and put in baking dish. Cover with cheese sauce. Bake ½ hour at 350° or until hot. Cheese sauce: Melt 2 Tbsp. butter, stir in 2 Tbsp. flour, whisk in 1½ cups milk, add ¼ tsp. salt, ¼ tsp. mustard, and pepper to taste. Add 1 cup grated cheddar cheese. Allow to melt, then stir in.

Lamb's-Quarter Onion Pie

ANNA RUTH KING

herbs

140

1 prepared pie crust
2-3 cups frozen greens
    or 4 cups fresh greens, chopped
2 bunches green onions, chopped
3 Tbsp. butter

2 eggs
1 cup milk
1 tsp. salt
dash of pepper
shredded cheese (optional)

Preheat oven to 425°. Cover crust with foil and fill it with something so it doesn't puff up (I've used another glass pan). Bake for 10 minutes. Remove foil. Sauté onions in butter, spread over crust. Put greens in blender with eggs, milk, salt and pepper. Blend, then pour over onions and top with shredded cheese if desired. Bake for 20-25 minutes. I just fill the pie with chopped greens and then pour the blended eggs and milk over it, instead of blending with the greens. Note: We made this with chopped watercress. My husband thought it was a better treat than fish, which was a big compliment because we all love fish!

TIP

Frozen Onion Cubes—One of my favorite time-saving tips came from a friend who shared how to freeze grated/chopped onions. Chop onions in a food processor until mushy. Scoop into ice cube trays (purchase an extra set to be used for this purpose only). Double bag, place in airtight container (I use an old Tupperware® Cold Cut Keeper, and keep it just for that purpose) and freeze. Transfer frozen cubes to a large plastic jar (peanut butter jars work well) and keep frozen. I chop extra onions and keep them in glass jars in fridge to fill onion cube trays for a few days. Frozen cubes are so handy to add to soup, sloppy joes, or in any recipe that calls for onion. I don't have to bother storing onions for the winter, nor take time for peeling and chopping (and crying) each time I prepare a dish calling for chopped onion. Great time-saver!

—Susie Wiebe, Manitou, MB

Cheesy Chickweed Fritters

Anna Ruth King

1 cup milk	¾ tsp. salt
1 egg	½ tsp. paprika
2 cups flour	1½ cup chickweed, chopped
2 tsp. baking powder	fat for frying

Beat first 6 ingredients together. Add to chopped chickweed. Drop mixture by tablespoons into deep hot fat (375°). Fry a few at a time until golden brown, about 4 minutes. Serve with cheese on top. Cheese sauce: 2 Tbsp. butter, 3 Tbsp. flour, 1 cup milk, 4 oz. cheese, grated. Melt butter, stir in flour, add milk and whisk over medium heat until thickened. Add cheese, stir occasionally until smooth. Remove from heat. Our children really like these.

Nettles

Anna Ruth King

nettles	bread slices
butter	eggs

Young nettles 6-12" tall are good to eat. Wear gloves and use scissors to snip them off. Wash nettles well. Chop them and sauté in butter. The heat takes the sting out. Serve over fried bread slices with poached eggs on top.

141

herbs

To Freeze Nettles

Anna Ruth King

Wash, chop, and steam nettles until wilted. Put on cookie sheets to cool, then bag the amount you want to use. I often put them in spaghetti or make lasagna with them.

Nettle Broth

Anna Ruth King

4 pints water	leeks
beef or lamb	pepper
1 cup barley	salt
1 cup nettles, chopped	flour
1 bunch green onions	

Cook meat in water with barley for 2 hours. When tender, add greens. Thicken with flour and add seasonings. Delicious served with cooked potatoes.

Batter-Fried Milkweed

ANNA RUTH KING

2 eggs
2 Tbsp. milk
3 Tbsp. butter
6 Tbsp. olive oil

salt to taste
pepper to taste
firm milkweed pods

Mix eggs and milk with whole wheat flour to make a thick batter. Wash pods well, boil 3-4 minutes. Drain. Dip pods in batter, fry in hot oil.

Meat and Potatoes with Peppergrass

ANNA RUTH KING

14 boiled new potatoes
2 cups cooked ham, chicken or beef
½ cup sliced green onion
1 cup finely chopped peppergrass
2 Tbsp. chopped green pepper
1 tsp. dry mustard
1 tsp. salt

¼ tsp. pepper
3 Tbsp. vinegar
½ cup water
1 cup homemade mayonnaise
  (pages 126-127)
⅓ cup chopped sweet pickles

herbs 142

Sauté onion and peppers. Blend in mayonnaise, salt, pepper, mustard, and peppergrass. Add water and vinegar, and cook until bubbly. Fold in pickles and pour over potatoes and meat.

Lamb's Quarter Cream Sauce for Pasta

ANNA RUTH KING

4 cups lamb's-quarters, washed
  and chopped
2 cloves garlic
1 cup mashed potatoes
½-1 cup milk

3 oz. cream cheese
½ tsp. salt
1 Tbsp. chives
1 tsp. fresh or dried oregano

Steam lamb's-quarters in butter until tender with garlic. Put mashed potatoes, milk, cream cheese, and salt in blender, and blend until smooth. Add to hot greens and cook for 1 minute, until bubbling. Add chives and oregano. Serve immediately with 1 lb. cooked wide noodles. When it's garden weeding time, we often have lamb's-quarters growing in the rows, so we cut a big bowlful before we weed. We all love this green.

Crumb Topping

ANNA RUTH KING

2 eggs (hard-boiled, crumbled)
½ cup parsley
½ cup butter, melted
5 slices bread, cubed

Melt butter, add bread cubes and fry until browned. Blend together eggs and parsley and add to bread cubes. Stir until mixed and serve over poke greens.

Hollandaise Sauce (for wild greens)

ANNA RUTH KING

3 egg yolks
2 Tbsp. lemon juice
½ tsp. mustard
½ cup butter
dash of cayenne
salt

Beat yolks, lemon juice, mustard, and cayenne. Heat butter until almost boiling. Mix together slowly until thickened (with whisk). Add salt to taste. Serve over steamed greens. Try this on poke greens. Delicious with fried bacon bits added. Tip: Pick poke before stem turns red; after they are red they are too old.

143

herbs

Hollandaise

ANNA RUTH KING

3 egg yolks
2 Tbsp. lemon juice
½ tsp. prepared mustard
dash of cayenne
½ cup butter

Blend yolks, lemon juice, mustard, and cayenne. Heat butter until almost boiling, mix together slowly until thickened. This will enhance the flavor of many greens. Try this on steamed poke greens, salt to taste. Delicious with bacon. Pick poke before stem turns red. If red they are too old.

Watercress Dip

ANNA RUTH KING

¼ cup sour cream
12 oz. cream cheese
⅛ tsp. garlic salt
½ tsp. salt
¼ tsp. pepper

1½ tsp. horseradish
2 Tbsp. lemon juice
1 small onion
1 bunch watercress

Put all ingredients in food processor with ¼ of the watercress. Blend until mixture is partially blended. Add remaining watercress a little at a time. Blend until smooth. Serve with homemade chips and crackers.

Chickweed Dip

ANNA RUTH KING

½ cup celery, finely chopped
½ cup red pepper, diced fine
¼ cup onion, finely chopped
2 Tbsp. butter

½-1 lb. cheese, grated
4 cups chickweed, chopped
¼ tsp. rosemary, crushed

herbs 144

Sauté celery, peppers, and onion in butter. Melt cheese and stir in. Add chickweed and rosemary last. Serve hot with toast and vegetable dippers.

Mushroom Sauce

ANNA RUTH KING

1 cup sliced mushrooms
¼ cup butter
⅓ cup wheat flour
2 cups beef broth

½-1 cup milk
¼ tsp. salt
pepper
nutmeg

Sauté mushrooms in butter. Whisk together flour and broth. Add to mushrooms slowly and stir with whisk until it thickens. Add milk and seasonings and stir until smooth. Can be used as a filling for crepes.

Herbal Vinegars

Mrs. Daniel (Verna) King, Pembroke, KY

Equipment needed: Glass jars, quart size or smaller with wide mouth and plastic lid. Optional: Decorative glass jars with cork lid for storage of finished product. Straining material: Cloth, paper towel, or coffee filter. Plastic funnel, wooden or plastic spoon. NOTE: Vinegar reacts chemically to metal, so avoid anything copper or aluminum. Vinegar: Distilled white vinegar is well suited for making colored vinegars. It produces a strong, acidic flavor. Apple cider vinegar, which already has a flavor of its own, makes a rich, well-bodied vinegar. It will hide the vinegar's true color because it is dark. What herbs can you use? The possibilities are unlimited. Almost all herbs can be used, as well as herb combinations. The most commonly used parts are the leaves. Some other plant parts can be used. In chives the leaves and flowers can be used. The flowers are beautiful as a garnish in the finished vinegar. Basic Recipe:

1 part herbs	2 parts vinegar

First, collect clean, unblemished leaves in the morning after the dew has dried. Keep in mind the size of your batch and collect accordingly. When washing be sure to completely dry! Moisture will cloud the vinegar. Watch for insects!! Sterilize jar with hot water. Avoid a large jar that will allow a big space between vinegar and lid. Measure herb leaves and stuff into jars. Do not cut or mince them. Pour measured vinegar over herbs. Poke wooden spoon in the jar and bruise the leaves. Remove any air bubbles and cover with plastic lid. Label and date each jar. This is important! Place the jar in an area with indirect lighting. Sunshine will speed up the brewing process, but it will also cloud the vinegar. Give the jar a shake every few days. After about 4 weeks, open jar and taste. If you'd like it a bit stronger, let it age an additional two weeks. If even then it's too mild for you, strain the old herbs out and repeat the process with fresh leaves. If the vinegar is too pungent for your taste, dilute with unflavored vinegar. Once it is done, strain the vinegar twice to remove any and all particles. Insert a fresh sprig of herbs for looks, but after it is no longer covered with vinegar, toss to avoid mold. Store in a cool, dark place. Herbal vinegars will keep 18 months or longer if properly prepared and stored. Use in soups, salad dressings, barbecue sauces, and marinades. Experiment!

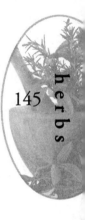

Herbal Vinegar

Veronica Weaver, Sears, MI

Choose your vinegar (we used white wine) and heat, but don't boil it. Then pour into a glass jar to which you have added your herb sprigs, garlic, or whatever. Use about three 2" sprigs of herbs for each cup of vinegar. Garlic, shallots, or chilies can be added as well, one for each cup of vinegar. Let the vinegar cool, then cover it, and store in a cool, dark place for up to a year. Use the vinegar in salad dressings, marinades, etc. You can use your own combinations but here are some suggestions: honey and mint, sage and parsley, garlic and oregano. Hint: Tie a pretty ribbon around the lid and give to others as gifts.

Thyme & Lemon Vinegar

SUSIE NISLEY, DANVILLE, OH

1 large sprig of fresh thyme
1 long spiral lemon peel

2 heaping tsp. black peppercorns
2 cups white wine vinegar

Put thyme, lemon peel, and peppercorns into 1 pint or 2-8 oz. bottles, add vinegar. Seal. Store 1 month.

Basil Vinegar

SUSIE NISLEY, DANVILLE, OH

4 large sprigs basil

2 cups white wine or champagne vinegar

A pattern to follow—you can use any fresh herb. Dill, for instance, is always enjoyed, as is chervil. Tarragon is one of the greatest vinegars of all and chives make a subtle vinegar. Be sure to use a lot of them in the bottles. For small-leaved herbs such as thyme, use an extra sprig or two.

Rosemary Tarragon Vinegar

SUSIE NISLEY, DANVILLE, OH

2 large sprigs rosemary
2 large sprigs tarragon

2 cups white wine vinegar

Make as you would the basil vinegar. If you're dividing between 2 bottles, make sure to put a sprig of each herb in each. White distilled vinegar is too strong, and overpowers the herbs.

Herb Seasoning

MARIE BEAR, PATRIOT, OH

3 Tbsp. basil (ground)
3 Tbsp. summer savory
2 Tbsp. celery seed
2 Tbsp. ground cumin
2 Tbsp. sage

1 Tbsp. thyme
2 Tbsp. marjoram
3 Tbsp. onion powder
1 Tbsp. garlic powder
1½ cup sea salt

Mix together well. Use all ground ingredients if possible.

Meats

AFTER MARVIN CAME HOME FROM HIS FASTING
experience, he didn't eat meat for fifteen years, so I'm not much of a
meat expert.

But I do know this, there is a vast difference between grass-fed healthy
beef and the hormone-laden alternative. Think of the implications
of your children eating hormones all their life. Not an interesting
thought!

Meat should be eaten more sparingly than most people do. If we're
not doing a lot of physically hard work, we certainly need less rather
than more.

We are blessed to have friends who raise organic beef, so each year
we order from them. We also order our chicken from friends who raise
and butcher them for customers. When David shoots a deer we get
hot dogs and beef sticks made out of it. I encourage you to give careful
consideration to your meat sources. Make it your business to find a good
organic source or raise your own if possible.

Basil Cream Chicken

KATHY SCHWEIHOFER, CHINA, MI

¼ cup milk
¼ cup bread crumbs
1 lb. boneless skinless chicken breast
3 Tbsp. butter
½ cup chicken broth

1 cup cream
½ cup grated Parmesan cheese
¼ cup chopped fresh basil
⅛ tsp. ground black pepper

Place milk and bread crumbs in separate bowls. Dip chicken in milk, then in bread crumbs. Fry on medium heat, both sides, until done. Add broth to skillet; bring to boil over medium heat. Stir in cream; boil; reduce heat. Add cheese, basil, and black pepper. Simmer and stir until heated through. To serve, pour the sauce over the chicken. Our entire family enjoys this dish. I serve it with brown rice and fresh steamed broccoli, cauliflower, and carrots.

Chicken Nuggets

LUCIA LAPP, BENTON, IL

1 cup whole wheat flour (or cornmeal)
4 tsp. seasoned salt
1 tsp. paprika
1 tsp. poultry seasoning

1 tsp. ground mustard
½ tsp. pepper
8 boneless skinless chicken
breast halves

Combine first 6 ingredients in bag. Pound chicken to ½" thickness and cut in 1½" pieces. Put chicken in bag and shake to coat. Heat oil in skillet and cook until juices run clear (6-8 minutes). Serve with your favorite sauces to dip them into.

149

meats

Chicken Nuggets

MRS. GLENN ZIMMERMAN, GREENWOOD, WI

1 cup whole wheat flour
3 tsp. seasoned salt
1 tsp. paprika
1 tsp. poultry seasoning
1 tsp. ground mustard

½ tsp. pepper
8 boneless, skinless chicken
breast halves
¼ cup olive oil

In a resealable plastic bag, combine the first 6 ingredients. Pound chicken to ½" thickness, and cut into 1½" pieces. Place chicken pieces, a few at a time, into bag, and shake to coat. Heat oil in a skillet; cook chicken, turning frequently, until browned and juices run clear, about 6-8 minutes. Yield: 8-10 servings. The seasoning can also be used on chicken breast halves to make yummy sandwiches.

Choices

Barbecued Chicken

Susan Stalter, Millersburg, OH

5 lb. chicken leg quarters	1 tsp. salt
1 cup ketchup	1 Tbsp. Worcestershire sauce
⅓ cup honey	2 tsp. chili powder
1 onion, minced	½ tsp. garlic powder

Cut chicken legs and thighs apart. Bake at 350° for 1 hour, uncovered. Meanwhile, combine all other ingredients, and bring to a boil. Simmer for 20 minutes. Drain grease off chicken, and take off skin. Pour sauce over chicken and bake 15 more minutes.

Uncle Leroy's BBQ on the Grill

Kaylene Hartzler, Tennille, GA

8 chicken leg and thigh quarters

1st sauce:

6½ Tbsp. butter	1 tsp. salt
6½ oz. vinegar	½ tsp. pepper
6½ oz. water	

2nd sauce:

1 oz. lemon juice	¼ tsp. mustard
1 tsp. salt	1¼ tsp. Worcestershire sauce
½ tsp. pepper	3 oz. ketchup
2 tsp. sweetener	4 Tbsp. butter

Turn every 5 minutes on the grill, and apply sauce each time for one hour and 30 minutes. Time can vary for different grills. For the last 15 minutes use the 2nd sauce.

Oven Barbecued Chicken

Miriam Yoder, LaGrange, IN

cooking oil	1 Tbsp. honey
3-4 lb. chicken pieces	½ cup water
⅓ cup chopped onion	2 tsp. mustard
3 Tbsp. butter	1 Tbsp. Worcestershire sauce
¾ cup ketchup	¼ tsp. salt
⅓ cup vinegar	⅛ tsp. pepper

Heat a small amount of oil in a large skillet. Fry chicken until browned. Drain; place in a 9 x 13" baking dish. Sauté onions in butter until tender. Stir in remaining ingredients. Simmer for 15 minutes. Pour over chicken. Bake at 350° for 1 hour or until chicken is done, basting occasionally. This is our favorite way to fix chicken.

Healthy

Lisa's Meatloaf

LISA WEAVER

2 lbs. hamburger
1 tsp. salt
¾ tsp. pepper
1½ cup cracker crumbs
2 cups tomato juice
1 tsp. liquid smoke

¾ tsp. garlic salt
2 eggs
1 cup milk
1 Tbsp. Worcestershire sauce
¾ cup catsup
1 med. onion, chopped

Mix all together well and put in dish. Bake at 350° for 1½ hour. Put topping on right away and cover for ½ hour with tinfoil, then remove foil and bake uncovered for the rest of the time. Very moist and delicious!

Topping:

1½ cups catsup
2-3 Tbsp. sweetener
1 Tbsp. vinegar

2 tsp. mustard
1 tsp. hickory smoke

Meatloaf

SUSAN STALTER, MILLERSBURG, OH

155 meats

1½ lb. hamburger
1 cup tomato juice
¾ cup rolled oats
1 egg

1½ tsp. salt
¼ tsp. pepper
¼ cup chopped onion

Combine all ingredients and mix well. Bake in 9 x 13" pan at 350° for about 1 hour.

BBQ Sauce:

⅓ cup ketchup
1 Tbsp. fructose

1 tsp. mustard powder

Mix and put on top.

Savory Meatloaf

ELIZABETH STALTER, MILLERSBURG, OH

1½ lb. ground beef
¼ cup onions, minced
1 cup crushed crackers
1 tsp. salt

1 egg, beaten
1 tsp. mustard
½ cup ketchup
1 cup tomato juice

Mix all ingredients and place in cake pan. Put a few slices of bacon on top or glaze.

Glaze:

¼ cup honey
½ tsp. dry mustard

1 Tbsp. Worcestershire sauce
a little vinegar (opt.)

Spread over meatloaf and bake at 350°-375° for 1 hour.

Best Ever Meatloaf

LUCIA LAPP, BENTON, IL

2 eggs
⅔ cup tomato juice
3 slices bread, torn*
½ cup onion
½ cup grated carrot

1 cup mozzarella cheese (opt.)
1 tsp. parsley
1 tsp. salt
¼ tsp. pepper
1½ lb. ground meat

Topping:

½ cup tomato sauce
¼ cup sucanat

1 tsp. prepared mustard

Bake at 350° for 45 minutes. Spoon topping on top and bake another 30 minutes. Let stand 10 minutes before serving. Yield: 6 servings.

*½ cup oatmeal for gluten-free.

Saucy Meatloaf

MIRIAM YODER, LaGRANGE, IN

1 egg, slightly beaten
2 Tbsp. ketchup
1¾ tsp. salt
¾ tsp. chili powder
dash of pepper

¼ cup onion, chopped
½ cup milk
1 cup quick oats
1½ lb. ground meat

Topping:

¼ cup ketchup
½ Tbsp. honey

½ tsp. mustard

Bake at 350° for 45 minutes. Add topping. Bake for 15 more minutes.

Ground Beef Grand Style

MRS. SUSIE NISLEY, DANVILLE, OH

1½ lb. ground beef or pork
½ cup chopped onions
1-8 oz. pkg. cream cheese
1 can mushroom soup
¼ cup milk
¼ cup catsup
½ tsp. salt

Brown meat and onions, add rest of ingredients. Put in pan. Bake at 350° for 20 minutes then lay biscuits on top, which have been rolled out and cut.

Biscuits:

2 cups flour (spelt preferred)
½ tsp. salt
½ cup coconut oil
4 tsp. baking powder
½ tsp. cream of tartar
⅔ cup milk

Sift dry ingredients together, add oil until mixture resembles coarse crumbs, add milk and mix and roll out.

Chinese Pepper Steaks

MRS. CONRAD (MARTHA) KUEPFER, PLEASANTVILLE, TN

½ lb. round steaks
3 cloves garlic
1 cup celery, chopped
1 onion, chopped
1 red and 1 green pepper, chopped
2 carrots, julienned
1½ Tbsp. soy sauce
2 cups water
2 Tbsp. cornstarch
1 tsp. curry powder
2 tsp. beef bouillon

Cut steaks in strips. Fry in 4 Tbsp. oil on high heat for 5 minutes. Remove meat from pan. Add a little more oil and the vegetables. Stir fry 3-5 minutes, until crisp-tender. Combine last five ingredients and stir into vegetables; cook until thickened. Add meat and cook gently for 1 minute. Remove from heat and serve over brown rice. You can vary the vegetables according to what you have on hand.

Herbed Venison or Elk Roast

SANDRA SMUCKER, JOHN DAY, OR

1 roast (can be put in frozen)
2 tsp. garlic powder or juice
2 tsp. onion powder
2 Tbsp. liquid aminos or soy sauce
oregano (fresh or dried)
sage (fresh or dried)
rosemary (fresh or dried)
lemon balm (fresh or dried)
chives (small fistful)
2-3 cups water

Use a few sprigs each of the herbs, add water (can use more if you want broth for gravy). Bake at 290° for 4 hours. You can do it at a higher temperature for less time, but may be less tender.

Roast Goose with Potato Stuffing

IDA EDWARDS, LINDEN, TN

8-10 lb. goose
2 cups water
1 small onion, chopped
1½ tsp. salt
6 cups soft bread crumbs
2 large potatoes, chopped
2 stalks celery, chopped

1 med. onion, chopped
¼ cup butter, melted
1½ tsp. salt
1 tsp. ground sage
½ tsp. ground thyme
1¼ tsp. black pepper
¼ tsp. cayenne pepper

Trim excess fat from goose. Heat giblets, water, small onion, and 1½ tsp. salt to boiling; reduce heat. Cover and let simmer 1 hour or until giblets are done. Strain broth, cover and refrigerate. Chop giblets. Mix with remaining ingredients. Rub inside of goose with 1½ tsp. salt. Fold wings across back having the tips touch. Fill the inside of the goose loosely with stuffing. Fasten neck skin to back with skewer, and opening with skewers and lace and string. Tie drumsticks to tail. Prick skin all over with fork. Put the goose on the rack in a shallow roasting pan, breast side up. Roast 3-3½ hours uncovered at 350°, until the drumstick moves easily. Remove excess fat occasionally. Make a tent of aluminum foil to place over goose for the last hour so it doesn't get too brown. Serve with gravy and stuffing.

meats

158

Liver Patties

SANDRA SMUCKER, JOHN DAY, OR

1 lb. liver
2 slices bacon (optional)
1 small onion
1 green pepper (optional)

1 tsp. real salt
⅛ tsp. pepper
2 Tbsp. flour
1 egg

Grind first 4 ingredients in meat grinder. Add last 4 ingredients. Mix well and drop from a spoon on a greased griddle. Serves 6. (Since the liver is ground up, it makes it not so tough to eat.)

Fried Salmon Patties

LISA WEAVER

2 cups cracker crumbs
1 tsp. salt, scant
1½ cup milk

1 cup salmon or tuna
2 eggs, beaten
pepper to taste

Roll crackers until fine. Mix with other ingredients. Drop by tablespoonfuls and fry with butter on each side until nicely brown.

Healthy

Oven-Baked Fish

FRIEDA YODER, MILLERSBURG, OH

¼ cup butter, melted
1½ Tbsp. lemon juice
½ tsp. honey
¼ tsp. pepper
¼ tsp. paprika

¼ tsp. basil
⅛ tsp. garlic powder
½ tsp. salt
1 lb. fish
⅔ cup dry cracker crumbs

Combine butter, lemon juice, honey, and spices. Dip fish in butter and herb mixture; roll in crumbs. Lightly coat shallow baking dish with oil. Arrange fish in single layer in pan. Spoon remaining mixture over fish. Bake uncovered at 450° for 20 minutes.

Baked Fish

CHRISTY NOLT, DODGE CENTER, MN

1 lb. fresh or frozen fish fillets
3 Tbsp. oil
3 Tbsp. ketchup
3 Tbsp. Worcestershire sauce

3 tsp. lemon juice
⅛ tsp. fresh ground pepper
fresh chopped parsley

Grease 9" loaf pan with oil. Place fish in a single layer. Combine remaining ingredients except parsley. Pour over fish. Bake at 350° for 20-25 minutes, or until fish flakes easily. Sprinkle with parsley and serve.

159 meats

Salmon Loaf with Sauce

MONICA BAZEN, GRAND RAPIDS, MI

Loaf:

2 cans salmon (drain and reserve liquid)
1 cup oats
4 eggs
1 onion, chopped

4 Tbsp. fresh parsley
2 Tbsp. lemon juice
2 tsp. Worcestershire sauce
1½ cup milk

Combine all ingredients. Put in 9 x 4" loaf pan, and bake at 350° for about 45 minutes.

Sauce:

4 Tbsp. butter
4-6 Tbsp. flour
2 cups milk

juice from drained salmon
2-4 boiled eggs, chopped

Melt butter, whisk in flour and stir to make a paste. Gradually add milk and juice from salmon and keep stirring until thickened. Stir in boiled eggs. Serve over salmon loaf. Great with mashed potatoes and carrots!

Honey Lemon Chicken Marinade

MARTHA WINGERT, CHAMBERSBURG, PA

½ cup lemon juice
⅓ cup honey
¼ cup soy sauce
2 Tbsp. finely chopped onion
4 garlic cloves, minced

2 tsp. dried parsley flakes
2 tsp. dried basil
1 tsp. salt-free seasoning blend
1 tsp. white pepper
1 tsp. lime juice

Makes enough for 6 chicken breasts. Reserve a little for basting.

Sauce for Grilling Meat

BARBARA SUE TROYER, EVART, MI

1 cup melted butter or olive oil
2 tsp. garlic salt

1 tsp. paprika

Brush on meat while grilling.

Soy-Lemon Chicken Marinade

INA SCHROCK, GAP MILLS, WV

1 cup soy sauce
1 cup olive oil

1 cup lemon

Marinates about 4 lbs. of chicken.

Meat Substitutes

BECAUSE MARVIN DID NOT EAT MEAT FOR FIFTEEN
years, I became interested in alternatives. It is my desire to help another
wife and mother somewhere who is about ready to despair, feeling
bogged down with trying to find acceptable alternatives. Don't give
up; here's a person who cares. That's why I'm sharing Pecan Loaf (163),
Grain Burgers (164), and Bulgur Burger (168). Keep your eyes open!
You never know which avenue God may use to send you a little help.
That's one of the excitements of a Christian, watching how uniquely
God once again addresses a need!

The Pecan Loaf I got out of a local newspaper, the Grain Burgers
were first served to us in Michigan, and one day I picked up a *Creation
Magazine* and stumbled on the Bulgur Burger. We have used this recipe
many times and it's so versatile. It freezes well and can be used for pizza,
in spaghetti, tacos, chili soup, and sloppy joe sandwiches and tastes
better in taco salad than hamburger!

Pecan Loaf

MRS. MIRIAM WENGERD, SUGARCREEK, OH

1 cup chopped pecans	1 cup dry bread crumbs

Chop pecans by hand or grind in blender to equal 1 cup. Put in a bowl and add bread crumbs.

1½ cups tomato juice	1 small onion
2 medium potatoes	

Combine in blender container, then chop. Stir all ingredients together. Add, mixing well:

½ cup flour	1 tsp. salt
2 eggs, beaten	½ tsp. sage

Pour into a large, greased loaf pan. Dot top of mixture with a bit of butter. Bake at 350° for 30 minutes. Slice and serve with brown gravy or ketchup.

Grain Burgers

MRS. JUNIOR KAUFFMAN, REDDING, IA

⅔ cup rice, uncooked	⅓ cup cornmeal
2 cups water	⅓ cup oats
1 tsp. salt	⅓ cup wheat germ
⅓ cup green pepper, chopped	soy flour or other flour
⅓ cup onion, chopped	salt to taste
⅓ cup celery, chopped	cayenne pepper to taste
1 egg (optional)	

Rice should be sticky when cooked. Cook rice in a pot with water and salt, cool and add vegetables. Stir in egg if desired. Add grain and enough flour to hold mixture together. Season to taste; make into patties. If too sticky, dip in flour. Brown in oil in hot skillet. Serve with lettuce and tomato. If desired, add a slice of cheese.

Grain Burgers

Mrs. Miriam Wengerd, Sugarcreek, OH

6 cups cooked millet

6 cups cooked barley

3 cups mashed potatoes

3 cups quick oats

1 cup chopped onions

5 tsp. salt

4 tsp. parsley

6 Tbsp. Vogue Vege-Seasoning

Bring 3¾ cups water to boil, add 1½ cup millet and bring to boil again. Reduce heat to low and cook 25 minutes. This will make a little more than 6 cups cooked millet. Bring 4½ cups water to boil, add 1½ cups barley. Bring to boil again, reduce heat to low, cook 40 minutes. This will make a little more than 6 cups cooked barley. Meanwhile, chop onions. When millet is ready, put in large bowl. Pour on onions, and add quick oats. Add while millet is hot; this will soften onions and oats. Put mashed potatoes on top, add ½ of salt and seasonings. When barley is done, add to bowl and put rest of salt and seasonings on top. Stir together with spoon, until it cools enough to mix with your hands. Mix thoroughly. Using your hands, form patties, using ⅔ cup for each patty. This recipe makes 19 large patties and 1 small one. If you want smaller patties, use ⅓ cup per patty. Coat patties with cornmeal on both sides, and bake on oiled cookie sheet at 350° for 20 minutes. Flip and bake 20 minutes longer. Serve on buns with mayo, thinly sliced onion, tomatoes, and cheese. Very good and very filling!

Lentil Nut Loaf

Martha Wideman, Listowel, ON

3 cups lentils (med.-soft puree)

1½ cups raw nuts, chopped

½ cup ground sunflower seeds

1 Tbsp. onion powder

½ cup raw oatmeal

1 tsp. sage

1 tsp. salt

½ tsp. celery seed

1 Tbsp. soya sauce

4 Tbsp. oil

Mix well. Bake in oiled loaf pan for 1 hour at 350°. Good served with gravy. We bake this in round pineapple or soup cans, then slice when cold and serve with warm gravy.

Meatless Sandwich

Martha Wideman, Listowel, ON

1 cup cornmeal

1 cup whole wheat flour

Heat cornmeal and flour in dry skillet on low heat until slightly browned. Mix or blend together:

¾ cup peanut butter

1 qt. tomato puree or juice

1½ tsp. salt

1½ cups warm water

Mix together well and bake in cans or steam in small greased tin cans about 1½ hour. Better the second day. Good sliced for sandwiches.

Healthy

Lentil Loaf

½ cup lentils
1 cup water
1 can black beans, drained
1 small onion, chopped
2 cloves garlic

⅓ cup oats
½ tsp. sage
1 tsp. mustard
1 Tbsp. ketchup
1½ tsp. chili powder

Cook lentils in water, mash. Add beans. Add rest of ingredients. Shape into loaf. Bake at 350° for 45 minutes. Slice when chilled.

Bar-B-Qed "Meat" Balls

Shape lentil loaf (preceding recipe) into balls. Sauce:

8 oz. tomato sauce
½ cup water
2-3 Tbsp. vinegar

¾ cup onion
1 Tbsp. Worcestershire sauce

Bake at 350° for 30-45 minutes.

Meatless Meatballs

B. GARBER, FAYETTEVILLE, PA

1 cup grated mozzarella cheese
½ cup pecan meal
3 egg whites (or 2 whole eggs)
½ cup chopped onions

1 cup bread or cracker crumbs
½ clove garlic, minced
¼ cup oat bran
1 tsp. salt

Sauce:

8 oz. tomato sauce
8 oz. tomato soup

1 cup water
1 pinch cumin

Combine all but sauce; shape into balls. Place in 7 x 11" baking dish. Bake at 350° for 14 minutes. Meanwhile mix sauce ingredients, pour over meatless balls after 15 minutes of being baked and bake 20 more minutes. Sprinkle additional cheese on top if desired. These are also delicious with BBQ sauce, sweet and sour sauce, or even pizza sauce. A delicious meat alternative.

substitutes

165

Oat Pecan Burgers

SHARON HOCHSTEDLER, KOKOMO, IN

4 cups water	¼ cup nutritional yeast flakes
1 Tbsp. basil	2 tsp. garlic powder
1 tsp. coriander	2 tsp. onion powder
1 tsp. sage	¼ cup olive oil
1 cup ground pecans	¼ cup Braggs

Place in a large kettle and bring to a boil. Remove from heat then add 4 cups rolled oats. Cover and let stand for 1 hour, then form into patties and place in two 9 x 13" baking pans. Bake at 350° for 25 minutes. Flip and bake another 20 minutes.

Vegetable Nut Roast

MRS. JUNIOR KAUFFMAN, REDDING, IA

1 cup carrots, grated	1 Tbsp. tomato juice
1 small onion, finely chopped	1 cup bread crumbs
½ cup celery, diced	1 tsp. salt
¼ cup sunflower seeds	½ tsp. pepper
¼ cup walnuts, coarsely chopped	1 tsp. chicken base
2 Tbsp. oil	1 cup water

Combine all ingredients in a bowl. Lightly grease a loaf pan and press in mixture. Bake 45 minutes in 325° oven. Variations: Replace celery with ½ cup chopped green pepper, replace carrots with 1 cup leftover vegetables, add ½ cup chopped mushrooms, replace nuts with ½ cup cashews. This is a very good substitute for dressing. Nuts take the place of meat.

Carrot & Sunflower Patties

MRS. ABBY ABBOTT RIDER, DELPHI, IN

2 large carrots, grated	2 Tbsp. oil
1 small onion, finely chopped	1 tsp. dried parsley
2 eggs, beaten	½ tsp. celery salt
½ tsp. dill	¾ cup ground sunflower seeds

Combine all ingredients and mix well. Chill, then shape into patties. Heat on a greased skillet.

No Meat Stromboli

MRS. MIRIAM WENGERD, SUGARCREEK, OH

1½ lb. bread dough
½ cup pizza sauce
1-2 cups Bulgur Burger (page 168)

1 cup shredded cheddar cheese
1 cup green peppers, chopped
1 cup onions, chopped

Sauté peppers and onions in a little butter. Grease 11 x 17" pan. Roll out dough in pan, not quite to edge. Spread pizza sauce down the center ⅓ of dough. Spread Bulgur Burger over this, then top with peppers and onions and cheese. Fold in ends and pinch tightly to seal. Bake 25 minutes at 375°. This is a delicious simple meal to make when you are baking bread anyway. Serve with applesauce.

Bean Burgers

MRS. ABBY ABBOTT RIDER, DELPHI, IN

2 cups cooked beans
⅔ cup ground sunflower seeds
¼ cup finely chopped onion
½ tsp. chili powder

1 tsp. salt
2 Tbsp. extra virgin olive oil
3 Tbsp. homemade catsup
⅓-½ cup wheat germ

I use kidney or pinto beans, ground. Combine all ingredients. Add enough wheat germ that the mixture will hold its shape. Place on a lightly greased baking sheet and bake at 350° for 15-20 minutes. May be cooked on a hot griddle or baked in oven. Can add cheese to each at end of cooking time.

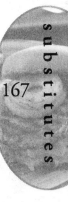

Bulgur Burger

Mrs. Miriam Wengerd, Sugarcreek, OH

2 cups bulgur wheat
1 cup water
1 cup tomato juice
½ med. onion, cut in pieces
1 garlic clove

1 cup pecans
2 Tbsp. Vege-Sal
2 Tbsp. sorghum molasses
2 Tbsp. taco seasoning (opt.)

Place bulgur in kettle. Blend all other ingredients in blender until smooth. Stir blended ingredients into bulgur in kettle. Cook over medium heat for 15 minutes, stirring frequently. Let set for 1 hour with lid on. Freezes well. This is a delicious recipe that closely resembles hamburger! It's wonderful on pizza, with spaghetti, tacos, or chili soup, or to use for sloppy joe sandwiches. I like to make large batches and freeze in measured portions.

Tofu Burgers

½ onion
¼ cup peppers

2 cloves garlic
12.3 oz. tofu

Fry first three ingredients together. Crumble tofu in bowl, then add:

fried mixture
2 pieces bread, crumbled fine

½-⅔ cup tomato sauce
2 Tbsp. egg replacer

Shape patties and fry.

Garbanzo Patties

2 cups garbanzo beans
½ cup onion, ground fine
1½ Tbsp. fresh parsley (1½ tsp. dried)

¼ cup cooked rice
4 Tbsp. egg replacer

Cook, mash and drain beans. Mix all ingredients together, shape patties, and fry. I use one can Great Northern beans, drained, and dump all ingredients into my food processor. If you want to be able to flip them easily, add ¼ cup flour. Serve with mustard and ketchup.

Casseroles

ALWAYS KEEP IN MIND TO INCORPORATE MORE vegetables into your diet. Casseroles are an easy way to do that. Don't just fill up on starches (noodles, potatoes, rice), but get lots of vegetables in there!

Keep a pretty dish on your counter to keep garlic in. Get a hand garlic press, then when making casseroles and side dishes press one clove, adding it to the vegetables you include. Just a little adds lots of flavor and health benefits. People use a lot of cream soups in casseroles, but they'd be better off making their own. Reading the labels on these cans is an enlightening experience: modified food starch, sodium phosphate, sugar, disodium guanylate, dextrose, thiamine hydrochloride, monosodium glutamate. These are a few of them! In the soup section you'll find some delicious homemade cream soups; try them. In the canning section you'll find more recipes that tell you how to can cream soups. Be prepared. Have them canned and handy so it's easier to reach for a healthy choice!

Taco Casserole

Mrs. Ruby Shetler, Homer, MI

4 cups cooked brown rice
5 cups cooked pinto beans
1-16 oz. bag frozen corn (or canned)
1½ qt. canned, diced tomatoes,
    processed in blender
1 Tbsp. chili powder

1 tsp. salt
1-15 oz. can olives, sliced (opt.)
½ tsp. onion powder
grated cheese
whole wheat flour tortillas

Mix and simmer first eight ingredients for 5 minutes. Put a scoop of mixture in the bottom of a casserole dish. Spread a layer of tortillas on top of the mixture. Spread another layer of mixture, cheese, and top with tortillas. End with mixture and top with grated cheese. Bake in 350° oven for 20 minutes or until bubbly.

Spaghetti Squash Casserole

1 med. spaghetti squash
½ cup chopped onion
1 large pepper, chopped (opt.)
1 cup shredded cheese
1 cup cottage cheese
1 large tomato, sliced

sliced mushrooms (opt.)
1 Tbsp. butter
1 Tbsp. flour
1 tsp. oregano
¼ tsp. basil
1 tsp. garlic salt

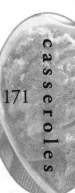

Boil squash 30 minutes in a little water. Slice lengthwise and remove seeds. Place face down on baking dish. Bake, covered, at 350° for 45-60 minutes. Melt butter and mix with flour. Add oregano, basil, and garlic salt. Mix all together and place in buttered dish. Bake at 350° for ½ hour.

Mock Burrito Casserole

B. Garber, Fayetteville, PA

1 pt. pizza sauce
4-5 whole grain flour tortillas
1 pt. pinto beans
½ tsp. chili powder
½ tsp. onion powder
½ tsp. garlic powder

½ tsp. cumin
½ cup frozen spinach (opt.)
⅓ cup pumpkin puree (opt.)
½ cup plain yogurt or sour cream
shredded cheddar cheese

Make refried beans by putting beans and seasonings in the blender. Add pumpkin and spinach if using and blend until smooth. Place ½ pint of pizza sauce in bottom of 9 x 13" dish. Break up 2 tortillas in pieces to cover sauce. Spread bean puree on top of tortillas. Spread ½ cup yogurt on bean puree. Top with remaining tortillas, broken in pieces. Cover with remaining pizza sauce and sprinkle with cheese to cover. Bake at 350° for 30 minutes.

California Blend Casserole

MRS. MIRIAM WENGERD, SUGARCREEK, OH

½ cup onions, chopped
4 cups carrots, chunked
4 cups broccoli, cut in small pieces
4 cups cauliflower, cut in small pieces
1 lb. bacon (optional)
4 Tbsp. butter

4 Tbsp. wheat flour
2 cups milk
1 cup cheese
1 tsp. salt
¼ tsp. pepper

Prepare vegetables and steam them just until tender. Fry bacon until crisp, drain on paper towels. Melt butter and stir in wheat flour with whisk. Add milk and bring to boil while stirring. Turn off heat. Add cheese, salt, and pepper, cover and let set until cheese melts. Stir in. Pour vegetables in 9 x 13" pan. Pour cheese over top and stir in slightly. Crumble bacon evenly over top. Spread crumb topping over all. Bake at 350° for ½ hour or until crumbs are golden. Crumb Topping: 4 cups crackers, crushed, 1 stick butter, melted. Mix well.

Chicken Broccoli Casserole

MRS. MIRIAM WENGERD, SUGARCREEK, OH

4 cups cooked, deboned chicken
4 cups broccoli, chopped
1½ cups carrots, diced
1 cup onions, chopped

½ cup red pepper, diced
1⅓ cups rice, cooked
2¼ cups chicken broth

Cheese Sauce:

½ cup butter
⅔ cup barley flour
1 qt. chicken broth

2 tsp. salt
½ tsp. pepper
1½ cups cheese

Melt butter, stir in flour, add broth and bring to boil over high heat, stirring with whisk until thickened. Add salt, pepper, and cheese. Turn off heat and let melt. Stir with whisk until smooth. Set aside until needed. For casserole: Bring broth to boil. Add rice, bring to boil again. Turn on low, cook 30 minutes. Steam carrots, peppers, and onions until tender, not too soft. Put chicken, rice, and vegetables into a bowl and add cheese sauce, mix and pour into casserole. Bake at 350° for 35 minutes. Serves 10 people. Delicious!

Lisa's Barbecue Beef Casserole

LISA WEAVER, LOGAN, OH

1-2 lbs. stew meat
2½ cups ketchup
2 Tbsp. sweetener
1 Tbsp. hickory smoke
2 tsp. prepared mustard
1 Tbsp. vinegar
1 tsp. garlic salt

6 large potatoes, peeled and cooked
¼ cup butter
½ cup sour cream
salt to taste
pepper to taste
¼ tsp. garlic salt
cheese

Cook stew meat until it's tender and falls apart. I usually put mine in the crockpot for overnight. Then make barbecue sauce and pour on meat. Put in bottom of 9 x 13" glass pan. Make mashed potatoes, add butter, sour cream, salt, pepper, and garlic salt. Layer in casserole pan and top with cheese slices. Bake at 350° for 45 minutes or until heated through. I was needing something new to make for my family, and had leftover stew meat and created this recipe on my own. We like it very well!

Butternut Squash Casserole

MRS. LARRY (LIANA) CABLE, TROTWOOD, OH

2-3 butternut squash, cooked and mashed
3 Tbsp. oil
1 large onion
½ lb. mushrooms
2 cloves garlic
1 tsp. oregano
salt to taste

pepper to taste
2 cups pizza sauce
1 cup cottage cheese
1 tsp. parsley
1 tsp. basil
1 cup bread crumbs
1 cup mozzarella cheese

Sauté onion, mushrooms, garlic, oregano, salt, and pepper in oil. Add the rest of ingredients. Mix well and put in a 9 x 13" baking dish. Bake at 375° for 30 minutes.

Shipwreck

1 large onion
4 cups cubed raw potatoes
2 Tbsp. white rice, uncooked
1 stalk celery

1 can kidney beans
salt
1 cup tomato juice

Kidney beans should be undrained. You may add more tomato juice if it's too dry. Layer in two layers in casserole dish. Bake at 350° for 1½ hours.

Stroganoff

Kari Wendt, Lake Ariel, PA

1 lb. ground beef or turkey	¼ tsp. pepper
½ cup finely chopped onion	2 Tbsp. parsley
1 clove garlic	1½ cups buttermilk
½ lb. mushrooms	3 Tbsp. whole grain flour
1 tsp. salt	3 Tbsp. butter

Brown meat slowly with onions, garlic, and mushrooms. Add salt and pepper. Over low heat, melt butter and add flour. Mix quickly and keep stirring until it has a slightly nutty aroma. Add buttermilk and whisk until smooth. Cook about 5 minutes on low heat, stirring constantly. Pour into meat mixture and simmer on low about 5 minutes. Serve over buttered brown rice or noodles (tossed with parsley). Hint: Buttermilk can be substituted for sour cream or yogurt in many recipes.

Ham & Swiss Stromboli

Mrs. Miriam Wengerd, Sugarcreek, OH

1½ lb. bread dough	¾ lb. thinly sliced ham
½ cup homemade mayonnaise (pages 126-127)	1 cup grated Swiss cheese

Grease 10 x 15" pan. Roll out dough in pan. Spread mayonnaise down center ⅓ of dough. Spread ham evenly over this, then top with cheese. Fold in ends and pinch tightly to seal. Bake 25 minutes at 375°. Variation: Replace ham with chicken breast chunks, and add pineapple tidbits and green peppers. Use BBQ sauce instead of mayonnaise.

Stromboli

Mrs. Rhoda Miller, Sugarcreek, OH

1½ lb. whole wheat bread dough	peppers
½ cup pizza sauce	pineapple (optional)
meat of your choice	onions
mushrooms	cheese

Roll out dough on 10 x 15" pan. Spread with pizza sauce down the center ⅓ of dough and top with toppings. Fold sides of dough over center. Fold in ends and pinch tightly to seal. Bake approximately 30 minutes at 375°. Or wrap in wax paper, then foil. Freeze. Thaw 6 hours before meal. Brush with beaten egg before baking.

Side Dishes

Amish Dressing

MRS. ANDY M. TROYER, MILLERSBURG, OH

1 loaf bread	1 pint chicken bits and broth
6 eggs, well beaten	2 tsp. chopped onions
2½ cups milk	2 tsp. chicken soup base
½ cup shredded carrots	parsley to taste
1 cup finely cut celery	salt to taste
1 cup cubed potatoes, boiled	pepper to taste

Cube bread and toast in butter, mix with remaining ingredients. Fry in butter until lightly browned, then bake in oven for 45 minutes at 350°.

Dressing

Gravy:

1½ cup boiling water	2 Tbsp. Chick-Nish
½ cup water	2 Tbsp. clear jel

Mix ½ cup water with Chick-Nish and clear jel. Add to boiling water. Cook until thickened.

Filling:

2 cups onion	2 tsp. poultry seasoning
2 cups celery	4 Tbsp. egg replacer
4 cups cubed whole wheat bread	gravy
2 Tbsp. dried parsley	

Fry onion and celery in a dab on butter. Add remaining ingredients. Place in greased casserole. Cover. Bake at 300° for 2 hours. Serves 3-4.

Dairy-Free Scalloped Potatoes

R.M.Z., THORP, WI

½ cup water	1 large sliced sweet onion
½ tsp. garlic powder	½ tsp. salt
1-4 oz. can mushrooms	black pepper (optional)

Combine all above ingredients and simmer 20 minutes in a covered skillet. Meanwhile slice thinly (or shred) 5-6 medium potatoes. Liquefy ingredients in blender, stir into potatoes, pour back into skillet and simmer ½-1 hour, or bake at 350° for 50-60 minutes. For variation, you may add vegetable broth or 1 lb. browned ground beef.

Scalloped Potatoes

18 medium potatoes
¾ lb. cheese, shredded
3 tsp. salt
1½ cup onion

¾-1½ cups milk
1 Tbsp. parsley
3 Tbsp. mustard
2 lb. ham (optional)

Cook, peel and shred potatoes. Combine all ingredients and put in casserole dish. May freeze ahead of time.

Scalloped Potatoes

Susan Stalter, Millersburg, OH

1¼ cups hot milk
2 cups grated cheddar cheese
¼ cup chopped onion (optional)

6 medium potatoes
3 Tbsp. butter
2 Tbsp. whole wheat flour

Scrub and slice potatoes. Layer potatoes, onion, butter, flour, cheese, and milk in a greased 9 x 13" pan. Cover and bake at 375° for 1 hour or until potatoes are tender.

Cheese Scalloped Potatoes

Elizabeth Stalter, Millersburg, OH

1¼ cups milk
2 cups shredded cheddar cheese
¼ cup onions

6 medium potatoes
3 Tbsp. butter
2 Tbsp. flour

Scald milk. Meanwhile, scrub and thinly slice potatoes (can leave peelings on). Layer in 9 x 13" pan: potato slices, salt, onion, milk, butter, flour, and cheese. Cover and bake at 375° for 1 hour or until potatoes are tender. Yummy!

Cheesy Broccoli Potatoes

Mrs. Ruby Shetler, Homer, MI

8 large red potatoes
3 stalks broccoli
½ cup whole wheat flour

2 tsp. salt
2 cups milk
3 cups cheese, finely grated

Bake, boil, or pressure cook unpeeled, scrubbed potatoes. While potatoes are cooking, peel tough outer peelings from broccoli stalks. Dice broccoli and steam until tender. Save water from cooking broccoli and potatoes. Add enough water to make 2½ cups. In a large saucepan, mix flour, salt, milk, and cooking water and simmer until thickened. Stir in cheese over low heat until melted. Add drained broccoli. Serve as a gravy topping over potatoes. Serves 8.

Choices

Baked Potato Wedges

Mrs. Ervin (Hannah) Hostetler, Pleasantville, TN

1½ cups flour

3 tsp. salt

2 tsp. Cajun seasoning

½ tsp. oregano

3 tsp. parsley flakes

½ tsp. basil

potatoes

melted butter

Wash potatoes and cut in fourths, lengthwise. Mix together flour and seasonings in a large bowl. Place melted butter in another bowl. Toss potatoes in melted butter then in flour/seasoning mixture. Place on cookie sheet and bake at 325°-350° until done. Serve with ketchup.

Mashed Potatoes and Turnips

Sharri Noblett, Port Arthur, TX

Cut 2 lbs. potatoes into cubes. Core and peel and cut up 1½ lbs. of turnips. Cook in boiling salt water. Drain, add ¼-½ cup butter, ½ cup heavy cream, and salt to taste. Mash. Sprinkle with parsley.

Spicy Sweet Potato Unfries

Maria Weaver, Squaw Valley, CA

4 medium-large sweet potatoes

2 Tbsp. olive oil

1 tsp. salt

1 tsp. black or white pepper

1 Tbsp. curry powder

Scrub sweet potatoes and cut in half. Cut each half in ¼" strips. In bowl combine ingredients and mix well until potatoes are evenly coated. Spread on cookie sheet and bake at 375° for 20 minutes or until tender. Serve hot.

Oven Baked French Fries

Miriam Yoder, LaGrange, IN

1 baking potato

2 tsp. olive oil

paprika

salt

Scrub potatoes, but do not peel. Cut into strips for french fries. Soak in cold water for 20 minutes. Blot potato strips on paper towel, then place in small bowl. Sprinkle with oil and paprika. Stir to coat. Arrange evenly on a greased cookie sheet. Bake at 475° for 20 minutes, stirring frequently to brown evenly. Sprinkle with salt when finished.

Oven-Fried Potatoes

PATRICIA TAYLOR, STOYSTOWN, PA

6 medium potatoes, peeled and cubed
2 Tbsp. flour
2 Tbsp. Parmesan cheese
1 tsp. salt

½ tsp. garlic powder
½ tsp. paprika
¼ tsp. pepper

Place potatoes in a large resealable plastic bag. Combine the flour, cheese, and seasonings; add to potatoes and shake to coat. Pour 3 Tbsp. oil into a 15 x 10 x 1" baking pan. Pour potatoes into pan. Bake uncovered at 375° for 40-50 minutes or until tender. Yield: 6 servings. Use cornmeal instead of flour for gluten-free.

Baked French Fries

CHRISTINA EBY, MONTNEY, BC

Peel 12 potatoes. Slice julienne style. Soak in cold water 15 minutes to 1 hour. Dry thoroughly. (I wrap them jelly roll style in a clean towel.) Dump into large bowl. Toss with 2 Tbsp. oil. Spread on several pans that have been greased with liquid lecithin. Bake on two shelves in 450° oven. Stir frequently and rotate pans. Bake approximately 50 minutes. Serve with sour cream and homemade salsa. Yummy! We often peel 14-15 potatoes for our family of 8!

side dishes

Parmesan Oven Fries

MRS. MIRIAM WENGERD, SUGARCREEK, OH

6 cups red potatoes, cubed
1 cup Parmesan cheese
1 cup barley flour
2 tsp. salt

¾ tsp. pepper
1 Tbsp. parsley flakes
½ cup fresh chives, chopped
1 cup butter, melted

Melt butter. Mix cheese, barley flour, salt, pepper, parsley flakes and chives in a bowl. Cube potatoes and put in bowl. Stir until evenly coated. Pour melted butter over everything and stir until well mixed. Spread on cookie sheet. Bake at 350° for 40 minutes or until golden and a little crispy. Easy and delicious! Serves 5.

Latkes (Jewish Potato Pancakes)

MRS. HARRY (CINDY) WILKINSON, DIXON, IL

3-4 potatoes, grated and drained
2 eggs
2 Tbsp. whole wheat flour
salt to taste
2-4 Tbsp. chopped onion

Mix and drop by Tbsp. into ½" hot oil. Cook to a golden brown. Makes about 20 cakes. Good served as a side with meat and vegetables.

Potato Pancakes

MIRIAM YODER, LaGRANGE, IN

3 cups finely shredded, peeled potatoes
2 eggs, beaten
1½ Tbsp. whole wheat flour
⅛ tsp. baking powder
½ tsp. salt
½ tsp. grated onion

Mix together potatoes and eggs. In a mixing bowl, gently combine dry ingredients and onion. Stir into potatoes. Drop by tablespoonsful onto hot greased skillet. Brown slightly on both sides. Serve with applesauce or maple syrup. We like it with chicken broth gravy.

188

Sweet Potato Delight

SHARON HOCHSTEDLER, KOKOMO, IN

4 sweet potatoes, peeled
1 large green apple, peeled and diced
¼ cup cranberries
½ cup raisins
2 Tbsp. honey
½ cup orange juice

Preheat oven to 350°. Cut sweet potatoes into 1" chunks and place in an 11 x 7" baking pan. Top with diced apples, cranberries, and raisins. Drizzle with honey and pour orange juice over all. Cover and bake approximately 1 hour or until potatoes are tender.

Baked Sweet Potatoes

MRS. ERVIN (ELIZABETH) BEACHY

Wash sweet potatoes, place onto oven rack. Bake at 375° for 15 minutes, reduce heat to 350°. Bake 1 hour or until soft. Enjoy with fresh raw butter or coconut oil. I enjoy the taste of coconut oil; it is an excellent choice to obtain healthy fats, especially if you cannot tolerate dairy. Coconut oil has the same fatty acids as mother's milk. Try to obtain butter from cows that had plenty of fast-growing grass. Spring butter is best and higher in vitamins. Grass-fed spring butter also contains activator X, which helps utilize vitamins and minerals. Be sure to line your stove with tinfoil if you plan to bake sweet potatoes or regular potatoes. You may wish to put a pan beneath the sweet potatoes. These are especially sweet prepared this way.

Healthy

Gravy

VICKY SCHILLING, SCOTLAND, UK

2 med. onions, chopped finely
2 garlic cloves, chopped
2 Tbsp. olive oil
1 tsp. sweetener of your choice

2 cups boiling water
2 Tbsp. corn flour
2 Tbsp. soy sauce

Cook onions, garlic, and olive oil in a covered pan. When soft, add sweetener and water. Mix corn flour with cold water, add this to the hot mixture and stir over heat until thick, then add soy sauce.

Baked Beans

MRS. LARRY (LIANA) CABLE, TROTWOOD, OH

4-5 cups cooked beans of your choice
⅓ cup sorghum
1 Tbsp. seasonings
1 cup tomato sauce or juice

¾ cup onion
4 Tbsp. oil
1 tsp. dry mustard

Mix together well and put on top of rice crust.

Bar-B-2 Beans

DOREEN OTTO, GRAYSON, KY

1½ cup navy beans
½ cup chopped onion
1½ Tbsp. vinegar
¾ tsp. dry mustard

3 Tbsp. ketchup
2 scoops stevia
Braggs to taste
10 oz. tomato sauce

Cook beans until soft. Reserve excess liquid. Add rest of ingredients, with some reserved water to make it a little soupy. May add cheese to make it rich. Bake at 350° for 30-45 minutes. Serves 3.

Bar-B-2 Green Beans

1 can kidney beans, undrained
2 cups green beans
1 cup lima beans
1 small onion
1 Tbsp. vinegar
¾ tsp. dry mustard

3 Tbsp. ketchup
2 scoops stevia
½ Tbsp. Braggs
1 tsp. garlic powder
¾-1 15 oz. can tomato sauce

Bake at 350° for 30-45 minutes. Serves 2-3.

Mexican Garbanzo Beans

1 cup dry measure of beans
16 oz. canned tomatoes
1 tsp. oregano
1 tsp. basil
½ tsp. cumin
1-2 tsp. chili powder

1 medium onion
2 garlic cloves
1 stalk celery
1 green pepper
a little butter

Soak beans, then cook. Add tomatoes, oregano, basil, cumin, and chili powder. Sauté onion, garlic, celery, and pepper in butter, then mix all together. Bake 45-60 minutes at 350°. Serve over rice or baked potatoes.

Black Beans & Rice

INA SCHROCK, GAP MILLS, WV

6 cups cooked or canned black beans
1 onion, chopped
5 cloves garlic, chopped
3 Tbsp. chopped green pepper
1 tsp. paprika

½ tsp. oregano
½ tsp. cumin
1 Tbsp. red wine vinegar
salt
pepper

Heat oil in pan, and add onion, garlic, and pepper. Toss and fry about 90 seconds, then add paprika, oregano, cumin, salt, and pepper. Toss again and allow seasonings to become fragrant and a little toasted, then pour in beans. Stir and add vinegar. Let simmer for about 15 minutes, then serve on top of plain rice. Have some freshly chopped cilantro to sprinkle on top.

Wild Rice with Mushrooms

MRS. LARRY (LIANA) CABLE, TROTWOOD, OH

⅔ cup wild rice
2 cups water
¼ cup butter or olive oil
1 Tbsp. onion
1 Tbsp. parsley
1 Tbsp. chives

1 Tbsp. green pepper
½ lb. mushrooms
1 tsp. salt
½ tsp. pepper
dash of nutmeg

Cook wild rice in boiling water. Keep covered for 45 minutes or until water is all absorbed. Melt butter in skillet. Sauté onion, parsley, chives, and green pepper. Cook for 3 minutes. Add rice to vegetables. Add mushrooms. Sauté for 5 minutes. Add more salt if necessary. Add a dash of nutmeg.

Vegetable Medley in Rice Crust

Mrs. Larry (Liana) Cable, Trotwood, OH

3 cups cooked brown rice
1 Tbsp. olive oil
2 stalks celery
1 med. onion
2 garlic cloves

1 zucchini, diced thinly
3 cups broccoli
1 tsp. chicken seasoning
1 tsp. garlic powder
¼ tsp. salt

Egg Filling:

3 eggs
1 Tbsp. lemon juice
1 Tbsp. olive oil
1 Tbsp. honey

2 tsp. garlic powder
1 tsp. basil
¼ tsp. salt
2-4 Tbsp. milk

Press rice into a greased pie pan. In a large skillet, heat olive oil, celery, and onion until tender. Add garlic and cook 2 more minutes. Add rest of ingredients and cook until tender. Pour into crust. Blend filling ingredients in a blender. Pour over vegetables. Bake at 375° for 30-35 minutes.

Hearty Rice Skillet

Mrs. Larry (Liana) Cable, Trotwood, OH

2 cups cooked beans
2 cups tomatoes, diced
1 cup corn
½ cup peas
½ cup lima beans
½ cup green beans
1 cup water

¾ cup brown rice, cooked
½ tsp. thyme
salsa, optional
½ cup tomato puree
1 Tbsp. lemon juice
1 Tbsp. honey
⅓ cup roasted, slivered almonds

Combine beans, tomatoes, corn, peas, lima beans, green beans, water, rice, and thyme in a large skillet. Stir in desired amount of salsa. Bring to a boil; reduce heat; simmer until everything is tender and hot. Stir in tomatoes, lemon juice, and honey. Heat through. Serve with toasted almonds and cheese.

Fried Rice with Mushrooms

CHRISTINA EBY, MONTNEY, BC

¼ cup soy sauce
¾ cup water
2 tsp. sweetener of your choice
¼ cup olive oil
4 cups mushrooms, sliced

1 qt. peas or green soybeans
9 cups cooked brown rice
1 cup onion, finely sliced
sesame seeds (optional)

Combine soy sauce, water, and sweetener. Set aside. Heat skillet and add oil. Add mushrooms, stir fry 3 minutes. Add frozen peas and stir fry 3 more minutes. Quickly stir rice and soy sauce together, add to vegetables. Add onion. Mix well and serve hot. Sprinkle with sesame seeds. Serves 8.

Baked Brown Rice

MRS. ERVIN (HANNAH) HOSTETLER, PLEASANTVILLE, TN

2 cups brown rice
2 tsp. salt
herbs and seasonings of your choice
chopped onion and celery

2 cups chicken broth
4 cups water
olive oil

Preheat oven to 350°. Pour rice in greased casserole dish. Sprinkle with salt and seasonings. Add onion and celery. Drizzle with olive oil. Add broth and water. Bake, covered, for approximately 2 hours or until done. Fluff with fork.

Wild Rice Casserole

SUSAN DOTY, LOBELVILLE, TN

1 cup raw wild rice
1 cup grated cheddar cheese
4 cups canned tomatoes, chopped, with liquid
½ cup cooked mushrooms

¼ tsp. pepper
1⅛ cup beef broth
¼ cup oil
½ tsp. chili powder

Rinse rice. Let stand in water 1 hour. Drain. Combine all ingredients. Place in 2 qt. casserole dish. Bake at 350° for 1½ hours.

Rice & Beans

Mrs. Rhoda Miller, Sugarcreek, OH

1 cup dried beans	6 cups water
1½ tsp. salt	2 Tbsp. butter
½ tsp. black pepper	2 cups uncooked brown rice
⅛ tsp. cloves (optional)	

Wash the beans and put into a large pot with 6 cups water. Add ½ tsp. each of salt and pepper. Bring to boil. Reduce heat and simmer until the beans are tender but whole (60-90 minutes). Drain into a bowl and put the beans aside. Add water to the bean liquid to make 4 cups. In a large saucepan, stir and fry the rice in butter for 1-2 minutes. Stir in the 4 cups of liquid from beans and 1 tsp. salt, and bring to a hard boil. Reduce the heat, add the cooked beans, cover tightly, and simmer until the rice is tender and has absorbed all the liquid. Serve with a vegetable or meat sauce, or use for your rice in haystack supper. Delicious by itself also!

Chicken Curry for Rice

Doreen Otto, Grayson, KY

1 onion	2 tsp. salt
¼ cup green peppers	2 cups cooked chicken (opt.)
4 medium potatoes, cubed	1½ tsp. curry powder
2 cups chicken broth	2 cups canned tomatoes

Sauté onion and green peppers. Add potatoes, broth, salt, and cooked chicken. When nearly done, add curry powder and tomatoes. Tomatoes should be undrained. You may also add leftover green beans or fresh zucchini if you have it on hand. Serve over rice. Should be soupy.

197

side dishes

Green Chili Chicken Enchiladas

Mrs. Ervin (Hannah) Hostetler, Pleasantville, TN

¼ cup olive oil	2 cups diced green chilies
3-4 cloves garlic, minced	3-4 cups cooked chicken, chopped
1 cup chopped onion	12 corn tortillas
2 Tbsp. flour	1 lb. Jack cheese, grated
2½ cups water or chicken broth	1 pint sour cream

To make sauce: Sauté garlic and onion in oil until tender, blend in flour, add water and green chilies. Bring to a boil and simmer approximately 5 minutes. Stir in chicken. Heat tortillas on hot griddle to soften, keep warm under a towel. In 9 x 13" pan, layer ⅓ of sauce, 6 tortillas, ⅓ of sauce, half of cheese, 6 tortillas, remaining sauce and remaining cheese. Bake at 350° for approximately 20 minutes. Smother with sour cream and return to oven for 10 minutes. Serves 6.

American Enchiladas

Doreen Otto, Grayson, KY

4 cups dry beans	5-6 cloves garlic

Soak beans, and cook with garlic. If too much liquid, drain some, reserving in case needed. Add:

1½ Tbsp. chili powder	1½ tsp. oregano
1¼ tsp. cumin	2 Tbsp. butter
1¼ tsp. coriander	3 jalapeños with seeds

Mash beans. Sauté 1 large onion and 4 cloves garlic. Mix with 3 cans tomato sauce and 1½ tsp. oregano. Spread some sauce on bottom of glass 9 x 13" and 8 x 11"pans. Fill tortillas (approximately 32) with beans (⅓-½ cup). Dab a little sauce and roll as best as you can. Squish into pans. Cover with remaining sauce. Top with cheese. Bake. For Sunday after-church dinner bake under 200°. May freeze ahead. Can be made flat—put the whole thing in layers. It's faster. Serves 10 adults.

Chicken Black Bean Enchilada Casserole

Monica Bazen, Grand Rapids, MI

1 green bell pepper, chopped	1 tsp. ground cumin
1 onion, chopped	½ tsp. garlic salt
3 cloves garlic, minced	8 corn tortillas
2 cups shredded, cooked chicken meat	½ red onion, diced
4 cups cooked black beans, drained	1 cup black olives, chopped
2 cups tomato sauce	2 cups shredded cheddar cheese
2 cups Mexican-style stewed tomatoes, drained	sour cream
	chopped fresh tomatoes
1½ cups picante sauce, divided	

Preheat oven to 350°. In large skillet, sauté bell pepper, onion, and garlic until soft. Add chicken, beans, tomato sauce, stewed tomatoes, 1 cup of the picante sauce, cumin, and garlic salt. Simmer 15 minutes. Ladle enough of mixture in a greased 9 x 13" pan to coat bottom of pan. Arrange ½ of tortillas in bottom of dish. Top with ½ of remaining meat mixture. Sprinkle with red onion, half of the olives, and half of the cheese. Repeat with everything except cheese. Cover tightly with foil and bake for 20 minutes. Remove foil, top with remaining cheese. Bake 5 minutes more. Let sit 10 minutes after removing from oven. Top with sour cream, ½ cup picante sauce, and chopped tomatoes.

Healthy

Enchilada Sauce

MARIA WEAVER, SQUAW VALLEY, CA

3 Tbsp. oil

Heat in saucepan, then add:

2½ cups water
6 Tbsp. chili powder

Boil. One recipe=2 cans.

3 Tbsp. flour

¼ tsp. garlic powder
½ tsp. salt

Oven Beef Stew

JOANNE MARTIN, BROOTEN, MN

2 lb. cubed beef
1 onion
3 carrots, chopped
2 potatoes, diced

½ cup tomato juice
1 tsp. salt
1 Tbsp. sweetener
2 Tbsp. tapioca

Bake at 350° for 1 hour. Reduce heat to 250° for 3½-4 hours.

Carrot Pilaf

MRS. RHODA MILLER, SUGARCREEK, OH

1 cup shredded carrots
½ cup chopped onion
1 Tbsp. butter

1 cup uncooked rice
2 cups chicken broth
1 tsp. lemon pepper

Sauté carrots and onion in butter until tender. Add rice and stir to coat. Stir in broth and lemon pepper. Bring to boil and simmer until rice is tender.

Tasty Okra

INA SCHROCK, GAP MILLS, WV

1 qt. cut-up okra
1 tsp. salt
1 onion, sliced thinly

3 tomatoes, chopped
½-1 tsp. curry powder

Toss the cut-up okra and salt in a bowl. Set aside. Slice onion. Heat 2 Tbsp. olive oil in a pan and add onion. Sauté about 90 seconds then add curry powder. Toss and sauté until curry becomes very fragrant. Add chopped tomatoes. Then add okra. Simmer for 15 minutes.

Citrus Honey Carrots

Mrs. Crist Nisley, Danville, OH

1 bunch carrots
1 pinch salt
¼ cup melted butter

¼ cup honey
1½ tsp. grated orange peel
1½ tsp. grated lemon peel

Wash and scrape carrots. Cook in 1" of boiling water until crispy tender. Drain. Blend melted butter, honey, and citrus peels. Pour over cooked carrots and place over low heat until carrots are thoroughly glazed. Makes 4 servings.

Nicki's Squash Dish

Kendra Rokey, Sabetha, KS

2 butternut squash, baked and scraped out
½ cup heavy cream
¼ cup butter
cinnamon to taste

nutmeg to taste
salt to taste
pepper to taste
honey to taste

Mash the squash and add all other ingredients and mix well. Rewarm if necessary, and enjoy!

Dad's Favorite Squash

Minna Friesen, Nova Scotia

2½ lb. butternut squash
¼ cup olive oil
3 Tbsp. pesto

1 tsp. salt
2 cloves garlic, crushed

Turn oven to 400°. Peel squash, and with vegetable slicer, cut into ¼" thick slices. In a large bowl, toss slices with olive oil mixture (last 4 ingredients). Put one layer on 10 x 15" cookie sheet and bake 15-20 minutes. Makes 3 cookie sheets full.

Scalloped Cabbage

Ida Edwards, Linden, TN

1 med. head cabbage	½ cup grated cheddar
5 slices bacon, crumbled	salt
1½ cup white sauce	pepper

Chop cabbage and fry in a cast-iron pan with 4 Tbsp. olive oil until soft. Remove from pan and put in a medium serving bowl. Melt cheddar into hot, freshly made white sauce (recipe below), add bacon, and pour over cabbage. Salt and pepper to taste, stir well.

White Sauce:

¼ cup oil	1 med. onion
1 cup milk	4 cloves garlic
⅓ cup flour	salt and pepper to taste

Heat oil, add chopped onion and crushed garlic. Sauté until soft. Add flour and pepper, mix well, then add milk. Heat to boiling and boil 1 minute, stirring constantly. Remove from heat and add salt.

Quick Beef & Noodles

Mrs. Ivan J. Yoder, Millersburg, OH

1 lb. hamburger	1 cup water
½ cup chopped onion	½ cup sour cream
8 oz. noodles	⅛ tsp. pepper
4 cups tomato juice	1 tsp. salt

In 5 quart kettle brown beef and onion. Add the rest of ingredients except sour cream and cover. Simmer 15-20 minutes until noodles are tender. Add sour cream and heat again.

Easy Spelt Noodles

Leah Nisley, Danville, OH

Measure out 14 cups flour into a large bowl. In a separate bowl, beat 3 dozen egg yolks. Add 1 Tbsp. salt and 1½ cup boiling water. Beat with wire whisk until foamy. Make sure water is boiling hot. Beat quickly. Pour this into the bowl of flour and stir with a large fork. Cover the bowl and let stand for 30 minutes. Put through noodle maker, first at number 3, then last at number 5.

Whole Wheat Noodles

Mrs. Kathryn Hershberger, Clare, MI

Put flour in bowl to weigh 3½ lbs. including bowl. Beat egg yolks from 3 dozen eggs (at least 2 cups) and 1½ cups boiling water until foamy. Pour into flour mixture and mix with a large fork to make crumbly. Shape into ball and cover, let set for 30 minutes then knead for 3 minutes. This dough is easy to handle and not sticky.

Whole Wheat Noodles

Mrs. Ruby Shetler, Homer, MI

6-7 whole eggs, measuring 1¾ cup
⅓ cup water

6 cups whole wheat flour
dash of salt

Beat eggs, add water and mix well. In a large bowl, measure flour and salt. Add egg mixture, stirring and kneading until a ball forms.

BB2 Lentils

Darla Reena Stoll, Odon, IN

5 cups water
½ tsp. salt
1 bay leaf
1½ cups lentils
⅛ tsp. garlic salt
½ cup brown rice
1 cup chopped onion

4 grated carrots
¼ tsp. thyme
¼ cup honey
½ Tbsp. sorghum
½ tsp. ginger
⅛ tsp. cloves
¼ cup vinegar

Simmer first 6 ingredients for 25 minutes, then add onions and carrots. Simmer 5 minutes, then add thyme, honey, sorghum, ginger, cloves, and vinegar. Simmer for 10 more minutes, uncovered.

Bulgur & Lentil Pilaf

¾ cup lentils
3 cups water or stock
1 tsp. salt (or Braggs)
3 Tbsp. oil

1 med. onion
1½ cups mushrooms
¾ cup bulgur

Combine lentils and water and cook. Add salt, then set aside. Sauté onion, mushrooms, and bulgur in oil for 5 minutes, then combine with lentils. Place in buttered casserole. Cover, then bake at 350° for 20 minutes. Serves 6.

Healthy

Red Lentils

MRS. LARRY (LIANA) CABLE, TROTWOOD, OH

Cook 2 cups red lentils in 8 cups chicken broth or bouillon for about 30 minutes. Sauté onion and garlic in olive oil until tender. Add to the lentils along with 2 vegetable bouillon cubes. Heat until bubbly. Serve with crackers, or bread and salad.

Squash Lasagne

MRS. ERVIN (HANNAH) HOSTETLER, PLEASANTVILLE, TN

6-8 small zucchini or yellow squash	1½ cups cottage cheese
16 oz. tomato sauce	½ cup sour cream
8 oz. cream cheese	½ cup chopped onion
2 lb. ground beef	¼ cup chopped green pepper
8 oz. tomato paste	grated Colby cheese

Peel squash, cut in slices lengthwise, and steam for a few minutes. Drain. Combine cheeses, sour cream, onion, and green pepper. Brown meat, drain. Add tomato sauces. Alternate squash, cheese, tomato/meat sauce. Sprinkle Colby cheese on top. Bake at 350° for 45 minutes.

Easy Lasagna

CYNTHIA KORVER, NEW OXFORD, PA

2 lb. lean hamburger (opt.)	½ onion

Brown and drain well, then add to sauce. Mix and simmer for 30 minutes:

1 gallon diced tomatoes, pureed	1 Tbsp. basil
8 cups tomato sauce	1 tsp. Italian seasoning
1½ cups tomato paste	1-6 oz. can black olives, sliced
1 cup frozen spinach	1 small can mushrooms

Drain mushrooms. Spinach, mushrooms, and olives are optional. Boil until tender:

2 lb. lasagna noodles

Optional:

24 or 48 oz. cottage cheese	grated mozzarella cheese

To assemble, begin with 1 cup sauce in bottom of 9 x 13" pan. Lay 3 lasagna noodles lengthwise. Top with more sauce. At this point you can dot with cottage cheese and sprinkle grated cheese before next layer of noodles. Repeat sauce, noodles, cheeses until dish is full. End with sauce and cheese. Bake at 350° for 45 minutes. Makes three 9 x 13" pans. Lazy method: Use uncooked noodles. Pour 2 cups water gently over each pan after assembling. Bake as usual. It really works.

Vegetable Lasagna

MONICA BAZEN, GRAND RAPIDS, MI

1 Tbsp. olive oil
3 cups grated zucchini
3 cups grated carrots
3 large eggs
1 cup Parmesan cheese

2-10 oz. pkg. frozen, chopped
   spinach, thawed, drained
1 large jar spaghetti sauce
½ lb. spaghetti noodles, cooked
8 oz. shredded provolone cheese

Sauté zucchini and carrots in olive oil until tender. Mix Parmesan and eggs. Combine ⅓ of egg mixture with spinach. Mix remaining egg mixture with sautéed carrots and zucchini. Spoon ⅔ cup of spaghetti sauce in 9 x 13" oven dish. Place half of noodles in pan. Layer spinach, half of the cheese, then zucchini mixture in pan. Top with remaining noodles, sauce, and cheese. Cover with foil, bake at 350° for 30 minutes. Remove foil and bake 10 minutes longer. Cool 10 minutes before serving.

Vegetable Lasagna

MRS. LARRY (LIANA) CABLE, TROTWOOD, OH

18 oz. box rice lasagna noodles
2 lg. carrots, sliced

2 cups broccoli pieces

Vegetable Tomato Sauce:

1 Tbsp. olive oil
2 stalks celery
1 lg. sweet bell pepper, chopped
2 small zucchini, sliced
2 small yellow squash, sliced
1 small onion, chopped
4-6 garlic cloves

4 tsp. dried basil
2 tsp. dried oregano
½ tsp. salt
8 cups diced tomatoes
1-6 oz. can tomato paste
4 Tbsp. lemon juice
4 Tbsp. honey

Herbed Tofu Cheese Mixture:

1 lb. tofu
2 Tbsp. olive oil
1 Tbsp. lemon juice

1 Tbsp. honey
2 tsp. garlic powder
1 tsp. basil

Steam carrots and broccoli until tender. Set aside. In a large skillet, heat olive oil. Add celery, red peppers, zucchini and yellow squash; cook until tender. Add onions, garlic, basil, oregano and salt. Continue to cook for 2 minutes. Add tomatoes, paste, lemon juice and honey. Add carrots and broccoli. In blender, combine tofu cheese ingredients. Blend until smooth. In 9 x 13" lasagna pan, oiled lightly, spread 3 cups vegetable sauce. Top with lasagna noodles. Put in 3 cups of vegetable sauce. Spoon half of tofu mixture on top of sauce. Repeat with second layer of noodles, the rest of sauce and remaining cheese mixture. Bake for 45 minutes at 350°. My family really enjoyed this lasagna. You could try replacing tofu with cottage cheese, ricotta cheese, or eggs.

Healthy

Stir-fry Cabbage

MRS. ERVIN (ELIZABETH) BEACHY

Cut cabbage fine. Sprinkle with salt or MSG-free seasoning salt. In heavy kettle, add water to barely cover the bottom. Toss cabbage with several tablespoons extra virgin coconut oil or olive oil. Place into kettle and cover with lid. Cook over fairly high heat until done. Stir several times throughout cooking time. Coconut oil lends an interesting flavor! Also coconut oil stays good with high heat, whereas vegetable, corn, and canola oils become rancid. For variations, you may want to add thinly sliced carrots, green beans, peas, or onions. Broccoli cooked with cabbage tends to give a strong flavor.

Stir-fry Dinner for Three

MARK & BETH WEAVER, NEWAYGO, MI

4 fresh medium potatoes
4 small carrots
1 medium onion
1 sweet pepper
2 Hungarian wax peppers
2 hot dogs or other meat (opt.)
cabbage (to make 1" layer on top)
2 tsp. salt
3 Tbsp. oil

Scrub unpeeled potatoes and cut into ¼" slices. Dice carrots and onion. Melt shortening in 10" frying pan and add vegetables. Cover and fry over medium heat until vegetables are partially tender, about 20 minutes. Stir occasionally. Add hot dogs that have been sliced and browned in small frying pan, and diced peppers. Top with a generous layer of coarsely cut cabbage. Reduce heat. Simmer about 30 minutes or until cabbage is tender. Serve. Note: The hot peppers will become milder the longer they simmer. I usually add those about the last 20 minutes instead of 30.

Stir-fry Zucchini

MRS. ERVIN (ELIZABETH) BEACHY

Slice zucchini into ⅛" rounds. If large, halve or quarter. However, 6-8" zucchini are the best! Place about 4 sliced zucchini in a large skillet when it is hot and oiled with olive oil or coconut oil. Add one onion, slivered, and 1 Tbsp. chopped garlic. Stir fry for about 3-4 minutes. Zucchini should be tender crisp. (I usually use a lid to cook, but be careful not to overcook.) Add 1 tsp. basil and salt and pepper to taste. Serve immediately. This is especially good with chicken. For those with extreme sensitivities you may want to go easy with the pepper and omit the onions and garlic. I just added a small dash of onion powder.

Stuffed Pepper Deluxe

EVA MAY YODER, CLARE, MI

8 green peppers
1 lb. ground beef
⅓ cup chopped onion
2 Tbsp. flour
1 Tbsp. maple syrup

⅛ tsp. pepper
2 tsp. salt
1 cup rice, cooked
1 cup tomato juice

Fry beef and onion together, then add flour, maple syrup, pepper, and salt. Stir, then add rice and tomato juice. Wash peppers, remove tops and seeds. Drop into boiling water for 1 minute. Drain and stuff with rice filling. Top with cheese and bread crumbs. Bake at 375° for 30 minutes. If you don't like that much green pepper, try chopping up a few and adding to filling. Put in a casserole, top with cheese and then bread crumbs. Bake until cheese is melted.

Stuffed Green Peppers

MRS. LEONA MILLER, ODON. IN

5-6 green peppers
¾ cup uncooked brown rice
1 lb. grass-fed ground beef
1 onion, chopped
8 oz. tomato sauce

¼ tsp. basil
¼ tsp. oregano
¼ tsp. thyme
1 tsp. salt
dash pepper

Remove tops and seeds from peppers and place in a kettle of boiling water. Cook 5 minutes, remove and drain. Cook rice according to directions. Brown beef and onion and drain. Add tomato sauce, herbs, salt, and pepper. Simmer 5 minutes, then stir in rice. Stuff peppers with beef mixture and place upright in a shallow baking pan. Bake at 375° for 15-20 minutes or until heated through.

Zucchini Special

MRS. LARRY (LIANA) CABLE. TROTWOOD, OH

4-6 small zucchini
2 qt. beef broth or bouillon

1 qt. pizza sauce
4 cups cooked beans

Slice the zucchini and cook in beef broth. Add the pizza sauce and beans. Heat until hot and bubbly. Serve over hot brown rice and sprinkle cheese on top. Brown rice: 2 cups brown rice, 5 cups water, a dash of olive oil. Put into a saucepan. Bring to a boil. Turn down to low. Leave lid on pan until water is absorbed, about 40 minutes.

Onion Patties

MRS. RHODA MILLER, SUGARCREEK, OH

¾ cup flour
1 Tbsp. cornmeal
2 tsp. baking powder
2 tsp. salt

2 tsp. honey
¾ cup milk
2½ cups onions, chopped

Mix dry ingredients together, then add milk and honey. Batter should be fairly thick. Add onions and mix thoroughly. Drop by tablespoon into ½" oil in skillet. Flatten slightly when you turn them. Brown on both sides until crisp.

Eggplant Parmesan

MRS. ERVIN (HANNAH) HOSTETLER, PLEASANTVILLE, TN

2 eggplants, peeled and sliced ½" thick

2 eggs, beaten

Coating Mix:

3 cups bread crumbs
1 tsp. salt
¼ tsp. black pepper
½ tsp. basil

½ tsp. oregano
1 pint spaghetti sauce
mozzarella cheese

Dip eggplants in beaten eggs and then roll in coating mix. Brown in olive oil. Layer in baking dish with sauce and mozzarella cheese. Bake at 350° for 30 minutes.

Baked Eggplant

MRS. ESTHER BEACHY, HUTCHINSON, KS

1 lb. eggplant, peeled and diced
½ lb. dried bread crumbs
⅓ cup cream
¼ cup milk
¼ cup chopped onion
¼ cup chopped green pepper
¼ cup chopped celery

½ cup butter
1 tsp. salt
½ tsp. sage
1 Tbsp. chopped pimiento
2 eggs, beaten
2 oz. shredded cheddar cheese

Cook eggplant in a small amount of water until tender; drain. Combine eggplant and remaining ingredients in a buttered casserole dish. Bake at 350° for about 40 minutes.

Scalloped Eggplant

Mrs. Ervin (Hannah) Hostetler. Pleasantville. TN

1 eggplant (1½ lb.)
2 Tbsp. butter
1 small onion, chopped fine
2 cloves garlic, chopped fine

salt and pepper
1 Tbsp. fresh parsley
buttered bread crumbs
Parmesan cheese

Preheat oven to 375°. Peel eggplant, and cut into ½" cubes. Place eggplant in a pot and boil with a little water for 5-10 minutes or until tender. Drain. Melt butter in a skillet, add onions and garlic. Cook until soft, stir in eggplant, parsley, salt and pepper. Spoon into baking dish, cover with lots of bread crumbs and cheese. Bake 20-25 minutes. Serves 4.

Eggplant

Rosalee Blair

2 eggplants
2-3 cups chopped ham (depends on
    size of eggplant)
2-3 cups grated white cheese (depends on
    size of eggplant)

1 qt. potatoes
½ cup chopped onion
1 qt. chicken bouillon water or broth

Partially peel 2 young, shiny eggplants. Cut 4 long slits into each and stuff with chopped ham and cheese. Put olive oil in 4 qt. pot and brown eggplants all over. Drop 1 qt. small new potatoes all around eggplants. Now add chopped onions, keep turning and lightly brown potatoes and onions. Then add hot chicken bouillon water (or broth). Cover and let cook until tender. Serve with cornbread or biscuits.

Tomato Sauce

Ina Schrock, Gap Mills, WV

2 cups tomato juice
⅓ cup ketchup
2 cloves garlic, chopped

1 onion, chopped
salt
pepper

Simmer for 15 minutes. Delicious over a Sunday "Chicken & Rice" lunch.

Healthy

Soups

WHAT'S BETTER ON A CHILLY FALL DAY THAN COMING in to a bowl of warming soup? Or maybe you've been outside on a snowy winter day, and as you step into the basement a whiff of spicy chili meets you. Your mouth starts watering for the first hot bite!

Soups are a good way to use leftover rice, or outside stalks of celery, carrots that are a little old and leftover casserole bits. When using up leftovers only make small amounts of soup so it isn't left over again!

Quick breads are a good way to round out a soup meal. Our family enjoys biscuits, muffins and cornbread with butter and honey. They are filling and satisfying.

Soups can also be canned for an instant meal in a jar. In our canning section you will find Chili, Chunky Beef, Rice, Vegetable, Tomato and Chicken Noodle Soup. Can a few different kinds and be ready for those times when you need something NOW! Then you can run to the basement and grab a jar of your own homemade soup, and relax knowing supper's ready in ten minutes.

Chili Soup

Mrs. Sam Stoner, Scottsville, KY

1 lb. ground beef
1 pt. kidney beans
1 pt. tomato juice
1 cup spaghetti sauce
1 Tbsp. chopped onion

1 tsp. chili powder
½ tsp. garlic powder
1 Tbsp. sorghum molasses
salt to taste

Brown beef with onions. Add the rest of ingredients. Bring to a boil. Keep at a low boil for 5 minutes. We like to eat it with cornbread.

Vegetarian Style Chili

Mrs. Junior Kauffman, Redding, IA

1 lb. pinto beans
6 whole tomatoes, peeled
1 onion, chopped
1 clove garlic, chopped

salt to taste
cayenne pepper to taste
3 Tbsp. chili powder
1 tsp. cumin seed

Soak beans overnight and cook until tender. In a large pot, mix all ingredients and simmer a few hours until mixture is very thick. Excellent with cornbread.

Chili Soup

Mrs. Miriam Wengerd, Sugarcreek, OH

3 lb. hamburger
2 cups onions, chopped
1 cup barley flour
2½ qt. tomato juice
1-19 oz. can kidney beans
1 Tbsp. cumin

2 Tbsp. chili powder
3 tsp. salt
1 Tbsp. taco seasoning
2 tsp. paprika
½ tsp. black pepper
½ cup sorghum

Fry and chop hamburger in 6 qt. kettle, add onions and fry a little longer. Sprinkle barley flour over this and stir with spoon to mix. Add tomato juice and turn on high, stirring frequently until it thickens and boils. Reduce heat, adding rest of ingredients. Simmer on low for 1 hour to develop flavor. Stir occasionally. Optional: If you like a sweeter chili soup, add ¼ cup sucanat. If you love fiery soup, add red pepper. This makes around 5 quarts of nice, thick soup.

White Chili Soup

LISA WEAVER, LOGAN, OH

1 lb. ground turkey burger
1 large can chicken broth
1-15.5 oz. can Great Northern beans
2 cups milk
1½ tsp. chili powder

½-¾ tsp. garlic salt
salt to taste
pepper to taste
2 cups cheese
2 chicken bouillon cubes

Brown turkey burger and add chicken broth, beans, chili powder, garlic salt, salt, and pepper. Bring to a boil, then let boil and let simmer for a while. Then add cheese and milk and heat through.

Meatless Chili Soup

SERENA YODER, GOSHEN, IN

1 pt. beans
1 onion
1 qt. tomato juice

2 tsp. chili powder
1 pt. mock pineapple

Combine ingredients in small kettle. Cover and simmer 20-30 minutes.

Raw Chili

SHARON HOCHSTEDLER, KOKOMO, IN

2 tomatoes
¼ sweet/red onion
4 cloves garlic
20 sun-dried tomatoes
½ cup raisins
2 Tbsp. chili powder
2 tsp. ground cumin
1 tsp. oregano
⅓ cup olive oil
handful fresh cilantro

1 jalapeño, optional
1 tsp. sea salt
2 stalks celery, finely diced
2 zucchini, finely diced
2 cups frozen corn, thawed
½ red bell pepper, finely diced
1 cup walnuts
1 carrot, finely chopped (opt.)
1 tomato, chopped (opt.)

Presoak walnuts for at least 4 hours. Presoak sun-dried tomatoes for at least 1 hour. Blend first 11 ingredients (down to salt) until smooth. Put chopped and grated vegetables and nuts into a bowl then mix in sauce. Allow to set at least 6 hours or overnight to allow for spices to fully contribute their flavor.

Split Pea Soup

Mrs. Ervin (Hannah) Hostetler, Pleasantville, TN

8 cups green split peas
8 cups water
4 tsp. seasonings
2 med. carrots, diced
¼ tsp. pepper
½ cup celery stalks, diced
1 onion, chopped

1 tsp. garlic powder
2 med. potatoes, diced
1 tsp. poultry seasoning
1 tsp. sage
½ tsp. basil
½ tsp. salt
2 cups bacon bits

Simmer 1¼-1½ hours. Delicious soup!

Jamie's Vegetable Soup

Mrs. Daniel Byler, Middlefield, OH

2 lbs. ground beef
½ cup chopped onion
28 oz. can diced or whole tomatoes
    with juice
2 small cans beef broth
½-¾ cup barley

1 lb. bag frozen mixed vegetables
1 bay leaf
10-12 whole allspice
½ tsp. salt
½ tsp. pepper

Brown meat and onion, drain fat and add tomatoes with juice, beef broth, barley, and spices. If you want to use canned vegetables, add after soup has simmered ½ hour, otherwise add frozen vegetables with other ingredients. Add water until it looks soupy. Barley soaks up a lot of broth. Simmer 1 hour. This is a delicious and hearty vegetable soup that we all enjoy. I like to make large amounts and can it. I got the recipe from my husband's work supervisor's wife. They sent us supper one time and sent a pot of this soup along.

Italian Vegetable Soup

MARTHA WINGERT, CHAMBERSBURG, PA

1 lb. ground beef or canned beef
1 cup diced onion
1 cup sliced celery
1 cup sliced carrots
½ tsp. oregano
½ tsp. basil
2 cups shredded cabbage
½ cup macaroni (optional)
1 pt. homemade tomato sauce or ketchup

2 cloves garlic, minced
2 cups water
5 tsp. beef bouillon
1 Tbsp. parsley
¼ tsp. pepper
1 cup frozen green beans
1 pt. whole tomatoes
15 oz. kidney beans, rinsed and drained

If using ground beef, brown with onion and drain. Add all the rest of ingredients except cabbage and green beans (and macaroni). Bring to a boil; reduce heat and simmer 20 minutes. Add cabbage, beans, and pasta if desired. Simmer until all vegetables are tender. Sprinkle with Parmesan cheese when serving.

Frijoles Charros

CHRISTY NOLT, DODGE CENTER, MN

2 onions, minced
2 Tbsp. lard
3 cups cooked pinto beans
6 slices bacon, minced
1 slice ham, diced (optional)

½ cup chorizo*
2 cups chopped tomatoes
chili powder to taste
salt to taste
jalapeños to taste (opt.)

Fry onions in lard, then add beans and cook over medium heat 5 minutes, stirring occasionally. In another skillet, fry bacon, ham and chorizo. Add to beans with tomatoes and spices. Add enough water to reach desired consistency. Heat thoroughly.
*Chorizo is available in the Mexican food section. It is packaged similar to sausage.

Italian Soup

MRS. RHODA MILLER, SUGARCREEK, OH

1 lb. ground beef
1 cup chopped onion
1 qt. spaghetti sauce
2 cups beef broth
1 cup chopped celery

1 tsp. salt
½ tsp. pepper
2 cups diced tomatoes
2 cups mixed vegetables

Brown beef with onion and drain. Add spaghetti sauce, beef broth, celery, salt and pepper. Simmer 20 minutes. Add tomatoes and vegetables and simmer an additional 15 minutes.

Healthy

Halibut Chowder

CHRISTY NOLT, DODGE CENTER, MN

½ cup chopped onion
½ cup chopped celery
¼ cup chopped green pepper
1 garlic clove, minced
2 cups chicken broth
1 cup potato, peeled and thinly sliced
1 cup carrot, peeled and thinly sliced

½ tsp. dried dill
½ tsp. salt
½ tsp. ground pepper
1½ cups milk
2 cups corn
2 cups cooked, flaked halibut

In a large saucepan, sauté onion, celery, green pepper, and garlic in butter until tender. Carefully stir in broth. Add potato, carrot, dill, salt, and pepper. Bring to a boil, reduce heat. Cover and simmer until vegetables are tender, about 20 minutes. Stir in milk, corn, and fish. Heat through. Note: Salmon or other fish can also be used in place of halibut.

Green Chili & Corn Chowder

CHRISTY STENGER, SALINAS, CA

225 soups

1 small can green chilies, chopped
1 cup butter
2 Tbsp. sweetener (opt.)
1 small onion, diced
1 small carrot, diced
1 small celery stalk, diced
1 clove garlic, minced
½ cup flour

3 cups frozen or fresh corn
3 cups chicken stock
2 cups cream
pinch of grated nutmeg
salt and pepper to taste
1 cup Monterey Jack cheese
1 cup bacon bits

Melt ½ cup of butter in a large skillet over medium heat. Add onion, celery, carrot, and garlic, and sauté for 2 minutes. Add flour and stir to make a roux. Cook until the roux is lightly brown, set aside and cool to room temperature. Meanwhile, combine corn and chicken stock in a saucepan, and bring to a boil. Simmer for 10 minutes. Pour boiling stock with corn into the skillet with the roux, a little at a time, whisking briskly so it doesn't lump. Bring to a boil. Add green chilies and sweetener. The mixture should become very thick. In a small saucepan, gently heat the cream; stir into the thick corn mixture. Add nutmeg, salt, pepper, and bacon bits to taste. Just before serving, cut the remaining butter into large chunks. Add it to the soup, stirring until the butter melts. Add Monterey Jack cheese and stir. I also add 1½ lbs. hamburger or ground turkey to make it more of a meal.

Lisa's Vegetable Soup

LISA WEAVER, LOGAN, OH

1½ lb. ground beef
salt and pepper to taste
2 Tbsp. sweetener of your choice
1 tsp. chili powder
1 tsp. garlic salt
2 qts. tomato juice
1 large onion, chopped
5 large potatoes, peeled and diced

2-3 carrots, peeled and diced
1 large green pepper, diced
1 qt. frozen green beans
1 pt. frozen corn
1 pt. frozen lima beans
4 beef bouillon cubes
2 Tbsp. parsley flakes
1 tsp. seasoning salt

Fry hamburger with onion until browned. Then add tomato juice and seasonings; add vegetables and cook until soft. Then simmer for a while. Flavor is better when simmered for awhile before serving. I often simmer for an hour or more. You may add water and more tomato juice if desired. You may add more seasoning to your liking.

Chicken Wild Rice Soup

PATRICIA TAYLOR, STOYSTOWN, PA

2 cups wild rice, cooked
1 cup diced chicken or turkey
1 med. onion, diced
2 stalks celery, diced
2 carrots, diced

½ cup butter
½ cup flour
4 cups chicken stock
2 cups milk
salt and pepper

Sauté the onion, celery and carrots in butter until onion is transparent. Reduce heat. Blend in flour. Cook over low heat. Stir mixture. Do not brown. Using wire whisk, blend in chicken stock. Heat to boiling, stirring occasionally, for 1 minute. Add cooked wild rice, milk, and chicken. Season with salt and pepper; simmer 20 minutes, but do not boil. Garnish with parsley. Makes 8 servings.

Cabbage Bean Soup

MRS. LEONA MILLER, ODON, IN

½ cup diced onion
2 cups water
1 cup diced, cooked ham (optional)
2 cups shredded cabbage
2 cups canned tomatoes, with juice

1 tsp. chili powder
¼ tsp. pepper
dash salt
16 oz. can Great Northern beans, drained
1-2 Tbsp. canola oil

In a large saucepan, sauté onion in cooking oil until tender. Add water, ham, if desired, cabbage, tomatoes, and seasonings. Bring mixture to a boil. Lower heat. Cover and simmer 15 minutes. Add beans. Continue simmering for 20 minutes or until cabbage is tender. Could also use smoked turkey instead of ham. May add 1 cup diced carrots.

Healthy

Tasty Reuben Soup

Mrs. Dennis (Miriam) Nolt, Pine Grove, PA

7½ cups chicken broth
4-6 cups shredded cabbage
2 cups uncooked whole grain
 spaghetti noodles
1 lb. fully cooked bulk sausage or links
½ cup chopped onion
¼ tsp. garlic powder
1 cup shredded Swiss cheese (opt.)

If using sausage links, cut into thin slices. Combine all ingredients in a kettle (except cheese). Bring to a boil, then simmer for 15 minutes or until cabbage and noodles are soft. Garnish with cheese if desired. Our family does not appreciate cabbage, but they like this soup!

Potato and Cheddar Cheese Soup

Martha Wideman, Listowel, ON

2 Tbsp. butter
½ cup chopped onion
1-2 cloves garlic
4 med. potatoes, peeled and diced
1½ cups chicken stock
¼ tsp. dried thyme
1½ cups milk
1½ cups grated cheddar cheese
salt and pepper to taste
2 Tbsp. fresh chopped parsley

Melt butter in a large saucepan or Dutch oven. Add onions and garlic. Cook until tender, do not brown. Add potatoes and combine well. Stir in chicken stock and thyme. Bring to a boil. Reduce heat. Cook gently, covered, 20 minutes or until potatoes are tender. Put half the soup in blender (or all of it) and puree. Return to saucepan. Stir in milk and heat just until mixture comes to a boil. Stir in cheese. Cook gently, stirring, until cheese melts. Add salt and pepper. Garnish with parsley. Serves 4-6. We often make this without the grated cheese and like it just as well. This is one of our family favorites when served with fresh biscuits. Yum!

227 soups

Chicken Noodle Soup

Mrs. Miriam Wengerd, Sugarcreek, OH

3 qts. chicken broth
1 pt. canned chicken bits
1 cup diced carrots
1 cup diced celery
1 cup diced potatoes
1 cup chopped onions
2 Tbsp. butter
2 tsp. salt
¼ tsp. pepper
2 tsp. parsley
8 oz. bag medium noodles

Melt butter in a 6 quart kettle. Sauté chopped onions about 10 minutes. Add broth and turn on high. While you wait for this to boil, dice carrots, celery, and potatoes. When it boils add vegetables and noodles, bring to a boil then immediately reduce heat to low. Add chicken. Add salt, pepper, and parsley. Simmer until noodles are tender and vegetables are soft, about 20 minutes. This makes about 5 quarts. Serves 10.

Chicken Rice Soup

MRS. MIRIAM WENGERD, SUGARCREEK, OH

4½ cups chicken broth, divided
½ cup uncooked rice
½ cup celery, diced
½ cup carrots, diced
1 pt. canned chicken, diced

parsley
pepper
salt
¼ cup barley flour
½ cup onion, chopped

Heat 3 cups broth until boiling, add rice and cook on low for 25 minutes. Meanwhile prepare celery, carrots, and onions. Add vegetables and chicken to rice and cook on low until rice and vegetables are tender, approximately 20 minutes. Whisk flour into remaining 1½ cups broth. Add to soup stirring with spoon, over high heat until it thickens. Add salt and pepper to taste and a little parsley for color. Makes 2 quarts.

Zucchini Soup

MRS. ERVIN (ELIZABETH) BEACHY

1 qt. or more of cooked, blended zucchini
browned hamburger
your favorite cooked vegetables

salt and pepper to taste
basil

Always use zucchini that are small (6-10"). These can be frozen. Lightly steam, slice, cool and freeze to enjoy on those wintry days.

Instant Cream of Tomato Soup

MRS. JEREMY (ROSE) MILLER, ST. IGNATIUS, MT

8 oz. can no-salt tomato sauce
½ cup rice milk
¼ tsp. oregano

¼ tsp. basil
1 tsp. onion powder

Mix and simmer for 3 minutes. Do not boil. Can add salt and more or less spices to suit your taste. My two-year-old often requests this soup for lunch.

Cream of Chicken Soup

MIRIAM YODER, LAGRANGE, IN

½ cup butter
1 onion, chopped
1½ cup whole grain flour
1 cup milk

2 cups chicken broth
3 Tbsp. chicken bouillon
1 Tbsp. salt

Melt butter, add onion and flour. Stir well. Add milk, chicken broth, soup base, and salt. Cook until thick. Use in recipes calling for cream of chicken soup. You can also can this by spooning into pint jars and cold packing 20 minutes. You can also freeze it. Variations: Cream of Mushroom Soup: 2 cups chopped mushrooms. Cream of Celery Soup: 2 cups chopped celery. Cream of Onion Soup: 2 cups chopped onions.

Chicken Bouillon

3 cups yeast (brewer's or nutritional)
5 Tbsp. salt
3 Tbsp. minced dried onion
3 Tbsp. parsley
5 tsp. dried bell pepper
2½ tsp. sage
2½ tsp. celery seed

2½ tsp. garlic powder
2½ tsp. thyme
2½ tsp. marjoram
2½ tsp. rosemary
2½ tsp. tarragon
2½ tsp. paprika
1 tsp. basil

Blend in blender. Use in soups or for white sauce to make cream soups.

229 soups

Cream Soup

MRS. LAMAR (NANCY) ZIMMERMAN, STEVENS, PA

3 Tbsp. butter
½ cup flour
¼ tsp. salt

⅛-¼ tsp. black pepper
3 cups milk or stock

Melt butter. Blend in rest of ingredients, cooking and stirring until bubbly. Can be frozen. Cheese Soup: Add 1 cup cheese and ¼ tsp. dry mustard. Cream of Mushroom: ½ cup chopped mushrooms and ¼ cup onion. Cream of Celery: ½ cup celery and 1 Tbsp. onion. Cream of Chicken: broth and ¼ tsp. sage or poultry seasoning.

Homemade Mushroom Soup

MRS. DALE (TWILA) YODER, ELKFORK, KY

¼ cup butter
¼ cup whole grain flour
½ tsp. salt

2 cups broth (beef or chicken)
1 can mushrooms, blended

Melt butter, add flour. Cook for 3 minutes. Add salt, broth, and mushrooms.

Basic Cream Soup

MRS. RHODA MILLER, SUGARCREEK, OH

3 Tbsp. butter
3 Tbsp. whole grain flour
1½ tsp. chicken bouillon

½ tsp. salt
⅛ tsp. pepper
2 cups milk or water

In saucepan mix all ingredients except milk. Heat until bubbly. Slowly stir in milk, stirring constantly until thickened. Mushroom Soup: Add 2 oz. canned mushrooms, finely chopped. Celery Soup: Add ½ cup finely diced, cooked celery.

Cream of Mushroom Soup

MRS. RUBY SHETLER, HOMER, MI

3 cups water
1 cup milk or cream
½ cup whole wheat flour

½ tsp. salt
¼ cup finely chopped mushrooms

Sauté mushrooms in a teaspoon of olive oil, butter, or just a few tablespoons of water. In a saucepan, mix all ingredients except mushrooms. Whisk until smooth and thickened over medium heat. Add mushrooms. Use in place of cream of mushroom soup in casseroles, recipes, or as gravy. Makes equivalent of a quart of reconstituted cream of mushroom soup.

Healthy

Dairy-Free Cream Soups

R.M.Z., THORP, WI

6 Tbsp. olive oil
½ cup flour
1 Tbsp. chicken bouillon
½ tsp. salt
¼ tsp. pepper
4 cups rice milk

In skillet, mix all ingredients except milk. Heat until bubbly. Remove from heat and slowly blend in part of milk. Return to medium heat and stir in rest of milk as it thickens. Boil 1 minute. Add 4 oz. finely chopped mushrooms, or ½ cup finely chopped chicken, or ½ cup chopped, cooked celery. Store in refrigerator up to a week or freeze in 1-2 cup containers up to a month.

Homemade Cream Style Soup Mix

MALINDA MAST, LOBELVILLE, TN

2 cups non-fat dry milk powder
½ cup + 2 Tbsp. cornstarch
½ cup potato flakes
¼ cup chicken bouillon
2 tsp. parsley flakes
2 tsp. minced onion
1 tsp. dried celery flakes
1 tsp. minced garlic
1 tsp. onion powder
½ tsp. dried marjoram
¼ tsp. garlic powder
⅛ tsp. white pepper

In a small bowl combine all ingredients. Store in an airtight container in a cool dry place for up to a year. Yield: 3 cups (16 batches). Note: Use as a substitute for half a can of condensed cream of chicken, mushroom, or celery soup. Cook together ⅔ cup water and 3 Tbsp. soup mix until thick and bubbly, whisking occasionally. For mushroom soup: Add ¼-½ cup sautéed, sliced, mushrooms. For celery soup: Add ⅛ tsp. celery salt or one sautéed, chopped celery rib.

Cream Soup Mix

JOANNE MARTIN, BROOTEN, MN

2 cups dry milk
¾ cup cornstarch
¼ cup chicken bouillon
1 tsp. onion powder
½ tsp. dried thyme
½ tsp. dried basil
¼ tsp. black pepper

Combine all ingredients. Mix well. Store in airtight container. Yield: 3 cups dry mix. For condensed cream soup substitute, blend ⅓ cup mix and 1¼ cup water until smooth. Bring to a boil, stirring occasionally. Use as a substitute for 10¾ oz. can condensed cream of celery, chicken, or mushroom soup. Note: I like to sauté celery or mushrooms in butter and add to the soup, whichever kind the recipe asks for. Note: If using chicken bouillon (from page 229) omit thyme and basil.

Choices

Cream Soup

MRS. IVAN (CLARA) YODER, MILLERSBURG, OH

1¼ cups liquid (broth or milk)
1½ Tbsp. cornstarch (or 3 Tbsp. flour)

1 tsp. salt
⅛ tsp. pepper (opt.)

Bring 1 cup liquid to a boil. Shake thickening with ¼ cup of remaining liquid. Then stir into hot liquid. Stir constantly. Boil 3 minutes, then add to casseroles, etc. Equivalent to 1 can of cream soup.

Split Pea Soup Mix

16 oz. jar with lid and ring
¼ cup split peas
⅛ cup beef bouillon granules (beef seasoning)
⅛ cup pearl barley
¼ cup dried lentils

⅛ cup onion flakes
¾ tsp. Italian seasoning
¼ cup long grain white rice
1 bay leaf
¼ cup tiny pasta (alphabet)

Layer all ingredients except pasta in jar. Close tightly. Place pasta in small ziplock. Instructions: ½ lb. ground beef, fried; season with garlic and black pepper. Add 14 oz. canned tomatoes, 3 oz. tomato paste, 1¼ quart of water. Add the jar ingredients and cover. Simmer for 45 minutes. Add pasta and salt and simmer 20 more minutes.

Zucchini Soup Stock

MARIE BEAR, PATRIOT, OH

3 cups diced zucchini
½ cup chopped onion
1 tsp. salt

½ cup water
2 tsp. chicken bouillon

Cook until tender. Blend until well mixed. Multiply as much as wanted, and freeze. When serving, add white sauce: ½ tsp. salt, 2 Tbsp. butter, 2 Tbsp. flour, 2 cups milk.

Pizza & Sandwiches

Healthy

PIZZA IS A PERENNIAL FAVORITE WITH EVERYBODY!
Children seem to enjoy it best if it doesn't have too many toppings.

Marvin doesn't feel well when he eats hot tomato sauce so I sometimes make pizza with pesto sauce. This recipe is on page 238 and it is delicious! Try it for something different.

Sandwiches are so easy to make if you have good homemade bread on hand. We eat lots of lettuce sandwiches, or egg sandwiches are a good quickie. If you want sandwich buns check out our bread recipe on page 57. We use this same dough to make buns. Grilled hamburgers are a summer favorite. Top with lettuce and thinly sliced tomatoes, or peppers are good too.

Always be on the lookout for ways to add fresh foods to your menus.

235 pizza

Choices

Pizza

BBQ Chicken Pizza

Mrs. Miriam Wengerd, Sugarcreek, OH

Pizza Crust:

- 1 cup warm milk
- 1 Tbsp. instant yeast
- 1 tsp. honey
- 1 tsp. salt
- 2 Tbsp. olive oil
- ½ cup barley flour
- 1¾ cup wheat flour

Dissolve yeast in milk. Add honey, salt, and oil. Stir in barley flour until smooth. Add wheat flour. Sprinkle dough with more flour and knead a little in your hands. Put on greased pizza pan, spread with hands, dusting with flour to prevent stickiness. Let rise ½ hour and bake at 350° for 12 minutes. Add toppings. Nice, soft crust.

Toppings:

- 2 chicken breasts, fried and cut in chunks
- 1 cup green peppers, julienned
- 1 cup red peppers, julienned
- 1 cup onions, chopped
- 1 cup mushrooms (opt.)
- 1 tsp. Italian seasoning, dried
- 1 tsp. basil, dried
- 1 cup pineapple tidbits, drained
- 1½-2 cups BBQ sauce
- 3 cups mozzarella cheese

Prepare vegetables and mushrooms. Sauté in 1 Tbsp. oil until tender. Add basil and Italian seasoning. When crust is ready, spread with BBQ sauce. Put on vegetables and chicken, and layer pineapples over all. Last top with cheese and bake until done. Delicious!

BBQ Pizza

Monica Bazen, Grand Rapids, MI

- 1 pizza crust, unbaked
- 1 cup BBQ sauce
- diced chicken breast (1½ cup per pizza)
- green pepper, diced
- 4-5 slices bacon, fried
- ½ cup red onion, diced
- 1-2 cups cheddar cheese

Spread your pizza crust with the BBQ sauce. Sprinkle on remaining ingredients, adding cheese last. Bake at 425° until crust is golden and done in middle.

Healthy

Rice & Bean Pizza

B. Garber, Fayetteville, PA

Crust:

2 cups cooked rice
2 Tbsp. melted butter
1 egg, beaten

½ tsp. salt
¼ tsp. oregano

Mix ingredients together and press into bottom of greased 9 x 13" dish. Spread 1 pint of pizza sauce on top. Set aside. Blend in blender to make refried beans:

1 pint pinto beans
½ tsp. cumin
½ tsp. chili powder

½ tsp. onion powder
½ tsp. garlic powder

Spread beans over pizza sauce and top with cheese. Bake at 350° for 30 minutes. To add nutrition, sometimes I add ½ cup of pumpkin puree and/or ½ cup frozen chopped spinach to the beans before blending.

Rice Pizza

Mrs. Larry (Liana) Cable, Trotwood, OH

2 cups cooked brown rice
2 Tbsp. butter

1 egg, beaten

Mix together and put in the bottom of a 9 x 13" baking dish. Put baked beans on top. Add mushrooms and black olives. Sprinkle with shredded cheese. Sift pizza seasoning on top of cheese. Bake at 350° for 30 minutes.

Whole Wheat Pizza Crust

Mrs. Kathryn Hershberger, Clare, MI

1 Tbsp. yeast
1 cup warm water
1½ tsp. salt

1 tsp. honey
2 Tbsp. olive oil
2 cups whole wheat flour

Dissolve yeast in water, add honey, oil, and salt, then add 1 cup flour and beat well. Gradually add last cup of flour. Knead on floured surface for 5-10 minutes. Do not make too stiff. Put in bowl and cover and let rise until double in size, about 1 hour. Roll out for 1 large cookie sheet. Bake at 425° for 15-20 minutes.

Whole Wheat Pizza Crust

2½-3 cups wheat flour, divided
1½ tsp. salt
1 Tbsp. rapadura

1 Tbsp. yeast
2 Tbsp. olive oil
1 cup warm water

Mix 1 cup flour with other dry ingredients. Add oil and water. Add more flour as needed to form a soft dough. Let rise ½ hour, then roll out onto large bar pan or 2 round pizza pans. Bake 5 minutes then add some cheese and your favorite toppings.

Herb Pizza Crust

BARBARA SUE TROYER, EVART, MI

1 Tbsp. honey
1 Tbsp. oregano
½ Tbsp. garlic powder
1 cup water

1 Tbsp. salt
1 Tbsp. basil
1 Tbsp. yeast
2½ cups whole wheat flour

Mix honey, water, and yeast. Let stand 10 minutes until bubbly. Mix in seasonings, then add flour gradually until a smooth, elastic ball of dough is formed. Knead on floured board a few minutes. Use fingers or rolling pin to spread on pizza pan. Bake at 350° for 15-20 minutes or until crust is done. Top with pizza sauce, cheese, and your choice of toppings.

Pizza Crust

MARLENE ZIMMERMAN, ORCHARD, IA

4 cups wheat, spelt, or Kamut flour
1 Tbsp. yeast
1 Tbsp. honey

1½ cups warm water
1 Tbsp. olive oil
1½ tsp. salt

In mixing bowl, add water and then remaining ingredients, adding enough flour to clean sides of bowl. Knead dough for 3-5 minutes or until gluten develops. Divide dough in half. Roll out and put in pizza pan. Brush crust with oil and prick with fork. Prebake 5-8 minutes. Top with favorite toppings or put in freezer for later use.

Yorkshire Pizza

MABEL ZIMMERMAN

Bake the Yorkshire Pudding* for 15 minutes then pour on hot pizza sauce and add any other pizza toppings and finish baking 10-15 minutes more.

*Recipe on page 33.

Healthy

Herb Pizza Crust

MRS. MIRIAM WENGERD, SUGARCREEK, OH

1 Tbsp. honey
1 Tbsp. oregano
½ Tbsp. garlic powder
1 cup warm water
1 egg

1 Tbsp. salt
1 Tbsp. basil
1 Tbsp. yeast (instant)
1½ cup wheat flour
1 cup barley flour

Mix honey, water, yeast and egg. Mix in seasonings, then add flour gradually. Knead on floured surface. Spread on greased cookie sheet. Let rise 15 minutes. Bake 10 minutes then top with pizza sauce and Bulgur Burger (page 168). Spread cheese on top and bake until pizza is ready. This crust can be baked then topped with cheese and put in oven until melted then cut in strips to use as bread sticks. Dip in pizza sauce—yummy!

Sandwiches

241

pizza

Fried Tomato Sandwiches

SUSIE NISLEY, DANVILLE, OH

8 slices firm spelt bread
3 oz. cream cheese
1 Tbsp. homemade Miracle Whip (pages 128-129)

½ tsp. snipped chives
½ tsp. dried dill weed

Butter each side of bread. Combine cream cheese, Miracle Whip, chives, and dill weed; mix until smooth and put thickly on 4 buttered slices; top with tomato slices large enough to fit bread and put remaining bread on top. Press down slightly. Dip sandwiches in a mixture of: 2 beaten eggs, ¼ cup milk, salt and pepper. Fry in butter or coconut oil. Very good!

Onion Sandwiches

MISS MARY NISLEY, DANVILLE, OH

1 large onion, chopped
1 cup homemade Miracle Whip
   (pages 128-129)
1 Tbsp. vinegar

1 Tbsp. honey
2 Tbsp. horseradish
1 tsp. celery seed

Soak onion in milk overnight and rinse. Then, next day, mix the rest of ingredients, toast like you would toasted cheese sandwiches. Very good!

Choices

Eggplant Pizza Sandwiches

Spread each slice of bread generously with tomato sauce, sprinkle generously with oregano and Italian seasoning. Slice and peel eggplant ¼-½" thick, 1 slice per sandwich. Chop onion, garlic (opt.), mushrooms (opt.), and cheese (opt.). Wrap sandwiches in foil and bake at 350° for 45 minutes (or 400° for ½ hour) or until eggplant is starting to get soft. Variation: Toast bread. Fry eggplant. Put sandwiches together and omit baking unless to melt cheese on top. Eggplant is good on pizza crust, too. Season and top with cheese.

Grilled Hamburgers

KAYLENE HARTZLER, TENNILLE, GA

3 eggs, lightly beaten
1 Tbsp. dried minced onion
1 tsp. Worcestershire sauce
½ tsp. salt

pinch pepper
¼ tsp. liquid smoke
½ cup pizza sauce

Mix together and add bread crumbs until the consistency of hamburger. Add 1 lb. hamburger, shape into patties, and grill.

Sloppy Joes

SUSAN STALTER, MILLERSBURG, OH

1½ lb. hamburger
¾ cup rolled oats
1 tsp. salt
½ cup chopped celery
½ cup chopped green peppers
½ cup chopped onion

1 cup ketchup
1½ cups water
2 Tbsp. fructose
2 Tbsp. vinegar
1 Tbsp. Worcestershire sauce

Brown meat. Drain off most of grease. Add everything else and bring to a boil. Simmer ½-1½ hours. Serve with whole wheat bread.

Beef & Zucchini Burgers

MRS. JOHN (EVA MAY) YODER, CLARE, MI

1 lb. ground beef
1 small zucchini, shredded (6 oz.)
½ cup oatmeal
1 tsp. salt

1 large egg
½ tsp. black pepper
minced onion or garlic (opt.)

Mix and fry as usual.

Healthy

Open-Faced Turkey, Apple, Cheese Sandwich

MONICA BAZEN, GRAND RAPIDS, MI

4 slices rye bread
½ cup salad dressing
2 tsp. honey
½ tsp. prepared horseradish sauce

2 cups cooked turkey or chicken
12 thin slices red or green apple
4 large slices Swiss cheese

Preheat broiler. Place bread slices on broiler pan. Lightly toast bread (1-2 minutes). Remove from oven and set aside. In small bowl, whisk together salad dressing, honey, and horseradish. Add turkey and stir to coat. Top each bread slice with turkey mixture, sliced apples, and cheese. Return pan to oven and broil for 5 minutes or until golden brown.

Grilled Hamburgers

MRS. IVAN (NANCY) PEIGHT, McVEYTOWN, PA

2 lb. ground hamburger
2 eggs
1 cup bread crumbs

1 tsp. garlic salt
1 tsp. onion powder
1 tsp. steak seasoning salt

Mix all together and form patties. Brush with Italian dressing while grilling. This makes 8 or 10 burgers, depending on how big you make them.

243

pizza

Chicken Salad

CHRISTY NOLT, DODGE CENTER, MN

2½ cups cooked, diced chicken
1 stalk celery, chopped
⅓ cup chopped onion
1 tsp. garlic salt

1 tsp. pepper
1½ cup homemade mayonnaise
  (pages 126-127)

Mix all ingredients together. Great for sandwiches or as a spread for crackers.

Salad Roll-Ups

MRS. JOE GARBER, PRATTSBURGH, NY

1-6" piece romaine lettuce
3 Tbsp. mashed banana
1 Tbsp. sauerkraut
1 Tbsp. onion, chopped fine
1 Tbsp. radish, chopped fine

1 Tbsp. carrots, chopped fine
2 leaves spinach, diced
1 clove garlic, diced (opt.)
sprinkle of salt

Place lettuce on plate, layer ingredients in order given, onto leaf. Roll up. A unique and nutritious finger food!

Choices

BLT Bites

16-20 cherry tomatoes
1 lb. bacon, cooked and crumbled
½ cup homemade mayonnaise
   (pages 126-127)

⅓ cup chopped green onions
3 Tbsp. grated Parmesan cheese
2 Tbsp. snipped fresh parsley

Cut a thin slice off each tomato top. Scoop out and discard pulp. Invert the tomatoes on a paper towel to drain. In a small bowl combine all remaining ingredients; mix well. Spoon into tomatoes. Refrigerate for several hours.

Burritos

I lived in Mexico for three years. The standard school lunch was pinto beans, cooked, then mashed. (Add garlic while cooking.) Season with salt, taco seasoning, and hot pepper as desired. Cheese can be mashed into beans. Meat is optional. This should neither be dry nor soupy. Fill flour tortillas and serve hot or cold. May be kept frozen until needed. To reheat, spread a little butter on burrito and toast on frying pan or griddle.

Dairy

WE ALL HAVE OUR DREAMS, DON'T WE? ONE OF MINE IS
to have a family cow...someday! Meanwhile I enjoy learning about
making butter and all the other goodies that can be made with milk.

When dealing with milk and yogurt I like to use glass jars and bowls.
I don't like to use plastic. Milk kept in glass jars will stay fresh longer.
Don't skim off the top of your set yogurt and throw it away! This is real
cream and should not be discarded. I put it in the blender with some
of the yogurt. Whiz until smooth, and stir into the rest of the yogurt
for rich creamy results.

Raw milk is great for smoothies, and so is yogurt. Cold yogurt with
granola and frozen blueberries is a winner for breakfast. A good way to
use up canned peaches that are a little old is to put them in the blender
with some yogurt. Use to pour over baked oatmeal, top with berries
and you have a summer supper.

It seems healthy choices always involve fresh ingredients and dairy
foods are no exception.

247 dairy

Butter

Butter

Collect cream until you have enough to fill your blender or churn ⅓ full. Set the cream out until it reaches 62°. When it is ready to churn, wash your churn with hot, then cold, water. This helps prevent sticking to the paddles and sides. Pour in your cream and churn it. You should have butter within ten minutes. Churn until it forms big clumps of butter. Take the butter out of the churn and put it in a bowl. Rinse with cold water, working it until the water is clear. Put butter on a cutting board and work until all the water is out of it. Add salt to taste. Save the buttermilk for drinking or baking. It makes delicious pancakes, whoopie pies, cakes, muffins, etc. Use buttermilk instead of milk in any baked goods that use it.

Renee's Cultured Butter

MRS. ELMER (RENEE) KROPP, HARRISON, AR

Skim cream off raw milk yogurt and churn. Strain off buttermilk and wash as desired. Add salt to taste. We love this butter! For a delicious snack, melt cultured butter and dribble over popcorn. Salt to taste. Enjoy!

Susan's Butter

SUSAN STALTER, MILLERSBURG, OH

Whip 2 gallons cream in Bosch mixer, 8 cups at a time using cookie whisks. Whip until it has passed through the whipped cream stage, and the butter is in balls on the whisks. Drain buttermilk. Put all the 4 chunks of butter back in mixer and knead with dough hook to get out all the buttermilk you can. Drain. Add 1 pint water and knead to wash the butter. Drain. Repeat until water comes off clean. Mix in 1 tsp. real salt. Freeze in 1 cup portions.

TIP

Mom used to churn all our butter and said it seemed to make butter faster if set out of fridge until it was 62° to 63°, then churn it. She used to let the cream sour first, but we have found sweet cream makes good butter and isn't quite as bitter.

— Mrs. Emery (Naomi) Stutzman, Hickory, KY

Healthy

Sandra's Cultured Butter

SANDRA SMUCKER, JOHN DAY, OR

raw cream   whey (opt.)

Let cream set at room temperature for around 2 days, sometimes it will be thick. Churn until butter forms. Drain off buttermilk (the buttermilk will be cultured). Rinse and work butter to get all the buttermilk out. Add salt to taste. Cultured butter has many good bacteria like yogurt and sauerkraut.

Preserving Butter

EDNA MILLER

Form butter into patties, then place them in a crock with salty brine, so strong that an egg can be floated on the surface of the water. Keep in cool place. In this way butter can be kept for months.

Cynthia's Butter

CYNTHIA KORVER, NEW OXFORD, PA

1½ quart cream, room temperature   ½ tsp. salt

In ½ gallon jar or blender, pour 1½ quart cream. Place on blender. Blend on high until glass on top of jar comes clean, about 10 minutes. If in blender jar, pour into ½ gallon jar. Put regular lid on jar and shake or roll on lap gently, for about 10 minutes or until butter collects in smooth, shiny balls. Pour off buttermilk into another jar. Dump butter into a bowl. With back of spoon, squish butter against side of bowl until as much buttermilk as possible is squeezed out. (Butter will be sweeter longer if all buttermilk is out.) Mix in salt. Refrigerate or freeze. Makes about 1-1¼ cups butter, depending on density of cream. Tip: Let milk sit for 24 hours or longer for thicker cream, the longer the thicker. Buttermilk may be used in baking bread or anything else calling for buttermilk.

Lorene's Butter

MRS. MAYNARD (LORENE) MAST, DALTON, WI

To make butter: Take cream off fresh milk and heat until scalding, cool and refrigerate for a couple of days. Set out until it reaches 60-70 degrees. Churn until butter forms, wash well and salt it. 4-5 day old cream seems to turn to butter faster when churned. To can cream: Boil cream a little bit, put in jars and cold pack for 1 hour. Can be used like fresh cream and has the same flavor.

Yogurt

Berry Yogurt

MRS. MIRIAM WENGERD, SUGARCREEK, OH

1 gal. milk
2½ Tbsp. unflavored gelatin

½ cup plain yogurt
1 cup sweetener (opt.)

Heat milk in 6 qt. kettle to 180°. Remove from heat, let cool to 130°. Meanwhile, soak gelatin in ½ cup cold water. When milk reaches 130°, stir in gelatin, yogurt, and sweetener. Beat well. Set in oven for 8 hours (on pilot). Raspberry Sauce: 6 cups frozen black raspberries (any berry can be used), 1 cup sweetener (opt.). Bring to boil and cook for 7 minutes. Then put in blender and blend 45 seconds. Strain to remove seeds, if using raspberries. Chill.

When yogurt has set for 8 hours, chill 4 hours. Then put in blender with raspberry sauce and pour into bowl. Chill until set. Marvin was skeptical about homemade yogurt, so I knew if I started making it, it would have to be absolutely delicious! This yogurt passed with flying colors!

Raw Milk Yogurt Starter

MRS. ELMER (RENEE) KROPP, HARRISON, AR

1 qt. raw milk

1 sterilized quart jar, lid, ring

Pour milk into jar. Cover with lid and ring and place in oven with light on (approximately 90°) for 12-36 hours or until set. For best results, use milk that has not yet been cooled. Starter only needs to be made once. Following batches of yogurt may be used for starter. Note: Good starter has no bubbles. If it looks bubbly, discard and try again.

Raw Milk Yogurt

MRS. ELMER (RENEE) KROPP, HARRISON, AR

1 qt. raw milk   2 Tbsp. yogurt starter

Stir yogurt starter into milk. Cover with lid and ring and place in oven with light on (approximately 90°) for 8-12 hours or until set.

Yogurt

MARTHA BEILER, QUARRYVILLE, PA

Heat 1 gallon milk to 180°. Mix ½ cup tapioca starch with water. Stir quickly into hot milk. Add ½ cup sweetener and vanilla. Cool to 100° then mix in ⅛ tsp. yogurt culture. Put in oven for 10-12 hours, then stir in flavoring if desired.

Simple Yogurt

MRS. D.E.B., BONDUEL, WI

1 cup store bought yogurt (for starter)   2 qts. raw milk

Heat milk in medium-sized saucepan over medium heat. Check frequently with candy thermometer until it reaches 185°-190°. Take off stove and let cool down to 110°. Add the yogurt and stir with wire whip very well. Dump into a large glass jar if available. If not, a plastic or other container works too. Put lid on, and place in oven on rack, with oven on pilot. Let set undisturbed for 8 hours. Take out and place in refrigerator. Do not stir until it is very cold. When only 1 cup is left, later on, reserve that for starter for the next batch, instead of store bought. Only when yogurt begins tasting sour or strong, do you need to buy other starter. We keep this on hand constantly and we all love it, served with real maple syrup as a sweetener, or thickened, canned fruit. We especially like the yogurt/maple syrup mixture on top of pancakes and french toast! We hope you enjoy this yogurt as much as we do.

251

dairy

TIP

When I make my yogurt, I use an insulated cooler (a small ice chest), fill it with hot water, set jars of yogurt in it for several hours. When an inserted knife comes out clean, it's done. Sometimes I let it set overnight. I found it useful as I don't have a pilot light, since I have an electric stove. Any yogurt recipe of your choice could be used. I put mine in a 2 quart jar. I like the results.

—Mrs. Wanda Fox, Ephrata, PA

Choices

Yogurt

Mrs. Bennie (Rebecca) Weaver, Apple Creek, OH

2 qts. goat milk
2 Tbsp. active yogurt
1 cup sweetener

1 Tbsp. gelatin
⅓ cup cold water

Heat milk in saucepan to 180°. Remove and let cool to 130°. Meanwhile, soak gelatin in cold water, add to milk at 180°. Mix sweetener and yogurt and add to milk at 130°, mixing well. Put lid slanting on dipper and put in oven with pilot on for 8 hours or overnight. After taking it out, beat with egg beater to make it smooth. Put in containers, jars, etc, and chill. To begin process again, use 2 Tbsp. of this yogurt. For different flavors, add 1 cup pie filling before beating with egg beater.

Homemade Yogurt

Mrs. Ivan (Nancy) Peight, McVeytown, PA

1 gal. milk
2 Tbsp. unflavored gelatin

1 cup plain yogurt
1 cup sweetener

Heat milk to 180°. Cool to 130°. Soak gelatin in ½ cup cold water. Add gelatin mixture, sweetener, and yogurt. Pour into 5 quart jars. Fill an ice chest (or a 5 gallon thermos works well) with hottest tap water. Put your filled jars into the hot water, making sure that the water comes to the neck of the jars. (If you are using the 5 gallon thermos you will need to lay one jar on top of the other 4 jars.) Let set 12 hours, then refrigerate. The jars will often seal which keeps the yogurt fresh. Serve with pie filling or add a Tbsp. of jelly.

Homemade Yogurt

Mrs. Allen R. Byler, Smicksburg, PA

2 qt. milk (whole or skim)
6 Tbsp. plain yogurt with active cultures

1 Tbsp. plain gelatin
¼ cup xylitol sweetener (opt.)

Soak gelatin in 1 cup cold milk. In a heavy saucepan over low heat, heat milk until tiny bubbles appear around the side of pan, about 180°. Put gelatin mixture into the hot milk and stir. Cool to 100°-110°. If sweetener is desired, add it now. Remove scum from surface and discard. Stir in yogurt until well mixed. Pour into a stainless steel or glass container with cover. Wrap with a heavy towel and set in a warm place for 5 hours or longer, until it thickens. An insulated bag is great. Hint: Can be put on the iron kettle or hot water tank. Can serve with thickened fruit.

Healthy

Yogurt

Mrs. Rhoda Miller, Sugarcreek, OH

1 gal. milk
2 Tbsp. unflavored gelatin

½ cup plain yogurt
sweetener of your choice

Heat milk to 180°. Let cool to 130°. Soak gelatin in ½ cup cold water. Add gelatin mixture, plain yogurt, and sweetener. Beat all together and set in oven with pilot on for 8 hours. Skim off skin on top and beat well. Add pie filling or flavoring of your choice. Chill. Beat well before serving and you will have delicious, smooth yogurt.

Cheese

Ricotta Cheese

sweet cheese whey (fresh or frozen)
sour whey or lemon juice

whole sweet milk
buttermilk

Begin by heating sweet whey. Add ¼ cup whole milk for each quart used. Heat to about 200°. When it reaches this temperature, stir in sour whey or lemon juice. A scum of coagulated albumin will appear on the top of whey. Scoop off with slotted spoon. Continue to add lemon (small amounts) until ricotta ceases to appear. Put the ricotta in cheesecloth and allow to drain. Salt. Add buttermilk, but don't make it too moist. Put in press for 6-7 hours.

253

dairy

Pepper Cheese

1 gal. milk
¼ cup vinegar
1 Tbsp. salt
4 Tbsp. diced jalapeños

3 Tbsp. diced olives
2 Tbsp. chopped pimento
1 clove chopped garlic

Slowly heat milk to boiling. Add vinegar. Let stand until curd forms (couple hours or overnight). Strain and drain off whey. To curd, add salt and vegetables. Press.

Muenster Cheese

BARBARA SUE TROYER, EVART, MI

Let 2½ gallons sour milk set until thick like junket. Scald until it's too hot to hold your hand in, then pour into a cheesecloth. Let hang until curds are really dry—overnight or 24 hours. Crumble curds and mix 2 heaping tsp. soda and ½ cup butter into them. Let set for 2 hours, then put in double boiler. Add 1 cup sour cream and melt. When melted, add another cup of sour cream and 1 Tbsp. salt. Mix well; pour into a buttered mold. Let set until completely cold and slice. Sometimes I use cheese powder for extra flavor.

Raw Cheese

MRS. JUNIOR KAUFFMAN, REDDING, IA

Let 1 gallon raw milk set until sour (thick and whey divided), put in cheesecloth bag and hang to drip, or put in a colander lined with cheesecloth for 6-12 hours. Add salt and herbs if desired. If dry, cream can be added. To take more of the sour taste out, soak cheese in water overnight and then drain again. You can produce a tasty dessert cheese by adding the following:

½ tsp. cinnamon
2 Tbsp. honey (or maple syrup)
¼ tsp. allspice

¼ tsp. nutmeg
¼ tsp. vanilla

For a flavorful herb cheese, add:

2 Tbsp. chopped fresh chives or onions
1 tsp. chopped fresh dill leaves
1 small clove garlic, chopped

¼ tsp. black pepper
salt to taste

Delicious Hard Cheese

Martha Wideman, Listowel, ON

4 gal. milk
4-5 oz. culture
½ tsp. cheese color

1 tsp. rennet mixed with ½
   cup cold water
4 Tbsp. salt

Heat milk to 88-90°. Add culture, mix well. Add color, mix well. Add rennet and water. Stir no longer than 1 minute. Let stand ½-1 hour. Chop curds into small pieces. Heat on high, stirring constantly, to 98°-100° (not higher). Remove from heat and let set 10 minutes, then pour off whey. Okay if a little stays in. Break up curds and mix in salt. Dump in cheesecloth lined mold—DO NOT press. After 1 hour flip cheese upside down, then let sit in mold for 24 hours. Remove from mold. Keep at room temperature for a week. Turn cheese daily. Store in cool place. Usually ready in two weeks.

Simple Slicing Cheese

Mrs. Rebecca Zook, Myerstown, PA

2 gal. whole milk
1 pkg. direct set or
   4 oz. prepared mesophilic starter

¼ rennet tablet dissolved in
   ¼ cup cool water
2 Tbsp. real salt

255

dairy

Heat the milk to 90°. Add the starter and diluted rennet. Stir with an up and down motion for 1 minute. Allow to set for 30-45 minutes, or until curd gives a clean break. Using a knife, press down into the curd at a 45 degree angle. If the curds separate cleanly and clearly around the inserted knife, you have a clean break, and the curds are ready for cutting. Cut into ¼" cubes. Cut ¼" strips, making sure to use a long knife to reach to the bottom of your kettle. Next, cut the ¼" strips the other way through the kettle. When you are done, you'll have a checkerboard pattern of ¼" square cubes. Then with the knife at a slant and using the previously cut lines, cut the curd at a 45 degree angle. Turn the pot around and repeat the 45 degree angle cutting. Over the next 20 minutes, gradually increase the temperature to 95°, stirring gently every few minutes to keep curds from matting. Let the curds set for 5 minutes, undisturbed. Drain off the whey. Add the salt and keep the curds at 95° for 30 minutes. Line a mold with cheesecloth and fill with curds. Press at 35 lbs. pressure for 6 hours. Remove the cheese from the mold and store covered in refrigerator for up to 2 weeks.

Easy Cheese

Barbara Sue Troyer, Evart, MI

Heat 2 gallons milk to 180°. Remove from heat and add ¾ cup apple cider vinegar. Stir until it separates. Pour curds into a colander lined with a cheesecloth, and set on pail. Mix in 2½ tsp. salt, and ¼ cup powder cheese if you want yellow cheese. We use a cheese press, but you can use a #10 can with both ends cut out and set in a colander. Fill a 2 quart jar with water and set on top of curds. Curds must be hot so they will hang together.

Easy Homemade Soft Cheese

Sandra Smucker, John Day, OR

1 gal. skim raw milk   4 Tbsp. whey (optional)

Place the milk in a clean glass container and let stand at room temperature for 1-4 days, until it separates. Line a large strainer with a clean dish towel and set over a bowl. Pour in the separated milk. Cover and let stand at room temperature for several hours. Tie up the corners of the towel over a wooden spoon being careful not to squeeze it. Place across the top of a container to let more whey drip out. When the bag stops dripping, the cheese is ready. I like to add some organic sour cream to make it more creamy. Also I add garlic and onion powder, salt, and any dried herbs that sound good. This tastes excellent on crackers and baked potatoes. The whey is very good for you. Save it for your next batch or use in bread, etc. It lasts for 6 months in the refrigerator.

Farmhouse Cheese

Esther Oberholtzer, Penn Yan, NY

Warm Milk: Pour 2 gallons whole milk into a stainless steel pot, set in warm water, stir, and add more hot water until milk temperature reaches 90°. Ripen Milk: Cover pot and leave for 45 minutes to ripen at 90°. (Add cheese color at this point if you wish.) Add Cheese Rennet: Dissolve ¼ of a cheese rennet tablet in ¼ cup of cooled sterile water, break and crush until completely dissolved. Add to milk and stir for 1 minute. Keep pot at 90° by regulating water. Protect pot from drafts. Let set until curd breaks clean: Let set undisturbed until a firm curd forms, 30-45 minutes. Test firmness with finger; it is ready to cut when curd breaks clean. Cut curd 4 ways: Cut curds into ½" cubes with a long bladed knife that reaches to the bottom. Cut curds one way, then across to form ½" blocks. Hold knife at a 45° angle, and cut in both directions. When curd is cut, gently stir, turning them over, bottom to top, cutting anything that is still too big. Scald Curd: Run hot water in sink, put pot in and raise temperature slowly to 100°. Temperature must not rise more than 2° every 5 minutes, nor exceed 100°. Stir gently, as it warms, should take 30 minutes. Drain Whey: Cover and let curd settle 5 minutes, pour whey off. Pour curds in a cheesecloth. Hang Curds: Knot corners of the cloth together and hang to drain 1 hour at 70°. Salt Curds: Pour drained curds into a scalded bowl, break gently with fingers into walnut-sized pieces. Mix 2 Tbsp. salt in thoroughly. Molding and Pressing Curd: Line mold with cheesecloth, put curds in, fold cheesecloth neatly over top when full. Place under 20 lb. pressure for 10 minutes, turn upside down and increase pressure to 30 lb. for 10 minutes. Repeat twice at 10 minute intervals and increase 10 lbs. each time. The last time, leave cheese under 50 lbs. pressure for 14-16 hours. Finishing Cheese: Remove from mold and carefully peel cheesecloth away, being careful not to rip surface of cheese mat until a rind has developed and surface is dry. Turn several times a day. After 3-5 days it will be ready to wax. Waxing and Curing Cheese: Paint melted cheese wax on a cool, dry cheese. Cover cheese completely. Cure your Farmhouse Cheese at 50° for at least 2 months. Turn cheese daily for 2 weeks and several times thereafter until it is eaten. A delicious hard cheddar-type cheese.

French Soft Spread Goat Cheese

Kathy Lotter, Silverwood, MI

1 gal. goat's milk
½ cup buttermilk or kefir

½ tsp. liquid rennet

Warm the milk to room temperature, about 72-80°. Stir in the buttermilk or kefir. Mix well; add ½ tsp. liquid rennet, and stir well into milk; cover and let set. Leave at room temperature for 12-18 hours, usually overnight. The cheese is ready to start draining when it looks like thickened yogurt. There will probably be a layer of whey floating on the top. Line a large bowl with cheesecloth or an old, clean pillowcase, cut in half. Pour mixture into bowl, and tie the ends of cloth, and hang to drain for 6-8 hours. You can speed up the draining process by scraping the sides of the bag towards the middle once or twice during the hanging time. When the bag has stopped dripping, the cheese should be the consistency of cream cheese. From this you can make a variety of flavored cheese balls and other goodies. This is a soft, mild cheese. It can be shaped into logs or rolled into balls, or can be used in recipes that ask for cream cheese.

Cheese Seasonings

Kathy Lotter, Silverwood, MI

Chive & Garlic:

1 lb. soft spread cheese
1 tsp. sea salt

¼ tsp. garlic powder
2 tsp. dried chives (2 Tbsp. fresh)

French Onion:

1 lb. soft spread cheese
3 Tbsp. minced onion

1 tsp. sea salt

Dill:

1 lb. soft spread cheese
1 tsp. dill weed

1 tsp. sea salt
chopped pickle (opt.)

Pineapple Walnut:

1 lb. cheese
¾ cup drained, crushed pineapple

1 tsp. sea salt
½ cup chopped walnuts

These seasonings are for the preceding cheese recipe.

Smear Cheese

Mrs. Esh, PA

20 cups dry cottage cheese crumbs
(takes about 6-7 gal. skim milk)
6 tsp. baking soda

12 tsp. Celtic sea salt
6-8 cups hot cream

Make sure curds are very dry or it won't take any cream, then it isn't as rich. Work the crumbs in cheesecloth, squeeze and punch until no more whey can be squeezed out. Note: This is very important for a rich tasting cheese. Work soda into dry crumbs, let stand 3 hours. Melt 1 lb. butter in large kettle over boiling water or use a burner plate. When melted and hot, add cheese and stir until melted and smooth. Add hot cream a little at a time, very slowly. Test if thick enough by putting some in freezer to chill. Add more salt if you had to add more than 6-8 cups cream, or to suit taste.

Buttermilk Cheese

Mrs. Glenn Zimmerman, Greenwood, WI

Let ½ gallon buttermilk set out approximately 12-24 hours until very thick, being careful not to disturb it. Pour into a kettle and heat slowly to 160°. Strain through cheesecloth until curds are dry. Work ½ tsp. soda into curds. Melt 2½ Tbsp. butter in a kettle and add curds. Stir well. Heat in double boiler until curds are melted, stirring often. Add ½ tsp. salt and 1 Tbsp. cheddar cheese powder (opt.), and beat well until blended. Pour into small containers. Chill.

259

dairy

Mozzarella Cheese

Mrs. Ervin (Hannah) Hostetler, Pleasantville, TN

2 gal. whole milk
2½ tsp. citric acid, diluted
in ¼ cup cold water

½ gal. water, heated to 170° with 1 cup salt
⅛ tsp. rennet (or ¼ tablet, dissolved
in ¼ cup cool water)

Stir citric acid into cold milk. Mix 2 minutes. Heat milk to 88°. Remove from heat and add rennet. Stir 15-20 minutes. Let stand ½ hour, until it coagulates, then cut into ½" squares. Let set 5-10 minutes, until whey separates from curds. Heat slowly to 108°. Keep well stirred. Remove from heat and let set 20 minutes, stirring occasionally. Drain in colander 15 minutes. Cut drained curds in strips and lay crisscross in bowl. Pour hot salt water over curd strips and stretch with wooden spoon, pulling up and down until nice and soft. Remove from water and knead until smooth. Shape into ball. Put in mold and refrigerate.

Mozzarella Cheese

KAREN MILLER, PARTRIDGE, KS

2 level tsp. citric acid
1 gal. whole milk
⅛-¼ tsp. lipase powder (opt.)

¼ tsp. liquid rennet
1 tsp. cheese salt

Dilute rennet in ¼ cup cool water. Add citric acid to milk and mix thoroughly. If using lipase powder, dissolve in ¼ cup cool water and allow to sit for 20 minutes, then add to milk. Heat the milk to 88°. (The milk will start to curdle.) Gently stir in diluted rennet and continue heating, *without stirring*, until temperature reaches 105°. (Warning: The temperature rises very quickly at the last.) Turn off heat and let curd set, covered, for 10-30 minutes. (Curds should look like thick yogurt.) Pour off whey and lift out curds into microwavable bowl. Press the curds gently with hands, pouring off and squeezing out as much whey as possible. Microwave on HIGH for 1 minute. Knead whey with spoon and pull curds like taffy. Sprinkle salt on top. Microwave on HIGH two more times, 35 seconds each. After each time, taste a bit and add more salt, if necessary. Knead in bowl and then pull like taffy (if too hot, use rubber gloves) until it's smooth. When it's smooth and shiny, it's ready to eat. Grease bowl lightly, add cheese. Cover lightly with plastic wrap and cool. (Or better yet, slice while still warm and enjoy your own string cheese!)

Kraft Cheese

ESTHER OBERHOLTZER, PENN YAN, NY

5 cups real dry cheese curds
2 tsp. soda
½ cup butter

1 cup hot cream
2½ tsp. salt

Work soda into curds. Let stand several hours. Melt butter in saucepan and have it hot. Add curds. Stir constantly until it's melted and smooth. Put in the cream, a little at a time. Add salt last. Add more milk if a spreading cheese is preferred.

Cottage Cheese

Cottage Cheese

B. Garber, Fayetteville, PA

Let 2 gallons fresh, raw milk set out all day to bring to room temperature. Skim cream and add 2 cups cultured buttermilk. Heat to 72°. (If your house is warm enough, it may not need to be heated at all.) Let set out at room temperature (above 72°) all night (at least 12 hours) until cheese is firm, and watery around edges. Cut through curd with knife both ways, making a ½" grid. Let set 10-15 minutes. Heat slowly to 115° and stir occasionally. (Ideally, 5° every 5 minutes.) Cook at 115° until curds feel firm; they should not stick together when squeezed, and the inside of the curds should be dry and granular. This may take 20 minutes. Let set ½ hour. Strain through cheesecloth into container big enough to hold whey. Gather up corners and work gently with hands to get whey out. Rinse in fresh water (dip cheesecloth in and out and work gently). Hang and let drip for about an hour. Add 1 Tbsp. salt and reserved cream that was skimmed (may use milk). May need to add extra milk.

Cottage Cheese

Mrs. Emery (Naomi) Stutzman, Hickory, KY

Heat 1 gallon milk to lukewarm 100°-110°. The sooner you can get it to thicken, the better the flavor. To speed up the thickening process add 1-2 Tbsp. buttermilk. Keep in a warm place. (Setting it in warm water in an ice chest helps.) If done in the evening, it's usually thickened by the next morning. Then heat ¾ gallon water to boiling, 110°, and pour over milk. Let set just a little, ½-1 minute. Then stir a little, and pour into a strainer or drainer to drain. Stir several times to make sure holes are opened and can drain. Refrigerate. Add 1 tsp. salt or to taste. Add ½ cup cream, or until it suits you. We prefer whipping cream first. The quicker it's made, the better tasting the cottage cheese will be, not as sharp-tasting.

Cottage Cheese

Karen Miller, Partridge, KS

1 gal. milk
1 cup white vinegar
salt to taste
cream/milk

Heat milk to 190°-200°. (The hotter the milk, the harder the curds.) Turn off heat, add vinegar and stir well. Let set for 1-2 hours, drain well, and rinse with water several times. You may need to break up curds if too hard. Add salt and cream/milk until it tastes and looks right to you.

Raw Milk Cottage Cheese

MRS. ELMER (RENEE) KROPP, HARRISON, AR

raw milk yogurt   salt
cream

Gently pour raw milk yogurt into a 4½ qt. kettle. Place 4½ qt. kettle into a 6 qt. kettle and fill 6 qt. with water to level of yogurt. Leave undisturbed for 15 minutes. Cut yogurt into ¼" cubes with long, sharp knife. Place over low heat. Gradually bring to 100°, not more than 2° every 5 minutes, stirring occasionally. Keep at 100° for 30 minutes. Pour into cheesecloth-lined bowl and hang up to drain for 6-8 hours or until as dry as desired. Place the curds in a bowl and break up any pieces that are matted together. Add several Tbsp. of heavy cream to produce a creamier texture. Salt may be added to taste.

Cottage Cheese

SUSAN STALTER, MILLERSBURG, OH

Heat 1 gallon milk to exactly 190°. While constantly stirring, add ½ cup apple cider vinegar. Cool to room temperature. Drain all the whey out of the curds. Grate curds and refrigerate in tightly sealed container. To serve, add cream to the amount you are going to use until it reaches desired consistency. Note: Whey is an excellent soil fertilizer.

Cottage Cheese from Goat's Milk

MARIE BEAR, PATRIOT, OH

Use 1 gallon goat's milk, 2 days old or older. Set out on countertop until clabbered (separated). Pour into a 12 x 17" cake pan. Put into oven at 200° for 1 hour. Turn oven off and leave in for another hour. Drain through cloth. Refrigerate.

Cottage Cheese

SANDRA SMUCKER, JOHN DAY, OR

1 gallon skim milk (raw)   1 cup cultured buttermilk

Stir together and let sit for 2-4 days until clabbered. Pour into large kettle and heat slowly to 110°, stirring often. Take off heat and drain through a strainer until curds are dry (at least 2-4 hours). Put into container and add cream and salt to taste. Refrigerate.

Healthy

Cream Cheese

Cream Cheese

MRS. JUNIOR KAUFFMAN, REDDING, IA

Take 1 quart of thick, raw cream; mix in 1 level Tbsp. of Redmond real salt. Tie in a piece of muslin and hang in a cool place to drip for 3 days. Keep refrigerated.

Cream Cheese

EDNA MILLER

1 qt. light cream   ¼ cup fresh sour milk

Mix well in top of double boiler or stainless steel bowl. Cover and let stand at room temperature until thick. Skim thin layer off top, if necessary. Cut in squares; heat over warm water to 110°. Make a few strokes across the bottom while warming. Handle carefully so cream doesn't get thin and drain off with the whey. Pour into cloth bag. After 15 minutes place bag on rack in refrigerator with bowl underneath to catch whey. Drain 10 hours. Press curd with weight on top of bag, until curd is pasty. Turn into bowl. With fork or mixer work in salt to taste (about ¾ tsp). Mix thoroughly. Good with crushed pineapples.

263

d a i r y

Cream Cheese

MISS MARY NISLEY, DANVILLE, OH

After yogurt has been refrigerated overnight, put colander in 6 qt. kettle with cheesecloth. Pour in yogurt, put lid on, and return to refrigerator. Drain until thick like cream cheese. Note: This does not work with yogurt made with gelatin unless drained while still warm.

Cream Cheese

MRS. SAMUEL (MARTHA) BRUBAKER, DUNDEE, NY

2 cups dry curds   ½ cup cream, sweet or sour
water   ½ tsp. salt

Blend curds, adding water until it's a thick, creamy texture. Add salt. Run on high until all lumps are gone. Just before shutting off blender, add ½ cup cream.

Dairy Extras

Kefir

MRS. ERVIN (ELIZABETH) BEACHY

2 cups whole milk	1 packet kefir powder

Follow directions on box if using cow's milk. Heat milk, but do not boil. Cool, mix kefir powder to milk, pour into glass 1 quart jar. Let stand at room temperature until a little thick. Refrigerate. (Or freeze ½ for later use.) Now add scant ½ cup kefir to scant ½ gallon of raw milk. (Do not fill quite full.) Leave on your kitchen worktable until it's slightly thick and has a pleasant sour smell. When the house is cool I like to set the jar in the oven, away from the pilot. Temperature will affect how fast it gets ready and how sour it becomes. Also do not add more starter as it gets more sour. Before your pasteurized kefir is all gone, heat 1 pint milk, cool and add ⅛ cup kefir. Repeat until your starter is too sour, then use your frozen portion, or a new packet again. Kefir can be obtained from Body Ecology. Call 1.800.511.2660.

Kefir and Dairy Intolerance: According to Pam Craig in her letter to *Wise Traditions,* Winter/Spring issue, kefir is a wonderful food to reestablish healthy flora, to digest milk. This was a very exciting thought for me as a mother with gluten and dairy sensitive children. Our second son suffered much from allergies from about one year old on. By the time he was two years old, he was doing better, and at about 2½ years we introduced raw goat kefir into his diet, in small amounts at first, maybe once a week and gradually increasing. Later we added raw goat's milk, and to our great joy he added some much needed pounds. Pam writes that in Russia, infants are given kefir mixed with water at 4 months, and school children are given kefir every day. I plan to continue using kefir to insure the children's ability to digest dairy throughout their life. According to another study in a country where kefir is part of the everyday diet, 10% of the population lives to be over 100 years.

Still another kefir story has it that slightly tainted meat was put into kefir, and the kefir was changed daily to keep it fresh. The meat kept for 20 years. Kefir has the ability to destroy putrefying bacteria.

Kefir can be used in smoothies, or enjoyed straight from the jar, like buttermilk. I like to add a little stevia to sweeten, stir in with a fork, and shake jar well. A wonderful breakfast food or snack. These healthy bacteria are passed from mother to baby, so it is a great idea for mothers to be.

Together we can make a difference in our children's lives and the lives of future generations. Enjoy your kefir!

Berry Smoothie

Mrs. Ervin (Elizabeth) Beachy

1¼ cup plain whole-milk yogurt or kefir
1-3 raw high-omega eggs
1 Tbsp. extra-virgin coconut oil

1 Tbsp. flaxseed oil
1-2 Tbsp. unheated honey
1-2 cups fresh/frozen berries

If you desire a sweeter finished product, add a little stevia. Combine ingredients in a high speed blender. This smoothie is a source of easy to absorb nutrition. It contains live enzymes and proteins, and a full spectrum of essential fatty acids. Smoothies should be consumed immediately or refrigerated for up to 24 hours. If frozen in ice cube trays with a toothpick inserted into each cube, smoothies can make a special treat. Note: A banana adds extra sweetness. Peaches can also be used, 1 cup peaches or 1 cup berries, as desired.

Sour Cream

Put 1 Tbsp. plain yogurt to 1 cup of cream. Let it set for 12-18 hours or until it reaches desired thickness. It will thicken some more after being refrigerated. You can also add some milk if you don't want to use all cream.

Canned Cream

Edna Miller

When there's an overabundance of cream during the summer months, can it and keep it for the winter. First, cook the cream, then seal it in pint or quart jars. Cold pack 1 hour. This cream can be whipped and used same as fresh cream, and has a good flavor.

265

dairy

TIP

If you are whipping cream and it doesn't want to become whipped, try pouring it into a quart box, put in freezer for 10 minutes then whip in the quart box.

Whipping cream triples its volume as it gets whipped.

— Ina Schrock, Gap Mills, WV

Lacto-Fermented

I DON'T HAVE A LOT OF EXPERIENCE WITH THE PROCESS of lacto-fermentation except for making sauerkraut.

The idea behind fermenting foods has two good things going for it. One, it is a way of preserving food without freezing or canning; two, these foods promote the growth of healthy flora throughout the intestine. These foods are not meant to be eaten in large amounts but as condiments. Two tablespoons of sauerkraut eaten with your meal will help the digestive process. A 93-year-old man in our area eats a little sauerkraut with each meal. Try it sometime.

Remember, it is best not to can these foods; they need to be unheated to retain their friendly bacteria. Since old habits die hard we have included recipes that do call for canning sauerkraut, but the best choice is to leave it unheated.

In Praise of Sauerkraut

Mrs. Vernon Schrock, Lewistown, IL

Do you like sauerkraut? We do!

Let's start at the beginning. . .

I had problems with digestion before our sixth child was born, which resulted in anemia because I didn't get the full value of all the supplements I was taking. A chiropractor and nutritionist helped get us on the right track, and the climb back to good health began, to make a long story short.

Somewhere along the line we found out that eating sauerkraut helps aid digestion. So we began. We got a few recipes here and there and now use our own version and it works very well, besides being very simple.

We raise our own cabbage, and it takes dozens of heads to last for a year. Once cabbage is ready, wash and trim, making sure all spoiled parts are cut out very well. Otherwise you might be pouring out hard work later! Shred cabbage with Salad Master, using shoestring cone, then add 1 Tbsp. sea salt per quart. Sometimes this is guesswork as a lot of cabbage goes into a jar, but be sure you have 1 Tbsp. per finished quart. Mix and let set in bowl for 10 minutes or until water forms. Now pack into clean jars, pressing it in to bring liquid to the top of cabbage, leaving at least 1" air space. If they are too full it will spew out in the fermenting process. Close very tightly. Lacto-fermentation is an anaerobic (without oxygen) process and the presence of oxygen, once fermentation has begun, will ruin the finished product. Keep at room temperature for 3 days, then move to your can shelves. That's all! It's important not to open the jars in the first three days. You can then begin to eat it, but it's better as it ages. The jars may not look like they have sealed, but it still keeps. It has kept for more than a year for us. Occasionally there are several that will spoil.

Don't cook the kraut, as that kills the good bacteria that's so important in our bodies. We serve it out of the jar, 1-3 times daily. (Keep in refrigerator after opening.) Each one takes a tablespoonful, more or less. We've had little ones who want second or third helpings, or they just eat it alone; and we have teenagers who think they don't like it. We wouldn't want to be without it for us and our family.

The benefits? We believe there are several. A change was noticed in bowel movements; softer, larger stools and more regular. Results are varied. We feel we don't get sick with flu or colds as often or as hard, simply because the bowels are working better and have the friendly bacteria to fight it off. Also, cabbage helps prevent cancer. We also try to eat healthy otherwise, like using fresh ground flour and less sugar.

I think back to when I was a little girl and Mom had us drink store-bought sauerkraut juice. We thought it was pretty bad—very sour and undesirable. While one of us ran around the table, the other drank her portion out of the small, teeny glass to see if she could finish by the time the other was back! That's just a memory now and something to smile about. But I think I'd still choose to eat our own homegrown, homemade sauerkraut any day!

Choices

Sauerkraut

MARIE BEAR, PATRIOT, OH

Wash cabbage. Cut in wedges, then shred. Use the following chart to see how much pickling salt you will need:

1 lb.	2 tsp. salt
2 lb.	4 tsp. salt
5 lb.	3 Tbsp. salt
8 lb.	4 Tbsp. + 2 tsp. salt
10 lb.	6 Tbsp. salt
25 lb.	15 Tbsp. salt

Mix salt in cabbage until juice forms. Pack firmly into sterilized 1 quart jars, ¾ full, until juice covers cabbage. Place a piece of clean cheesecloth on shreds, making sure it's in juice. Keep the jars at 65°-72°. Check in two weeks. Freeze in pint containers. (To sterilize jars, place in oven at 200° for 20 minutes. Cool before using.)

Sauerkraut to Can

MRS. IVAN J. YODER, MILLERSBURG, OH

Shred cabbage rather coarsely. Place a layer of it in a large stainless steel cake pan. Sprinkle 2 tsp. salt over it and chop it up with a little round hand chopper until juice begins to run. Now use your hands and just squeeze the cabbage until it's very, very juicy. Pour into a stainless steel kettle. Repeat until you have your desired amount of kraut. When your kettle is 3" near full, take a large new plastic bag and put water in it and place it on top of kraut to make it airtight. Leave set at room temperature 7-8 days or until desired sourness. Pack into jars and cold pack 5-10 minutes. This is an old recipe.

Sauerkraut

SANDRA SMUCKER, JOHN DAY, OR

1 med. cabbage, cored and shredded
1 Tbsp. caraway seeds (opt.)
1 Tbsp. sea salt
4 Tbsp. whey (if not available use an additional 1 Tbsp. salt)

In bowl, mix cabbage, caraway seeds, salt, and whey. Pound with wooden pounder for about 10 minutes to release juices. Place in wide-mouth, quart-sized jar, and press down firmly with pounder until juices come to the top of cabbage. The cabbage should not be more than 1" from the top of the jar. Cover tightly and keep at room temperature for 3 days before putting in refrigerator. Sauerkraut may be eaten immediately, but improves with age. The recipe can be done in larger batches in a crock. After 3 days put in jars and refrigerate. Do not process!! This sauerkraut has many good enzymes and a small portion eaten with each meal will help digestion immensely. Yield: 1 quart.

Healthy

Homemade Sauerkraut

MARTHA STOLTZFUS, BLAIN, PA

You will need 5 lbs. cabbage for every gallon of your crock. Cut cabbage in quarters and shred with a fine shredder. Place 5 lbs. shredded cabbage and 3½ Tbsp. pickling salt in a large pan. Mix well with hands. Pack gently in large crock, using a potato masher to press it down. Repeat above until crock is filled to within 5 inches from the top. Press cabbage down firmly with potato masher to extract enough juice to cover. Fill a large plastic bag with cold water and secure firmly with a twister. Place on top of cabbage in crock, making sure all cabbage is covered. Keep crock at 65° to ferment. Fermentation will be complete in 10-12 days. (If no bubbles rise, fermentation has ended.) Pack in quart jars to within 1" from top. Pour any leftover juice into jars with sauerkraut. Process in boiling water 15 minutes. 50 lbs. makes about 15 quarts.

Fresh-Pack Pepper Mix

MRS. URIE (LIZZIE ANN) MILLER, MIDDLEBURY, IN

8 qt. mildly hot peppers, cut into rings
4 qt. sweet peppers, cut into strips

2 cans ripe black olives (opt.)

Brine:

2 cups olive oil
5 cups white vinegar
5 cups water

1 cup salt
2⅓-3 Tbsp. chopped garlic
¼ cup dried oregano

Mix all together and pour over vegetables in a large non-metal container. Let set to marinate for 24 hours. Put into jars with a tight lid. No need to seal or heat. Should keep for up to a year. Refrigerate or store in a cold place. If you don't care to use that many hot peppers, you may substitute some sweet peppers, or some cauliflower, carrots (sliced or baby carrots) or onions. Yield: 10-11 quarts.

Lacto-Fermented Pickle Brine

FANNIE BONTRAGER, MANTON, MI

1½ Tbsp. dry dill weed
2½ cups liquid whey
4 Tbsp. real salt

2½ qt. filtered water
3½ Tbsp. dry mustard powder
1 Tbsp. dry turmeric

This mixture equals 3 quarts of brine. Pour over raw, sliced, not peeled, cucumbers in jars. Put on lids (as to can), flats and rings. Leave at room temperature 1½-2 days, then refrigerate. The whey works best off milk that has been set at warm place (like on top of your refrigerator) when still warm from milking, until it separates. If done this way, it does not even taste sour! The jars will sometimes seal because the cucumber brine causes a rise and then a shrink as it ferments, then calms down and contracts. We keep our pickles and sauerkraut in our cave. If we ferment pickles earlier than September, we do refrigerate them as the cave isn't cold enough. Most of our pickles turn out mushy, but still have a hamburger dill flavor. We even drink the juice for a digestive aid.

Beet Kvass

3 med. or 2 large organic beets
¼ cup whey

1 Tbsp. salt
water

Peel and chop up beets coarsely. Place beets, whey, and salt in a 2 quart glass container. Add water to fill the container. Stir well and cover securely. Keep at room temperature for 2 days before transferring to refrigerator. When most of the liquid has been drunk, you may fill up the container with water and keep at room temperature another 2 days. The resulting brew will be slightly less strong than the first. After the second brew, discard the broth and start again. You may, however, reserve some of the liquid and use this as your inoculant instead of the whey. Makes 2 quarts. Note: Do not use grated beets in the preparation of beet tonic. When grated, beets exude too much juice, resulting in a too rapid fermentation that favors the production of alcohol rather than lactic acid. This drink is valuable for its medicinal qualities and as a digestive aid. Beets are just loaded with nutrients. One 4 oz. glass, morning and night, is an excellent blood tonic, promotes regularity, aids digestion, alkalizes the blood, cleanses the liver and is a good treatment for kidney stones and other ailments. Beet kvass may also be used in place of vinegar in salad dressings and as an addition to soups. Lubow A. Kyivska, in *Ukrainian Dishes,* says, "No Ukrainian home was ever without its beet kvass. The kvass was always handy and ready when a pleasing, sour flavor had to be added to soups and vinaigrettes." Sick people lack digestive juices, not only during their illness but also for a long time afterwards. Thus, lacto-fermented foods, rich in vitamins and minerals, as well as enzymes, are a valuable aid. Beets have a regenerating effect on the body. Beet kvass, with its liver-supporting properties, is useful in preventing future morning sickness.

Cakes

WE MOMS LOVE THE SIMPLICITY OF WHIPPING
together a cake. Not as time consuming as making individual cookies.
If not using sugar and white flour, cakes are not so unhealthy and can
be served as summer suppers with fruit and milk.

Cakes made with fresh ingredients are hard to beat. In twenty-two
years of married life I've never bought a single cake mix. Yes, it's possible
to live without them!

If you like mixes go ahead and make some. Just mix the dry ingredients
of a cake recipe, put them in a ziplock bag, writing wet ingredients and
baking instructions on the outside. Make several and keep them on
hand on your pantry shelf. (A good job for girls.) When you want to
make a cake fast, just grab a bag and go for it! Grandmas, this would
be something you could do for your married daughters who are busy
with raising little ones. Would make a good gift for a new mom as well!
Healthy choices must be planned; they don't just happen.

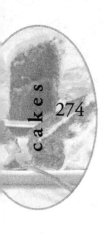

Sun Gold Cake

Mrs. Miriam Wengerd, Sugarcreek, OH

3 cups barley flour
3 tsp. baking powder
½ tsp. salt
1 tsp. vanilla

1 cup butter, melted
1 cup milk
1 cup honey
4 eggs, separated

Put first three ingredients in bowl, stir with whisk. Add rest of ingredients, except egg whites. Beat well until smooth. Beat egg whites until stiff and fold in. Pour into greased 11 x 17" pan and bake 20-30 minutes. Makes a delicious shortcake!

Blueberry Coffee Cake

Mrs. Miriam Wengerd, Sugarcreek, OH

2¼ cups wheat flour
¾ cup sucanat
1½ tsp. baking powder
1½ tsp. cinnamon
¾ tsp. salt

2¼ cups frozen blueberries
2 eggs
¾ cup milk
6 Tbsp. butter, melted

Topping:

6 Tbsp. butter
1½ cup sucanat

1½ Tbsp. flour
¾ cup chopped pecans

In a large mixing bowl, combine flour, sucanat, baking powder, cinnamon, and salt. Gently fold in blueberries. In a small bowl, whisk together eggs, milk, and butter. Add to flour mixture and stir well. Spread in a greased 9 x 13" pan. Combine topping ingredients and sprinkle over batter. Bake at 350° for 30 minutes, or until golden brown. Delicious served warm as breakfast dessert.

Strawberry Rhubarb Coffee Cake

Lucia Lapp, Benton, IL

Filling:

3 cups diced rhubarb	½ cup honey
4 cups mashed strawberries	⅓ cup cornstarch
2 Tbsp. lemon juice	

Cake:

3 cups pastry wheat flour	1 cup butter or coconut oil
½ cup sweetener	1½ cup buttermilk
1 tsp. baking powder	2 eggs
1 tsp. soda	1 tsp. vanilla
½ tsp. salt	

Topping:

¼ cup melted butter	½ cup sucanat
¾ cup flour	

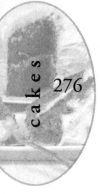

In a large saucepan, combine fruit and lemon juice and cook 5 minutes. Combine honey and cornstarch and stir into fruit. Cook until thick. In a bowl combine dry ingredients. Cut in butter until mixture resembles crumbs. Mix rest of liquid into batter. Spread half of cake in a greased 9 x 13" pan. Carefully spread filling on top. Drop remaining batter on top and sprinkle crumbs over all. Bake at 350° for 40-45 minutes. Best served warm.

cakes 276

Apple Coffee Cake

Mrs. Rhoda Miller, Sugarcreek OH

3 eggs	2 tsp. baking soda
¼ cup honey	1 tsp. cream of tartar
½ cup oil	½ tsp. salt
1½ cup apple juice	1 qt. apple pie filling
3 cups whole wheat flour	2 tsp. cinnamon

Mix pie filling and cinnamon and set aside. Combine remaining ingredients. Pour ½ of batter into greased 9 x 13" pan. Spoon ½ of pie filling onto batter, then repeat with remaining batter and filling. Sprinkle with chopped walnuts. Bake at 350° for 45-60 minutes.

Peach Cobbler Cake

Leah Nisley, Danville, OH

½ cup maple syrup
⅓ cup butter
¼ cup water
¼ cup milk
3 egg yolks
1 tsp. lemon extract

¼ tsp. almond extract
1 tsp. vanilla
1½ tsp. baking powder
2 cups flour
3 egg whites (beaten stiff)
1 qt. fresh or canned peaches

Cream maple syrup and butter, add egg yolks, milk, water, and flavorings. Add flour and baking powder. Fold in stiffly beaten egg whites. Pour over peaches in a greased pan. Bake at 350°.

Apple Cake

Mrs. Miriam Wengerd, Sugarcreek, OH

4 cups shredded apples
¾ cup honey
2 tsp. vanilla
1 cup butter, melted
2 tsp. cinnamon

½ tsp. salt
2 beaten eggs
*2 cups barley or wheat flour
1 tsp. baking soda
1 cup chopped nuts (opt.)

Sauce:

½ cup butter, melted
1½ cup sucanat

1 cup sour cream

Peel and shred apples. Place in bowl, add honey, vanilla, melted butter, cinnamon and salt. Beat eggs and stir in well. Add soda and flour. Stir thoroughly with spoon. Add nuts if you wish. Pour into greased 9 x 13" pan and bake at 350° for 25 minutes or until cake springs back. For sauce, melt butter, add sucanat. Will be thick and chunky. Add sour cream and heat on low, stirring with whisk until mixture is smooth. You can also use honey in sauce instead of sucanat. It's easier to stir in, probably use smaller amount. Serve cake with sauce—yummy! * Barley flour is made by grinding barley grain. It makes a whiter flour than wheat berries do.

277

cakes

Choices

Honey Applesauce Cake

DARLA REENA STOLL, ODON, IN

½ cup oil
1 cup honey
2 eggs
3 cups whole wheat flour
1½ tsp. baking powder

¼ tsp. salt
1½ cups applesauce
1 tsp. cinnamon
1 cup raisins
½ cup chopped nuts

Cream oil and honey until well blended. Beat eggs into creamed mixture, adding one egg at a time and mixing well. Add dry ingredients alternately with applesauce. Add nuts and raisins last. Pour into well-greased 9 x 13" pan. Bake at 325° for 40 minutes.

Apple Cake

MRS. JOHN (NORLEEN) HOOVER, OWEN, WI
MRS. JEREMY (ROSE) MILLER, ST. IGNATIUS, MT

2 cups mashed bananas or grated zucchini
1 cup honey
¾ cup applesauce
2 tsp. vanilla
½ tsp. sea salt

1 tsp. cinnamon
2 tsp. baking soda
2 cups whole wheat flour
3 cups diced apples
2 cups walnuts

Cream bananas or grated zucchini, honey, and applesauce. Add vanilla, salt, cinnamon, and soda. Beat until well blended. Gradually add flour. Fold in apples and walnuts. Pour into a 9 x 13" glass baking dish. Bake at 350° for 30-45 minutes. Very yummy!

Apple Cake

MRS. EMERY (NAOMI) STUTZMAN, HICKORY, KY

2 tsp. stevia
1½ cup olive oil (scant)
2 large eggs
2½ cups spelt flour
2 tsp. baking powder

1 tsp. soda
1 tsp. salt
1 tsp. vanilla
3 cups chopped apples
½-1 cup chopped pecans (opt.)

Place stevia in bowl. Add oil and eggs; beat well. Sift together flour, baking powder, baking soda, and salt. Add flour mixture to egg mixture and blend. Add apples and nuts. Pour batter into a greased, floured 9 x 13" pan. Bake at 350° for 40 minutes. This cake is good sprinkled with a little nutmeg before baking. Needs no frosting.

Pineapple Cake

MRS. MARVIN WENGERD, SUAGRCREEK, OH

Cake:

2 cup spelt flour

2 tsp. baking soda

1 tsp. vanilla

¾ cup honey

1-20 oz. can crushed pineapple with juice

1 cup unsweetened coconut

1 cup nuts, chopped

Mix well and pour into buttered 9 x 13" cake pan.

Topping:

½ cup nuts, chopped

½ cup oatmeal

¼ cup butter, melted

½ cup coconut

1 cup sucanat

Mix and spread evenly over cake batter in pan. Bake at 350° for 40 minutes or until done.

Susan's Shoofly Cake

MRS. JOE GARBER, PRATTSBURGH, NY

3 cups whole wheat flour

1 cup oat flour

½ cup oil

1 cup sucanat

3 tsp. baking powder

1 cup milk

1 cup molasses

1 cup boiling water

½ tsp. salt

vanilla

Mix first 5 ingredients. Save 1 cup for topping. Then add the rest and mix well. Add 1 tsp. cinnamon to the topping before sprinkling on cake. Bake at 350°.

Choices

Oatmeal Cake

Mrs. Miriam Wengerd, Sugarcreek, OH

1 cup oatmeal
½ cup butter
1¼ cups boiling water
1¼ cups honey
1 tsp. vanilla
2 eggs

1⅔ cups barley flour
1 tsp. soda
1 tsp. cinnamon
½ tsp. nutmeg
⅛ tsp. salt

Put butter and oats in bowl. Pour boiling water over it and let set 15 minutes. Beat well. Add honey, vanilla, and eggs. Beat until smooth. Add rest of ingredients and pour into greased 9 x 13" pan. Bake at 350° for 30 minutes. Spread coconut topper on cake and pop under broiler for 5 minutes, turning pan once to brown evenly. Delicious with chilled peaches and cold milk.

Coconut Topper:

2 cups fine shredded coconut
½ cup honey
½ cup butter, melted

½ cup cream
1½ tsp. vanilla

Mix all ingredients together well.

Hawaiian Carrot Cake

Mrs. Miriam Wengerd, Sugarcreek, OH

2 cups wheat flour
2 tsp. baking powder
1½ tsp. baking soda
1 tsp. salt
2 tsp. cinnamon
½ cup pecans, chopped

¾ cup oil
¾ cup honey
4 eggs
2 cups carrots, finely grated
2 cups coconut flakes, unsweetened
1 cup crushed pineapple

Mix dry ingredients. Add oil, honey and eggs. Mix thoroughly. Stir in carrots, coconut and pineapple, mixing well. Pour into greased and floured 9 x 13" pan or divide evenly between 9" round layer pans. Bake in preheated 350° oven for 35-40 minutes. Cool before turning out on racks (layers). If baking in 9 x 13" pan, set on rack to cool.

Cream Cheese Frosting:

8 oz. cream cheese, softened
6 Tbsp. butter, softened

4 Tbsp. honey
1 tsp. cinnamon

Beat cream cheese until smooth. Add softened butter and beat until fluffy. Add honey and beat until creamy. Add cinnamon, mixing in well. Spread on cooled 9 x 13", or double the recipe and use between layers. May need another batch or two to finish frosting top and sides. This cake is good chilled in fridge.

Carrot Cake

MISS. LEAH NISLEY, DANVILLE, OH

3 cups flour
1½ cup honey
2 tsp. soda
2 tsp. cinnamon
1 cup chopped pecans

1 tsp. salt
1 cup vegetable oil
4 eggs
3 cups grated carrots

Sift flour, soda, and salt with cinnamon. Add oil, honey, and eggs. Mix well. Fold in carrots, add nuts. Pour into 9 x 13" pan or 2 layer pans. Bake at 325° for 30 minutes or until done. Frost when cool, with:

8 oz. cream cheese
⅓ cup honey

1 tsp. vanilla

Beat cream cheese with honey and vanilla until smooth. Spread on cake.

Carrot Cake

KARI WENDT, LAKE ARIEL, PA

1 cup (scant) maple syrup
¾ cup (scant) oil
4 eggs
3 cups grated carrots
⅓ cup ground flax seed
1 tsp. baking soda

1 tsp. baking powder
½ cup brown rice flour
1½ cup whole wheat flour
¾ tsp. salt
½ tsp. nutmeg
1½ tsp. cinnamon

Preheat oven to 350°. Mix dry ingredients and set aside. Mix wet ingredients and then slowly pour in dry ingredients. Mix quickly and pour into greased 9 x 13" pan. Bake for 30 minutes or until lightly browned and firm to the touch.

Carrot Cake

Kathryn Hershberger, Clare, MI

4 eggs, beaten
¼ cup honey
¾ cup maple syrup
1 cup olive oil
3 cups shredded carrots

2 cups whole wheat flour
1¼ tsp. soda
1 tsp. cinnamon
½ tsp. salt

Beat eggs with beater, add sweeteners, beat well. Add olive oil and beat thoroughly. Mix in dry ingredients. Last add carrots. Pour into a 9 x 13" pan and bake at 300° for 1 hour or less. Frosting:

8 oz. cream cheese, softened
2 Tbsp. butter, softened

maple syrup (enough to make it creamy)

Beat cream cheese and butter until fluffy. Add maple syrup until nice, spreading consistency.

Chocolate or Spice Cake

Mrs. Beechy, LaGrange, IN

2 cups sucanat
½ cup applesauce
2 eggs
1 cup hot water
½ cup sour milk or cream

4 Tbsp. cocoa
2 cups whole wheat flour
2 tsp. soda
½ tsp. salt
1 tsp. vanilla

For a spice cake, omit the cocoa and add 1 tsp. cinnamon and ½ tsp. each of nutmeg and ginger. Mix in order given. Pour into a greased 9 x 13" pan. Bake at 350° for 35 minutes or until done.

Very Good Chocolate Cake

Kathryn Hershberger, Clare, MI

½ cup olive oil
½ cup honey
¾ cup maple syrup
2 eggs
pinch of salt

2 cups boiling water
½ cup cocoa
3 tsp. soda
2 tsp. baking powder
2½ cups whole wheat flour

Mix in order given. Batter will be thin. Bake at 350° for 38 minutes. This cake is very moist and delicious. Chocolate frosting:

8 oz. cream cheese
2 Tbsp. butter

¼ cup cocoa
maple syrup (enough to make it creamy)

Cream together cream cheese and butter until fluffy. Add maple syrup to right consistency and beat well. Add cocoa, mix, then add more syrup if necessary.

Oatmeal Pone

Mrs. Urie Miller, Middlebury, IN

2 cups rolled oats
1 cup whole wheat flour
1 tsp. baking soda
1 tsp. salt

¼ cup natural sweetener
1 egg
1¼ cup milk or cream

Blend dry ingredients. Add sweetener, egg, and milk. Bake in an 8" square pan at 350° for 25-30 minutes or until done. Variation: Add approximately ¾ cup chopped apples to batter. A good supper cake to eat with fruit and milk.

Yummy Oatmeal Cake

Susie Nolt

1 cup quick oats
1½ cup boiling water
1 cup sucanat
½ cup xylitol
½ cup butter
1 egg

1 tsp. vanilla
1⅓ cup spelt flour
1 tsp. baking soda
1 tsp. baking powder
1 tsp. cinnamon
1 tsp. sea salt

Cream together first 7 ingredients. Add remaining ingredients and bake in a greased 9 x 13" pan at 350° for 30-35 minutes.

Crumb Topping:

1 cup sucanat
¼ cup butter, softened
1 cup coconut

½ cup chopped nuts
5 tsp. milk or cream

Mix together. Spread on cake while still warm and place under broiler until bubbly and brown.

Crazy Carob Cake

2 cups spelt flour
1¼ tsp. baking soda
½ cup carob
½ cup oil

⅓ cup honey
1⅓ cup water
1¼ tsp. vanilla
1¼ tsp. vinegar

Stir together flour, baking soda, and carob. In a separate bowl, mix oil, honey, water, vanilla, and vinegar. Mix. Then mix all together and pour in an ungreased 8 x 8" pan. Bake at 350° for 30-40 minutes.

Molasses Cake

MISS LEAH NISLEY, DANVILLE, OH

Crumble together:

4 cups flour   ¾ cup butter
2 tsp. baking powder

Divide in 2 pans. Keep 1¾ cup crumbs out for top. Mix 2 cups hot water and 1 cup molasses and add 2 tsp. soda just before pouring over crumbs. Then add remaining crumbs on top. Bake at 400° for 10 minutes. Turn down to 350° to finish baking.

Autumn Pumpkin Cake

MARY BETH HEISEY, PUEBLO WEST, CO

⅔ cup oil   2 tsp. baking powder
1 cup honey   ½ tsp. salt
4 eggs   2 tsp. cinnamon
2 cups pumpkin   1 tsp. baking soda
2 cups whole wheat flour

Beat together first 4 ingredients. Add dry ingredients. Mix well. Pour into one 9 x 13" pan or make 2 dozen cupcakes. Bake at 350° until done. Frost with:

Cream Cheese Frosting:

½ cup butter, softened   8 oz. cream cheese, softened

Add honey to sweeten to taste.

Whole Wheat Famous Jiffy Cake

MRS. JOE GARBER, PRATTSBURGH, NY

¼ cup applesauce   ½ tsp. salt
1 egg   ⅓ cup cocoa
½ cup sucanat   ½ tsp. soda
¼ cup oil   1 tsp. baking powder
½ cup milk   1 tsp. vanilla
1½ cup whole wheat flour   ½ cup boiling water

Mix applesauce, egg, sucanat, and oil. Add milk and mix again. Then add rest of ingredients, except for water, and mix well. Last, add water and beat real well. Bake in 8" square pan at 350°.

Frosting:

1 Tbsp. honey   1 Tbsp. peanut butter

Spread on warm cake. Sprinkle with ½ cup coconut and ½ cup chocolate chips.

cakes

284

Healthy

Graham Cake

MRS. ALLEN R. BYLER, SMICKSBURG, PA

½ cup honey
1½ cups whole wheat flour
½ tsp. soda
pinch of salt
1 cup milk
½ cup butter or olive oil

Mix and bake in hot oven (about 400°) for 20-25 minutes. Serve warm with milk. Also good with fruit of your choice.

Angel Food Cake

JUANITA WEAVER, JOHNSONVILLE, IL

2⅓ cups egg whites
1 tsp. salt
2 tsp. cream of tartar
2 tsp. vanilla
¼-½ tsp. almond extract

Note: Eggs will beat fluffier at room temperature. Beat all above ingredients in mixing bowl until soft peaks form. Gradually beat in 1¼ cup slightly warmed honey. Sift 1¾ cup of soft wheat flour. Add to egg mixture in several additions, folding lightly and carefully after each addition. Bake in tube pan at 350° for 35-40 minutes. This cake has gotten lots of comments. Great with strawberry Danish. I put flour in a fine sieve and shake lightly to let the finest flour through. I use that in icing, angel food cakes, gravy, etc. The coarser flour I use in the rest of baking. *(Try using barley flour for a white cake. -Mrs. Marvin Wengerd)*

Maple Nut Angel Food Cake

LEAH NISLEY, DANVILLE, OH

2⅓ cups egg whites
2 tsp. cream of tartar
¾ cup maple syrup
¼ cup sorghum
¾ cup pecans
1¾ cup sifted flour

Beat egg whites and cream of tartar. Slowly add maple syrup, sorghum, pecans, and flour. For Carob Angel Food Cake, omit nuts and put in ⅓ cup carob and ¾ cup honey instead of maple syrup and sorghum.

Whole Wheat Angel Food Cake

MRS. URIE MILLER, MIDDLEBURY, IN

2 cups egg whites
1¼ tsp. cream of tartar
¼ tsp. salt
1 tsp. vanilla
1 cup honey, maple syrup, or sorghum
1 cup whole wheat flour

1 tsp. baking powder
¼ cup arrowroot powder or cornstarch
2 Tbsp. carob powder or flour
1 tsp. cinnamon
¼ tsp. nutmeg

Beat together first 4 ingredients until stiff peaks form. Add sweetener in 3-4 additions. (You may prefer using a scraper to mix in sweetener as it tends to settle to bottom of bowl.) Sift together dry ingredients 5 times; fold in (do not beat) in several additions. Turn batter into ungreased angel food tube cake pan. Bake at 350° for about 1 hour or until done.

Best Gingerbread

MRS. MIRIAM WENGERD, SUGARCREEK, OH

½ cup butter
¼ cup honey
1 egg, beaten
1½ tsp. baking soda
1 tsp. cinnamon
1 tsp. ginger

½ tsp. cloves
½ tsp. salt
1 cup sorghum
1 cup hot water
2½ cups wheat flour (sifted)

Preheat oven to 350°. Cream butter and honey. Add beaten egg. Measure and sift dry ingredients. Combine sorghum and hot water. Add dry ingredients to first mixture alternately with sorghum, beating after each addition until smooth. Pour into greased 9 x 9" pan and bake at 350° until done, about 30 minutes. Cut into squares and serve with plain yogurt and chilled applesauce spooned on top. A special treat first served to us by Marianne Savage.

Healthy

Whole Wheat Gingerbread

Jessica Strite, Cochise, AZ
Cynthia Korver, New Oxford, PA

1 cup molasses
¾ cup honey
¾ cup oil
3 eggs
3 cups whole wheat flour
1 Tbsp. baking powder

1 tsp. salt
1½ tsp. ground cinnamon
1½ tsp. ground cloves
1 tsp. ground ginger
2 cups milk
whipped cream

In large mixing bowl, beat molasses, honey, oil, and eggs until well mixed. Combine dry ingredients and add alternately with the milk to the egg mixture. Pour batter into a greased 9 x 13" cake pan. Bake at 350° for 45-50 minutes or until toothpick inserted in the center comes out clean. Serve warm or at room temperature with chilled whipped cream. Yield: 12-15 servings.

Strawberry Shortcake

Mrs. Marvin Wengerd, Suagrcreek, OH

4 cups barley flour or wheat
1 tsp. salt
6 tsp. baking powder
2 eggs (opt.)

1½ cups milk
½ cup butter
½ cup maple syrup or honey

Put first three ingredients in bowl. Mix with whisk. Cut in butter until mixture is crumbly. Add milk and maple syrup, mixing well. Pour into greased 9 x 13" pan and bake in preheated 350° oven for 20-30 minutes. Serve with cold milk and chopped strawberries, sweetened with maple syrup. Can be used with other in-season fruits—black raspberries, peaches and blueberries. When made without eggs this cake is like biscuits, we like it both ways.

Strawberry Shortcake

Cynthia Korver, New Oxford, PA

2 eggs
1 Tbsp. butter
1 cup sucanat
6 cups whole wheat flour

4 tsp. cream of tartar
1 tsp. baking soda
2 cups milk

Beat eggs, butter, and sucanat. Add dry ingredients, then milk. Will be thick. Put in 10 x 15" pan. Bake at 350° for 30-35 minutes or until pick comes out clean. Note: This recipe came from my mother-in-law. She passed away before we were married. This is all I make for strawberry shortcake, because to my husband nothing else tastes right.

Pumpkin Cake

MRS. MIRIAM WENGERD, SUGARCREEK, OH

1½ cups wheat flour
2 tsp. baking powder
1½ tsp. cinnamon
1 tsp. baking soda
½ tsp. salt
½ tsp. nutmeg

¾ cup honey
⅔ cup milk
½ cup oil
2 eggs
1 cup cooked pumpkin

Put first six ingredients in bowl. Stir with whisk. Add rest of ingredients all at once and beat thoroughly. Pour into greased 9 x 13" pan and bake at 350° until center springs back, 20-30 minutes. This cake is so easy to make and so good! Delicious served warm with cold peaches. Excellent served with the following frosting.

Cream Cheese Frosting

MRS. MIRIAM WENGERD, SUGARCREEK, OH

8 oz. cream cheese
cinnamon

honey

Soften cream cheese. Beat with potato masher until smooth. Add enough honey to make creamy and add cinnamon to taste. Use food processor if you have one. Spread on cooled cake. Goes well with the preceding cake.

Pumpkin Cupcakes

4 eggs
1 cup oil
¾ cup honey
3 cups whole wheat flour
2 tsp. cinnamon
3 tsp. baking powder

2 tsp. soda
½ tsp. salt
1 tsp. ginger
2 cups pumpkin
1 cups raisins and/or nuts

Beat eggs, oil and honey well, until frothy. Add remaining ingredients. Bake at 350° for 15 minutes. Makes 24 cupcakes. Frosting:

4 oz. cream cheese
⅓ cup honey

¼ cup soft butter

Note: This frosting works well to decorate cakes, too. Also, in many recipes applesauce can be substituted for up to ½ the oil.

Ruth's Frosting

MRS. ESH, PA

3 Tbsp. flour
1 cup milk
1 cup rapadura
1 cup butter, softened

Mix flour and milk well, stir and bring to a boil until thick, cool. Beat rapadura and butter well, then add flour mixture and beat well.

Chocolate Fudge Icing

JUANITA WEAVER, JOHNSONVILLE, IL

½ cup fructose
¼ cup cocoa or carob
¼ cup butter
¼ cup cream or milk
½ tsp. vanilla

Boil all ingredients except vanilla for 2½ minutes. Remove from heat, add vanilla. Cool and stir until slightly thick. Pour over cake before it gets too hard.

Chocolate Frosting

MRS. BEECHY, LaGRANGE, IN

¼ cup cocoa
¾ cup sweetener of your choice
2 Tbsp. cornstarch
½ tsp. salt
1 cup milk
1 tsp. vanilla
1 Tbsp. butter

Mix dry ingredients; add milk and cook to thicken. Add butter and vanilla. Spread on a 9 x 13" cake while it's still warm.

Beat n' Eat Frosting

½ cup honey
¼ tsp. cream of tartar
1 tsp. vanilla
1 egg white, unbeaten
¼ cup boiling water

Place first 4 ingredients in deep bowl. Mix and add boiling water. Beat well until mixture stands in stiff peaks. Makes 3 cups frosting. Sprinkle cake with shredded coconut. I also use this for Cool Whip in recipes, though food tends to get watery after several days. Recipes that take cream cheese keep this Cool Whip firm. Do not mix cream cheese with all of mixture, though, or it will fall. Beat cream cheese with small amount of "Cool Whip" then fold in with the rest of it. It will lose some volume, but will be okay. Refrigerate a few hours before using to make more firm.

Choices

Buttercream Frosting

MARY BETH HEISEY, PUEBLO WEST, CO

3 rounded Tbsp. cornstarch
1 cup milk

½ cup maple syrup

Combine in a small saucepan. Bring to boil and boil until thick, stirring constantly. Cool.

½ cup butter, softened

1 tsp. vanilla

Beat. Add cooled cornstarch mixture. Beat until fluffy. Use for cakes and cupcakes.

Honey Cream Icing

KENDRA ROKEY, SABETHA, KS

8 oz. cream cheese, softened
⅓ cup honey

2 tsp. vanilla

Stir all together until smooth and well blended. Use to frost cinnamon rolls, cakes, and breads.

cakes

290

Frosting

½ cup carob
¾ cup milk (or water)
⅓ tsp. stevia (1-2 scoops)

⅓ cup peanut butter
1 tsp. vanilla

Heat first 3 ingredients on low for 7 minutes. Remove from heat and add peanut butter and vanilla.

Frosting for Cake

MRS. GLENN ZIMMERMAN, GREENWOOD, WI

Let 8 oz. cream cheese warm up to room temperature. Beat with mixer until creamy, add honey or maple syrup to desired sweetness. Add 1 tsp. vanilla, or other flavoring. Spread on cake. This stays creamy and sticky, and should be refrigerated if there are leftovers.

Quick & Easy Frosting

Lucia Lapp, Benton, IL

1 pkg. cream cheese
½ cup butter

¼ cup honey

Whip until creamy.

Sucanat Icing

Julia Engle, Oklahoma City, OK

8 oz. cream cheese
¼ cup butter

½-1 cup sucanat
1 tsp. vanilla

Cream together the cream cheese and butter. Add vanilla. Slowly add sucanat until you reach the desired sweetness. Spread on cake.

Honey Frosting

Mrs. Ruby Shetler, Homer, MI

⅓ cup honey
2-4 egg whites
dash of cream of tartar

1 tsp. flavoring (vanilla,
    almond, anise or lemon)
salt to taste

Beat egg whites, salt, and cream of tartar until stiff peaks form. Gradually add honey and flavoring. Use to frost 9 x 13" or 2 layer cake.

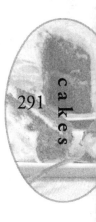

291

cakes

Honey Frosting

Beat 1 egg white until stiff. Heat ½ cup of honey to 238°. Drizzle honey into egg white, beating all the time. Add carob powder for brown icing. Makes enough for a tube cake.

Choices

Cookies

"MOM, I'M HUNGRY. CAN I HAVE A COOKIE?" WE moms can hardly resist that question. I like to say yes if I know there is no white sugar or flour involved.

We don't have cookies all the time, but occasionally I like to fill up our clear glass cookie jar when the weekend comes around. Little Jonathan just loves it when his eyes light on a cookie! He gets so excited when he is allowed to have a treat!

Cookies are so handy because you can grab one and eat it on the run. Or stick a few in your pocket when you go on a walk. They definitely pass the test for picnics too.

When your family is used to rich, gooey, sugary cookies it's a little hard to get them used to a healthier version. In recognition of that we have printed a few recipes that include chocolate chips as an option, even though they don't make it through the sieve of our no-sugar rule! Maybe you need the chocolate chips in there as bait to get them used to eating whole grain cookies.

Don't give up though; keep trying. For those of you with young children, begin now to introduce healthy choices to them. It really makes a difference and is worth the effort.

Mary's Mouthwatering Whole Wheat Cookies

SUSAN BYLER, MUNFORDVILLE, KY

1 cup oil
1 cup maple syrup
2 eggs
1¾ cup whole wheat flour
1 tsp. soda

1 tsp. cinnamon
2 cups quick oats
1 cup raisins
½ cup nuts

Mix together and bake at 350°-375° for 10-15 minutes. Do not overbake. Easy to make and delicious.

Health Rounds

MIRIAM YODER, LaGRANGE, IN

1 cup butter or ¾ cup oil
1 cup honey
2 eggs, beaten
½ tsp. salt
2 tsp. vanilla
1 tsp. baking powder

3 cups whole wheat flour
1 cup rolled oats
1 cup sunflower seeds
1½ cups nuts, chopped
2 cups raisins

Cream butter or oil and honey. Add eggs, salt, and vanilla. Blend in dry ingredients. Stir in seeds, nuts and raisins. Drop by teaspoonsful onto an ungreased cookie sheet. Bake 10-12 minutes at 375°. Delicious!

Carob Mint Drop Cookies

KARI WENDT, LAKE ARIEL, PA

3½ cups whole wheat flour
¼ cup ground flax seed
1½ tsp. baking powder
¾ tsp. salt
½ cup carob powder

1 cup milk
2 eggs
½ cup oil
¾ cup maple syrup
1 tsp. peppermint flavoring

Preheat oven to 350°. Mix wet ingredients and set aside. Mix dry ingredients and pour into wet ingredients, stir well. Drop by teaspoonfuls onto greased cookie sheet. Bake 10-15 minutes. Check carefully as you can't see these browning.

Date Drop Cookies

ELAINE ROPP, ONTARIO

1½ cups dates
2 tsp. vanilla
2 eggs
½ cup melted butter
¼ cup oat bran
1 tsp. soda

½ cup raw sunflower seeds
¼ cup whole grain flour
1-1½ cup rolled oats
½ cup raisins
½ cup chopped walnuts

Blend dates, vanilla, and eggs in blender until smooth. Pour into mixing bowl. Add rest of ingredients and mix. Drop by spoonfuls onto greased cookie sheet. Bake at 350° for 10-12 minutes. Yields: 1½ dozen cookies.

Sugar Free Cookies

PAULINE SAUDER, LATHAM, MO

½ cup chopped apples
½ cup dates, chopped
1 cup raisins
1 cup water
⅓ cup oil
3 eggs

½ tsp. salt
1⅓ cup whole wheat flour
1 tsp. vanilla
1 tsp. soda
1 tsp. cinnamon
½ cup walnuts, chopped

cookies

296

Cook together apples, dates, raisins, and water 3 minutes. Cool. Add remaining ingredients and mix well. Drop on greased cookie sheet. Bake at 350° for 15 minutes. Do not overbake.

Oatmeal Coconut Chewies

MRS. MIRIAM WENGERD, SUGARCREEK, OH

1½ cup butter, softened
2 cups sucanat
1½ cup honey
2 eggs
1 cup milk
4 tsp. vanilla
2 tsp. soda

1 tsp. baking powder
1 tsp. salt
2 tsp. cinnamon
6 cups quick oats
1 cup fine coconut
7 cups barley or wheat flour
2 cups currants

In Bosch mixer: Beat sucanat and honey into butter. Add eggs and beat until fluffy. Add milk and vanilla and beat again. Add soda, baking powder, salt, cinnamon, and 2 cups oatmeal. Beat well. Add 2 more cups oatmeal, beat again. Add last 2 cups oatmeal and coconut and beat well. Remove mixers and put in dough hooks. Mix in flour thoroughly. Let set ½ hour. Preheat oven 10 minutes at 350°. Drop cookies by small scoop onto cookie sheet, 12 scoops on each 11 x 17" sheet. Flatten slightly with wet fork and bake until lightly browned, 12-15 minutes. This is the best sugarless cookie recipe I've used! Soft and chewy. If your family must have chocolate chips, you can substitute them for currants. If your family doesn't like raisins in cookies, they might still enjoy currants, as they are smaller and not so dominant.

Oatmeal Molasses Cookies

MRS. URIE MILLER, MIDDLEBURY, IN

1 cup butter
2 cups sorghum
2 eggs
2½ cups whole wheat flour
4 tsp. baking powder
4 tsp. baking soda

½ tsp. salt
2 tsp. cinnamon
1 tsp. nutmeg
5 cups rolled oats
2 cups raisins

Melt together butter and sorghum; add eggs. Sift together and add dry ingredients. Stir in rolled oats and raisins. Drop by teaspoon on cookie sheet. Bake at 350° for 12-15 minutes, or until done.

Choices

Oatmeal Wafers

FANNIE BONTRAGER

1½ cups rolled oats
¾ cup spelt flour
¼ cup honey
1 tsp. cinnamon
⅛ tsp. salt

½ cup coconut oil
1½ Tbsp. maple syrup
⅛ tsp. vanilla
¼ tsp. nutmeg
¼ tsp. cloves

Grease pans. Bake at 375° for 8 minutes, or until lightly browned, spacing them 2" apart on cookie sheet and patting down to form ½" thick rounds. It is a known fact that baking soda and powder deplete the body of B vitamins, and here is a cookie recipe without either! Stir together 24 hours before baking to help break down phytic acid in grain for better assimilation.

Emma's Oatmeal Cookies

MRS. JOE GARBER, PRATTSBURGH, NY

2 cups sucanat
½ cup honey
2 eggs
1½ cup butter
½ cup water
2 tsp. vanilla

4 tsp. baking powder
6 cups oatmeal
2 cups wheat flour
2 tsp. cinnamon
nuts or raisins (opt.)

Mix first 6 ingredients together well, then add rest of ingredients. Form in balls. Place on cookie sheet and flatten slightly. Bake at 375°.

cookies

298

Simple Peanut Butter Oatmeal Cookies

⅔ cup peanut, almond, or cashew butter
2 tsp. vanilla

½ cup honey
2 cups rolled oats

Mix peanut butter and honey until smooth. Add vanilla and oats. Form balls. Grease pan. Flatten balls. Bake 8-9 minutes. Makes 3 dozen.

Special Oatmeal Cookies

KATHRYN HERSHBERGER, CLARE, MI

1 cup butter	3 tsp. cinnamon
½ cup honey	2 eggs
¾ cup maple syrup	1½ tsp. soda
1 cup sour milk	2 cups oatmeal
3 cups whole wheat flour	1 cup raisins
¾ tsp. salt	1 cup nuts (opt.)

Cream butter and sweeteners, add eggs and milk. Mix well. Add flour, salt, cinnamon, and soda. Mix, then add oatmeal, raisins, and nuts. Bake at 375° until done.

Apple Oatmeal Cookies

AUDREY DANTZLERWARD, VA

¼ cup flour	1 apple, peeled and chopped
1 egg	½ tsp. baking soda
1⅓ cup oatmeal	scant ¼ cup honey

Mix honey, egg, and apple; in separate bowl, mix flour, oatmeal, and baking soda. Add wet mixture to dry mixture—if it's too wet, add more flour, a little at a time. Roll into 1-1½" balls; place on greased cookie sheet. Bake for 10-15 minutes at 400°. Enjoy!

Date Oatmeal Cookies

MRS. SAM (LYDIA) MILLER, FREDERICKSBURG, OH

1½ cup dates	½ cup raw sunflower seeds
2 eggs	¼ cup natural sweetened carob chips
2 tsp. vanilla	¼ cup whole spelt flour
½ cup butter, melted	1 cup quick rolled oats
¼ cup oat bran	½ cup chopped nuts
1 tsp. soda	½ tsp. salt

Grind dates; add eggs and vanilla. Process in Salsa Master until smooth. Pour in mixing bowl. Add remaining ingredients. Mix and drop onto greased cookie sheet. Bake at 350° for 15-20 minutes. Yield: 1½ dozen cookies.

Oatmeal Cookies

MRS. JUNIOR KAUFFMAN, REDDING, IA

1 cup butter
1½ cup sweetener
3 unbeaten eggs
2 tsp. vanilla
2 Tbsp. milk
2 cups whole wheat flour

2 tsp. baking powder
1 tsp. soda
1 tsp. salt
3 cups rolled oats
½ cup chocolate chips (opt.)

Put soft butter, sweetener, eggs, vanilla and milk into a mixing bowl, mix well. Sift flour, baking powder, soda, and salt together. Add sifted dry ingredients to creamed mixture. Mix well, add rolled oats and mix. Stir in chocolate chips. Bake in 375° oven.

Oatmeal Raisin Cookies

MRS. MIRIAM WENGERD, SUGARCREEK, OH

1½ cup butter, softened
1½ cup honey
1½ cup sucanat
4 eggs
2 tsp. vanilla
1 tsp. salt

2 tsp. soda
1 tsp. baking powder
6 cups spelt flour
4 cups oatmeal
2 cups raisins

Cream butter and honey. Add sucanat and beat. Mix in eggs and beat until fluffy. Add vanilla, salt, soda, and baking powder. Add 4 cups flour, stir well. Stir in oatmeal and raisins. Add last 2 cups flour and mix well. Bake at 350° until golden. Do not overbake. You may substitute currants for raisins; they are smaller than raisins and add a spicy sweetness.

Molasses Cookies

MRS. ALLEN R. BYLER, SMICKSBURG, PA

2 qts. molasses
4 cups olive oil
8 tsp. soda
1 tsp. ginger

1 tsp. cloves
2 tsp. cinnamon
10 eggs
3 Tbsp. vinegar

Heat molasses and olive oil until you can mix it well. Cool, add 2 quarts whole wheat flour. Add eggs, pour vinegar over soda. Add to mixture. Add spices then add flour until thick enough dough to drop on cookie sheet. Bake at 350° for 10 minutes or until done.

Sweet Molasses Cookies

MRS. IVAN J. YODER, MILLERSBURG, OH

4½ cups flour
2 tsp. soda
⅛ tsp. salt
¼ tsp. cinnamon
½ tsp. ginger

1 cup butter
1½ cup molasses
2 eggs
⅓ cup milk

Cream molasses and butter, add eggs. Beat well. Add spices and soda. Add milk. Stir in flour. Mix well. Drop by teaspoonfuls on greased cookie sheet. Bake at 350° for 10-15 minutes, until they are light and golden.

Soft Molasses Cookies

MISS MARY NISLEY, DANVILLE, OH

3 cups molasses
1¾ cup butter or oil
4 eggs
2 tsp. vanilla
4 tsp. baking powder

4 tsp. soda (dissolved in ¼ cup hot water)
2 tsp. salt
3 Tbsp. ginger
2 tsp. cinnamon
8 cups flour

Cream the first 2 ingredients together. Gradually add eggs. Add vanilla, then the rest. Mix well. Chill dough. Shape into walnut-sized balls, flatten. Bake at 375° for 12 minutes.

301

cookies

Honey Supreme Cookies

Mrs. Aaron (Cynthia) Wise, Waterloo, NY

4 cups whole wheat flour	4 eggs
2½ tsp. soda	1 cup chocolate or carob chips (opt.)
2 tsp. salt	4 cups oatmeal
2 cups butter	2 tsp. vanilla
1¾ cup sweetening	½ cup nuts

Sweetening options are honey, maple syrup, 2 cups sucanat, or part dates. (Dates may be blended with liquids and stirred into dry ingredients.) Mix butter, honey and eggs. Stir dry ingredients together and mix into butter mixture. Add vanilla and mix well. Stir in nuts and chips. Bake at 350° for 12-14 minutes. Makes 5-6 dozen cookies.

Natural Tollhouse Cookies

1 c. butter	2 c. wheat flour
½ c. honey	2 c. carob chips or chocolate chips (opt.)
2 eggs	½ c. nuts, chopped
1 tsp. vanilla	½ c. unsweetened coconut
1 tsp. soda	½ c. quick oats
1 tsp. salt	

Cream together butter and honey. Beat in eggs and vanilla. Sift together soda, salt and flour and add to butter mixture. Fold in rest of ingredients. Drop with cookie scoop on cookie sheets. Bake at 350° for 12-15 minutes.

Ranger Joe Cookies

Mrs. Aaron (Cynthia) Wise, Waterloo, NY

1 cup shortening	1 tsp. vanilla
1 cup honey	2 cups oatmeal
2 eggs	2 cups rice crispies
2 cups flour	1 cup coconut (opt.)
½ tsp. baking powder	½ cup peanut butter (opt.)
1 tsp. baking soda	½ cup nuts (opt.)
½ tsp. salt	¾ cup chocolate or carob chips (opt.)

Mix honey, eggs, and shortening until smooth. Stir together first 4 dry ingredients, and add to honey mixture. Add vanilla and mix well. Stir in oatmeal, rice crispies, and any or all options. Bake at 350° for 12-14 minutes.

Triplet Cookies

MRS. JOHN SZKLARZ, DEVINE, TX

2 cups mashed bananas
¼-⅓ cup raisins (or try currants or dates)
¾ tsp. salt
1 tsp. vanilla

3 cups rolled oats
1 Tbsp. ground flax seed
¼ cup unsweetened coconut

Mix bananas, raisins, salt and vanilla together thoroughly. Add remaining ingredients and mix all together. Very easy. The children enjoy making these very much. Place teaspoon sized balls on parchment papered cookie sheet and bake in preheated 350° oven for 30 minutes or until done. Makes 2½ dozen.

Nut Cookies

⅓ cup butter
⅓ cup honey
½ tsp. stevia
1 cup whole wheat flour
dash of salt

1 tsp. soda (scant)
⅔ cup coconut
⅔ cup chopped nuts
¼ cup oatmeal

Melt butter, honey, and stevia. Mix soda with 2 Tbsp. water, then add flour, salt, and soda mixture to butter mixture. Mix well, then add coconut, nuts, and oatmeal.

303

cookies

Brother's Delights

LOVEDA BEAR, PATRIOT, OH

3 cups butter
2½ cups honey
3 eggs
3 cups finely ground walnuts
3 cups coconut
5½ cups barley flour

2 tsp. baking powder
1½ tsp. baking soda
3 cups oatmeal
2 cups crushed cornflakes
2 cups carob chips (opt.)

Melt butter. Mix with honey and eggs. Add the rest of ingredients. Bake at 350° for 15 minutes. Yields: 7 dozen.

No Bake Cookies

VICKY SCHILLING, SCOTLAND, UK

½ cup milk
½ cup maple syrup
1 Tbsp. peanut butter

3 cups rolled oats
½ cup raisins
1 tsp. vanilla

Melt first 3 ingredients in a pan and simmer. Stir until well mixed. Mix next 3 ingredients and then stir in first mixture. Once all is well mixed, form into heaping tablespoonful onto a cookie sheet and press flat with your fingers. Chill in the fridge. Makes 12-16 cookies.

Applesauce Cookies

MIRIAM YODER, LaGRANGE, IN

1 cup honey
½ cup oil
2 eggs, beaten
1 cup applesauce
2½ cups wheat flour

½ tsp. soda
½ tsp. baking powder
1 tsp. cinnamon
½ tsp. vanilla
1 cup sunflower seeds

Stir honey and oil until creamy. Add eggs and applesauce. Sift flour, soda, baking powder, and cinnamon together and add to first mixture. Mix vanilla and sunflower seeds together and add. Drop by teaspoonful onto a greased cookie sheet. Bake at 375° for 10 minutes. This is a favorite of ours; it's soft and moist.

Whoopie Pies

JUANITA WEAVER, JOHNSONVILLE, IL

1 cup honey
½ tsp. salt
½ cup butter
1 tsp. vanilla extract
2 eggs
¼ cup carob powder

¼ cup cocoa
1 cup barley flour
1¼ cup soft wheat flour
2 tsp. baking soda
1 cup sour milk

Cream all ingredients, except milk, until fluffy (about 3 minutes on medium-high). Add milk and beat lightly. For whoopie pies, drop by teaspoons onto greased cookie sheets. Bake at 400°. Can be baked as chocolate cake at 350° (add ½ cup more milk if desired). Frost with icing.

Icing:

1 cup butter
½ cup fructose or honey
7 Tbsp. sifted flour

1 tsp. vanilla
½ cup milk

Put all ingredients in bowl. Let set ½ hour. Beat for 5 minutes or until fluffy.

Healthy

Peanut Butter Cookies

MRS. JEREMY (ROSE) MILLER, ST. IGNATIUS. MT

1½ cup peanut butter
½ cup honey
¼ cup olive oil

½ tsp. salt
1½ cup quick or rolled oats

Blend oats into a flour. Stir together all ingredients, adding flour last. Drop onto oiled cookie sheet and flatten with fork. Bake at 350° for 8-12 minutes, or until golden brown. Makes approximately 30 cookies.

Cherry Winks

MRS. GLENN ZIMMERMAN, GREENWOOD, WI

1½ cup butter
¾ cup honey
4 eggs
¼ cup milk
2 tsp. vanilla
5 cups flour

2 tsp. baking powder
1 tsp. baking soda
1 tsp. salt
1¾ cup chopped pecans
2⅔ cup dried fruit
      (pineapple, apricot, papaya)

Mix dough, then drop by teaspoonsful into crushed cornflakes (takes about 5 cups to coat). Roll into balls and flatten on cookie sheet. Bake at 375° until golden brown.

Filled Date Cookies

MRS. JOE GARBER, PRATTSBURGH, NY

2 cups spelt flour
4 cups wheat flour
4½ cups oatmeal
2 tsp. soda
3 tsp. baking powder
2 tsp. cinnamon

1½ tsp. salt
2 cups honey
1½ cup olive oil
6 eggs
2 tsp. vanilla

Cook oil and honey for 1 minute. Cool. Beat in eggs and vanilla. Combine with dry ingredients. Chill dough. Form balls and flatten slightly on cookie sheet before baking. When cookies are cold, spread one cookie with filling and top with another cookie.

Date Filling:

1 cup water
1½ cup finely chopped dates
1½ Tbsp. cornstarch

1 cup maple syrup
1 Tbsp. lemon juice

Cook until thick.

Choices

Gingersnaps

¼ cup molasses
½ cup raw honey
½ tsp. ground cinnamon
½ tsp. ground cloves
¼ cup oil
⅛ tsp. ground nutmeg

2 Tbsp. water
⅛ tsp. ground allspice
2 cups whole wheat flour
½ tsp. soda
1-2 tsp. ginger

Combine wet ingredients to dry ones. Refrigerate 30 minutes. Preheat oven to 375°. Make 1" balls and put on greased cookie sheet. Flatten to ⅛" thick. Bake 7-9 minutes. Makes 3 dozen. May substitute barley (2 cups) or spelt (1½ cups).

Ginger Spice Cookies

LEAH NISLEY, DANVILLE, OH

1 cup shortening
2 cups sorghum
2 eggs
2 tsp. baking soda
½ tsp. salt

1 Tbsp. ginger
1 tsp. cinnamon
1 tsp. nutmeg
½ tsp. hot water
5 cups flour

Cream together shortening and sorghum. Add eggs, beat until well blended. Stir baking soda and hot water together. Add to creamed mixture. Next add salt and spices blending thoroughly. Add flour and mix well. Drop dough from a teaspoon onto an ungreased baking sheet. Flatten. Bake in a preheated 375° oven for 8-10 minutes. These will keep for some time. Makes 7-8 dozen.

Gingersnaps

MRS. IVAN J. YODER, MILLERSBURG, OH

2 cups molasses
1 cup butter
2 eggs
1 tsp. vanilla
2 tsp. baking powder

3 tsp. baking soda
1 tsp. cinnamon
¼ tsp. salt
2 tsp. ginger
5½ cups spelt flour

Cream butter and molasses. Add eggs, vanilla, and sifted dry ingredients. Chill dough. Roll in small balls and bake at 350° for 10-15 minutes. Do not overbake. I use a small ice cream scoop to shape cookies.

Healthy

Chocolate Mints

MARTHA WIDEMAN, LISTOWEL, ON

⅔ cup butter
½ cup fructose
1 egg
½ tsp. salt

1½ cups spelt or barley flour
½ cup carob powder
½ tsp. soda
4 drops mint flavor

Cream butter and fructose together. Add egg and beat until smooth. Add remaining ingredients. Form into rolls and chill overnight. Slice thin and bake at 375° for 8-10 minutes. When cool, put 2 cookies together with mint frosting.

Mint Frosting:

2 egg whites
¼ tsp. cream of tartar
¼ cup honey

2 tsp. mint flavor
1 cup milk powder

Beat egg whites and cream of tartar until frothy. Beat in honey and mint flavor. Gradually beat in dry milk. If icing is not firm enough, add more dry milk.

Moist Date Cookies

MARTHA WIDEMAN, LISTOWEL, ON

1 cup raisins
½ cup dates
1 cup water
2 eggs
½ cup butter

3 tsp. honey
1 tsp. vanilla
¼ tsp. cinnamon
1 cup pastry or barley flour
1 tsp. baking soda

Combine raisins, dates, and water in saucepan. Boil 3 minutes, cool. Cream together eggs, butter, honey, and vanilla. Sift together cinnamon, flour, and baking soda. Add dry ingredients to creamed mixture alternately with date mixture. Beat well, then chill several hours. Drop from spoon onto cookie sheet. Bake at 350° for 10-12 minutes. These cookies stay soft.

Davy Crockett Bars

Pauline Sauder, Latham, MO

¾ cup butter
2 tsp. vanilla
1 cup applesauce
3 eggs
1 Tbsp. honey
2 cups oatmeal
1⅓ cup whole grain flour
½ cup water

1¼ tsp. stevia
1 tsp. salt
1 cup unsweetened coconut
1 tsp. soda
1 tsp. baking powder
1½ cup chopped nuts
1 cup raisins

Cream butter, vanilla, applesauce, eggs, and honey until fluffy. In a separate bowl, combine dry ingredients and nuts and mix thoroughly. Add to applesauce mixture. Cook raisins in water, and mix with rest of the ingredients. Spread in 9 x 13" cookie sheet. Bake 10-15 minutes at 350°. Do not overbake!

Coconut Dream Bars

Mrs. Miriam Wengerd, Sugarcreek, OH

Crust:

½ cup butter, softened
1 cup sucanat

2 cups wheat flour

Cream butter and sucanat. Then stir in flour. Press into lightly greased 9 x 13" pan. Bake at 350° for 12 minutes. Cool for 30 minutes.

Filling:

4 eggs, well beaten
⅔ cup honey
1 cup sucanat
2 tsp. vanilla

1 tsp. baking powder
6 Tbsp. wheat flour
1 cup chopped pecans
1 cup coconut

Beat eggs in bowl. Add honey, beat until smooth. Beat in sucanat, vanilla, baking powder, and wheat flour. Beat until smooth. Stir in pecans and coconut. Pour onto cooled crust and return to oven. Bake 20-25 minutes. Cool 15 minutes. Cut while warm. Serve when cool. These bars are reminiscent of pecan pie. Sweet and scrumptious!

Healthy

Fruit Bars

MRS. LAMAR (NANCY) ZIMMERMAN, STEVENS, PA

1 cup dates
1 cup raisins
1 cup apples, peeled and chopped
2 cups apple juice
1 cup butter
1 cup chopped walnuts

2 cups whole grain flour
2 tsp. baking soda
½ tsp. salt
4 eggs
2 tsp. vanilla

Boil fruit and juice. Add butter. Mix eggs, vanilla, and dry ingredients. Add fruit mixture. Bake in greased jelly roll pan at 350° for 25-30 minutes. Don't overbake. Cool slightly and cut in bars. I use a glass 9 x 13" pan.

Applesauce Spice Squares

1½ cups flour
2½ tsp. soda
2 tsp. cinnamon
½ tsp. cloves
½ cup butter
2 eggs

½ cup apple juice concentrate
2 tsp. vanilla
1½ cups applesauce
1 cup nuts
1 cup raisins or dates

Bake at 350° for 25 minutes. Frost when cool.

311

cookies

Basic Brownies

SUSAN STALTER, MILLERSBURG, OH

1 cup softened butter
1⅓ cups fructose
3 eggs
1 tsp. vanilla

¼ cup cocoa, rounded
1½ cups whole wheat flour
¼ tsp. real salt
¾ cup chopped nuts

Cream butter and fructose together. Add eggs and vanilla and mix. Add rest and mix well. Pour into greased 9 x 13" pan. (Push batter into corners well.) Bake at 350° for 30 minutes.

Blond Brownies

Lucia Lapp, Benton, IL

¾ cup softened butter
1 cup sucanat
4 eggs
2 tsp. vanilla

2 cups wheat pastry flour
2 tsp. baking powder
1 tsp. salt
1 cup chopped pecans

Cream butter and sucanat. Add eggs and vanilla. Combine dry ingredients and slowly add to creamed mixture. Stir in pecans. Spread in a greased 9 x 13" pan. Bake for 25-30 minutes.

Maple Cream Sauce:

1 cup maple syrup
2 Tbsp. butter

¼ cup milk or cream

Bring syrup and butter to boil and cook 3 minutes. Remove from heat and stir in milk. Best eaten the same day. Serve with sauce drizzled on top and sprinkle with pecans.

Rice Krispie Squares

Juanita Weaver, Johnsonville, IL

½ cup sorghum
½ cup honey
½ cup butter

2 cups peanut butter
10-12 cups cereal
   (rice krispies, puffed rice, etc.)

Boil first 3 ingredients 1 minute. Add peanut butter. Stir until melted. Stir in cereal. Spread in large buttered cookie sheet. Can add sunflower or pumpkin seeds, or nuts.

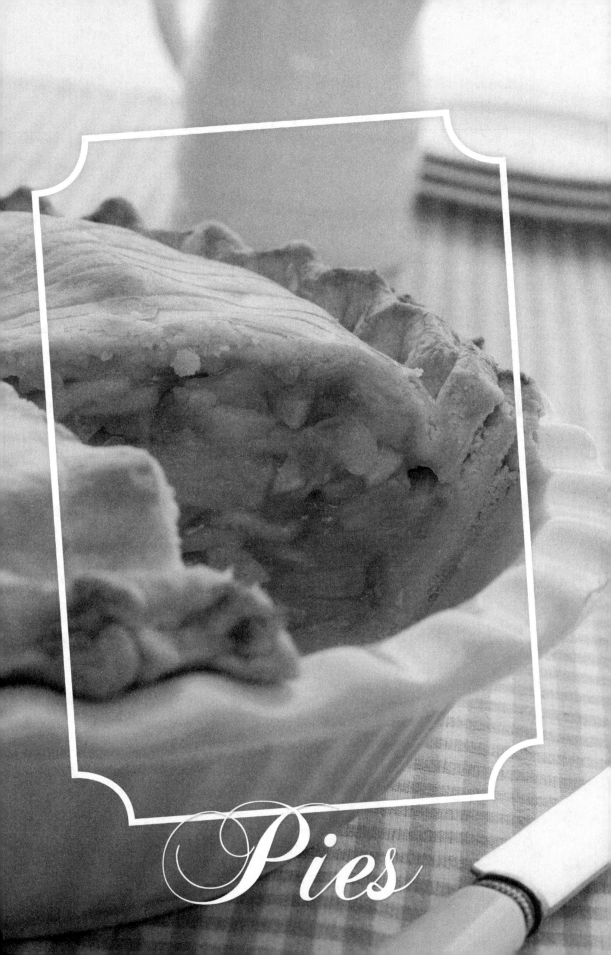

Pies

IS THERE A MAN ALIVE WHO DOESN'T ENJOY A GOOD piece of pie? There's something special about pie. It's such an old-fashioned idea, something we moms like to make as a treat for our families.

Each fall I look forward to eating my mom's and my mother-in-law's delicious pumpkin pie at Thanksgiving time. Pumpkin pie is one of my favorites. Fruit pies are great too. I enjoy cream pies too, but I don't like to eat whip topping; it's so artificial. I like the idea for canned cream in the dairy section. I'd really like to try that sometime. I'm always looking for ways to eliminate one more artificial food from our diet.

It's a little tricky to make perfect crusts with whole wheat flour, but it can be done. Mrs. Urie Miller's tip at the end of the pie section is a good one that I've used—it works!

Roll up your sleeves, don your kitchen apron, get out your rolling pin and surprise your honey with a scrumptious pie.

Choices

Pies

Pumpkin Pie

MRS. MARVIN (KATIE) MILLER

1½ cup pumpkin
1 cup sucanat
½ cup maple syrup
3 Tbsp. flour

3 eggs
1 tsp. salt
1 tsp. pumpkin pie spice
3 cups milk

Mix pumpkin, sucanat, maple syrup, flour, spices, and salt. Add egg yolks, then milk. Beat egg whites and fold in last. Bake at 350° until firm. Yield: 2 pies.

Pumpkin Pie

LUCIA LAPP, BENTON, IL

2 cups pumpkin
½ tsp. salt
1½ cup milk
3 eggs
2 Tbsp. sucanat

⅓ cup honey
1¼ tsp. cinnamon
½ tsp. allspice
1 Tbsp. cornstarch (heaping)

Blend ingredients in blender. Pour into unbaked pie shell and bake at 350° for 45 minutes or until done.

Pumpkin Pie

MRS. KATHRYN HERSHBERGER, CLARE, MI

1 cup pumpkin
1 cup maple syrup
2 tsp. cornstarch (heaping)
⅓ tsp. cloves and allspice

½ tsp. cinnamon
2 eggs, separated
2 cups warm milk
½ tsp. salt

Beat together pumpkin, maple syrup, cornstarch, spices, egg yolks, and salt. Add warm milk. Beat egg whites until stiff and fold in last. Bake at 350°.

Healthy

Pumpkin Cream Pie

LAURA MILLER, ARTHUR, IL

2 cups milk
½-¾ cup honey
2 cups mashed pumpkin*
2-3 eggs
½ cup milk

dash of salt
3 Tbsp. cornstarch
1 Tbsp. flour, rounded
vanilla
pumpkin pie spices

Heat 2 cups milk, honey, and pumpkin in 2 quart kettle. Shake up eggs, ½ cup milk, salt, cornstarch and flour in Tupperware® shaker. Add to hot milk mixture. Stir briskly, and bring to boil. Add vanilla and pumpkin pie spices. Serve warm with graham crackers or cool and fill your favorite crust and add topping (opt.). Enough for two 8" pies.

*Canned, mashed sweet potatoes can also be used.

Homemade Pumpkin Pie Spice

MALINDA MAST, LOBELVILLE, TN

4 tsp. ground cinnamon
2 tsp. ground ginger

1 tsp. ground cloves
½ tsp. ground nutmeg

Combine all ingredients. Store in an airtight container. Use as a substitute for the spices called for in your favorite pumpkin pie recipe.

Grandma's Pumpkin Pie

MRS. IVAN J. YODER, MILLERSBURG, OH

1 cup pumpkin
2 eggs, separated
2 Tbsp. spelt flour
1 cup maple syrup
1/2 tsp. cinnamon

¼ tsp. cloves
¼ tsp. nutmeg
1 cup milk
⅛ tsp. salt

Mix spices into pumpkin; add flour, syrup, and milk. Beat eggs separately. Beat into pumpkin mixture. Pour into unbaked pie shell. Bake at 425° for 10 minutes, then finish at 375°.

Dried Apple Pies

BETTY LONON, MARION, NC

This is actually a "non-recipe." We cook dried apples in apple juice (that is the only sweetening we use), mashing with potato masher several times during the cooking time.* When the apples are the desired consistency, add cinnamon and nutmeg to taste. Then refrigerate this mixture overnight so that it thickens slightly and is less juicy. Make pie dough of your choice, roll out and cut in circle about 5" in diameter. Place this circle on a greased baking sheet, fill ½ with dried apple mixture, fold over and seal edges. Do this until you have used all the pie dough or pie filling. Bake at 400° for 30-40 minutes, until lightly browned. Remove from baking sheet immediately and let cool. Best when eaten while still warm!

*Note: This can be done with any amount that suits your family size. Generally, we use about 1½ quart jars of packed, dried apples (we store our dried apples in quart jars). We cover the apples with apple juice about 1" above the apples. If this is not enough as the apples cook, we add more juice; if it is too much, we can tilt the lid and let some evaporate out. With this amount, we would use about 2-3 tsp. ground cinnamon and 1-2 tsp. ground nutmeg. Start small and add until it is a taste pleasing to you. We use a pie crust recipe for a double crust with this amount of apples. If there is crust left over, we sometimes roll it out thin, sprinkle with salt, cut into squares, prick with a fork, and bake like crackers.

No Sugar Apple Pie

LISA WEAVER, LOGAN, OH

1 cup raisins
4 cups sliced apples
3 Tbsp. minute tapioca
⅓ cup water
½ tsp. cinnamon
¼ tsp. salt
1 pie crust

Cook raisins in ½ cup water for 5 minutes. Blend raisins. Mix with apples. Add tapioca, water, cinnamon, and salt. Pour into pie crust. Bake for 10 minutes at 425°, then 30-35 minutes at 350°.

Shoestring Apple Pie

MIRIAM YODER, LaGRANGE, IN

1 cup honey
2 rounded Tbsp. cornstarch
3 eggs, beaten
pinch of salt
4 cups shoestring apples

Mix together and put in two 8" unbaked pie shells. Sprinkle with cinnamon on top. Bake at 325° until done.

Healthy

Apple Pie

Mrs. Miriam Wengerd, Sugarcreek, OH

1½ cup cider, divided
1½ cup maple syrup
½ tsp. salt
1 cup raisins
3 heaping Tbsp. clear jel

3 eggs, separated
1 tsp. cinnamon
1 tsp. nutmeg
9 cups apples, peeled and
shredded

Heat 1 cup cider, maple syrup, salt, and raisins. Mix clear jel, egg yolks, ½ cup cider, cinnamon, and nutmeg together. Add to first mixture. Boil until thick, then cool. Mix into peeled, shredded apples. Add beaten egg whites last. Pour into crust and top with pie crumbs. Bake at 350° for 40 minutes, or until pie filling bubbles.

Crumbs:

2 cups oatmeal
⅔ cup butter, melted
⅔ cup nuts

⅔ cup sucanat
1 tsp. cinnamon

Mix and sprinkle on top of pie filling.

Honey Apple Pie

Susie Nolt

5-6 Granny Smith apples
1 tsp. cinnamon

⅓ cup whole wheat flour
⅔ cup honey

Do not bother to peel apples, simply core and dice fine. Toss apples with flour and cinnamon. Heap 9" pie shell with apples and drizzle honey over top. Bake at 350° for 10-15 minutes. Put a crumb topping over it:

½ cup sucanat
½ cup whole wheat flour

¼ cup butter

Bake at 425° for 30-40 minutes longer, or until apples are soft.

Best Apple Pie

Mrs. Ivan J. Yoder, Millersburg, OH

1 qt. chopped apples
⅔ cup maple syrup
½ tsp. cinnamon
½ tsp. nutmeg

2 Tbsp. spelt flour
⅛ tsp. salt
1 Tbsp. butter

Prepare apples. Place in bowl. Add rest of ingredients and mix well. Pour into unbaked 9"pie shell. Top with another piece of pie dough. Seal and crimp edges. Brush top of dough with milk. Bake at 425° for 10 minutes. Turn heat down to 350° and bake until crust is light golden brown.

Pecan Pie

Miriam Yoder, LaGrange, IN

3 eggs
¾ cup maple syrup
2 Tbsp. butter, melted

1 tsp. vanilla
1 cup pecans
1 unbaked 8" pie shell

Beat eggs, add syrup, and beat again. Stir in butter, vanilla, and pecans. Pour into unbaked pie shell. Bake at 350° for 35-45 minutes, or until browned and center is just a little jiggly. I have used this for oatmeal pie, too. I use ¾ cup honey instead of syrup and 1 cup oatmeal instead of pecans.

Pecan Pie

Mrs. Ivan J. Yoder, Millersburg, OH

3 eggs
1½ cup maple syrup
1 tsp. vanilla
¼ tsp. salt

2 Tbsp. butter
1 cup chopped nuts
2 Tbsp. spelt flour

Beat eggs, add maple syrup and rest of ingredients. Pour into unbaked pie shell. Bake at 350° for 40 minutes.

Pecan Pie

Mrs. Kathryn Hershberger, Clare, MI

4 eggs
1 cup maple syrup
2 Tbsp. butter, melted

1 tsp. vanilla
½ tsp. salt
1 cup pecans

Beat eggs well, add syrup and beat again. Stir in rest of ingredients and pour into 8" pie shell. Bake at 350° for 35-45 minutes or until browned and center is just a little jiggly.

Rhubarb Cream Pie

Mrs. Glenn Zimmerman, Greenwood, WI

2 Tbsp. butter
2 cups diced rhubarb
½ cup honey
2 egg yolks

¼ cup honey
¼ cup milk
2 rounded Tbsp. flour
pinch of salt

Cook butter, rhubarb, and ½ cup honey in saucepan until rhubarb is tender, then mix together rest of ingredients. Add to cooked rhubarb, and boil 3 minutes, stirring constantly. Cool and pour into a baked pie shell. Top with a meringue made from:

2 egg whites
2 Tbsp. fructose

¼ tsp. cream of tartar
½ tsp. vanilla

Brown in a preheated 425° oven. Serve warm or cool; either way, it's delicious!

321 pies

Ten Dollar Fruit Pie

Frieda Yoder, Millersburg, OH

½ cup oatmeal
1 cup whole wheat flour
1½ cup honey

1 cup milk
1 tsp. salt
1 Tbsp. baking powder

Melt ½ cup butter in 9 x 13" cake pan. Pour batter into this. Heat 1 qt. canned sour cherries or peaches (other fruit may be used if desired) and pour into batter. Bake at 375° for 30 minutes. This is delicious served warm with milk or ice cream.

Blueberry Pie Filling

Mrs. Aaron (Cynthia) Wise, Waterloo, NY

2 qt. blueberries, fresh or frozen
3 cups water
1-1¼ cup honey

¾ cup clear jel
2 Tbsp. ReaLemon (opt.)

In a saucepan, combine ½ of the blueberries, water, and honey. Cook 5 minutes. Add enough water to clear jel to make a thin paste and add to blueberry mixture. Cook until thick enough for bubbles to "pouff". Stir in remaining berries and cool. Raspberry or cherry can be used, but increase honey for sour cherries.

Impossible Blueberry Pie

Mrs. Joe Garber, Prattsburgh, NY

¼ cup oil
½ cup wheat flour
2 eggs
1½ cup milk

¼ tsp. salt
½ cup maple syrup
1 tsp. vanilla
1½ cup blueberries

Mix liquid ingredients. Beat well. Add flour and salt. Beat again. Stir in blueberries. Pour into 9" pie plate. Bake at 375° until set.

Cherry Pie Filling

Susie Nolt

3 cups water
½ heaping cup Perma-flo

1½ cup honey

Combine above ingredients in a kettle and cook until thick, stirring constantly. Turn off heat. Add 3 oz. sugar-free cherry gelatin. Then add as many cherries as you like, 3-6 cups. Makes two 9" pies. Brings compliments from guests who'd never guess it's sugar free!

Fruit Custard Pie

⅓ cup whole wheat flour
½ cup honey
⅛ tsp. stevia
2 or 3 eggs, separated
pinch of salt

4 cups milk
1 tsp. vanilla
½ tsp. cinnamon
2 cups fruit (peaches, strawberries, raspberries, rhubarb)

Mix flour, stevia, salt, and cinnamon. Slowly add egg yolks, vanilla, honey, and milk to make smooth custard. Last fold in beaten egg whites. Divide fruit into 2 pie shells; then add custard. Bake at 325° until just firm in the middle, about 30 minutes. If it is too firm, it will be dry when cool. This is an old Swiss recipe.

Peach Custard Pie

MRS. IVAN J. YODER, MILLERSBURG, OH

2 cups sliced fresh peaches
⅔ cup maple syrup
2 Tbsp. spelt flour (or 1 Tbsp. wheat)
1 egg
⅛ tsp. salt

½ tsp. cinnamon
1 cup milk
2 Tbsp. butter, melted
1 tsp. vanilla

Beat egg, add flour, cinnamon, salt, milk, maple syrup, and vanilla. Add peaches and butter. Pour into unbaked 9" pie shell. Bake at 400° for 10 minutes, then finish at 350°. Pie is baked when the center is set.

323 pies

Sweet Potato Pie

MRS. URIE MILLER, MIDDLEBURY, IN

¼ cup butter, softened
⅓-½ cup sweetener
2 eggs
¾ cup evaporated milk
2 cups mashed, cooked sweet potatoes

1 tsp. vanilla
½ tsp. cinnamon
½ tsp. nutmeg
⅓-½ tsp. salt

Cream together butter and sweetener. Add eggs; mix well. Add milk, sweet potatoes, vanilla, cinnamon, nutmeg and salt; mix well. Pour into pie shell. Bake at 425° for 15 minutes. Reduce heat to 350°. Bake 35-40 minutes longer or until a knife inserted near the center comes out clean. To make your own evaporated milk, simmer milk on low heat in a heavy saucepan or kettle for several hours, until it reaches a nice cream color. When doing large amounts, it may be sealed in sterile jars. Process in boiling water bath for 1 hour.

Cream Pie

Mrs. John (Eva May) Yoder, Clare, MI

2 cups milk

⅓ cup cornstarch

½ cup maple syrup

2 egg yolks

In a saucepan, combine milk and maple syrup. Heat until scalding. Beat egg yolks and cornstarch together, adding a little cold milk if necessary. Stir into hot milk, stirring well until thickened. Remove from heat, add a chunk of butter and vanilla. When cool, but not cold, put into a baked pie crust, adding bananas or coconut, etc. Top with whipped cream.

Pie Crusts

Stir n' Roll Pie Crust

Susan Stalter, Millersburg, OH

2 cups whole wheat flour

¾ tsp. salt

¼ cup olive oil

¼ cup cream

¼ cup whole milk

2 tsp. liquid lecithin

Mix flour and salt. Pour oil, whole milk, cream, and liquid lecithin into one measuring cup (don't stir). Add all at once to flour. Stir until mixed. Press into smooth ball and divide into ⅓ and ⅔. Place ⅔ ball between wax paper (12" squares) and roll out. (Can dampen tabletop to prevent slipping.) Peel off top paper. (If dough tears, mend without moistening.) Place pastry paper-side-up in 9" pie pan. Peel off paper and trim edges. Repeat for top.

Whole Wheat Pie Crust

Kathryn Hershberger, Clare, MI

3 cups whole wheat flour

1 Tbsp. wheat gluten (opt.)

1 tsp. salt

1 cup butter or lard

1 Tbsp. vinegar

½ cup water

Mix dry ingredients together, mix in butter or lard. Put vinegar in water and add last. I think lard makes a flakier crust than butter.

Healthy

Whole Wheat Pastry

MRS. URIE MILLER, MIDDLEBURY, IN

3 cups whole wheat pastry flour
1 tsp. baking powder
½ tsp. salt
1 cup butter

1 egg, slightly beaten
1 Tbsp. vinegar
5 Tbsp. cold water

Combine flour, baking powder, salt, and butter. Blend together until crumbly. Combine egg, water, and vinegar. Stir into flour with fork until ingredients are moistened. With hands, mold into a ball. Chill at least 15 minutes before rolling. Divide pastry in half and press into a ball. Roll out between 2 squares of waxed paper. Remove top sheet of paper and invert pastry over a pie pan, easing the pastry gently into the pan. Remove waxed paper and fit pastry into pan without stretching. Roll out second half of pastry and place over filling, first having moistened edge of bottom pastry along rim of pan with milk to help secure bond. Press top and bottom pastry together along rim; trim off along edge and flute. Moisten top with back of spoon dipped in milk to aid browning. Make a few vents in top to allow steam to escape. Bake according to directions. Makes enough pastry for 2 two crust 9" pies or 3 or 4 single crust pies. For pie shells, fit pastry into pans, flute, and prick entire surface with a fork. Bake at 400° for about 10 minutes or until lightly browned, or until shell can easily be turned in pan.

Whole Grain Pie Crust

MRS. ERVIN (HANNAH) HOSTETLER, PLEASANVILLE, TN

4 cups oat flour
4 cups wheat flour
   (you can use pastry wheat)
2 tsp. baking powder
3 tsp. salt

1 cup butter
1 cup oil
2 eggs, slightly beaten
2 Tbsp. vinegar
1 cup cold water

Mix flours, baking powder, and salt. Cut in butter and oil. Add vinegar, eggs, and cold water. Mix together lightly. (This is a more crumbly dough to roll out.) You can use variation by adding ground flax seeds or other seeds to the flour. Oat flour can be made by putting quick oats in the blender.

Tender Flaky Pie Crust

LUCIA LAPP, BENTON. IL

5 cups whole grain flour
2 tsp. salt
1 cup butter

1 cup unflavored coconut oil
1 Tbsp. vinegar
1 egg and water to make ½ cup

Combine first 4 ingredients to make crumbs. Mix vinegar, egg, and water and add to flour mixture. Roll out. Makes three 9" double crust pies. Very handy to freeze extras.

Choices

Pie Dough

Mrs. John (Eva May) Yoder, Clare, MI

4 cups Prairie Gold flour
2 Tbsp. wheat gluten
1 tsp. baking powder
2 tsp. salt

1½ cups lard
1 egg
1 Tbsp. vinegar
1 cup water

Mix first 4 ingredients together, then cut in lard until crumbly. Beat last 3 ingredients together and add to flour mixture. Mix just until moistened. Depending on flour, you may need to add more water.

Whole Wheat Pie Crust

Elizabeth Stalter, Millersburg, OH

1¾ cups flour
¾ tsp. salt
2 tsp. liquid lecithin

⅜ cup olive oil
¼ cup cold whole milk

Mix flour and salt. Pour oil and milk into one measuring cup. (Do NOT stir.) Add all at once to flour. Stir until mixed. Press into smooth ball. Cut in half. Place each half between 12" squares of wax paper. Dampen tabletop to prevent slipping. Roll out ⅛" thick. Peel off top paper. If dough tears, mend without moistening. Flip into pie pan, take off top paper, and press into place. Do the same for top crust once pie has filling in. Place crust scraps in 9 x 13" pan, sprinkle with cinnamon sugar and bake for 10 minutes at 350°. For single crust: 1⅓ cups flour, ½ tsp. salt, ⅓ cup oil, 3 Tbsp. milk, 1 Tbsp. dough enhancer.

Mom's Perfect Pie Dough

Joyce Strite, Cochise, AZ

6 cups whole wheat flour
2 cups shortening (lard or butter)

1 tsp. baking powder
1 tsp. salt

Mix together until crumbs resemble the size of peas. Beat together 2 eggs, 1⅓ cups water, and 4 Tbsp. vinegar. Add liquid mixture to dry ingredients until a nice tacky ball. Roll out thinly on floured pie board and fill pie plates. Makes approximately 4 one crust pies and 3 two crust pies.

TIP

If you have problems when rolling out whole wheat pastry, try rolling out between two layers of waxed paper. Remove one sheet of waxed paper. Fit gently into pie pan. Remove second sheet.

—Mrs. Urie Miller, Middlebury, IN

Desserts

SOMETIMES YOU WANT TO MAKE A SWEET TREAT FOR A special occasion. Other times you want to serve dessert to dress up an ordinary meal. Or maybe you want a bedtime snack for the family.

You'll find a variety of delicious possibilities in this section. Pumpkin Pie Squares and Pineapple Rings sound like something the Wengerds would enjoy at Thanksgiving and other holiday meals. I would imagine the Basic Crepes to be perfect to serve using summer fruits as a filling. Need a frozen dessert that can be made in advance? Minty Ice Cream Dessert will fill the bill! It's so good you might not realize it doesn't have any sugar in it.

Why not choose one evening a week to have as dessert night and then try out some of these healthy choices?

Date Pudding

FRIEDA YODER, MILLERSBURG, OH

1 cup dates, chopped
1 cup boiling water
1 tsp. soda
1 cup cane molasses

1 tsp. baking powder
1 Tbsp. butter, melted
1 cup whole spelt flour

Pour boiling water over soda and dates and let stand until cool. Add molasses, baking powder, butter, and flour. Bake in a 9 x 9" pan at 350° for 20 minutes or until done. Cut in squares when cool and layer in bowl with sweetened whipped cream to serve.

Date Pudding

MRS. URIE MILLER, MIDDLEBURY, IN

1 cup boiling water

1 cup dates, cut up

Pour boiling water over dates. Set aside to cool. Measure and sift into bowl:

1½ cups whole wheat flour
1 tsp. soda

1 tsp. baking powder
½ tsp. salt

Add:

¼-⅓ cup sorghum or maple syrup
1 egg
2 Tbsp. melted butter

date mixture
1 cup chopped nuts

Mix and pour into 9 x 13" baking pan. Pour sauce over top made up of the following:

1½ cups boiling water
2 Tbsp. butter

⅔ cup maple syrup

Bake at 350° for 30-35 minutes, or until done. Serve with whipped cream.

Vanilla Pudding

ELIZABETH STALTER, MILLERSBURG, OH

6 egg yolks, slightly beaten
6 Tbsp. butter
1 Tbsp. vanilla
6 cups cold milk

6 Tbsp. cornstarch
1⅛ cup fructose or ¾ cup honey
¾ tsp. salt

Measure out egg yolks, butter, and vanilla. In saucepan or double boiler, mix together rest of ingredients and bring to a low boil for 1 minute over medium heat, whisking constantly. Gradually stir at least half of the cooked mixture into egg yolks, whisk back into saucepan with remaining mixture: boil again for 1 minute. Remove from heat and stir in butter and vanilla. Chill. If desired, put a topping or coconut on top, or mix in fresh fruit.

Coconut or Vanilla Pudding

Mrs. Ivan J. Yoder, Millersburg, OH

2 cups milk
2 Tbsp. butter
1 heaping Tbsp. flour
¾ cup coconut

2 eggs, separated
¾ cup maple syrup
1 tsp. vanilla or maple flavor

Put 1½ cup milk, syrup, and butter in a 3 qt. saucepan. Heat. Take remaining ½ cup of milk and make a paste with it and flour. Separate eggs. Add the yolks to paste and blend well. Pour slowly into milk mixture and bring to a boil. Boil 2-3 minutes. Turn off heat. Beat egg whites stiff and beat into hot pudding. Cool and serve with crushed crackers and whipped cream if desired.

Maple Syrup Pudding

R.M.Z., Thorp, WI

1¾ cup milk
¼ cup cornstarch or clear jel
¾ cup maple syrup
1 tsp. salt

2 Tbsp. butter
2 egg yolks
1 cup whipping cream

Heat milk and maple syrup. (Do *not* make too hot! Milk will curdle badly!) Mix cornstarch, salt, and ¼ cup milk. Add to hot mixture. Cook until bubbly then remove from heat and add beaten egg yolks. Return all to stove, stirring constantly until first bubble appears, then remove from heat. Stir in butter and cool thoroughly, then add whipped cream. Delicious!

Maple Syrup Pudding

Mrs. Kathryn Hershberger, Clare, MI

8 cups milk, divided
¾ cup Perma-flo
1¾ cup maple syrup

1 tsp. salt
8 egg yolks
¼ cup butter

Bring 7 cups of milk to a boil. Mix 1 cup milk with Perma-flo, maple syrup, and salt. Add to boiling milk. Take out 1 cup and mix with the beaten egg yolks. Return to hot milk mixture. Stir until thickened on low heat. Add butter and stir to mix. This is good to use for pie filling for peanut butter, banana, and coconut cream pies.

Rice & Raisin Pudding

SUSIE NISLEY, DANVILLE, OH

1 cup brown rice
6 cups milk
2 beaten egg yolks
1 cup sweet cream

½ cup maple syrup
½ tsp. salt
½-¾ cup raisins

Cook brown rice in milk until soft. Add beaten egg yolks with sweet cream. Add maple syrup and salt. Cook raisins in a little water until soft, add to rice mixture. Do not boil after adding eggs, just until thick.

Yorkshire Pumpkin Cobbler

MABEL ZIMMERMAN

Pour Yorkshire Pudding* into prepared pan and carefully spoon pumpkin custard on top. For custard, mix together:

2 eggs
1 cup milk
3 cups pumpkin puree
1-2 cups sucanat

1 Tbsp. flour
1 tsp. cinnamon
½ tsp. salt

Bake at 350° for 1 hour or until done. The cake will then be on top and custard on bottom. Serve warm or cold with or without ice cream. A delicious way to use lots of pumpkin. *See page 33 for Yorkshire Pudding recipe.

Cherry Pudding

MRS. URIE MILLER, MIDDLEBURY, IN

1 cup sifted whole wheat flour
1 tsp. baking powder
⅛ tsp. salt

1 Tbsp. butter, melted
½ cup + 1 Tbsp. milk
¼-⅓ cup honey or sorghum

Sauce:

1 cup pitted sour cherries, sweetened
 to taste

½ cup hot cherry juice
1 Tbsp. butter, melted

Sift together flour, baking powder, and salt. Add butter, milk, and sweetener; mix until blended. Pour into 9" square baking pan. Cover with cherry sauce. Bake at 375° for 30-40 minutes or until done. Serve warm with milk or ice cream. For an extra-special dish, sprinkle top with pecans before baking.

Chocolate Pudding

Mrs. Marvin (Katie) Miller

2 cups milk

3 Tbsp. cornstarch

½ cup sucanat

1 heaping Tbsp. cocoa

Heat milk to boiling. Mix together cornstarch, sucanat, and cocoa. Add a little milk. Slowly add to hot milk. Stir until boiling and add 1 tsp. vanilla.

Vanilla Pudding

Mrs. Marvin (Katie) Miller

3½ cups milk

¾ cup maple syrup (or 1 cup honey)

2 egg yolks

⅓ cup cornstarch

1 tsp. vanilla

Heat milk to boiling, then add maple syrup, bring to a boil. Mix egg yolks with some milk then add cornstarch. Add to milk. Stir until boiling, add vanilla.

Sweet Potato Pudding

Loveda Bear, Patriot, OH

4 cups mashed, cooked sweet potatoes

¼ cup honey + 1 tsp. orange rind

1 tsp. vanilla

1 tsp. cinnamon

½ cup chopped nuts

½ cup chopped dried apples

½ cup raisins or dates

Mix together and cover mixture. Refrigerate for 3 days. May serve with whipped cream.

Molasses Pudding

R.M.Z., Thorp, WI

5 cups milk

½ cup maple syrup

1 cup molasses

5 eggs

1 scant cup flour

½ tsp. salt

1 Tbsp. vanilla

Mix flour and maple syrup. Add ½ cup milk, molasses, eggs, salt, and vanilla, and beat. Bring 4½ cups milk to a boil and pour egg mixture in. Stir until thick.

Indian Pudding

SHARRI NOBLETT, PORT ARTHUR, TX

1 qt. milk	⅔ cup yellow cornmeal
¾ cup maple syrup	1 tsp. ground ginger
2 Tbsp. butter	¼ tsp. ground nutmeg

Grease shallow 2 qt. casserole or pan. In saucepan, combine 3 cups milk and syrup. Heat mixture to boiling over medium heat. Then add butter. In small bowl, combine cornmeal and spices. Add gradually to milk mixture. Reduce heat to low. Cook about 10 minutes. Stir constantly. Spoon into the prepared casserole dish. Pour the remaining milk over pudding. Do not stir. Bake at 300° for 2½ hours or until milk has been absorbed and top is golden brown.

No Cook Pudding

SANDRA SMUCKER, JOHN DAY, OR

4 cups milk (I use raw goat milk)	2 tsp. vanilla
1 cup rapadura	½ cup cocoa*
⅓-½ cup no cook clear jel	

Mix rapadura, clear jel, and cocoa together and slowly pour into milk while stirring with a whisk. Add vanilla. Mix well and let set in fridge for at least 10 minutes before serving. Should be eaten in 1-2 days as the enzymes in the milk will break it down and it will become runny.

*For chocolate pudding.

335

desserts

Caramel Raisin Pudding

MRS. VERNON SCHROCK, LEWISTOWN, IL

Batter:

3 cups whole wheat flour	1 tsp. salt
1 cup rolled oats	½ cup olive oil
¾ cup honey	1 egg
2 tsp. soda	2 cups milk

Mix dry ingredients, then add oil, egg, and milk, and mix well. In saucepan, boil together until browned:

¾ cup sucanat	2 cups water
3 Tbsp. butter	½ tsp. vanilla

Boil until sucanat is dissolved. Spread 2 cups raisins in bottom of 10 x 14" cake pan. Add syrup mixture, then spoon batter on top. Bake at 325° for 45 minutes. This disappears at our table! It's a 1-piece dessert, and we serve it with milk.

Peanut Butter Pudding

¾ cup water
2 tsp. rice flour
½ of 12 oz. pkg. firm tofu
2 Tbsp. peanut butter

1 Tbsp. honey
1 tsp. vanilla
2 tsp. stevia

Heat water and rice flour to boiling. Blend rest of ingredients in blender. Mix with water mixture, simmer for 1 minute. Chill. When I doubled the batch, it did not set up as well. Maybe use a little gelatin.

Rhubarb Bread Pudding

Mrs. Abby Abbott Rider, Delphi, IN

2 cups diced rhubarb
⅓ cup honey
2 cups whole wheat bread
1 cup milk

1 egg
1 tsp. lemon or orange peel
1½ tsp. lemon juice

Mix all together and bake in a casserole dish at 375° for about 1 hour. This is nice with rhubarb sauce over it—rhubarb cooked with enough honey to taste.

Maple Tapioca

Mrs. Kathryn Hershberger, Clare, MI

2 eggs, beaten
1 cup maple syrup
4 cups milk

½ tsp. salt
½ cup tapioca or
   3 Tbsp. minute tapioca

Beat eggs and add rest of ingredients in heavy saucepan. Cook until thick, stirring almost constantly.

Tapioca Pudding

Mrs. Urie Miller, Middlebury, IN

¼ cup maple syrup
3 Tbsp. minute tapioca, slightly rounded
⅛ tsp. salt

2¾ cups milk
¾ tsp. vanilla or maple flavoring

Mix maple syrup, tapioca, salt, and ¾ cup milk together in bowl. Let set for 15 minutes. Meanwhile, bring 2 cups milk to a boil in heavy saucepan. Add tapioca mixture. Bring to boil over medium heat, stirring almost constantly. Simmer on low for a minute or two. Remove from heat; add flavoring. Chill. May add whipped cream for an extra special dish.

Healthy

Strawberry Tapioca

MRS. IVAN J. YODER, MILLERSBURG, OH

2 qt. water
1½ cup tapioca

1½-2 cups fructose or maple syrup

Bring water to a boil. Add tapioca. Boil 10 minutes. Stir it several times. Turn off heat and add sweetener. Let set 20 minutes. Now add 1 qt. frozen strawberries, ⅛ tsp. salt, and 1 tsp. vanilla. Let it set until strawberries are thawed, mix, and then refrigerate. Whip 1 cup whipping cream sweetened with 2-3 Tbsp. of sweetener and mix into tapioca! This is very refreshing. Oftentimes we eat it without the cream.

Strawberry Rhubarb Tapioca

LUCIA LAPP, BENTON, IL

1 can frozen apple/berry concentrate
4 cups rhubarb
2-4 cups strawberries

½-1 cup honey or fructose
½ cup (heaping) tapioca

Mix everything but strawberries and cook until soft and tapioca is clear. Add strawberries and cool.

Pumpkin Roll

DOREEN OTTO, GRAYSON, KY

2 eggs
¼ cup honey
2 scoops stevia
½ cup blended pumpkin

⅔ tsp. soda
⅔ tsp. cinnamon
½ + ⅛ cup spelt flour

Blend eggs, honey, and stevia well. Add remaining ingredients. Put greased wax paper on 9 x 13" cookie sheet. Bake 10 minutes at 350°. Dump on tea towel sprinkled with 10x sugar. Roll up and cool. Filling:

6-7 oz. cream cheese
¼ tsp. vanilla

2½ Tbsp. melted butter
3 scoops stevia

Beat well. Serve with topping: ¼ cup ReaLemon, ¼ cup water, clear jel. Heat ReaLemon to boiling, add water and thicken with clear jel as desired. Add 4-5 scoops stevia. Then cool.

Frozen Pumpkin Dessert

JUANITA WEAVER, JOHNSONVILLE, IL

2 cups pumpkin
¾ cup sorghum
½ tsp. salt
½ tsp. nutmeg

2 tsp. cinnamon
¼ tsp. ginger (optional)
1 qt. cream, whipped to 2 qt.
1 tsp. vanilla

Fold all ingredients together carefully. Do not overmix. Fills 9 x 13" pan. Freeze by itself or on top of graham cracker crust. Also good on top of crust made with crushed gingersnaps or molasses cookies mixed with butter and toasted.

Pumpkin Pie Squares

ROSALYN NOLT

Crust:

1½ cup whole wheat flour
¾ cup oatmeal
⅜ cup sucanat

⅜ cup honey
¾ cup butter, softened
⅛ tsp. sea salt

Combine all ingredients and press into a greased 9 x 13" pan.

Filling:

3 cups cooked pumpkin
⅜ cup whole wheat flour
3 eggs
3 tsp. vanilla

¾ cup honey, scant
¾ tsp. sea salt
1 Tbsp. cinnamon
2 cups milk

Put all ingredients into blender and blend until smooth. Pour over crust. Bake at 350° for 45 minutes-1 hour, or until done. Note: This pumpkin filling also makes good pies. Double the filling for three 9" pies.

Creamy Baked Custard

SUSIE NISLEY, DANVILLE, OH

10 egg yolks, well beaten
1½ cups maple syrup
8 Tbsp. spelt flour, sifted fine

1½ tsp. salt
flavoring if desired
2 qts. boiling milk

Add maple syrup, flour, salt, and flavoring to egg yolks, and beat together until smooth. Add milk while stirring briskly. Pour into cake pan, set in hot water in 350° oven. Do not let water boil, or custard will curdle. Sometimes I add cold water until custard is set to keep from boiling. Sprinkle with cinnamon before baking. Chill 12 hours.

Healthy

Egg Custard

Mrs. John Allgyer, Drumore, PA

4 cups cream	pinch of salt
3 cups milk	¾ cup honey
1 Tbsp. vanilla	8 eggs

Beat eggs, then add cream, vanilla, salt, honey, and 1 Tbsp. cinnamon. Beat well then add milk last. Beat again. You need to bake this in hot water on a cookie sheet with sides. I have about one cup size glass containers I usually put it in. Bake at 325° for 1 hour. Enjoy! It's delicious.

Quick Marbled Cobbler

Lucia Lapp, Benton, IL

1½ cup whole grain flour	pinch of salt
¾ cup fructose	1½ Tbsp. oil
1 Tbsp. baking powder	¾ cup yogurt or milk

Spread dough on bottom of a greased 8 x 11" pan and spread a jar of your favorite canned pie filling on top. Bake at 350° for 20-30 minutes. Serve warm with fresh whipped cream.

Danish Dessert

Mrs. Aaron (Cynthia) Wise, Waterloo, NY

¾ cup honey	⅔ cup clear jel
6 cups fruit juice	1 Tbsp. plain gelatin

Bring honey and juice to a simmer. Put ⅓-½ cup water into clear jel to make a thin paste. Stir into simmering mixture and continue stirring until thick. Remove from heat and sprinkle gelatin in while stirring. Cool, then add frozen and partly thawed fruit. Orange juice with peaches or mixed fruit, apple juice with cherries or strawberries, etc.

Vanilla Pudding

Mrs. Aaron (Cynthia) Wise, Waterloo, NY

2 qt. milk	½ cup whole wheat flour
2 eggs	½ tsp. salt
½ cup honey	2 tsp. vanilla
½ cup cornstarch	

Warm all but 2 cups milk in kettle. Put 2 cups milk and remaining ingredients into the blender. Blend and pour slowly into warmed milk, stirring constantly until thick. Remove from heat and cool. Whole wheat flour will leave a speckled appearance, but it's delicious anyway.

Tofu Cheesecake

12 oz. tofu
1½ Tbsp. cornstarch
¼ cup honey
1 Tbsp. oil

1¼-1½ Tbsp. ReaLemon
½ Tbsp. vanilla
dash salt

Blend together. Crush 1½ cup graham crackers. Add ⅛ cup melted butter. Mix well and press into 8 x 8" pan. Bake at 350° for about 10 minutes. Pour on tofu and bake again for 45 minutes.

Strawberry Cheese Dessert

SUSIE NISLEY, DANVILLE, OH

8 oz. cream cheese
1 cup creamed cottage cheese
2 Tbsp. honey
½ cup heavy cream

1 env. unflavored gelatin
¼ cup cold water
1 qt. sliced strawberries

Beat cream cheese, cottage cheese, and honey together. Gradually add cream, beating until thick. Soften gelatin in water, dissolve over low heat. Add to cheese mixture, blending well. Pour into lightly oiled 1 quart mold until firm. Unmold and put strawberries on top. Serve date sugar separately.

Tofu Maple Cheesecake

BECKY COBLENTZ, LIBBY, MT

⅓ cup orange juice concentrate
1 Tbsp. plain gelatin
2-10.5 oz. containers mashed tofu
1 large ripe banana

⅔ cup maple syrup
½ tsp. vanilla
2 Tbsp. fresh lemon juice

Pour orange juice concentrate into top of double boiler. Sprinkle unflavored gelatin over orange juice and dissolve. Set aside. In a blender, mix the rest of the ingredients and then add the orange gelatin, blend until smooth.

Crust: Take enough rolled oats and mix with some of the filling to make it stick together and line a 10" glass pie pan. Pour tofu filling into pie pan. You may add chopped flax seed to sprinkle on top. Refrigerate several hours. Better the second day, because maple flavor mellows.

Pineapple Rings

2-20 oz. cans pineapple rings
5 tsp. plain gelatin

1 cup boiling water or juice

Drain pineapple rings. Soak gelatin in ¾ cup juice. When softened, dissolve gelatin mixture in boiling water. Stir until dissolved. Keep pineapple in original cans and pour gelatin over to fill. Refrigerate until set. To serve: Cut out bottom of can and run lukewarm water over can to loosen gelatin. Not so hot that gelatin melts. Slide tube of pineapple out and slice. Serve with cottage cheese. Simple and delicious! Note: Use your imagination for flavored liquid. Fruit juice (orange, peach, cherry, grape) makes it attractive, too. You may want to sweeten it some.

Pineapple Rings

MRS. RUBY SHETLER, HOMER, MI

8 slices pineapple
¾ cup natural peanut butter
¼ cup plain yogurt
¼ cup maple syrup

¾ cup whipping cream
2 Tbsp. maple syrup
⅛ tsp. cinnamon
⅛ tsp. salt

Mix together peanut butter, yogurt, and ¼ cup maple syrup until creamy. Spoon on top of pineapple rings. Whip the cream until desired stiffness; add 2 Tbsp. maple syrup, salt, and cinnamon. Put on top of rings. Chill and serve. Tip: For good peanut butter, mix 16 oz. natural peanut butter and ¼ cup sorghum. Stir well to mix. We have used Honey Frosting instead of whipping cream with success.

Sugar-Free Fruit Pizza

MRS. KATHRYN HERSHBERGER, CLARE, MI

½ cup butter
1 egg
1⅓ cups whole wheat flour
1 tsp. baking powder
pinch of salt

8 oz. cream cheese, softened
3 Tbsp. maple syrup
2 cups pineapple juice
2 Tbsp. gelatin
fresh or canned fruit

Cream butter and egg together. Add next 3 ingredients, pat into greased pizza pan. Bake at 375° for 10 minutes. Cool. Cream together cream cheese and maple syrup and spread over cooled crust. Cover with fruit. For glaze, cook pineapple juice and gelatin together until clear. Allow to cool until slightly thickened. Pour onto pizza. Refrigerate.

Fruit Pizza Crust

Juanita Weaver, Johnsonville, IL

¼ cup honey
¼ cup fructose
1 cup butter
2¼ cups soft wheat flour

½ tsp. cream of tartar
½ tsp. baking soda
2 Tbsp. cornstarch

Beat all ingredients together and spread evenly into an 11 x 16" cookie sheet, well greased. Bake at 350° until lightly golden colored on top, about 10 minutes.

Fruit Pizza Crust

Juanita Weaver, Johnsonville, IL

½ cup sorghum
½ cup butter
1 egg
⅛ tsp. salt
½ tsp. cinnamon

½ tsp. baking soda
⅛ cup hot water
1 cup oatmeal
1 cup barley or wheat flour

Beat all ingredients together until well mixed. Press or spread into an 11 x 16" greased cookie sheet. Bake at 350° for 8-10 minutes.

Fruit Pizza Filling

Juanita Weaver, Johnsonville, IL

8 oz. cream cheese, softened
½ cup plain yogurt
1 cup cream, whipped to 2 cups

¼ cup honey
⅛ tsp. pure vanilla

Whip cream separately until peaks stand formed. Cream remaining ingredients together until smooth. Stir in cream carefully by hand. Enough for one large pan. Do several hours ahead of time so it has time to stiffen.

Banana Cream

MRS. GLENN ZIMMERMAN, GREENWOOD, WI

2 Tbsp. plain gelatin
1¼ cups milk
½ cup hot water
2 cups mashed banana pulp

2 Tbsp. orange juice
3 Tbsp. honey
pinch of salt

Mash bananas until a smooth cream is formed. Add milk, orange juice, honey, and salt. Blend thoroughly. Stir in gelatin, dissolved in hot water. Pour into mold and refrigerate. Serve garnished with whipped cream, lightly sprinkled with nutmeg.

Strawberry Cream

MRS. GLENN ZIMMERMAN, GREENWOOD, WI

1 cup cold milk
1 cup hot milk
1 Tbsp. plain gelatin

¼ cup honey
1 tsp. vanilla
1-3 cups frozen strawberries

Put cold milk in blender, add gelatin. Heat 1 cup milk while gelatin soaks. Add hot milk to cold milk and blend well. Add next ingredients, one at a time, and blend until well blended. Let set in fridge for 15-20 minutes. Ready to eat!

Fruit Glaze

EDNA MILLER

Soak 1 Tbsp. gelatin in 2 Tbsp. water. Thaw 1½ cups frozen fruit, or use fresh fruit. Press through sieve. Bring to a boil in saucepan. Remove from heat and add gelatin. Stir until gelatin is dissolved. Chill until set but not firm. Pour over desserts such as puddings, pies, or whatever desired.

Mom's Mixed Fruit Slush

MRS. IVAN J. YODER, MILLERSBURG, OH

2 qt. fresh or canned peaches
3-20 oz. cans pineapple
12 apples, peeled and shredded
7-8 lbs. bananas, sliced

2 cans orange juice concentrate
1 qt. water
1 cup fructose

Mix and freeze. Yield: 8 quarts.

Fruity Delight

MRS. AARON (CYNTHIA) WISE, WATERLOO, NY

2 pkg. graham crackers, crushed
¼ cup melted butter (opt.)
8 oz. cream cheese

¼-½ cup honey
1 tsp. vanilla
1 cup whipping cream

Mix cracker crumbs and melted butter together. Press lightly into serving dish or 9 x13" pan. Mix cream cheese in mixer until smooth. Add honey and vanilla. Beat until smooth before adding whipped cream. Spread over graham crust. Pour 1½-2 quarts of blueberry pie filling over cream for a very fruity dessert.

Pineapple Rice Cream

LOVEDA BEAR

1 cup boiling water
1 Tbsp. plain gelatin
3 eggs
½ cup honey

¼ cup butter
2 cups cooked rice
1 cup crushed pineapple
1 cup marshmallows

Blend water and gelatin in blender to dissolve gelatin. Continue to blend, while adding eggs, honey, and butter. Then add ice cubes until thickened. Pour mixture in bowl. Stir in rice, pineapple, and homemade marshmallows (following recipe). Serve as a healthy dessert.

Marshmallows

LOVEDA BEAR

2 Tbsp. gelatin
5 Tbsp. cold water
¾ cup boiling water

½ cup honey
½ tsp. vanilla flavoring

Soak gelatin in cold water. Add remaining ingredients, pouring boiling water over all and beat until mixture holds a soft peak. Pour into an 8 x 8" pan that is wet. When chilled, cut. This cannot be remelted. This recipe goes well with Pineapple Rice Cream (preceding recipe).

Healthy

Cottage Cheese Salad

JUANITA WEAVER, JOHNSONVILLE, IL

2 Tbsp. gelatin
¼ cup cold water
6 oz. frozen orange or grape juice concentrate

1 cup boiling water
1 cup cold water or fruit juice

Soften gelatin in cold water. Pour on boiling water and stir to dissolve. Add cold liquid and frozen juice. When partially set, beat in the following:

1 qt. pears, drained
1 can crushed pineapple, drained

8 oz. cream cheese
1 cup cottage cheese

Carefully fold in:

1 cup cream, whipped to 2 cups with a tsp. vanilla

¼ cup honey

Variation: Substitute 1 cup of crushed strawberries for juice concentrate.

Tomato Jelly Salad

MARTHA WIDEMAN, LISTOWEL, ON

3 cups tomato juice
1¾ Tbsp. gelatin

sweetener

Bring ½ of juice to a boil. Stir in gelatin that has been dissolved in ¼ cup water for 5 minutes. Stir well and let set. A very quick and pretty salad for company when put in molds.

Citrus Salad

MRS. SUSIE NISLEY, DANVILLE, OH

1 cup fresh pineapple chunks
1 cup fresh orange pieces
1 cup fresh tangerine pieces

1 cup sour cream
½ cup pecan halves
½ cup flaked coconut

In a large bowl, combine the fruit, sour cream, nuts, and coconut. Cover and refrigerate for several hours. If desired, serve in lettuce lined bowl. Yield: 6-8 servings.

Carrot Salad

MARIE BEAR, PATRIOT, OH

8 cups carrots
2 cups homemade mayonnaise
  (pages 126-127)

20 oz. crushed pineapple
1 cup raisins

Wash and peel carrots (approximately 2 lbs.). Shred, and add mayonnaise, pineapple, and raisins. Sprinkle sunflower seeds on top if desired. Serves 12.

Fresh Garden Salad

MRS. CRIST (SUSIE) NISLEY, DANVILLE, OH

1 can crushed pineapple
½ cup maple syrup
6 Tbsp. water
2 pkg. Knox gelatin (1 Tbsp.)
1 cup shredded carrots
1 pint cream, whipped

1 cup cut-up celery
1 cup nuts
1 cup cottage cheese
1 cup homemade Miracle Whip,
  scant (pages 128-129)

Mix gelatin with water. Let set 5 minutes. Bring pineapples and maple syrup to a boil. Add soaked gelatin. Stir until dissolved, set aside to cool. Add rest of ingredients. Chill overnight.

Cranberry Jell-O Salad

JUANITA WEAVER, JOHNSONVILLE, IL

1-12 oz. bag cranberries, chopped
3 cups shredded apples
3 cups green grapes, sliced in rings
½ cup fructose or honey

12 oz. juice concentrate
1 can crushed pineapples
3 Tbsp. plain gelatin
1½ cup sunflower seeds (opt.)

Soak gelatin in 1 cup cold water. Add 1 cup boiling water. Stir until dissolved. Add pineapple juice and water to make 5 cups. Chill until partly set. Stir in remaining ingredients. For juice concentrate you can use pineapple, apple raspberry, apple cherry, apple kiwi strawberry or white grape juice.

Healthy

Honey Banana Mold

SUSIE NISLEY, DANVILLE, OH

2 Tbsp. gelatin
¼ cup cold water
1½ cups milk
1 Tbsp. lemon juice

½ cup honey (not raw)
3 bananas, mashed
1 cup whipped cream

Soak gelatin in cold water until soft. Heat milk, remove from oven and stir in gelatin. Add honey, bananas, and lemon juice. Set in a cool place. When it begins to thicken, fold in the whipped cream. Chill thoroughly.

Basic Crepes

MARY BETH HEISEY, PUEBLO WEST, CO

4 eggs
1½ cups milk
1½ tsp. honey

⅛ tsp. salt
1 cup whole wheat flour

Blend together. Let stand in the refrigerator overnight. In the morning, fry like pancakes on a non-stick griddle. To serve, put any kind of pie filling, nuts, etc. inside, and roll up. Drizzle cream sauce on top. Sprinkle with cinnamon.

Cream Sauce:

1 egg
¾ cup cream

1 Tbsp. honey
½ tsp. vanilla

Beat together and cook until thick.

Lemon Refresher

MRS. JOHN SZKLARZ, DEVINE, TX

¾ cup water
1½ lemons, peeled

3 Tbsp. honey
2 cups honey

Blend in blender. Start on low and go to high. Do not overmix or it will melt. Serve immediately. Makes seven ½ cup servings.

Graham Cracker Crumb Crust Substitute

RACHEL NOLT

1 cup whole wheat flour
½ cup quick oatmeal
¼ cup honey
¼ cup sucanat
½ cup butter

Mix all together and pat into 9 x 13" pan. Bake at 350° for 15 minutes. Then top with your favorite cheesecake, etc.

Graham Cracker Crumbs

JUANITA WEAVER, JOHNSONVILLE, IL

½ cup oil
½ cup honey
1 Tbsp. black molasses
2 tsp. vanilla
½ tsp. salt
3½ cups wheat flour
1½ tsp. baking powder
1 tsp. baking soda
2 tsp. cinnamon
⅓ cup milk

Mix all ingredients in large bowl. Dough should be stiff. To make crackers, add up to ½ cup more flour and roll out ¼" thick. Place on cookie sheets, prick with fork. Bake at 300° until edges are browned. Cool before removing from pan. For cake, bake in large cookie sheet until good and done. Crumble into several pans and bake in slow oven until dry. Mix with butter to make graham cracker crusts. 2½ cups crumbs to ½ cup butter for 9 x 13" pan.

Minty Ice Cream Dessert

MRS. MIRIAM WENGERD, SUGARCREEK, OH

Crust:

1 cup quick oats
1 cup wheat flour
1 cup ground pecans
¼ tsp. soda
⅔ cup butter
1 Tbsp. cocoa
2 Tbsp. honey

Combine oats, flour, nuts, cocoa, and soda. Cut in butter until mixture is crumbly. Add honey. Divide evenly and pat into 9 x 13" pan. Bake at 350° for 15-20 minutes. Cool.

Filling:

2 cups cream
4 eggs, separated
½ cup maple syrup
½ tsp. mint flavoring

Beat cream, egg whites, and egg yolks in separate bowls. Fold a little cream into egg yolks first, then fold all together. Fold in maple syrup and mint flavoring. Pour into one crust. Crumble remaining crust evenly over top and freeze 8 hours. Delicious!

Mabel's Ice Cream

Susan Doty, Lobelville, TN

1½ qts. light cream
1 qt. milk
1 cup maple syrup

1½ tsp. salt
4 beaten eggs
1 Tbsp. vanilla

Mix together. Freeze in ice cream freezer, using 5 parts ice and 1 part salt.

Our Favorite Ice Cream

Mrs. John (Eva May) Yoder, Clare, MI

7 cups milk
2½ cups maple syrup
1½ Tbsp. plain gelatin

3 eggs
5 rounded Tbsp. cornstarch

Heat milk and maple syrup until scalding. Add gelatin, after soaking in a little cold water. Beat eggs, then add cornstarch. Stir into hot milk, stirring until thick. Cool pudding, then add enough cream to fill 1½ gallon freezer, 4 inches from top. Freeze and enjoy.

Vanilla Ice Cream

Susan Stalter, Millersburg, OH

½ cup warm water
2 pkgs. unflavored gelatin
4 eggs
1½ cups fructose

4 cups cream
4½ tsp. vanilla
½ tsp. real salt
5 cups milk

Dissolve gelatin in warm water. In large bowl, beat eggs. Add gelatin mixture and mix thoroughly. Add fructose gradually, and beat until mixture is fairly stiff. Add all but milk and mix thoroughly. Pour into 1 gallon ice cream freezer. Fill to fill line with whole milk. Freeze. Variation: For other flavors, put in half as much vanilla and add pureed fruit before milk.

Maple Ice Cream

MRS. IVAN J. YODER, MILLERSBURG, OH

10 cups milk

1 cup sweet cream

5 eggs

2½ cups maple syrup

2 rounded Tbsp. plain gelatin

½ cup cold water

2 tsp. maple flavoring

⅛ tsp. salt

Soak gelatin in cold water 2-5 minutes. Heat 1 cup milk, mix gelatin into hot milk. Stir to completely dissolve. Separate eggs. Beat yolks in a 6 quart mixing bowl. Add milk, then maple syrup, cream, gelatin mixture, flavoring, and salt. Beat egg whites to stiff peaks. Beat into ice cream mixture. Pour into freezer can (5 quart) and let set 2-6 hours. Leaving it set makes a creamier ice cream.

Ice Cream

MRS. MARVIN (KATIE) MILLER

10 cups milk

1 cup sucanat

2 cups maple syrup

½ cup cornstarch

8 eggs

½ tsp. salt

2 tsp. vanilla

6 cups cream

Heat milk, add maple syrup, bring to boil. Mix together rest of ingredients except for cream and vanilla. Add to milk, stir until boiling. Add vanilla. Cool, then add cream and freeze. Fills a 2 gallon freezer.

Frozen Yogurt

MRS. ERVIN (ELIZABETH) BEACHY

Heat ½ gallon milk to 180°. Soak 1 Tbsp. gelatin in ¾ cup water. Add to hot milk. Cool to lukewarm and add ¼ cup yogurt. Set in warm water, about 105°-110°. Leave undisturbed 4-6 hours. Add stevia to sweeten. Add fruit when almost frozen.

Dips, Spreads & Salsa

IT'S A MUGGY DAY IN AUGUST. NOBODY WANTS TOO
much food, but everybody wants to eat. Solve the problem by serving
tortilla chips with one of these dips. Or pair crackers with a cheese ball.
Make popcorn and a smoothie to go with it. It'll be a winner and keep
everybody smiling while the heat is on!

Our family enjoys a colorful platter of vegetables and dip. I don't like
all those not-good-for-you ingredients listed on the back of dip mixes,
so I look forward to trying out Ranch Powder (page 402) and Hidden
Valley Ranch Mix (page 356).

Make up a batch of Herb Butter and keep it cold in the fridge until
you bake your next batch of bread. Set it out to soften while your bread
is baking. Then grab a chair, put up your feet and relax as you savor
that first bite of warm bread and herb butter. Sure to become a family
favorite!

Fresh Avocado Salsa

Monica Bazen, Grand Rapids, MI

3 large avocados, chopped
3 tomatillos, washed, patted dry, and diced
1 small onion, finely chopped
2 cloves garlic, minced

juice of 2 limes
1 jalepeño, minced
1 tsp. salt
1 bunch cilantro, washed and finely chopped

Combine all ingredients and chill 30 minutes before serving. Serve with tortilla chips. Note: Tomatillos are found in the produce section of most grocery stores. They are not green tomatoes, but look like a small green tomato with a loose paper-like skin around it (which you remove before using).

Chips and Dip

Mrs. Miriam Wengerd, Sugarcreek, OH

16 oz. sour cream
8 oz. cream cheese
3 Tbsp. taco seasoning

lettuce
tomatoes
1 bag tortilla chips

Mix first 3 ingredients in food processor until smooth. Pour onto shallow serving platter. Top with chopped lettuce and diced tomatoes. Serve with tortilla chips. A good light supper for summer evenings.

355

dips & salsa

Fruit Dip

Mrs. Miriam Wengerd, Sugarcreek, OH

4 oz. cream cheese
¾ cup peanut butter (fresh ground)

¾ cup maple syrup

Put all ingredients in food processor and blend until creamy. Good with apples and bananas.

Cracker Spread

Mrs. Miriam Wengerd, Sugarcreek, OH

½ cup sunflower seeds
½ cup hot, cooked millet
¾ cup water
1 tsp. salt

1½ tsp. onion powder
½ tsp. garlic powder
¼ tsp. dillweed
⅓ cup lemon juice

Blend until smooth. Add ¼ cup yeast flakes and ½ cup homemade mayonnaise (pages 126-127). Spread on crackers or use on baked potatoes.

Vegetable Dip

MIRIAM YODER, LAGRANGE, IN

1 cup sour cream
1 Tbsp. parsley flakes
½ tsp. onion salt

1 cup homemade Miracle Whip
   (pages 128-129)
½ tsp. garlic salt

Mix all ingredients together. Chill and serve.

Hidden Valley Ranch Mix

MRS. LAMAR (NANCY) ZIMMERMAN, STEVENS, PA

5 Tbsp. dried, minced onion
7 tsp. parsley flakes

4 tsp. garlic
1 tsp. garlic powder

Combine and store in an airtight container. For dressing, combine 2 Tbsp. mix, with 1 cup homemade mayonnaise (pages 126-127) and 1 cup sour cream. For dip: 2 Tbsp. mix with 2 cups sour cream.

Herb Butter

MRS. MIRIAM WENGERD, SUGARCREEK, OH

1 cup butter, softened
1 tsp. lemon juice
2 tsp. dried basil

2 tsp. dried oregano
1 tsp. garlic powder

Very good on bread, especially when serving with spaghetti. Serve spreadable.

Pesto

MINNA FRIESEN, NOVA SCOTIA, CANADA

1 cup virgin olive oil
1 tsp. sea salt

4 cloves garlic
4 cups fresh basil leaves

Put first 3 ingredients in blender, and while running it, add basil leaves. This is very good on rice, pasta, or popcorn.

Snacks

snacks

358

LOOKING FOR GRAB AND GO SNACKS? SOMETHING to put in a baggie and send out to the sandbox? Needing a treat for a little girls' tea party out under the shade tree?

Maybe it's pouring down rain and you want to brighten up your children's play time? Or the sun is beating down on a few youngsters toiling to hoe those weedy corn rows. Another possibility—you want to plan a little treat for a "date" with your one and only, one of those "let's wait until everyone else is in bed, then let's have a snack as we enjoy the silence" evenings. The snack recipes will fill the need for any of the above scenarios. Pick one and try it today!

Healthy

Healthy Snack Mix

Mrs. Miriam Wengerd, Sugarcreek, OH

3 cups whole cashews, roasted and salted   2 cups organic raisins
2 cups peanuts, roasted   2 cups unsweetened banana chips
2 cups dried pineapple tidbits

Mix together in bowl. Banana chips should only be mixed in one day ahead, then they are not stale and hard. Delicious! A good mix (not messy) to take along when traveling. Can put in ziplock snack bags in advance.

Snack Mix

Elizabeth Stalter, Millersburg, OH

1½ cups raisins   1 cup peanuts
1½ cups walnuts   1 cup pumpkin seeds

Mix all together, using the ingredient combinations your family likes. Store in freezer for a quick treat.

Delicious Party Mix

Mrs. Ivan J. Yoder, Millersburg, OH

6 oz. pretzels   2 tsp. garlic powder
6 oz. puffed corn   ½ tsp. seasoned salt
6 oz. puffed rice   9 Tbsp. tamari sauce
6 oz. puffed kamut   1 cup melted butter
6 oz. Oatios

Combine cereal in a large tub. Melt butter, add seasonings and pour over cereal. Mix well. Put party mix in large cake pans and bake 1 hour at 250° . Stir every 15 minutes.

Grape Finger Jello

Marie Bear, Patriot, OH

1 cup cold water   ¾ cup honey
8 Tbsp. plain gelatin   1 qt. grape juice
2 cups boiling water   1 cup water

Dissolve gelatin in 1 cup cold water. Mix gelatin and honey in boiling water. Add grape juice and extra cup of water. Stir. Pour into a 9 x 12" cake pan.

Apple Fritters

Juanita Weaver, Johnsonville, IL

5 cups peeled, chopped apples
1 cup raisins
1 cup boiling water
2 cups apple juice concentrate
6 eggs
2 Tbsp. lecithin
2½ Tbsp. yeast

1½ Tbsp. cinnamon
1¼ cups oil
2½ tsp. salt
2 cups mashed potatoes
8 cups Golden 86 flour
2 cups soft wheat flour

Boil raisins in 2 Tbsp. water for 2 minutes. Add apples. Cover with lid and remove from heat. Mix all ingredients, except flour and potatoes, in mixer bowl. Add 4 cups flour. Beat for several minutes. Pour in larger bowl and stir in potatoes. Knead in as much flour as needed to make a slightly sticky dough. Let rise until double. Add more flour if needed to roll out. Cut in rings or squares. Let rise again and fry in olive oil or lard, sprinkled generously with ginger so they absorb less oil.

Glaze:

2 cups fructose
3 Tbsp. cornstarch

1 tsp. cinnamon

Blend in blender on high 1 minute. Coat fritters just before serving.

Peanut Butter Balls

Sandra Smucker, John Day, OR

1 cup natural peanut butter
1 cup powdered milk

1 cup honey

Mix together. May add chocolate chips and/or sesame seeds, sunflower seeds, etc.

Carob Peanut Fudge

Mrs. Ivan J. Yoder, Millersburg, OH

1 cup carob chips
2 Tbsp. butter

1 cup peanut butter
1 tsp. vanilla

In a small saucepan, melt butter. Add carob chips, melt them. Add vanilla and peanut butter and mix well. Put into a buttered pan. Cool, cut in squares.

Healthy

Cashew Crunch

MRS. JOHN (EVA MAY) YODER, CLARE, MI

½ cup butter   1 cup maple syrup

Boil together until hard crack (295°) on your candy thermometer. Meanwhile, grease a flat pan and sprinkle with 1 cup cashews in a thick layer. When candy is done, stir in ⅓ tsp. soda. Immediately pour onto cashews, spreading evenly. When cool, break into pieces, store in airtight container.

Popcorn Crunch

MIRIAM YODER, LaGRANGE, IN

½ cup butter, melted   3 qt. popped corn
½ cup honey   1 cup nuts, chopped
1 tsp. cinnamon

Blend butter, honey, and cinnamon. Heat until well blended. Pour over popcorn/nut mixture. Mix well. Spread over cookie sheet in thin layer. Bake at 350° for 10-15 minutes or until crisp. Variation: 2 Tbsp. peanut butter can be used and also sorghum can be used instead of honey.

Caramel Popcorn

JUANITA WEAVER, JOHNSONVILLE, IL

1 cup butter   ½ tsp. soda
1½ cups sucanat   1 tsp. vanilla
½ cup honey   ¼ tsp. cream of tartar

Bring butter and sweeteners to a boil in medium saucepan. Boil 4 minutes or less, stirring occasionally. Remove from heat. Add remaining ingredients and pour over 5-7 quarts of popped corn. Stir until coated. Bake in several pans at 225° for 1 hour. Stir every 10-20 minutes while baking and cooling.

Garlic Popcorn

IVAN WEAVER FAMILY, SEARS, MI

¼ cup butter   8-10 large garlic cloves

Thinly slice garlic. On low heat, stir the garlic and butter with a small metal or wooden spoon. Be very attentive, as it burns easily. Brown until the garlic is a nice golden brown. Pop one popper of popcorn. Pour garlic mixture all over the bowl of hot popcorn, which has been salted and seasoned to taste. Optional: When the popcorn is hot, sprinkle liberally with Parmesan cheese for added goodness. Yummy! Eat this during the winter months to help chase away those colds and flus.

Yogurt Pops

Mrs. Rebecca Zook, Myerstown, PA

1 cup plain yogurt
¾ cup fruit juice, undiluted

¾ cup milk

Combine all ingredients and pour into 6 small paper cups. Insert a wooden stick in the center of each. Freeze until firm.

Juice Jigglers

Mrs. Ivan J. Yoder, Millersburg, OH

3 Tbsp. unflavored gelatin
1 cup cold fruit juice (grape, orange, or cherry)

3 cups fruit juice

Soak gelatin in 1 cup cold juice for 2 minutes. Heat up 1 cup fruit juice. Add gelatin to it and stir to dissolve. Add the last 2 cups of juice. If you prefer fructose, 2 Tbsp., or 4 drops stevia may be added. Pour into a pan and let set.

More-ish Apples

Miriam Yoder, LaGrange, IN

4 apples
¼ cup peanut butter

¼ cup honey

Mix honey and peanut butter. Spread in core (holes) in apple halves. Enjoy!

Edible Playdough

Beth Weaver, Narvon, PA

⅓ part natural peanut butter
⅓ part dry powdered milk

⅓ part honey

Mix well and knead for a few minutes until dough sticks together. Refrigerate leftovers in airtight container to keep for a week or more.

Campfire Cooking

I WILL NEVER FORGET THE TIME OUR FAMILY WENT camping in the Doughty Valley. This is one the most picturesque places in this area. You enter a narrow, deep valley by a steep lane. A wide, shallow, clear creek goes running through the midst of it. We pitched two tents and stayed one night and the next day. It was one of those perfect September days with blue skies—a wonderful family memory.

We made pancakes and eggs over an open fire using iron skillets. It really isn't hard to cook over an open fire if you have the proper equipment.

At home, around our fire ring we like to make Campfire Stew (367). So simple, fast and really good. This recipe can be found in this section. Try it! There's something special about sitting around a fire with family and friends, watching the stars come out, singing songs and making happy memories together.

Healthy

Bannock Bread

VERNON SCHROCK, LEWISTOWN, IL

1 cup whole wheat flour   ¼ tsp. salt
1 tsp. baking powder

Add water until you have a heavy batter. Fry like pancakes in a greased skillet over campfire. Or add some sweetener and drop into boiling fruit for campfire dumplings.

Wilderness Biscuits

JESSICA STRITE, COCHISE, AZ

2 cups whole wheat flour   2 tsp. baking powder
2 tsp. sweetener of your choice   ½ tsp. cream of tartar
½ tsp. salt

Blend ingredients together. Add ½ cup butter and mix together until crumbs. Then add ⅔ cup milk, and 1 egg. Stir together. Form into balls, about the size of a walnut. Bake in skillet over fire or grill. Bake until firm and golden brown, about 10-12 minutes. These are delicious with butter and honey, eaten with a soup, or served with hickory smoke flavored gravy.

Pie Iron Sandwiches

MRS. JOHN (EVA MAY) YODER, CLARE, MI

Spread both bread slices with salad dressing. Sprinkle on bread: Italian seasoning, oregano, salt, pepper. Layer with thinly sliced meat, cheese, tomato slices, lettuce. Toast your sandwich in your pie iron for a delicious campfire treat.

Chicken Pizza Packets

MARTHA WINGERT, CHAMBERSBURG, PA

1 lb. boneless, skinless chicken breasts
2 Tbsp. olive oil
1 small zucchini, thinly sliced
16 pepperoni slices
1 small green pepper, julienned
1 small onion, sliced
½ tsp. dried oregano

½ tsp. dried basil
¼ tsp. salt
¼ tsp. garlic powder
¼ tsp. pepper
½ cup shredded mozzarella cheese
½ cup shredded Parmesan cheese
1 cup halved cherry tomatoes

Cut chicken into 1" pieces. In a large bowl, combine the first 11 ingredients. Coat 4 pieces of heavy-duty foil (about 12" square) with cooking spray. Place a quarter of the chicken mixture in the center of each piece. Fold foil around mixture and seal tightly. Grill, covered, over medium hot heat for 15-18 minutes or until chicken juices run clear. (Or could be done in coals of campfire.) Carefully open each packet. Sprinkle with tomatoes and cheeses. Seal loosely; grill 2 minutes longer or until cheese is melted.

Venison on the Grill

KAYLENE HARTZLER, TENNILLE, GA

You will need: Venison cubed steaks, enough for your family. Grill and baste with this sauce: ½ cup butter, melted, chopped garlic, black pepper, cilantro, parsley, Cajun seasoning, garlic salt; season to your taste. Make a trough or packet of double layers of aluminum foil. Cut steak into bite-sized pieces. Put in foil and add: ½ cup butter, 2 medium onions, sliced, garlic powder, garlic salt, pepper, parsley, cilantro, 4 cups canned, chopped tomatoes, sliced potatoes, peppers, and carrots, sliced. Seal and simmer 1 hour or until vegetables are soft.

Campfire Potatoes

FRIEDA YODER, MILLERSBURG, OH

5 med. potatoes, thinly sliced
1 med. onion, sliced
2 Tbsp. butter
2 Tbsp. minced fresh parsley
1 Tbsp. Worcestershire or tamari sauce

salt to taste
pepper to taste
⅓ cup shredded cheddar cheese
⅓ cup chicken broth

Put potatoes and onion on a large piece of heavy-duty foil, about 20" x 20". Combine the cheese, parsley, sauce, salt, and pepper. Sprinkle over potatoes, tossing to coat. Dot with butter. Fold foil up around potatoes and add broth. Seal the edges of foil well. Grill covered over medium coals for 35-40 minutes or until tender.

Healthy

Campfire Stew

Mrs. Miriam Wengerd, Sugarcreek, OH

potatoes, chunked
carrots, chunked
smoked sausage,
    cut diagonally in chunky pieces

peas
onions, wedges
1 qt. chicken broth
1 qt. water

Prepare vegetables in amounts you need. Cut up sausage. Put everything in iron kettle. Pour broth and water over all. Put lid on. Set in good hot fire. Will be ready in 15-20 minutes. Serve with Herbamare seasoning or other salt if desired. Deliciously simple!

Campfire Stew

Vernon Schrock, Lewistown, IL

1½ qt. water
5 large potatoes
3 med. carrots
¼ head cabbage
2 large bell peppers
1 large onion

½ cup celery
1 cup peas
1 cup beans
1 small zucchini
1 clove garlic
1 pkg. Little Smokies

Get your campfire good and hot. Heat water in cast-iron pot (my first batch was made in a large skillet) while you dice, slice, and chop your ingredients with a paring knife, pocket knife, or whatever you have. Add potatoes, carrots, cabbage, celery, peas, and beans first, boil until they start getting soft, then throw in the onion, pepper, garlic, and zucchini. Add Little Smokies whenever you want to. Salt to taste. Boil in an open pot to get the true campfire flavor. You may have to add more water, as it evaporates. Ingredients can vary according to taste and availability. When ready, serve with hot bannock bread. If your family is like ours, they will clean the pot!

Picadillo

Our standard campfire meal is made on a "disco." (A large disk with legs welded to it and a fire built under it.) We simply cube raw potatoes, chopped onions, peppers, and garlic, and add as much raw hamburger as desired. Fry all together. Lay corn tortillas on top to warm them when picadillo is nearly done. Serve with salsa. (Once after butchering day we used cubed liver instead of hamburger. A great way to eat liver.)

Onions on the Grill

MRS. LEONA MILLER, ODON, IN

3 large onions, sliced

2 Tbsp. honey

½ tsp. salt

½ tsp. ground mustard

In a large bowl, combine all ingredients; toss to coat. Place on a double thickness of heavy-duty foil (about 18" square). Fold around onion mixture and seal tightly. Grill, covered, over medium heat for 20-25 minutes or until onions are tender, turning once.

Bundle of Veggies

MRS. LEONA MILLER, ODON, IN

8 oz. whole, fresh mushrooms

8 oz. cherry tomatoes

1 cup sliced zucchini

1 Tbsp. olive oil

1 Tbsp. butter, melted

½ tsp. salt

½ tsp. onion powder

½ tsp. Italian seasoning

⅛ tsp. garlic powder

dash pepper

Place mushrooms, tomatoes, and zucchini on a double thickness of heavy-duty foil (about 18" square). Combine remaining ingredients and drizzle over vegetables. Fold foil around vegetables and seal tightly. Grill, covered, over medium heat for 20-25 minutes or until tender. You may substitute other vegetables of your choice if desired. Just experiment.

Canning

CANNING IS A LOT OF HARD WORK, BUT IT'S WORTH it! It makes meal planning so simple. You can literally have a meal ready in minutes, which is very important if you live on the corner of two busy streets and get lots of company like we do!

It is very convenient to use a tablet to keep record of your canning. For example, write down how many bushels/boxes of peaches you got and how many quarts that made. Keep track of how much you had left over by the end of the year. This really is very helpful when canning season is in full swing and your mind is busy with hundreds of details. When your tablet is filled, keep it! It's very interesting to look back over and see how many hundreds of jars you filled! If any of you are just married, purchase a brand-new tablet, write "Canning Tablet" on the outside and keep track from day one—a real keepsake later on!

Feeling overwhelmed with a large canning job on the horizon? Plan ahead to have neighbors, family or friends come and help. This is such an encouragement to our girls when the aunts and girl cousins come to help. It turns a mountain of work into an enjoyable day together.

Let's try to help each other stock up our canning shelves, so we can enjoy practicing hospitality.

Canning Soups

Chili Soup

MRS. URIE MILLER, MIDDLEBURY, IN

10 lbs. hamburger
6 cups onions, chopped
4 Tbsp. salt
2 Tbsp. pepper
4 qt. tomato juice
2 qt. water

4 cups ketchup
1 gal. kidney or other beans
3 tsp. chili powder
2 Tbsp. salt
1½-2 cups sorghum

Brown hamburger, onions, salt, and pepper. Add rest of ingredients. Thicken slightly with a cup or so of Perma-flo or some other thickener, blended with water before adding. May add extra tomato juice or water if desired. Put in jars, leaving about 1¼" headspace. Pressure can at 10 lbs. pressure for 30 minutes. Yield: 18 quarts.

Chunky Beef Soup

MRS. RUTH WANNER, CONNEAUTVILLE, PA

8 cups diced potatoes
8 cups diced carrots
6 qt. water
¼ cup + 2 tsp. salt
⅓ cup beef soup base
1 gal. beef broth
2 qt. tomato juice
sweetener (opt.)
1 cup butter
½ cup ABC noodles

4 lbs. hamburger
3 cups peas
½ cup dry beans
¾ cup dry brown rice
2 tsp. celery flakes
1 Tbsp. pepper
1 Tbsp. celery salt
2 qt. drained beef chunks
onions, minced

Cook potatoes and carrots with 2 tsp. salt and 1 quart water until slightly tender. Bring 5 quarts water, soup base, broth, tomato juice, sweetener, and butter to a boil. Add vegetables and rest of ingredients. Bring to boil again and thicken with ⅓ cup clear jel and ⅔ cup cornstarch, dissolved in cold water. Cold pack 2 hours. Pressure cooking makes it too mushy. Yield: 16 quarts. We enjoy this soup; it's more mild than tomato soup.

Chunky Beef Soup

Mrs. Urie Miller, Middlebury, IN

8 lbs. hamburger
2 large onions, chopped
3 Tbsp. salt
pepper or seasoning to taste
2 qt. navy beans
4 qt. potatoes, diced
2 qt. carrots, diced
2 qt. whole kernel corn
2 qt. peas
1-2 qt. celery, diced
6 qt. beef broth
2½ gal. water
4 qt. tomato juice
⅔ cup sweetener
⅓ cup salt
1-2 Tbsp. chili powder

Brown hamburger, onions, salt, and pepper. Boil vegetables separately, not too soft. Bring beef broth and water to a boil, thicken with 4 cups (more or less) of desired thickener. Combine all ingredients, ladle into jars, leaving 1¼" headspace. Process in hot water bath for 2 hours. Let jars set in water for up to 15 minutes after turning off burner to prevent soup from bubbling out beneath lids. Yield: 27 quarts.

Kettle Stew

Mrs. Rebecca Weaver, Apple Creek, OH

1 lb. butter
6 large onions, chopped
20 lb. sausage
9 gal. water
1½ cups ham, cubed
20 lb. cubed potatoes
15 lb. cubed carrots
10 lb. peas
4-5 Tbsp. salt
1 Tbsp. pepper
2 Tbsp. seasoned salt

Place kettle over open fire and melt butter. Add onions and sausage and brown it. Then add 9 gallons water, potatoes, carrots, salt and pepper. Cook until vegetables are soft, adding peas and ham last. Mix 3 quarts flour with 1 gallon water and pour slowly into soup to thicken. Put into jars and cold pack quarts for 2 hours. Makes around 64 quarts.

Rice Soup to Can

Marie Bear, Patriot, OH

⅓ cup rinsed rice
⅓ cup chopped carrots
⅓ cup chopped celery
¼ cup chopped onions
½ cup cooked, chopped chicken
1 tsp. salt
1 Tbsp. chicken bouillon (page 229)

Put all ingredients in a 1 quart jar. Fill jars with hot water to neck. Seal. Can 10 lb. pressure for 90 minutes. To rinse rice, put in sieve and let water run through.

Canned Cream of Celery Soup

MIRIAM STOLTZFOOS, GARNETT, KS

3 qt. celery	½ cup chopped onion
3 qt. beef stock	½ lb. flour
½ lb. butter	2 Tbsp. salt

Cook celery in beef stock until very tender. Melt butter, fry onions in butter until delicately browned. Blend in flour and salt; add hot celery stock gradually, and cook until mixture thickens, stirring constantly. Put in jars. Process pints in pressure cooker for 30 minutes at 10 lbs. pressure. When opening, dilute half and half with milk, unless you use it for a casserole. One pint is about 1½ cans store-bought soup. I canned this and think it's very good. Makes 8 pints.

Cream of Celery Soup to Can

B. GARBER, FAYETTEVILLE, PA

2 cups diced celery, divided	2 tsp. salt
2 Tbsp. oil, divided	½ cup dry milk powder (not instant)
2 Tbsp. chopped onion	1½ cup water, divided
5 cups chicken stock or broth	8 Tbsp. cornstarch
1 cup cream	3 Tbsp. flour
2 Tbsp. butter	

Sauté 1 cup finely diced celery in 1 Tbsp. oil. Set aside. Sauté 1 cup celery and 2 Tbsp. chopped onion in 1 Tbsp. oil. Put sautéed celery and onion in blender and blend until you have a smooth puree (use part of cream in blender if needed, to help form puree). Combine 5 cups chicken stock, the remainder of 1 cup of cream, 2 tsp. salt, 2 Tbsp. butter, and the puree in a large, heavy kettle. Combine milk powder and 1 cup of water, stirring with a whisk to blend and add to kettle. Heat over medium heat. Mix cornstarch and flour in ½ cup water. Add to hot liquid and stir to thicken. Add the sautéed celery and bring it to a boil. Boil 5 minutes. Put in pint jars. Process at 10 lbs. pressure for 40 minutes. Yields: 4 pints. You may substitute 1¼ cups of milk for the milk powder and 1 cup of water.

Vegetable Soup

Mrs. Andy M. Troyer, Millersburg, OH

1 qt. celery, cut fine
1 qt. potatoes, shredded
1 qt. carrots, shredded
1 qt. fresh or canned sweet corn
1 pt. onions, cut fine
1 qt. pork and beans

6 lb. hamburger
1 cup alphabet macaroni
2 tsp. chili powder
2-3 tsp. salt
7-8 qt. tomato juice

Fry hamburger with salt and pepper to taste. Cook first 4 ingredients to boiling. Drain all water, except potato water. Add to soup. Soak onions in cold water until rest is ready. Don't cook onions. Add each ingredient as it is ready in large canner, cover macaroni with boiling water a few minutes. Mix all together. Add more juice if you like. Fill jars. Cold pack for 2 hours. Makes 15 quarts.

Vegetable Soup

Mrs. Rhoda Miller, Sugarcreek, OH

1 qt. potatoes
1 qt. celery
1 qt. cooked pinto beans
1 qt. carrots
2 cups onions, chopped
3 qt. tomato juice

4 cups broth
4 tsp. chili powder
½ cup sorghum
salt and pepper to taste
seasonings to taste
2 cups whole wheat ABC pasta

Put vegetables together raw. Add broth, seasonings, and pasta. Cold pack for 3 hours.

canning

375

Canned Vegetable Soup

Mrs. Jessica Eby, Elora, ON

6-9 lbs. ground beef
3 qt. green and/or yellow beans
3 qt. carrots
3 qt. corn
3 qt. peas
2 bunches celery
5 lbs. potatoes
1 qt. navy beans,
   soaked overnight or precooked

10 med. onions
2 med. heads cabbage
4 large green peppers
2 large red peppers
11 qt. tomato juice
1 tsp. salt for each quart
parsley for each quart
1 cup pot barley, soaked
   overnight (opt.)

Fry ground beef until red color disappears. Dice and cook (slightly) each of the vegetables separately, then mix everything together in large container. (I usually use a large plastic bushel-sized container.) Put soup in jar size of your choice. If vegetables seem dry when packing, add more tomato juice. Do NOT overfill jars! Process 75 minutes at 10 lbs. pressure. Makes 30-35 quarts. Enjoy your quick winter meal.

Potato Soup to Can

Rachel Yoder, Millersburg, OH

ham
potatoes

salt

Shred the potatoes; cube the ham. Put 3 cups potatoes in a quart jar, then add 1 cup ham, put ½ tsp. salt on top, then fill jar with water. Cold pack for 2 hours. When you open a jar, melt 3 Tbsp. butter in a kettle then add ¼ cup flour. When bubbly add 4 cups milk. Bring to boil, then add canned potatoes, water and all. Heat again. Can also add some cheese and onions. Serves 6.

Cream of Chicken Soup to Can

B. Garber, Fayetteville, PA

5 cups chicken stock or broth
1 cup cream
2 Tbsp. butter
1 Tbsp. vegetable or olive oil
2 tsp. salt
⅛ tsp. garlic powder
1 tsp. kelp (opt.)

½ cup dry milk (not instant)
1½ cup water, divided
8 Tbsp. cornstarch
3 Tbsp. flour
2 cups diced chicken, divided,
  using 1¼ cup for puree

Put cooked, diced chicken in blender with part of the cream and blend until you have chicken puree. Combine chicken stock, remainder of cream, butter, oil, salt, garlic powder, kelp, and 1 cup of puree in a large, heavy kettle. Combine milk powder and 1 cup water, stirring with a whisk to blend, and add to kettle. Heat over medium heat. Mix cornstarch and flour in ½ cup water. Add to hot liquid and stir to thicken. Bring to boil and boil 5 minutes. Then add ¾ cup diced chicken. Put in pint jars and process at 10 lbs. for 40 minutes. Can be frozen. Yield: 4 pints. This can be doubled, tripled, etc. for large batches to can. This is very good to subsitute in recipes instead of store-bought. I use regular milk instead of powdered milk, omitting dry milk and 1 cup water, and using 1¼ cups regular milk.

canning

Cream of Chicken Soup

Mrs. Rebecca Zook, Myerstown, PA

½ cup butter
1 onion, chopped
1 cup whole grain flour

1 cup milk
2 cups chicken broth
1 Tbsp. salt

Melt butter, add onion and flour. Stir well, add milk, chicken broth, and salt slowly, and cook until thick. You can add more or less flour, depending on how thick you want it. You can also can this. Put in pint jars and cold pack for 1 hour.

Carrot Tomato Soup

Martha Wideman, Listowel, ON

5-6 qt. carrots
3 qt. onions
1 qt. parsley

basil (opt.)
2½ Tbsp. salt
½ Tbsp. pepper

Put in a 12 qt. kettle, fill up with tomatoes. Bring to a boil and put through strainer or blender. Add cooked noodles or macaroni if you like. Put in jars and steam 20 minutes.

Choices

Chicken Noodle Soup

MARTHA WIDEMAN, LISTOWEL, ON

3-5 chickens
1 gal. potatoes, cubed
2 pkg. noodles
2-3 qt. celery, chopped

2 qt. carrots
20 tsp. chicken bouillon (page 229)
salt to taste

Cook each item separately. Cool. Mix everything together. Put in jars. Steam 2 hours. Cook chicken in a *lot* of water, and use that stock.

Home-Canned Cream Soup

AMANDA WITMER

¾ cup olive oil
1 (4 lb. 4 oz.) can mushrooms (or fresh)
2-3 onions, chopped fine
30 cups broth or stock (any kind)
12 tsp. salt
pepper to taste
10 tsp. garlic powder
3 cups dry milk powder (not instant)

6 cups cream
6 cups water
1 cup regular clear jel
½ cup dry milk powder
3 cups cornstarch
1 cup + 2 Tbsp. flour
4 cups water

Sauté onions and mushrooms in oil. Add broth, salt, pepper, garlic powder, milk powder, cream, and 6 cups water. Heat until boiling. Mix clear jel, dry milk powder, cornstarch, flour, and 4 cups water. Add to hot mixture. Stir until thick. Pour into pint jars. Process 40 minutes at 10 lb. pressure. To make celery or chicken soup, put in 12 cups of celery or chicken instead of mushrooms. This is delicious! It doesn't have MSG and all the preservatives that store-bought cream soups do.

Canned Cream of Mushroom Soup

MIRIAM STOLTZFOOS, GARNETT, KS

⅓ cup butter
1 lb. chopped mushrooms
¾ cup flour (can add more)
1 Tbsp. salt

⅛ tsp. pepper
2 qt. meat stock
pinch cayenne
1 tsp. lemon juice

Fry mushrooms in butter until brown. Blend in flour. Add meat stock and seasonings. Whip until thoroughly mixed. Heat until it boils. Put in jars. Pressure can 40 minutes at 10 lb. pressure. When opening, dilute half and half with milk, unless you use it for a casserole. 1 pint equals about 1½ cans store-bought soup. Makes about 6 pints. I think this is very good! I substituted some meat stock with vegetable broth.

Cream of Mushroom Soup

B. GARBER, FAYETTEVILLE, PA

1½ cup finely diced raw mushroom caps
½ Tbsp. + 1 tsp. oil, divided
1 cup raw mushroom caps and stems, chopped
¼ cup chopped onions
5 cups chicken stock or broth
1 cup cream
2 tsp. salt
1 Tbsp. butter
¼ tsp. garlic powder
½ cup dry milk (not instant)
1½ cups water, divided
8 Tbsp. cornstarch
3 Tbsp. flour

Wash mushrooms, separate caps and stems. Finely dice raw mushroom caps and sauté in ½ Tbsp. oil for 2 minutes; set aside. (Should equal about ½ cup sautéed mushrooms.) Coarsely chop stems and remaining caps to equal 1 cup; add chopped onions and sauté in 1 tsp. oil for 2 minutes. Put sautéed mushrooms and onions in blender, and blend until you have a smooth puree (use part of cream in blender if needed to help form smooth puree). Combine stock, remainder of cream, salt, puree, butter, and garlic powder in large, heavy kettle. Combine dry milk powder with 1 cup water, stirring with whisk, and add to kettle. Heat over medium heat. Dissolve cornstarch and flour in ½ cup water. Add to hot stock mixture and stir to thicken to desired consistency. Add ½ cup sautéed mushrooms. Bring to a boil and boil 5 minutes. Put in pint jars and process at 10 lb. pressure for 40 minutes. Yields 4 pints. Can be frozen. I use 1¼ cup water instead of milk powder and 1 cup water.

canning

Mushroom Soup to Can

MARIA WEAVER, SQUAW VALLEY, CA

½ lb. butter
1 lb. mushrooms
1 med. onion
1 cup chopped celery
1 cup butter
¾ cup whole wheat flour
1 gal. milk
3 tsp. salt
½ tsp. black pepper
3 cups water
2½ cups whole wheat flour

In heavy bottom 8 quart kettle, melt ½ lb. butter until just starting to brown. Dump in chopped vegetables and sauté until mushrooms are shrunk. In another skillet, brown ¾ cup flour and 1 cup butter together until well browned. Add browned flour, milk, salt, and black pepper to vegetable kettle. Bring to boil, stirring occasionally. Beat together water and 2½ cups flour with mixer to get all the lumps out, then add to kettle. Cook 2 minutes. Fill jars. Pressure cook at 10 lb. for 30 minutes. Even if I have to buy milk from the store, this recipe costs me about half of what I would have to pay for mushroom soup from the store.

Canning Meats

Sausage Mix

Miss Leah Nisley, Danville, OH

2½ cups salt
1 cup + 2 Tbsp. dry mustard
12 Tbsp. black pepper (slightly rounded)

1 cup sage
4 Tbsp. red pepper

Mix and grind. For 20 gallons meat.

Sausage Mix

Ida Edwards, Linden, TN

10 lb. ground pork
3 Tbsp. black pepper
5 tsp. garlic powder
2 Tbsp. ground sage

¼ cup maple syrup
3 tsp. dry mustard
3 Tbsp. sea salt
¼ cup fennel seed

Put the ground pork in a large mixing bowl. Sprinkle with seasonings, one at a time, mixing well after each addition. Mix until you find no more clumps of spice. Now it is ready to can, freeze, or use as you wish.

TIP

To keep jars free from grease when cold packing meat, add vinegar to the water.
When boiling meat on the bones for broth, letting the broth cool several hours or overnight with the bones still in it will result in a firmer gelled broth. The broth may be reheated to melt it, if necessary, to take out all the bones.

—Mrs. Urie Miller, Middlebury, IN

Healthy

Venison Jerky

SUSAN DOTY, LOBELVILLE, TN

1 cup soy sauce
¼ cup Worcestershire sauce
1½ tsp. black pepper

2 tsp. garlic powder
2 tsp. onion powder
3 Tbsp. hot pepper sauce

Fill one cookie sheet with a single layer of raw, thinly sliced meat. Mix sauce and pour over meat. Marinate 24 hours. Drain, and dry jerky as desired. May use 8 cloves pressed garlic instead of garlic powder. If you want it hot, add more hot pepper sauce.

Chicken Burger

MRS. URIE R. MILLER, MIDDLEBURY. IN

24 lb. ground chicken burger
10 Tbsp. salt
1 tsp. cayenne pepper

½ tsp. garlic powder
½ tsp. ground mustard
½ tsp. poultry seasoning

Add seasonings to chicken burger. Mix well.

Canning Chicken Tidbits

MRS. MIRIAM WENGERD, SUGARCREEK, OH

Put chicken in large kettle and cover with water. Put lid on. Bring to boil, turn heat down and simmer for one hour or until fork tender. You don't want it cooked too little, which makes it hard to pick off, yet you don't want it overcooked either, which makes it hard to keep the small bones separated from the meat. When done remove from heat and spread on cookie sheets to cool. Strain broth and set aside. Begin de-boning right away, as it is easiest to pick off when hot. After de-boning, cut into tidbits, removing any small bones, etc. Pack tidbits in clean jars and cover with strained broth, adding ½ tsp. salt per pint. Put lids on and pressure can at 10 lbs. pressure for 65 minutes for pints, 75 minutes for quarts. Pour remaining broth in jars, adding ½ tsp. salt per pint, seal and cold pack 30 minutes for both pints and quarts. This chicken is so handy; use it in soups, casseroles and noodles.

TIP

After deboning your chicken put your bones and scraps back in a kettle and cover with water again. Simmer 2 hours and strain. You will get lots more broth this way and it's very good. If it looks like too much work for canning day, save bones and scraps overnight and cook the next day instead.

—Mrs. Miriam Wengerd, Sugarcreek, OH

Canned Meatballs

MRS. IVAN J. YODER, MILLERSBURG, OH

15 lb. hamburger
6 Tbsp. salt
40 squares crackers finely crushed
1 tsp. black pepper
4 cups tomato juice

2 tsp. liquid smoke
1 Tbsp. Worcestershire sauce
1 tsp. garlic powder
1 tsp. onion powder
2 tsp. rubbed sage

Mix juice and seasonings, add crushed saltines. Add hamburger and mix well. Shape into small balls. Put in rows in cake pans and bake 35-40 minutes or until baked, pour off broth. Put balls in quart jars and divide broth among each jar. Put lids and rings on jars and pressure cook at 10 lb. pressure for 45 minutes.

Sausage or Hamburger Seasoning

MRS. URIE MILLER, MIDDLEBURY, IN

34 lb. meat
1 cup salt
1 Tbsp. black pepper

1 tsp. cayenne
1 tsp. ground mustard

Mix well.

Spicy Bologna

MISS LEAH NISLEY, DANVILLE, OH

25 lb. deer meat
6 lb. pork
1½-2 med. bulbs garlic
2½ qt. water
1 pint sorghum
5 cups cornstarch
1 cup dry milk

1¼ cup salt
1 Tbsp. paprika
¼ cup black pepper
1 Tbsp. coriander
6 Tbsp. dry mustard
1 Tbsp. curry

Grind deer meat, pork, and garlic once, then mix together the rest of the ingredients. Pour this into meat and mix together, then grind again. Stuff into links and smoke. Or, for an easier way, add 4 Tbsp. liquid smoke. Put in jars. Pressure can 30 minutes. *Do not* let set long after mixing all together.

Bologna

Mrs. John (Eva May) Yoder, Clare, MI

25 lb. hamburger
¾ lb. salt, minus ½ cup
1¼ cup maple syrup
1½ tsp. salt petre (optional)*
5 Tbsp. liquid hickory smoke
4 qt. water
2 cups powdered milk

1½ tsp. mace
1½ tsp. sage
1 Tbsp. garlic powder
3 Tbsp. black pepper
2 Tbsp. powdered mustard
2 Tbsp. Spike
1½ tsp. onion salt

Mix all together except meat, then mix with meat. Let set in a cold place for 2-3 days. To can, pack firmly in wide-mouth quart or pint jars and pressure can 1½ hours at 10 lb. You can freeze it, too, and when ready to use, thaw and bake in bread pan (glass or stainless steel) for 1¼ hour at 350°, or until done. This may also be used to stuff into casings, then smoked and cooked. If you plan on smoking it, do not add liquid hickory smoke.

*Salt petre helps the bologna to stay a nice red color, but it does not affect the flavor if you leave it out.

Bologna

Mrs. Urie Miller, Middlebury, IN

50 lb. beef
15 lb. pork
1 lb. salt
½ lb. seasoned salt
1¾ Tbsp. black pepper
4 Tbsp. ground coriander seed

1 Tbsp. mace
1 Tbsp. garlic powder
10 Tbsp. liquid smoke
1½ lb. cornstarch
1¾ lb. fructose
2¼ gal. water

Grind meat once. Put a layer of meat, then salt in containers. Repeat. Chill for 24 hours, then grind twice. Mix all spices, starch, and sweetener in 1 gallon of water. Mix into meat; add rest of water and mix for 15-20 minutes. Pack into jars, leaving approximately 1½" of headspace. Process as for meat. Chicken, chevron, or venison may be used instead of beef and pork. For a more moist finished product, leave some fat in with the meat. Venison tends to be a bit dry.

To Can Salmon

Mrs. John (Eva May) Yoder, Clare, MI

Cut fish into 1" cubes; pack jars full, then add ⅓ cup vinegar and 1 tsp. salt to a quart. Pressure cook 1½ hours at 10 lb. This is great for soup, etc. If the meat has bones, they are usually dissolved with this process.

Choices

Canning Vegetables & Fruits

Salsa

MRS. RHODA MILLER, SUGARCREEK, OH

14 lb. tomatoes, skinned, seeded, chopped
  (no juice)
10 green peppers
6 hot peppers
1 cup cider vinegar
1½ cups molasses
¼ cup salt
2 Tbsp. chili powder
5 cups onions
8 cloves garlic
2½ Tbsp. cumin
4 Tbsp. oregano

Combine everything and bring to a boil. Remove 4 cups juice and set aside. Boil remaining mixture for 20 minutes. Add ¾ cup clear jel to the 4 cups juice. Stir into salsa to thicken. Pour into pint jars and hot water bath for 40 minutes. Yield: 15 pints.

Salsa

MRS. IVAN J. YODER, MILLERSBURG, OH

14 lb. tomatoes
10 green sweet peppers
5 cups onions
⅓ cup vinegar
¾ cup honey or fructose
5 Tbsp. salt
3 Tbsp. seasoned salt
5 cloves garlic
3 Tbsp. chili blend powder
2 Tbsp. taco seasoning
1 Tbsp. cumin
3 Tbsp. oregano
1¾ tsp. red pepper, or to taste
1¾ cup Perma-flo

Grind all the vegetables with coarse blade. Drain the peppers. Then mix all of them together. Add the rest of ingredients except Perma-flo. Bring to a boil. Put Perma-flo into enough water to make it pourable (2-3 cups) and add to salsa. Ladle into pint jars. Put on lids and rings. Cold pack 30 minutes.

canning

Healthy

Zucchini Relish

Mrs. Rhoda Miller, Sugarcreek, OH

30 cups zucchini, shredded
2 cups onion
2 cups green pepper, diced
2 cups red pepper, diced
¾ cup salt
4½ cups vinegar

4 cups honey
2 tsp. celery seed
2 tsp. dry mustard
1 tsp. nutmeg
1 tsp. black pepper

Combine the first five ingredients and let set several hours. Rinse thoroughly. Add the remaining ingredients and cook 30 minutes. Put into pint jars. Hot water bath 10 minutes.

Spaghetti Sauce

Susan Stalter, Millersburg, OH

8-10 qt. tomato juice
3 lb. (4 cups) onions
4 sweet peppers
1 carrot, chopped
2 cups olive oil
2 Tbsp. basil flakes
1 Tbsp. oregano

1 cup fructose
¼ cup real salt
½ tsp. red pepper
1½ cups tomato paste
2½ cups clear jel (opt.)
5 cups water (opt.)

Blend onions, peppers, and carrots into juice (in blender, 1 quart at a time). Place in large kettle. Add oil, fructose, salt and spices. Cook 1 hour. Add tomato paste. Combine clear jel and water and add to sauce, if you want it to be thick. Fill 1 qt. jars. Add 1 bay leaf to each jar, if desired. Pressure can at 10 lb. for 5 minutes.

385

canning

Spaghetti Sauce

Mrs. Ivan J. Yoder, Millersburg, OH

2½ gal. thick tomato juice
2 cups chopped onions
4 cloves garlic (or 1 tsp. garlic powder)
1 Tbsp. basil
1 Tbsp. rosemary

⅓ cup salt
1½ cup honey or fructose
1½ lb. raw roast
1 Tbsp. oregano

For the juice, I skim off 1-2 quarts of the clear liquid after the tomatoes are cooked, but before I juice them. The juice should be a little bit thick. Add all the rest of the ingredients, and cook 5-6 hours, until roast falls apart and sauce is thick. Remove roast and eat for supper. Ladle sauce in pint jars and seal. Cold pack 15 minutes. For the roast, I freeze the meat when we butcher. It adds a delicious flavor to the sauce.

Choices

Sandwich Spread

MRS. IVAN J. YODER, MILLERSBURG, OH

12 red sweet peppers
36 med. sized green tomatoes
2 large onions
1 pint vinegar

5 cups fructose
4 Tbsp. salt
1 Tbsp. celery seed
1 pint prepared mustard

Grind vegetables, drain. (I put them in a colander to drain.) Now place vegetables, fructose, salt, celery seed, mustard, and vinegar in a 12 quart kettle. Bring to a boil. Take 6 Tbsp. Perma-flo, add enough water to make it pourable and add to vegetables. Add more thickener if needed. Put in pint jars, with lids and rings. Cold pack in boiling water bath for 15 minutes; leave set 15 minutes before removing from water.

Pizza Sauce to Can

MRS. KATHRYN HERSHBERGER, CLARE, MI

½ bushel tomatoes, cooked and juiced
1 gal. tomato paste
3 lb. onions
5 green peppers
4 hot peppers
½ cup salt
2 cups maple syrup

1 cup olive oil
2 Tbsp. oregano
2 Tbsp. sweet basil
2 tsp. garlic powder
2 tsp. paprika
½ cup parsley flakes

Cook onions and peppers together in 1 quart tomato juice until soft. Mix all ingredients thoroughly and simmer a bit. Put in quart jars and pressure cook at 5 lb. pressure for 10 minutes.

Pizza Sauce

MRS. GLENN ZIMMERMAN, GREENWOOD, WI

2½ gal. tomato juice
4 green bell peppers
8-10 onions
1 pint oil
2 Tbsp. basil
1 cup honey
2 Tbsp. oregano

6 bay leaves, crushed
2 Tbsp. red pepper, crushed
3 Tbsp. pizza seasoning
1 Tbsp. Italian seasoning
½ gal. tomato paste
1 tsp. garlic powder
½ cup salt

Cook tomato juice, peppers, and onions together for 1 hour. Strain through Victorio strainer. Return to kettle and add rest of ingredients. Cook together for 1 hour, then add ½ gallon more tomato paste and mix well. Ladle into jars and process in hot water bath for 10 minutes. Yield: 25 pints. This tastes very much like Pizza Hut sauce. To make tomato paste, drain tomato juice, then put the thick pulp in the freezer. When frozen, take out and drain again. Use right away or process in boiling water bath for 15 minutes.

Pizza Sauce

PATRICIA TAYLOR

1 lb. fresh tomatoes, chopped
2 Tbsp. olive oil
1 cup tomato sauce
1 tsp. dried oregano

1 tsp. dried basil
1½ tsp. salt
¼ tsp. pepper
2 cloves garlic, minced

Cook minced garlic in olive oil for 1 minute, add other ingredients. Cook until it thickens, about 20 minutes. Makes 1 pint, enough for 2 pizzas. I multiply this by 16 to can. Water bath quarts for 20 minutes.

Pizza Sauce

MRS. LARRY (LIANA) CABLE, TROTWOOD, OH

2½ gal. tomato juice
4 bell peppers
8-10 onions
1 pint oil
2 Tbsp. basil
¼ tsp. stevia powder
2 Tbsp. oregano

6 bay leaves, crushed
3 Tbsp. pizza seasoning
1 Tbsp. Italian seasoning
½ gal. tomato paste
1 tsp. garlic powder
½ cup salt

Chop peppers and onions in blender, add to tomato juice, and cook for one hour. Add rest of ingredients and cook well for one hour. Add about ½ gallon more of tomato paste if needed. Mix well. Put into jars. Can at 5 lb. pressure for 5 minutes. Makes about 25 pints.

Ketchup

Mrs. John (Eva May) Yoder, Clare, MI

2 gal. cut-up paste tomatoes
1½ tsp. mustard
¼ cup salt
2 cups vinegar
pinch of cloves

½ tsp. pepper
1 tsp. celery seed
¼ tsp. cinnamon
½ tsp. onion salt
1-2½ cups maple syrup

Cook tomatoes. When soft, let set for 20 minutes. Then drain off watery liquid. Put through strainer, then add remaining ingredients. Simmer until thick enough. Remember, it's thicker when it's cold. Put in pint or quart jars and cold pack 20 minutes.

Ketchup

Mrs. Marvin (Katie) Miller

20 qt. chunked tomatoes
4 hot peppers
5 large onions
2 or 3 garlic cloves
3 Tbsp. cinnamon
2 Tbsp. dry mustard

6 cups honey
½ cup salt (slightly rounded)
1 tsp. pepper
3 Tbsp. pickling spice, put in
   a cloth and tied

canning

388

Fill a 20 quart kettle with chunked tomatoes, peppers, onions, and garlic cloves. Bring to a boil and boil for 2 hours, then put through a sieve. This should yield 12 quarts tomato juice. Add remaining ingredients to juice. Boil together for 2 hours, thicken with scant 2 cups clear jel mixed with 4 cups vinegar. Put in jars and cold pack for 20 minutes.

Ketchup

Mrs. Rebecca Zook, Myerstown, PA

8 qt. tomato juice
4 tsp. stevia powder
1 tsp. red pepper (scant)
1 tsp. black pepper
3 cups vinegar

2 Tbsp. salt
5 tsp. ground mustard
2½ cups arrowroot powder
1½-2 cups water

Mix first 7 ingredients together and heat. Thicken with arrowroot powder and water. Put in pint jars and cold pack 10 minutes. For barbecue sauce, add: 1 quart honey, 2 cups unsulfured molasses, 8 Tbsp. Worcestershire sauce. Omit the stevia.

Excellent Uncooked Pickles

MARTHA WIDEMAN, LISTOWEL, ON

Select good small pickles (or long pickles diced into 1" pieces). Wash and dry, pack into jars. Put ½ teaspoon salt in each quart jar. Make a brine of: 2 cups water, 1 cup cider vinegar, ½ cup sweetener. Double as many times as needed. Put jars in boiler in cold water and bring to a boil. When it starts boiling, take jars out of water, and tighten lid. This makes a very crisp pickle. Variations: Put dill or garlic clove or both in jars for flavor.

Garlic Dill Pickles

EDITH ZIMMERMAN, SCOTTSVILLE, KY

Select medium or small green cucumbers. Wash well. Let stand in cold water for 1 hour to harden. Dry and pack in jars. In bottom of each, put some dill and garlic. Then pack in cucumbers. Pour over them the following:

3 qt. water   1 cup salt
1 qt. vinegar

Boil together and fill jars with liquid. Process for 5 minutes or just until completely discolored.

Delicious Dill Pickles

MIRIAM YODER, LaGRANGE. IN

1 qt. water   ¾ cup maple syrup or ½ cup honey
1 cup vinegar   4 tsp. salt

Mix all together and bring to boiling. Pack sliced pickles into jars. Also to each quart jar, add a slice of onion, 2 large garlic cloves, and a few dill sprigs. Pour boiling mixture over pickles. Enough for 8 quarts. Put in hot water bath. Bring to a boil, then turn off heat and let set for 10 minutes.

canning

Cinnamon Pickles

JUANITA WEAVER, JOHNSONVILLE, IL

1 gal. cucumbers	5 sticks cinnamon
1 cup lime	1 Tbsp. salt
4½ qt. water	2½ cups fructose
2 cups vinegar	1 cup red beet juice

Peel and seed cucumbers and cut into rings (or cube). Mix lime and water, and soak cucumbers in lime water for 24 hours. Rinse well. Soak in ice water 2 hours. Drain. Rinse well. Combine rest of ingredients to make syrup, and bring to a boil. Pour over rings. Let set overnight. Bring syrup and pickles to a boil. Pack into jars, keeping syrup at a low boil the entire time. Screw lids on after each jar is full, and set upside down until cool. If any don't seal, put in kettle with several inches of water. Cover with lid and bring water to rolling boil. Remove from heat and let jars set until cool. Note: If using raw beet juice, double amount of juice. Amount of beet juice varies with different summers and kinds of beets. Add as much as you like.

Pickled Beets

MIRIAM YODER, LaGRANGE, IN

canning

390

1 qt. water	4 tsp. salt
2 cups vinegar	2½ cinnamon sticks
1 cup maple syrup or ½ cup honey	18 whole cloves

Combine all ingredients and bring to a boil. Pack cut-up cooked beets in jars. Cover with boiled brine. Hot water bath for 5 minutes. Yield: Enough for 8 quarts.

Pickled Red Beets

MRS. REBECCA ZOOK, MYERSTOWN, PA

3 cups white vinegar	2 tsp. stevia powder
8 cups red beet juice (add water to equal 8 cups)	3 Tbsp. salt

Mix ingredients together and bring to a boil. Makes enough juice for 10 quarts beets. Wash and cook beets until soft. Do not discard water after cooking. After beets are soft, slide off skins and put beets in jars. Pour juice in jars and process until boiling. Turn off burner and let set 5 minutes. These taste very similar to pickled beets canned with sugar.

Pickled Beets

Mrs. Rhoda Miller, Sugarcreek, OH

3 cups water
1 cup vinegar
2 cups sorghum

1 tsp. cinnamon
½ tsp. allspice

Scrub beets with brush. Cook until tender, but do not overcook. Put beets in cold water and peel off skins. Cut into desired size pieces. Pack into jars and cover with brine made of the above ingredients. Add 1 tsp. salt per quart. Process in hot water bath for 10 minutes. About 5 quarts.

Pickled Okra

Mrs. Vernon Schrock, Lewistown, IL

¼ cup salt
1½ cups vinegar

1½ cups water

Boil. Fill 7 pint jars with unstemmed okra, 2-3" long. In each pint, add 1 large clove garlic and 1 hot pepper or a strip of sweet pepper. Fill jars to neck with hot brine, cover, then cold pack for 5 minutes.

391

canning

Sweet Peppers

Mrs. Rebecca Zook, Myerstown, PA

4 cups xylitol
4 cups water

4 cups vinegar

Bring ingredients to a boil. Slice or chop pepper. Put in jars and pour in hot syrup. Cold pack 6 minutes.

Pepper Relish

8 qt. chopped peppers
a few onions
a few sticks celery
2 Tbsp. celery seed
2 Tbsp. celery salt

3 Tbsp. salt
2 Tbsp. ground mustard
5 cups white vinegar
3 cups water
¾ tsp. stevia

Mix all together. Put in jars and cold pack 10 minutes.

Canning Dry Beans

CHRISTINA EBY, MONTNEY, BC

1½ cups dry beans, scant
1 tsp. salt
sprinkle of ginger

water
chopped garlic (opt.)

Fill 1 quart jars with ingredients. Pressure can jars at 12 lb. for 75 minutes.

Dilly Beans

EDITH ZIMMERMAN, SCOTTSVILLE, KY

2 lb. trimmed, tender green beans
4 heads dill
4 cloves garlic
1 tsp. cayenne pepper

2½ cups vinegar
2½ cups water
¼ cup canning salt

Pack beans lengthwise into jars, leaving ¼" headspace. To each pint add ¼ tsp. cayenne pepper (or less), 1 clove garlic, and 1 head of dill. Combine remaining ingredients, boil, and pour over beans. Process in hot water bath for 10 minutes. Yields: 4 pints.

Canning Dry Beans

MARIA WEAVER, SQUAW VALLEY, CA

1½ cups dry beans

1 tsp. salt

Put ingredients into each quart jar. Fill each jar with water. Let soak approximately 10 hours. Put flats and rings on and pressure can at 10 lb. for 90 minutes. Very handy to open a jar to make your favorite chili soup, or mash for your favorite refried bean dish or hot bean dip to eat with tortilla chips. I often have my vpreschoolers fill the jars in the evening, then first thing in the morning, I put the canner on to help warm the kitchen up. It is one thing I can in the wintertime when we need the heat in the house.

TIP

In canning peaches, I use pineapple juice full strength instead of sugar. In canning pears, I use half pineapple, half water.

—Patricia Taylor, Stoystown, PA

Healthy

To Can Peaches

Mrs. Kathryn Hershberger, Clare MI

Fill quart jars with peeled and sliced peaches. Or just leave them in halves. Add ¼ tsp. stevia powder and fill jars with hot water. Cold pack for 10 minutes.

To Can Peaches

Mrs. Sadie Lapp

Save some of the nice peach stones and put a few on top of the peaches in each jar for more flavor. To each quart also add 400 mg (I used liquid) vitamin C (to keep the nice color) and a few stevia leaves.

To Can Peaches

Miriam Yoder, LaGrange, IN

Fill jars with peaches, then add pineapple juice that's mixed with water. I use 1 part pineapple juice and 2 parts water. You can even make it half and half. Cold pack for 10 minutes.

To Can Pears

Miriam Yoder, LaGrange, IN

Fill jars half full of pears, add 1 Tbsp. of crushed pineapples, then finish filling the jars with pears and another Tbsp. of crushed pineapples, and fill with pineapple juice. Cold pack 10 minutes.

Applesauce

Mrs. Kathryn Hershberger, Clare, MI

13 qt. applesauce
4 tsp. stevia powder

1½ tsp. salt
1 tsp. vitamin C powder

Fill jars and cold pack 10 minutes.

Canning Applesauce

Mrs. Leona Miller, Odon, IN

4 qt. apple puree
1½ tsp. stevia powder
⅓ cup raw honey

½ tsp. salt
1½ tsp. cinnamon

Combine all ingredients and mix well. Chill and enjoy. If canning, process quart jars in boiling water bath for 15-20 minutes.

Easy Crockpot Apple Butter

Cynthia Korver, New Oxford, PA

Wash, quarter, and core (no need to peel) apples. Use any variety available. A red-skinned apple will result in darker butter. (I prefer York.) Fill 6 quart crockpot with apple pieces and cover about ⅓ of apples with water. Cover and cook on low setting 10-12 hours (overnight). Puree all. Add ⅛ cup sweetener per cup puree (or to taste). Add juice of 1 lemon (3 Tbsp. lemon juice concentrate), ½ teaspoon ground cloves, and 2 tsp. cinnamon (adjusting spices to taste). Return to slow cooker and cook to desired texture, stirring often. The apple butter takes about 1 day to cook down to right thickness, but it has a great potpourri aroma while it cooks. You can offset the lid to allow steam to escape quicker. Process in 1 quart jars in boiling water bath 10 minutes. 6 quart crockpot makes about 5 pints.

canning

394

Apple Pie Filling for Canning

Susan Stalter, Millersburg, OH

12 qt. apples, peeled and cut into pieces
¾ cup flour
2 cups honey

¼ cup cinnamon
1 Tbsp. nutmeg

Mix all together. Put in quart jars. Fill jars with water, to replace air spaces. Water bath for 30 minutes. For a quick apple dessert, spread 2 jars apple pie filling in a greased 9 x 13" pan. Combine the following and spread on top: ⅔ cup whole wheat flour, 2 cups oats, ⅔ cup melted butter, ½ cup honey, 1 tsp. salt, and 2 tsp. cinnamon. Bake at 350° for 30 minutes. Serve warm.

Diabetic Jelly

WALTER SAUDER, LATHAM, MO

1 Tbsp. lemon juice (scant)
1 tsp. unflavored gelatin
2 tsp. cornstarch

dash of salt (opt.)
1 cup unsweetened fruit juice
1-2 Tbsp. honey

Combine all ingredients in a saucepan. Bring to a boil for two minutes, stirring constantly. Yield: 1 cup.

Tomato Juice Cocktail

SERENA YODER, GOSHEN, IN

8 lb. tomatoes
2 med. onions, peeled and chopped
4 stalks celery, chopped
2 small to med. carrots

4 cloves garlic
1 Tbsp. salt
½ tsp. oregano
1 sprig parsley

Quarter tomatoes, do not peel. Place them in an 8 quart pot, mashing them as you go to form juice. Add remaining ingredients. Simmer over low heat until vegetables are tender. Put through food mill or Victorio strainer. Put in jars and process 15 minutes. Note: If using a food mill, it works best to puree the raw vegetables in the blender. Pour them over the tomatoes in the pot and simmer until tomatoes are soft. With the Victorio, the vegetables just need to be chopped.

395

canning

Grape Juice

MRS. KATHRYN HERSHBERGER, CLARE, MI

Fill quart jars ¾ full with grapes. Add ¼ cup maple syrup, ⅛ tsp. stevia powder and ⅛ tsp. salt. Fill jars with hot water and cold pack for 10-15 minutes.

Green Beans to Can

MARTHA WISE, SENECA FALLS, NY

raw green beans
1 tsp. salt

1 Tbsp. size raw bacon
½ cup water

Fill a quart jar with raw beans. Add salt, bacon, and water. Put lids on jars and place in oven. Bake 3 hours at 250°. Turn oven off and allow to cool before removing jars. Store in a cool place.

Canned Corn

EDNA MILLER

Cut off corn, cover with water and cook 5 minutes. Put corn and liquid in pint jars. Add to each pint: 1 tsp. salt, 1 tsp. sweetener (opt.), and 1 tsp. lemon. Cold pack 3 hours.

Sauerkraut to Can

MRS. IVAN J. YODER, MILLERSBURG, OH

Shred cabbage rather coarsely. Place a layer of it in a large stainless steel cake pan. Sprinkle 2 tsp. salt over it and chop it up with a little round hand chopper until juice begins to run. Now use your hands and just squeeze the cabbage until it's very, very juicy. Pour into a stainless steel kettle. Repeat until you have your desired amount of kraut. When your kettle is 3" near full, take a large new plastic bag and put water in it and place it on top of kraut to make it airtight. Leave set at room temperature 7-8 days or until desired sourness. Pack into jars and cold pack 5-10 minutes. This is an old recipe.

Homemade Sauerkraut

MARTHA STOLTZFUS, BLAIN, PA

You will need 5 lbs. cabbage for every gallon of your crock. Cut cabbage in quarters and shred with a fine shredder. Place 5 lbs. shredded cabbage and 3½ Tbsp. pickling salt in a large pan. Mix well with hands. Pack gently in large crock, using a potato masher to press it down. Repeat above until crock is filled to within 5 inches from the top. Press cabbage down firmly with potato masher to extract enough juice to cover. Fill a large plastic bag with cold water and secure firmly with a twister. Place on top of cabbage in crock, making sure all cabbage is covered. Keep crock at 65° to ferment. Fermentation will be complete in 10-12 days. (If no bubbles rise, fermentation has ended.) Pack in quart jars to within 1" from top. Pour any leftover juice into jars with sauerkraut. Process in boiling water 15 minutes. 50 lbs. makes about 15 quarts.

Vegetable Stew to Can

MARIE BEAR, PATRIOT, OH

1 med. head cabbage	6 med. onions, chopped fine
1 gal. tomatoes	6 green peppers
1 bunch celery	6 red peppers
2 lb. carrots	2 tsp. salt

Chop all vegetables and mix all ingredients together. Fill 1 quart jars and seal. Process for 10 minutes at 10 lb. pressure. This stew is so versatile! Add to potatoes and hamburger, mixed beans and meat, or zucchini soup stock and white sauce.

Healthy

Crushed Pineapple (from Zucchini Squash)

1 gal. ground zucchini
1-46 oz. can pineapple juice (unsweetened)
1 cup honey

2 tsp. stevia
½ cup lemon juice
½ tsp. pineapple oil

Use large zucchini. Peel and remove seeds. Cut into long strips. Grate or grind coarsely. Drain and measure 1 gallon. Heat pineapple juice, honey, and stevia until boiling. Add lemon juice and pineapple oil. Add to ground zucchini and mix well. Dip into pint jars, leaving 1" headspace. Process at 10 lb. for 30 minutes or water bath for 3 hours. I use this in jello or most anywhere. Does not taste quite like the real thing in fresh fruit mixture. I have not been able to obtain pineapple oil. I use LorAnn Gourmet pineapple flavor, and some people say some brands of pineapple oil give a much better flavor than others.

Pineapple Butter

LOVEDA BEAR

8 qt. applesauce
2 cans crushed pineapple

3 cups honey
cinnamon (opt.)

Cook down until thick. Keep hot, and fill 16 pint jars. Screw on sterilized lids and let seal. (This does not need to be canned.) This can be made sweeter or less sweet by adjusting the amount of honey.

Sugar Free Pear Butter

MRS. IVAN J. YODER, MILLERSBURG, OH

4 lb. ripe pears
⅔ cup white grape juice concentrate
1 tsp. cinnamon
1 tsp. cloves

¼ tsp. allspice
⅛ tsp. salt
½ cup xylitol
⅛ cup lemon juice

Peel and cut up pears. Drain off juice. Put pears through sieve. Put juice in a saucepan and cook down separately. Watch carefully. Put pear mush in a kettle, add rest of ingredients and begin to cook. When juice is cooked thick, add to pear butter. Continue boiling, but on low until of spreading consistency. Stir often. Yield: 5 pints. Apples could be used instead of pears.

Dry Seasoning Mixes

TAKE A LOOK AT THE MIXES YOU ARE USED TO BUYING;
read the ingredients carefully and attempt finding out what some of
those strange words mean! You might become motivated to make your
own mixes. Three main mixes many people use all the time are Hidden
Valley Ranch Dip Mix, Chicken Seasoning and Taco Seasoning. In this
section you will find a good replacement for all three of these.

You'll also find homemade baking powder recipes. Before buying
baking powder check the ingredients. If it contains aluminum don't
buy it. I buy Rumford baking powder at a natural food store, which
does not contain aluminum.

Develop a habit of checking the ingredients on anything you buy.
Safeguarding your family's health is hard work, but it's important!

Chicken Dipping

Juanita Weaver, Johnsonville, IL

1 cup flour
¼ tsp. garlic powder
1 tsp. seasoning salt
½ tsp. black pepper
⅛ tsp. sage

2 tsp. dry mustard
⅛ tsp. poultry seasoning
1½ tsp. paprika
2-3 tsp. chicken bouillon
   powder (below)

Mix all together.

Chicken Bouillon Powder

Juanita Weaver, Johnsonville, IL

3 cups nutritional yeast flakes
5 Tbsp. salt
3 Tbsp. onion (dried)
3 Tbsp. parsley
2½ tsp. sage
2½ tsp. celery seed
2½ tsp. garlic powder

2½ tsp. thyme
2½ tsp. marjoram
2½ tsp. rosemary
2½ tsp. tarragon
2½ tsp. paprika
1 tsp. basil

Grind all ingredients together in blender. Use to flavor soups and gravies.

Aluminum-Free Baking Powder

Juanita Weaver, Johnsonville, IL

½ cup cream of tartar
¼ cup cornstarch

¼ cup baking soda

Mix together and store in tight container. Measures like store-bought.

Homemade Baking Powder

Mrs. Urie Miller, Middlebury, IN

2 cups arrowroot powder
2 cups cream of tartar

1 cup baking soda

Sift together several times. Use as any other baking powder.

Ranch Powder

JUANITA WEAVER, JOHNSONVILLE, IL

5 heaping Tbsp. dried onion
2½ Tbsp. parsley
2 tsp. paprika
1 Tbsp. salt

2 tsp. pepper
1 tsp. garlic powder
1 tsp. celery salt

Mix all ingredients in mini grinder or blender. Keep in airtight container. 1 tablespoon mix=1 envelope of Ranch dressing.

Taco Seasoning Mix

JOANNE MARTIN, BROOTEN, MN
EUNICE HALTEMAN, NEWVILLE, PA

¼ cup instant minced onion
3 Tbsp. chili powder
2 Tbsp. ground cumin
2 Tbsp. salt

1 Tbsp. hot red pepper flakes (opt.)
1 Tbsp. minced garlic
1 Tbsp. cornstarch
2 tsp. oregano, crushed fine

Combine and mix all ingredients. Divide into 6 equal portions and place in small ziplock bags. To use: Mix 1 lb. browned hamburger, 1 Tbsp. ketchup, ½ cup water, and 1 bag taco seasoning mix. Simmer and stir uncovered until water has evaporated.

Taco Seasoning Mix

LEAH NISLEY, DANVILLE, OH

1½ cup chili powder
1¼ cup cumin
½ cup + 2 Tbsp. garlic powder

½ cup + 2 Tbsp. paprika
¾ cup onion powder

This has no salt like the boughten packages, so allow for that. Also, it does not contain cornstarch as a filler. 7 teaspoons=1.25 oz. package.

Taco Seasoning Mix

SUSAN STALTER, MILLERSBURG, OH

1 tsp. chili powder
1 tsp. paprika
1½ tsp. cumin
2 tsp. parsley flakes

1 tsp. onion powder
½ tsp. garlic salt
½ tsp. oregano

Mix and use as 1 store-bought package.

Healthy

Taco Seasoning

JUANITA WEAVER, JOHNSONVILLE, IL

4 Tbsp. onion powder
2 Tbsp. salt
2 Tbsp. chili powder
1 Tbsp. garlic powder

1 Tbsp. cumin
1½ Tbsp. dried oregano
1 tsp. red pepper (opt.)
¼-½ cup cornstarch (opt.)

Use to season taco soup or meat for burritos or taco salad. 2 Tbsp. equals 1 envelope of boughten, if cornstarch is left out.

Taco Seasoning Mix

BECKY SCHWARTZ, BOURBON, IN

¾ cup chili powder
½ cup flour
8 tsp. cumin
8 tsp. oregano

2 tsp. onion powder
2 tsp. garlic powder
2 tsp. salt
2 tsp. red pepper

Makes some over 2 cups seasoning. Sprinkle on meat (to taste) while frying, or use as packaged store-bought mix. Store in airtight container.

Taco Seasoning

GIAN RYAN, CLINTON, KY

1 cup chili powder
2 Tbsp. garlic powder
3 Tbsp. paprika

10 Tbsp. cumin
6 Tbsp. salt
2 tsp. pepper

Use 2-3 Tbsp. per pound of ground beef, or to taste. We also like to add a couple of teaspoons to ⅓ cup mayonnaise, 1 Tbsp. vinegar, and 1 clove garlic to make a taco salad dressing.

Mexican Seasoning

MRS. MIRIAM WENGERD, SUGARCREEK, OH

2 Tbsp. chili powder
2 tsp. garlic powder
2 tsp. paprika
pinch of stevia (opt.)

2 tsp. oregano
1 tsp. salt
4 tsp. onion powder

I've used this recipe for years. Mix up several batches and store in container with tight fitting lid. I write the recipe on the outside—very handy.

Taco Seasoning Mix

THE B. SISTERS, OREGON CITY, OR

2 tsp. instant minced onion or
   onion powder
1 tsp. salt
1 tsp. chili powder

½ tsp. cornstarch or arrowroot powder
½ tsp. garlic powder
¼ tsp. dried oregano
½ tsp. ground cumin

This recipe is for 1 lb. ground beef. Can be tripled, etc. and stored until ready to use. When ready to make tacos, brown 1 lb. ground beef. (Optional: Brown with chopped onions and/or garlic.) Add 1 recipe mix, reduce heat and mix well. For a saucy filling, add ½ cup water and simmer for 10 minutes. When ready, fill warmed taco shells and top with favorite toppings. (Lettuce, shredded cheese, tomatoes, olives, onions, salsa, sour cream, avocados, etc.) This can be a very quick, easy, delicious meal. Makes 8-10 tacos. Note: Natural organic taco shells can be bought by the case from Azure Standard (delivers to 11 states) 79709 Dufur Valley Road, Dufur, OR 97021. Phone number: 541.467.2230.

Homemade Herb Seasoning

MARTHA WIDEMAN, LISTOWEL, ON

2 tsp. salt
8 Tbsp. dried parsley
4 Tbsp. dried chives
1 tsp. sage
1 tsp. oregano

½ tsp. thyme
1 tsp. basil
½ tsp. celery seed or dried lovage
1 tsp. garlic powder

Rub dried herbs through a sieve. Store in an airtight container. Garlic may sink to bottom, so shake before each use. We use this recipe to go by, and use any proportions of herbs to our liking. Our family-favorite all-purpose seasoning for buttered vegetables, etc.

Herb Seasoning

MARIE BEAR, PATRIOT, OH

3 Tbsp. basil (ground)
3 Tbsp. summer savory
2 Tbsp. celery seed
2 Tbsp. ground cumin
2 Tbsp. sage

1 Tbsp. thyme
2 Tbsp. marjoram
3 Tbsp. onion powder
1 Tbsp. garlic powder
1½ cup sea salt

Mix together well. Use all ground ingredients if possible.

Healthy

Seasoned Salt

B. Garber, Fayetteville, PA

8 Tbsp. salt
2 Tbsp. pepper
2 Tbsp. paprika

1 Tbsp. onion powder
½ Tbsp. garlic powder

Mix. Use to season green beans, eggs, meats, etc. May be doubled, tripled, etc.

Seasoned Salt

Mrs. Ivan J. Yoder, Millersburg, OH

1 cup salt (sea or mineral)
2 Tbsp. onion powder
1 tsp. garlic powder
1 Tbsp. powdered celery seed

2 tsp. paprika
1 tsp. chili blend
1 tsp. ground parsley

Mix well. Store in tight container. I dry my own parsley and press it through a very fine strainer for my parsley powder.

Seasoned Salt

Juanita Weaver, Johnsonville, IL

1½ cup sea salt
2 Tbsp. paprika
2 tsp. chives
1 Tbsp. parsley
2 tsp. thyme

2 tsp. marjoram
2 tsp. celery seed
2 tsp. garlic powder
2 tsp. onion powder
1 tsp. cumin (scant)

Put parsley, chives, thyme, marjoram, and celery seed in coffee grinder or food processor. Add enough salt to make it easy to grind. Stir all ingredients together, or put in container and shake.

No Salt Seasoning

MIRIAM YODER, LaGRANGE, IN

1 Tbsp. onion powder
1 Tbsp. garlic powder
1 Tbsp. paprika
1 tsp. thyme
1 tsp. oregano
½ tsp. pepper

½ tsp. celery seed
⅛ tsp. cayenne pepper
2 tsp. parsley flakes
½ tsp. cumin
1 tsp. basil

Combine all ingredients in a small jar with a shaker top. Use for seasoning fish, poultry, vegetables, stews, and soups. Yield: About 2 oz.

Seasoned Salt

LORETTA JESS, AVA, IL

1½ cup salt
2 Tbsp. onion powder
1 Tbsp. garlic powder
2 Tbsp. celery seed

1 Tbsp. paprika
1 tsp. chili powder
½ tsp. red pepper
1 Tbsp. dried parsley flakes

Mix well and store in a spice or salt shaker. Use your imagination by adding or subtracting any seasoning of your choice or by increasing the amounts. I use this to season all my soups, meats, and casseroles, and like it very well.

dry mixes

406

TIP

When using sun-dried sea salt, use only half of the amount called for in a recipe. Dissolve in liquid before using.

Soaps & Cleaners

Healthy

WANT TO HAVE SPARKLING WINDOWS? A CLEAN FRESH smelling bathroom? Pleasant smelling bed sheets and clothes? Me too! What I'd rather not do is pay for it with my health. So many cleaners are toxic poisons. Avoid them by making better choices.

We buy Basic H from Shaklee (a mild liquid soap) by the five gallon bucket. It's great to use for showers, baths and hand soap. We also use *Our* liquid laundry soap for washing our clothes. They also have an all-purpose liquid cleaner which we use in spray bottles for cleaning tubs and toilets. It works especially well for pretreating a garment just covered with grass stains. You know how it is when children are outside a lot during summer! Just spray all the dirty areas, let set five to ten minutes, lay on basement floor and scrub with brush and water. It'll do a great job!

This cleaner does not give off harmful fumes and can be used for all types of cleaning—walls, stove tops, etc.

If you prefer a powder rather than liquid, you can try Neo-Life's laundry soap. It's called G-One Laundry Compound. We've used this for years as well. It's available in fifty pound containers.

I will never forget how I met a seven-year-old girl and her mother. When this girl was younger she drank a cleaner that ate away the lining of her esophagus. She was unable to have anything to eat. All she could handle was clear liquids. How devastating this would be! Let's try to do our very best to avoid toxic cleaners so little children will not have to suffer for it. Not to mention our older daughters who inhale the fumes every week as they clean. Better choices *are* available. Let's find them and use them.

Resources

The following resources will help you get what you need for your soap-making endeavors.

Bio Pac
(800) 225-2855
Natural laundry products.

Earth Friendly Products
(800) 335-3267
Natural laundry and cleaning products.

Frontier Herb
PO Box 229, Norway, IA 52318
(800) 669-3275
30-year-old company offering bulk herbs and spices. Call for catalog.

Real Goods
(800) 762-7325
"Green" laundry products.

SunFeather Natural Soap Co.
1551 Hwy. 72, Potsdam, NY 13676
(315) 265-3648

Complete line of soaps, soap-making books, oils, waxes, colorants, essential and fragrance oils, soap molds. soap decals, soap stamps, soap-making equipment and soap kits. Also supplies ingredients to the home cosmetic and liquid shampoo maker, such as xanthan gum, vitamins, lecithin, surfactants, collagen, polysorbates and preservatives. Call for catalog—$2.00.

Rainbow Meadow
(800) 207-4047
Lots of soap making supplies. Call for catalog.

Soaps

Bath Soap

Mrs. Jr. Kauffman, Redding, IA

6 lb. oil or fat
3 cups water
18 oz. lye

essential oil
¼ cup borax
2 cups lemon juice

Place water and oil in kettle, add lye and stir well. When blended add borax; when it traces add lemon juice, essential oil, etc. Pour into molds. After about 2 hours cut into bars and when it releases, dump it out. This may be in 1-2 days. Allow to cure 4-8 weeks. I usually set it in cold water so it sets up faster. This soap is very easy to make and works well for a hand soap. Coconut and olive oil can be used with fat.

Homemade Bath Soap

Mrs. Jason Byler, Lobelville, TN

6 lb. fats of your choice
18 oz. lye
3 cups water
2 cups lemon juice

¼ cup borax
essential oils, scents, or any
    skin enhancing ingredients

Put water into a 6-8 quart kettle. Add lye, stir well. Add fats and stir until melted. Add borax and stir to dissolve. Blend in lemon juice and continue to stir slowly until it thickens enough to trace. It may be necessary to set it in cold water if it thickens too slowly. Add essential oils or extra ingredients. Pour into mold, and after 2 hours cut into bars. When it releases from sides, dump it out (usually 1-2 days). Cure in a dry, airy place for 4-8 weeks or until lye is no longer caustic. This is my favorite soap because it suds so well, and is so easy to make—no need to heat anything on the stove. I've added blended oatmeal, goat milk, and cucumbers. There are many common kitchen ingredients and vegetables that are good for the skin. Your imagination is the limit! I use any blend of whatever fats I have—lard, shortening, coconut oil, vegetable oil, etc. A kitty litter pan makes a good mold and is the perfect size for 1 batch of soap.

TIP

How to brighten linens—Delicate napkins, linens, and even white socks can be whitened on the stove. Fill a pot with water and a few slices of fresh lemon, and bring to a boil. Turn off the heat, add linens, and let soak for up to an hour, then launder as usual. For extra brightening, spread them out in the sunlight to dry.

Choices

Shampoo

EDNA MILLER

Flake 1 bar castile soap. Melt soap in 1 pint boiling water, then cool. Put soap mixture into mixing bowl and add 1 egg. Beat with beater. Put in jar. After it is settled, it is ready to use. This shampoo will keep.

Homemade Lye Soap

MRS. TIM SENSENIG

2-18 oz. cans lye in 2½ pints cold soft water. 12 lb. clean lard or tallow—if using half lard and half tallow, have tallow at 11° and lye water at 85°. If all tallow, have lye water at 95°. If sweet lard or soft fat, have it at 85° with lye water at 150°. Pour lye water slowly into lard, stirring with slow motion back and forth. Stir until light and thick. Pour into mold, which has been lined with plastic. Let set and cut into squares before entirely cold.

Homemade Soap

MARY YODER

10 lb. melted lard or tallow
5 pt. water
2 cans lye
1 oz. oil of sassafras
2 oz. glycerin

4 Tbsp. sugar
½ cup ammonia
½ cup Sal-Soda
½ box borax

Mix everything except tallow. When cooled, mix tallow with other ingredients. Try to have them close to the same temperature. Pour in pan; cut when firm. Let cure a few weeks before using. Floats on top of water. Smells good, too.

Crumbalized Soap

MRS. JR. KAUFFMAN, REDDING, IA

10 cups cold rain water
9 cups melted fat (or any grease)
½ cup ammonia

3 Tbsp. borax
½ oz. citronella
1 can Lewis lye

Mix these in above order. Sprinkle lye in last and let stand for 5-10 minutes. Stir frequently for the first 1½ hours; after that, once every hour throughout the day. Avoid inhaling fumes. Let set in crock for a few days, stirring often. Put in a tight container so it will not dry out. This is to be in crumbles ready to put in wash water. The citronella is mostly for a pleasant smell, works fine without. Be very cautious when handling lye.

Eucalyptus-Mint All-Purpose Disinfecting Soft Soap for Kitchen and Bath

SANDY MAINE*

This soap can be used for washing dishes, floors, stoves, refrigerators, sinks and hands. It's mild to the skin but effective enough to get cleaning jobs done. The eucalyptus and mint provide a disinfecting quality as well as a fresh scent. Any areas washed with this soap will be undesirable to crawling insects and flies. They'll stay away for a while.

5 cups grated castile soap
1 tsp. borax
1 tsp. eucalytus essential oil
½ cup baking soda
6 cups hot peppermint tea

Put grated soap into a three quart stainless steel saucepan and add hot mint tea. Simmer for 15 minutes on low heat. Add baking soda, borax and eucalyptus oil. Store in a labeled plastic jug or squirt bottle. Shake before using.

*Sandy Maine is author of "Clean Naturally" (Interweave Press) and founder and coed of SunFeather Natural Soap Company, www.sunfeather.com

Powder Soap

JUANITA WEAVER, JOHNSONVILLE, IL

10 cups soft water
9 cups melted lard (not hot)
½ cup ammonia
½ cup borax
1¼ cup lye

Mix all ingredients in a bucket. It is important to add the lye last. Stir every 5-10 minutes for 2 hours, then once an hour throughout the day until there is no liquid at the bottom. Let set for a few days, then put a tight lid on to keep from drying. This mixture looks separated at first, but moisture eventually absorbs and becomes crumbly with stirring. Batch does not double well, but after it sets a few days, you can put several batches in a 5 gallon bucket and seal tightly, to cure for a couple of weeks.

Soft Soap

JUANITA WEAVER, JOHNSONVILLE, IL

Fill a 5 gallon bucket ½ full of soft water. (I like to collect rain water.) Add 1¼ cup of lye and mix. Slowly stir in 7 cups of melted fat (half lard, half tallow). Fat should be just so it's melted, not at all hot, or it will separate. Add 1 cup ammonia, 2 cups borax, 2-3 cups of laundry detergent, ⅛ cup bluing. Mix well. Add more soft water until bucket is full. Stir well every day for one week. Ready to use. Great for clothes, dishes, and dirty hands.

Choices

Soft Soap

LEAH NISLEY, DANVILLE, OH
MRS. ROMAN RABER, BRINKHAVEN, OH

5 gal. water
1 can lye
7 cups melted grease

3 cups Wisk (or any soap)
2 cups borax
1 cup ammonia

Put 2 gallons water in container. Dissolve lye in water, add grease (have lye water and grease the same temperature). Add other ingredients gradually with other water. Stir thoroughly. Then stir once a day for a week. We really like this soap. It might look like a failure at first, but usually it is fine in a few days.

Dishwashing Soap

5 cups grated castile soap
½ cup baking soda
1 tsp. borax

6 cups peppermint tea
1 tsp. eucalyptus essential oil

Put grated soap in a 3 quart stainless steel pot and add hot mint tea. Simmer for 15 minutes on low heat. Add baking soda, borax, and eucalyptus oil. Shake before using.

Cold Homemade Soap

EDNA MILLER

1 can lye
3 pt. cold water
5½ lb. fat

½ cup powdered borax
½ cup turpentine
bluing

Have lye water cold and fat lukewarm before mixing. Stir until it starts to thicken, then add turpentine and borax. Add enough bluing to tint.

Granulated Soap

Mrs. John (Emma) Mullet, Burton, OH

9 cups very soft lard
3 Tbsp. 20 Mule Team borax
½ cup ammonia
1 can lye

10 cups water
1 cup liquid soap
1½ cup Clorox (opt.)
bluing (opt.)

Mix in order given in a large stainless steel bowl. Stir for 5-10 minutes, then let set for 5-10 minutes. Stir frequently for the first 1½ hours, then every few hours. Stir off and on for a few days. Store in tight container. This will be granular and white. I use 1 cup of soap in washing machine with very hot water for white clothes. Can also use for colored, but dissolve in hot water first.

Homemade Laundry Soap

Julia Engle, Oklahoma City, OK

2 bars Ivory soap, grated
1 cup washing soda

3 gallons boiling water

Grate Ivory soap, using a cheese grater. Put grated soap, washing soda, and boiling water into a 5 gallon bucket. Stir until soap gratings are melted. Let set until cool. It will turn into gel.

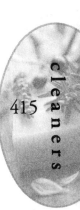

415

cleaners

Laundry Soap

Mrs. Esh, PA

4 lb. lard
12 oz. lye
2 qt. water

½ cup borax
1 cup Basic H

Mix lye and water and let stand to cool off to 98°. Takes around 2 hours, depending on the weather. Melt lard, make it 98°. Slowly add lye to the lard mixture while stirring. Add soaps and stir until you can trace on the soap. Pour into a cloth lined container and let set for 1 month. The longer you age the soap the more suds there will be. You can use stainless steel or glass and you are able to use the utensils and containers again with whatever.

Fels-Naptha Laundry Soap

CYNTHIA KORVER, NEW OXFORD, PA

½ bar Fels-Naptha soap*
¾ cup borax
¾ cup washing soda**

For 2 gallon plastic pail, heat 3 pints of water. Grate ½ bar soap into it and dissolve. Remove from heat and stir in ¾ cup borax and ¾ cup washing soda. Mix well. Mixture will thicken. Pour 1 quart hot water into 2 gallon plastic pail. Add Fels-Naptha solution, stirring well. Finish filling pail with cold water. Stir. Cover. Set aside, and stir occasionally. Ready to use in 24 hours. Use ½-¾ cup per load. Makes enough for 48-64 loads. *I found Fels-Naptha at my local Shurfine. **Washing soda may be found in the laundry aisle of grocery store. Note: I got this recipe out of *Countryside Magazine*. It's the only laundry detergent I use now. It's quick and easy to make. Clothes only smell fresh—no perfumes.

Household Cleaners

Spritz-and-Spray Toilet Bowl Cleaner

SANDY MAINE*

The baking soda and vinegar in this formula dissolve mineral buildup, while the oils loosen grime and give it a fresh, clean scent.

¼ tsp. sodium lauryl sulfoacetate
2 Tbsp. vinegar
1 tsp. grapefruit essential oil
2 Tbsp. baking soda
1 tsp. orange essential oil
2 cups water

Mix all ingredients in a four cup measuring cup or a bowl. When you mix the vinegar and baking soda, it will foam. Let this mixture stand for ten minutes before pouring into a spray bottle.

Sandy Maine is author of "Clean Naturally" (Interweave Press) and founder and coed of SunFeather Natural Soap Company, www.sunfeather.com

Tub & Tile Cleaner

SANDY MAINE*

1 cup baking soda
2 vitamin C tablets, crushed

¼ cup liquid castile soap
3-5 drops eucalyptus or tea tree oil

Use in an empty dish soap bottle. Add everything and just enough water to make paste. Use as you would any other cleaner.

*Sandy Maine is author of "Clean Naturally" (Interweave Press) and founder and coed of SunFeather Natural Soap Company, www.sunfeather.com

Soft Scrub

SANDY MAINE*

1 cup fine grade pumice
½ cup clay powder
2 Tbsp. grapefruit essential oil

¼ cup baking soda
¼ cup sodium lauryl sulfoacetate
½ cup boiling water

Mix all ingredients together and stir. Store in old dishwashing soap container.

*Sandy Maine is author of "Clean Naturally" (Interweave Press) and founder and coed of SunFeather Natural Soap Company, www.sunfeather.com

Lavender Soft Scrub

¾ cup baking soda
¼ cup powdered milk

½ cup castile soap
5 drops lavender oil

Combine in a soap bottle. Add enough water to make a paste. Shake, apply to surface, then wipe area clean. Clean with damp cloth. Rinse well.

Natural Fabric Softener

MRS. LAMAR (NANCY) ZIMMERMAN, STEVENS, PA

2 cups white vinegar
2 cups baking soda

4 cups water

Pour into plastic bottle, cover and shake. Use ¼ cup in rinse. Variation: Add 1 cup white vinegar to rinse water.

Choices

Woodwork Cleaner

MRS. DENNIS (MIRIAM) NOLT, PINE GROVE, PA

1 qt. water
¼ cup olive oil
½ cup vinegar

Mix well in a bucket. Rub into woodwork. Dry. Buff with a soft cloth until it shines. Works especially well on kitchen cabinets.

Stove & Oven Cleaner

MRS. RUBY SHETLER, HOMER, MI

2 Tbsp. lye, heaping
½ cup cold water
1 Tbsp. flour or cornstarch
½ cup cold water

Dissolve lye in ½ cup cold water, in glass jar. In another container stir flour or cornstarch in ½ cup cold water. Pour starch solution slowly into lye solution, stirring constantly. This cleaner may be used immediately or stored in a closed glass jar until needed. It works wells on stainless steel. Wear rubber gloves when using it. Keep away from children.

Window Cleaner

MRS. MIRIAM WENGERD, SUGARCREEK, OH

juice from one lemon
2 cups water
½ tsp. peppermint essential oil
1 tsp. cornstarch

Mix all ingredients and pour into plastic spray bottle. Shake well before using.

Window Cleaner

ESTHER OBERHOLTZER, PENN YAN, NY

1 pt. rubbing alcohol
2 Tbsp. ammonia (opt.)
2 Tbsp. liquid soap
3 drops blue food coloring

Add water to make 1 gallon. Use in a spray bottle. (I use this recipe without the liquid soap or food coloring. - Mrs. Miriam Wengerd.)

Healthy

Window Cleaner

JUANITA WEAVER, JOHNSONVILLE, IL

1 pt. rubbing alcohol
½ cup ammonia

1 tsp. dish soap

Add water to make 1 gallon.

Spray Cleaner

SANDY MAINE*

1 tsp. sodium lauryl sulfoacetate
1 tsp. borax
2 Tbsp. white vinegar
2 cups hot water

¼ tsp. eucalyptus essential oil
¼ tsp. lavender essential oil
3 drops tea tree essential oil

Mix all ingredients and stir until dry ingredients dissolve. Pour into spray bottle and use.

*Sandy Maine is author of "Clean Naturally" (Interweave Press) and founder and coed of SunFeather Natural Soap Company, www.sunfeather.com

Prewash

MRS. E. LAMBRIGHT, ARTHUR, IL

Mix equal parts of Wisk laundry detergent, ammonia, and water. Spray on garment. Works wonders for chocolate, blood, and other hard stains.

Household Cleaner

MRS. SAM (LYDIA) MILLER, FREDERICKSBURG, OH

We like to have a spray bottle with white vinegar handy. Before washing dishes, spray faucet, etc. and it will shine after wiping. Also good for lime deposits. Soak a cloth in hot vinegar and wrap around fixtures with mineral buildup for one hour.

Drain Opener

CHRISTINA EBY, MONTNEY, BC

Sprinkle 1 cup baking soda down drain. Pour 2 cups boiling vinegar down drain. Be ready with plunger if needed. When drain is clear, turn on hot water for a few minutes.

Clean Teakettles

MRS. URIE MILLER, MIDDLEBURY, IN

If you have a teakettle or kettles used for heating water with a mineral buildup inside, letting whey set in them for up to several days will do much to assist you with cleaning power! The heavier the buildup, the longer they need to soak.

Chicken Defeathering

EDNA MILLER

Put a handful of soda in boiling water to scald chickens. This will help remove pinfeathers. To make chickens easier to defeather, the water should be heated to 150°.

Silverware Brightener

EDNA MILLER

To brighten dull silver, rub it with a piece of potato dipped in baking powder. Save your potato water to soak your silverware in to brighten it.

Spider Be-Gone

MRS. REBECCA ZOOK, MYERSTOWN, PA

Put some lavendar oil into your water when housecleaning. It keeps the spiders away.

Bathroom Cleaner

MRS. REBECCA ZOOK, MYERSTOWN, PA

Mix lavender oil with water in a spray bottle for a natural bathroom spray. When using essential oils, only use a few drops until it's as strong as you prefer.

Home Remedies

IT IS A CHALLENGE TO FIND WAYS TO HELP KEEP
ourselves and our families healthy. This is a subject in which I have great
interest. Begin by eating lots of fresh fruits and vegetables. Make it your
goal to always include something fresh with each meal.

Wise moms think ahead and prepare for those times when family
members are not feeling well, fighting flu and colds or other contagious
diseases.

I always keep Flu Buster (page 423) on hand, which I make each
year. It's not hard to make and is very effective. For younger children
dilute with water. For many years we have made and used the Immune
Booster on page 429. It is so handy for children as the glycerin gives it
a sweet taste. I often give it after another less pleasant tasting medicine
to leave them with a good taste.

When dealing with illness, one benefits from asking questions of
others who have experienced what one is going through. Call a natural
food store, ask your midwife, study herbs, learn how to make your own
tinctures and how to use them. If I would offer advice I would suggest
making Immune Booster and Flu Buster and a good cough syrup. These
three will cover a lot of territory in chasing away common illnesses.

Remember to pray, asking God for wisdom in how to deal with
whatever situation is at hand. He has all the answers. Find them.

Whooping Cough Syrup

MRS. MIRIAM WENGERD, SUGARCREEK, OH

2 oz. marshmallow root
1 qt. distilled water
2 Tbsp. vinegar

2 oz. garden thyme
½ cup glycerin

Combine ingredients and simmer one hour on low heat. Strain and use.
This recipe originated from old-time herbalist Dr. Shook. His version included sugar. I changed it to no sugar, glycerin instead, and added vinegar. This is very effective and if used persistently it really helps to lessen the hard coughing. Must be refrigerated.

Herbal Whooping Cough Syrup

MRS. MIRIAM WENGERD, SUGARCREEK, OH

¾ cup slippery elm, cut & dried
¼ cup lobelia, cut & dried
½ cup peppermint tea leaves
1 cup glycerin

¼ cup licorice root, cut & dried
⅛ cup flax seed
2 cups water
4 Tbsp. vinegar

Combine and simmer two hours on low then strain. Use every two hours or as needed. One or two teaspoons for children, one tablespoon for adults. Give after each coughing episode as well. This formula tastes pleasant and it works to eliminate phlegm, thus lessening the hardness of the coughing. It really helps! When our nine-year-old got whooping cough, I looked through my herbal books and this combination came into my mind. It was one of those moments when I felt like God gave me a recipe. If children have whooping cough, rub their chest and back with mullein and garlic oil and antispasmodic tincture from Dr. Christopher three times a day. Also give them eucalyptus steam baths. Keep them on a cleansing diet, fruits, put watermelon in blender and blend into drink, avoid dairy products, white sugar and white flour. Makes a *big* difference! Keep this cough syrup refrigerated and use for all coughs.

Colds, Flu, & Fever

MRS. JUNIOR KAUFFMAN, REDDING, IA

Stop all foods, give fruit juices or herbal teas. No dairy foods of any kind, milk or eggs, as this is very mucus forming. If having fever, keep hydrated with warm baths, rub all over with olive oil and give pedialyte water. Fever is a natural way to burn up toxins, which are caused by mucus-forming foods.

Old Cough Remedy

1 tsp. cinnamon
1 tsp. cloves
1 tsp. allspice

1 tsp. nutmeg
½ tsp. ginger
½ tsp. mustard

Add enough lard to make a paste. Apply to chest and throat. Fold cloth so it won't fall out—it will get crumbly. Should work overnight.

Cough Syrup

JUANITA WEAVER, JOHNSONVILLE, IL

Slice 1 lemon in thin slices in small kettle. Add ¾ cup of flax seed and 1 pint water. Simmer for 2 hours. Do not boil! Strain while hot. Add ¼ cup honey. If water evaporated, add enough to make a pint. This spoils easily. Keep refrigerated. Good for chest colds and whooping cough. 1 tablespoon 3 times a day and after each severe cough. Soothing and tastes good. Good for sore throats—add slippery elm.

Bronchitis Tea

SANDRA MILLER, IONIA, MI

juice of one fresh lemon
3 slices fresh ginger

⅛ tsp. cayenne
2 cups boiling water

Steep and strain. Add honey to taste. Drink ¼ cup at a time—but don't linger to get the flavor! This makes a pint. If this is drunk over two days, it usually cures an adult. This tea is NOT for children.

Electrolyte Drink

JUANITA WEAVER, JOHNSONVILLE, IL

1 qt. water
2 Tbsp. honey
½ tsp. salt

1 tsp. baking soda
orange juice concentrate

Mix all together. Serve warm or cold. Good for fever, upset stomach, diarrhea, etc. Can use grape concentrate and/or less soda.

Healthy

Natural Pedialyte

MRS. JUNIOR KAUFFMAN, REDDING, IA

2 cups warm water
2 Tbsp. maple syrup

½ tsp. Redmond real salt

Mix all together, give as needed for fever and vomiting. If your child is dehydrating, rub him/her all over with pure olive oil and give this orally. This has kept our children out of the hospital already.

Natural Pedialyte

MRS. LAMAR (NANCY) ZIMMERMAN, STEVENS, PA

2 cups warm water
2 Tbsp. honey

¾ tsp. soda
½ tsp. salt

Mix all together. Give as needed for fever and vomiting. Note: Babies under a year old should not be given honey. Maple syrup may be substituted.

Sassafras Tea

ANNA RUTH KING

Scrub small sassafras roots carefully. Place handful in boiling water for 5 minutes or until water turns red. Sweeten with cream and sweetener (honey, etc.). We have only made it with dry sassafras. This is a great spring tonic, and very good as an iced tea.

Body Cleanse

MRS. LAMAR (NANCY) ZIMMERMAN, STEVENS, PA

Mix 2 tablespoons freshly squeezed lemon juice with 2 tablespoons maple syrup in a glass of water. Use daily as an energizer, a cleanser, and as a refreshing, nourishing drink.

Slippery Elm Milk

SUSAN DOTY, LOBELVILLE, TN

1 tsp. honey (or more)
1 tsp. slippery elm powder

1 cup hot milk
nutmeg and cinnamon

In mug mix honey and slippery elm into a paste. Add hot milk and spices to taste. A soothing drink for stomachache and diarrhea.

Liquid Garlic

MRS. JOHN (EVA MAY) YODER, CLARE, MI

Fill a pint jar ½ full of thinly sliced garlic cloves. Cover with vegetable glycerin, as much as you prefer. 1 cup garlic and 1 cup glycerin make a fairly strong finished product. Cover jar and let set at room temperature for 3 weeks or longer, shaking every couple of days. Strain off and bottle liquid. Use this when your little ones have been exposed to the flu, have a cold, or are sick. When sick, take every hour.

Anemia Prevention Drink

MARIA WEAVER, SQUAW VALLEY, CA

½ oz. dried nettle leaves
½ oz. dried parsley leaves
½ oz. dried comfrey leaves
½ oz. dried yellow dock root
¼ oz. peppermint leaves

Measure herbs and put in glass half-gallon jars. Pour boiling water until jar is totally full; cover tightly. Steep for at least 8 hours. This brew contains 3 excellent sources of iron: nettles, parsley, and yellow dock. It provides folic acid from the parsley, and vitamin B-12 from the comfrey. The green herbs all contribute Vitamin C which aids iron absorption. The mint makes it tasty. Drink freely, up to 4 cups daily.

Immune Booster

MRS. GLENN ZIMMERMAN, GREENWOOD, WI
MRS. MIRIAM WENGERD, SUGARCREEK, OH

2 cups Echinacea Purpurea
1 cup Echinacea root
1 cup peppermint leaf

1 cup stinging nettle leaf
1 gal. food grade glycerin

Mix the dry herbs together. These herbs can be used as a tea or made into a tincture. Fill a quart jar ⅓ full with your mixed herbs (save the rest for later use). Pour ½ cup of boiling water on the dry herbs, then fill the jar within one inch from the top with glycerin. Stir the thick goo until mixed, then cap with a tight lid. Place small kitchen towel in the bottom of a slow cooker so as to protect the jar from direct heat, then fill pot half full of water. Put the sealed jar on the towel in the water in the crockpot, then put on the crockpot lid. Turn on lowest heat for 3 days. It should not boil but be hot to the touch. Stir the hot goo every day. Do not let the crockpot get too low in water. After 3 days, strain the hot herb mixture through a cloth from the now dark, warm glycerin. Throw the used herbs away and store the liquid tincture in a tightly capped bottle. Be sure to label. Keep in a dark, cool place. Take 1 dropper every 2 hours when ill or exposed to illness. If you have stinging nettles around your place, you can gather and dry your own. Put on latex gloves, or any other gloves and wear long-sleeved clothing. Cut with a sharp scissors or pruning knife, and put in a clean pail or box. If you have an extra bed, spread a clean sheet over it and arrange the stinging nettles on it so they don't overlap. Make sure you're still wearing gloves! When dry and brittle they do not sting, but may make the hands itchy when handling a lot. Brush leaves off stems and store in glass jars in cool place. Crush when you want to use them. This recipe comes from Debi Pearl. An excellent place to buy herbs is from *The Bulk Herb Store*, 1.877.278.4257, 26 West 6th Avenue, Lobelville, TN 37097. They have a great catalog and potent herbs at good prices!

For Headaches

LORETTA JESS, AVA, IL

1 Tbsp. Epsom salt
1 tsp. bi-carbonated soda

1 pt. ice cold water

Dip washcloth in this and put on forehead. Dip again as soon as towel gets warm. Also drink lots of water.

Baby Powder

JUANITA WEAVER, JOHNSONVILLE, IL

2 cups cornstarch
¼ cup baking soda

several drops lavender essential oil
or whatever scent you prefer

Shake and stir all ingredients until thoroughly mixed. Fill your powder jar.

Diaper Rash

Mrs. Conrad (Martha) Kuepfer, Pleasantville, TN

Use coconut oil to clear up persistent and hard to heal diaper rashes.

B-Complex for Numbness

Edna Miller

For those who have sleeping and numb hands at night, try using B-complex in the morning with your meal and B-12 in the evening.

Vitamin B for Restlessness

Edna Miller

Vitamin B calms nerves. It is good for restlessness or cramps in the legs. Take one B-50 a day or more.

Peroxide Solution for Sore Mouth

Edna Miller

For a sore mouth, make a solution of ⅓ water, ⅓ mouthwash, and ⅓ peroxide. Swab mouth for babies and rinse for adults.

Calcium Tablets for Relaxation

Edna Miller

Take calcium tablets before going to bed. It makes you sleep well and relax.

Joy's Cream

Maria Weaver, Squaw Valley, CA

13 oz. Vaseline

6 tsp. oil of turpentine

1 scant tsp. oil of wintergreen

Set the container of Vaseline in a small saucepan of hot water on a very low burner. Watch closely until it is all melted. Add the oils. Combine well and pour into small containers. It is very healing for all the small cuts and scrapes children are masters at getting. It also relieves the topical pain. I originally received this recipe from an old friend in Texas who raised goats. Her name was Joy Kornagie so we named the cream Joy's Cream.

Healthy

Beeswax Lip Balm

MRS. MIRIAM WENGERD, SUGARCREEK, OH

¼ cup grated beeswax
3 Tbsp. coconut oil

2 Tbsp. cocoa butter
1 Tbsp. almond oil

Mix ingredients together and heat gently in a double boiler until everything is melted. Pour into small tins or lip balm tubes.

Chest Rub

SANDRA MILLER, IONIA, MI

½ oz. peppermint oil
½ oz. eucalyptus oil
½ oz. wintergreen oil

4 oz. olive oil
½ oz. beeswax
4 drops Benzoin Tincture

Heat olive oil, add oils, then beeswax. I use an old crockpot to melt this. I also add enough beeswax to fill a half pint jar. This runs about $13, but lasts all winter for us, and works well.

Plantain Salve

MRS. ALTA ZIMMERMAN, GREENWOOD, WI

Pack fresh plantain leaves in a quart jar and fill with olive oil. Cover all leaves with oil and dislodge all the air bubbles. Set jar in a bowl, as it will run over a bit, and put out of direct sunlight for 6 weeks. (Put date on jar.) After 6 weeks, pour off oil and squeeze out leaves. Discard leaves. For every ounce of oil, add: 1 Tbsp. grated beeswax, 1 Vitamin E capsule. Heat slowly in kettle, then pour into small wide-mouth jars or tins. I often add orange oil, or peppermint oil—our favorite. Use for ouchies, insect bites and stings, minor burns, etc.

Herbal Bath Bags

VERONICA ANNE WEAVER, SEARS, MI

Gather about 2 cups of dried herbs (any combination, such as lavender, sage, bee balm, mint, etc.). Using a 15" circle of material (such as old bed sheets), gather the edges together, making a little pouch, and tie with yarn, ribbon, or whatever. In a kettle, bring 2-3 quarts of water to a rolling boil. Pop in the herb bag and remove from heat. Let steep for 20 minutes. Pour everything into your bath water including the bag. Relax in your hot bath and enjoy. This is wonderful for treating flu and colds.

Herbal Hair Rinse

IDA ELIZABETH WEAVER, SEARS, MI

Fill a 32 oz. jar (with tightly fitting lid) half full with fresh herbs. You may use any combination, such as lavender, rosemary, or yarrow. Add apple cider vinegar or white vinegar. Before you put the lid on, put a bit of plastic wrap between the jar and lid, as the vinegar will corrode the lid. Now screw the lid on tightly and shake the jar every day for 2 weeks, then strain. The rinse is ready to use. Dilute half a cup rinse in 32 oz. of water. This is especially good for dry, hard to manage hair, and it also stimulates the scalp. Try it!

Natural Hair Spray

MRS. CONRAD (MARTHA) KUEPFER, PLEASANTVILLE, TN

1 tsp. plain gelatin
1 cup water, boiling

Stir until dissolved. Try adding essential oil for scent. Store in spray bottle in refrigerator and drop in hot water for a few minutes to use. Works well to keep little girls' hair in place. Spray it while combing.

Gardening Solutions

THE PERFECT GARDEN…EVERYTHING GREEN AND
growing, no bad bugs in sight! Delicious juicy strawberries, large crisp, sweet heads of cabbage, leafy green lettuce, tender young string beans… the list goes on. Doesn't it sound like a dream?

In this section you will find simple solutions to those pests that like to munch on your garden goodies. The only thing we can't provide you with is a bottle of time to do it.

Try some of these tips and see if the garden of your dreams doesn't materialize into reality. At least you'll get closer to it.

Here's our favorite tip on how to avoid weeding. Each fall we bag lots and lots of leaves, approximately sixty bags. We store them in the barn attic and in the spring once the corn is up we hoe it and put leaves between the rows. The same with potatoes, peas, etc. We could probably use twice this many bags if we had them. This is a good job for children—they'll do it a lot rather than hoeing weeds! The leaves let the rain through and keep the ground moist and cuts way down on the weeding.

Ant Deterrent

Spray apple cider vinegar on ants. Pour in spray bottle and mist on countertops or wherever you have ants.

Garden Hint

MRS. REBECCA ZOOK, MYERSTOWN, PA

Sprinkle salt on your cabbage, cauliflower, and broccoli transplants to keep them free from worms.

For Wormy Broccoli

For wormy broccoli, use 4 parts flour and 1 part red pepper, and dust plants with this mixture.

Cucumber Beetle Control

MRS. JASON WANNER

1 Tbsp. ammonia
1 tsp. Epsom salt
1 Tbsp. salt petre

1 tsp. soda
1 gal. water

Pour around roots. Drench roots every 2 weeks. Enough for 6 plants.

Melon Mixture

6½ Tbsp. Epsom salt
3½ Tbsp. borax

5 gal. water

This is for tasteless melons. Apply when vines start to run and again when fruit is 2 inches in diameter. Melons don't cross with cucumbers or pumpkins, so you can't blame flat taste on cross-pollination.

Potato Bug Remedy

For those of you who are concerned about all the chemicals we use on our food nowadays, here is a natural way to get rid of potato bugs! Dig wild mayapple plants with the roots and boil them in enough water to cover them for 30 minutes. Set aside until cool, then strain and spray on potato plants on a warm day. This will not hurt the potato plants and works well.

Bloodmeal

MRS. ERVIN (ELIZABETH) BEACHY

We experienced having our ripe strawberries cleaned out, and discovered deer tracks. So I sprinkled bloodmeal on the rows and around the patch. Later we noticed fresh tracks near the patch but not in it! The following year we put it on before the berries ripened and several times through the season, especially after a rain. We didn't experience the thieves again. Bloodmeal is also a wonderful nitrogen booster, especially for peas, green beans, and sweet corn. Broadcast around plants and hoe into ground. I like to do this before peas bloom so a lot of energy goes into production. We buy bloodmeal at our local co-op in 50 lb. bags.

Aphid Repellent

MRS. SADIE LAPP

1 Tbsp. oil   3-4 drops dishwashing soap

Mix oil and soap with a quart of water. Put in spray bottle and use for aphids on your lettuce, roses, etc.

Pepper Spray for Pests

MRS. SADIE LAPP

1 tsp. cayenne pepper   1 quart warm tap water
6 cloves garlic, chopped very fine

Mix, then let stand for one hour. Strain and put in sprayer.

Natural Bug Juice

½ cup marigolds   ½ cup garlic
½ cup geraniums

Put in blender and add enough water to blend. Strain. Mix with 10 gallons water. Sprinkle or spray over, around, and underneath vegetables, especially lettuce.

Tomato Worm Prevention

MRS. ERVIN (ELIZABETH) BEACHY

1 Tbsp. Epsom salt   1 handful of oatmeal

At planting time, put the above into each hole to keep away tomato worms.

Tomato Worm Repellent

MIRIAM YODER, LaGRANGE, IN

Add a tablespoon of cornmeal to each pepper and tomato plant and you won't find very many tomato worms, if any.

Soil Enhancer

MARLENE DETWEILER, ROME, OH

½ cup 35% peroxide   5 gal. water
½ cup apple cider vinegar

This is good to enhance soil to transplant. Moisten soil as needed. This is also good for bacteria in soil.

Ant Deterrent

MARLENE DETWEILER, ROME, OH

Cinnamon sprinkled on the routes of ants keeps them away.

Root Maggots

MARTHA WIDEMAN, LISTOWEL, ON

Mix 2 tablespoons ammonia to 2½ gallons water and pour some at each plant.

Choices

To Trap Earwigs

MARTHA WIDEMAN, LISTOWEL, ON

Crumple newspaper in a ball and moisten it slightly. The earwigs will crawl into the balls, and all you have to do is throw the whole thing in the garbage.

Insecticide

MARTHA WIDEMAN, LISTOWEL, ON

1 Tbsp. detergent   1 cup oil (sunflower, corn, etc.)

Mix 2½ teaspoons of oil mixture to 1 cup water. Spray on bug-infected plants.

For Powdery Mildew

MARLENE DETWEILER, ROME, OH

1 tsp. vinegar   3-4 drops soap
1 tsp. Lysterine

Mix into a bottle filled with water. Spray affected areas.

My Favorite Garden Spray

1 gal. of lukewarm water   1 Tbsp. liquid fertilizer
2 Tbsp. of Spray n' Grow   1 Tbsp. 3% peroxide
2 Tbsp. Pyola   2 Tbsp. soap shield

Mix lukewarm water and Spray n' Grow. Let set 15-20 minutes. Add remaining ingredients. Mix well and spray every 2 weeks after the sun is down or on a cloudy day. Do not spray in the sun, as it may burn plants. This spray is a plant food, pest control, and blight spray for all garden goodies.

For Melons, Cucumbers & Squash

1 Tbsp. ammonia   1 tsp. baking soda
1 Tbsp. salt petre   1 gal. water
1 tsp. Epsom salt

Mix and pour around roots of melons, cucumbers, and squash every two weeks, in early morning or in evening. This is for 6 plants. Start using this when plants start to bear fruits, or earlier if needed.

Healthy

Homemade Round-up

4 cups vinegar
¼ cup table salt

2 tsp. liquid dish soap

To kill weeds and grass. Combine ingredients and spray on.

Rose Feeding

Feed your roses by working rotten bananas, skins and all, into the soil near the base of your rosebushes. The potassium in the skins gives them a power packed boost. I've used the blender when planting. Blend banana peel with enough water (2 cups or so) to make it blendable. Dig a deep hole for roses. Pour your blender full of bananas into hole. Cover with 2-3" of dirt. Plant roses on top as usual. We tried this and the rosebush just grows and blooms.

How to Raise Raspberries

MRS. ERVIN (ELIZABETH) BEACHY

If you wish to trellis raspberries to a comfortable height for picking, you can do this by putting in 2 steel fence posts every 10-12 feet. The 2 steel posts should be 6-8" apart parallel. Stretch wire like you would for a clothesline, thus creating a fence for plants to grow inside. I have 2 strands, 1 about mid-height and another at about the height I want them for picking. Also short pieces about 10-12" can be bent, creating a hook at each end to keep the strands of wire together, as plants tend to push your fence away too far. Mix a gallon of wood ashes, 1 gallon lime, a handful of sulfur, and 1 handful of Epsom salt. Put a handful around each stalk once a month in February, March, April, and again when they have small berries and again in the fall. Trim new stalks by cutting off the top of the stalk a little taller than your top strand of wire fence. When new shoots come out from these canes, cut tops off again. But not later than July. You can trim out the old stalks when they are finished bearing. My mother used to wait until the following March.

Recipe for Fruit Trees

MARTHA WIDEMAN, LISTOWEL, ON

10 lb. lime
5 lb. wood ashes

2½ lb. sulfur
1 lb. coarse salt

Put tight around trunks of trees. Keeps insects from going up trees and keeps mice away.

Asparagus Food

MRS. ERVIN (ELIZABETH) BEACHY

3 parts green sand or granite sand   1 part bonemeal
2 parts cottonseed

Mix and scatter into row. For a fairly large patch (75-100 stalks) I mixed 20 lb. green sand, 14 lb. cottonseed, and 7 lb. bonemeal. Apply after the harvest. Also fertilize with manure then. The above recipe is from a lady who always had thick spears of asparagus!

Natural Vegetable Rejuvenator

MARTHA WIDEMAN, LISTOWEL, ON

Dilute 1 Tbsp. Epsom salt in 1 gallon water. With watering can, in evening, pour over plants and soil every week until plants look healthy and growing, then a few more times. If you have yellow leaves the yellow leaves will drop off, but the heart grows out healthy again. For cabbage, cauliflower, and broccoli.

Raspberry Treatment

MARTHA WIDEMAN, LISTOWEL, ON

15 lb. pail agricultural lime   1 heaping Tbsp. sulfur
½-1 lb. pail wood ashes

Put on in spring and in September.

How to Shell Popcorn

MIRIAM YODER, LaGRANGE, IN

Take a gunny sack, plastic or burlap, and put 6-8 ears of popcorn into it. Swing and hit bag on cement floor 3 or 4 times and most of your popcorn is shelled. There may be a little to shell off the ends. Dump out and repeat with more popcorn. Really saves your thumb and time.

Index

Beverages

Breads

Yeast Breads 56

Quick Breads 67

Muffins 75

Biscuits 80

Healthy

Breakfast

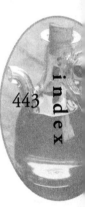

443

index

Choices

index 444

Healthy

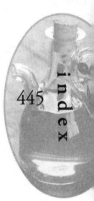

Choices

Casseroles

Cookies

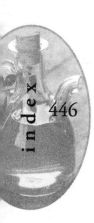

Cooking with Herbs

Dairy

447 index

Choices

Desserts

Lacto-Fermented

Meats

Meat Substitutes

Pies

Healthy

index 452

Healthy

Snacks

Soaps & Cleaners

453

index

Soups

Sourdough

Healthy